HMH SCIENCE DIMENSIONS™

Teacher Edition • Grade 1

Houghton Mifflin Harcourt™

Acknowledgments for Covers

All photos ©HMH unless otherwise noted

Back Cover: *chick hatching* ©wisawa222/Shutterstock

Teacher Edition Contents

About the Program

Units

Resources

Program Authors

Michael A. DiSpezio

Global Educator
North Falmouth, Massachusetts

Michael DiSpezio has authored many HMH instructional programs for Science and Mathematics. He has also authored numerous trade books and multimedia programs on various topics and hosted dozens of studio and location broadcasts for various organizations in the U.S. and worldwide. Most recently, he has been working with educators to provide strategies for implementing the Next Generation Science Standards, particularly the science and engineering practices, cross-cutting concepts, and the use of Evidence Notebooks. To all his projects, he brings his extensive background in science, his expertise in classroom teaching at the elementary, middle, and high school levels, and his deep experience in producing interactive and engaging instructional materials.

Marjorie Frank

Science Writer and Content-Area Reading Specialist
Brooklyn, New York

An educator and linguist by training, a writer and poet by nature, Marjorie Frank has authored and designed a generation of instructional materials in all subject areas, including past HMH Science programs. Her other credits include authoring science issues of an award-winning children's magazine, writing game-based digital assessments, developing blended learning materials for young children, and serving as instructional designer and co-author of pioneering school-to-work software. In addition, she has served on the adjunct faculty of Hunter, Manhattan, and Brooklyn Colleges, teaching courses in science methods, literacy, and writing. For HMH Science Dimensions, she has guided the development of our K-2 strands and our approach to making connections between NGSS and Common Core ELA/literacy standards.

Michael R. Heithaus, Ph.D.

Dean, College Of Arts, Sciences & Education
Professor, Department Of Biological Sciences
Florida International University
Miami, Florida

Mike Heithaus joined the FIU Biology Department in 2003, has served as Director of the Marine Sciences Program and Executive Director of the School of Environment, Arts, and Society, which brings together the natural and social sciences and humanities to develop solutions to today's environmental challenges. He now serves as Dean of the College of Arts, Sciences & Education. His research focuses on predator-prey interactions and the ecological importance of large marine species. He has helped to guide the development of Life Science content in HMH Science Dimensions, with a focus on strategies for teaching challenging content as well as the science and engineering practices of analyzing data and using computational thinking.

Cary I. Sneider, Ph.D.

Associate Research Professor
Portland State University
Portland, Oregon

While studying astrophysics at Harvard, Cary Sneider volunteered to teach in an Upward Bound program and discovered his real calling as a science teacher. After teaching middle and high school science in Maine, California, Costa Rica and Micronesia, he settled for nearly three decades at Lawrence Hall of Science in Berkeley, California, where he developed skills in curriculum development and teacher education. Over his career Cary directed more than 20 federal, state, and foundation grant projects, and was a writing team leader for the Next Generation Science Standards. He has been instrumental in ensuring *HMH Science Dimensions*™ meets the high expectations of the NGSS and provides an effective three-dimensional learning experience for all students.

Program Advisors

Paul D. Asimow, PhD
*Eleanor and John R. McMillan Professor
   of Geology and Geochemistry*
California Institute of Technology
Pasadena, California

Dr. Eileen Cashman, PhD
Professor
Humboldt State University
Arcata, California

Mark B. Moldwin, PhD
*Professor of Space Sciences and
   Engineering*
University of Michigan
Ann Arbor, Michigan

Kelly Y. Neiles, PhD
Assistant Professor of Chemistry
St. Mary's College of Maryland
St. Mary's City, Maryland

Dr. Sten Odenwald, PhD
Astronomer
NASA Goddard Spaceflight Center
Greenbelt, Maryland

Bruce W. Schafer
*Director of K-12 STEM Collaborations,
   retired*
Oregon University System
Portland, Oregon

Barry A. Van Deman
President and CEO
Museum of Life and Science
Durham, North Carolina

Kim Withers, PhD
Assistant Professor
Texas A&M University-Corpus Christi
Corpus Christi, Texas

Adam D. Woods, PhD
Professor
California State University, Fullerton
Fullerton, California

Classroom Reviewers

Michelle Barnett
Lichen K-8
Citrus Heights, California

Brandi Bazarnik
Skycrest Elementary
Citrus Heights, California

Kristin Wojes-Broetzmann
Saint Anthony Parish School
Menomonee Falls, Wisconsin

Andrea Brown
*District Science and STEAM Curriculum
   TOSA*
Hacienda La Puente Unified School
   District
Hacienda Heights, California

Denice Gayner
Earl LeGette Elementary
Fair Oaks, California

Emily Giles
Elementary Curriculum Consultant
Kenton County School District
Ft. Wright, Kentucky

Crystal Hintzman
*Director of Curriculum, Instruction and
   Assessment*
School District of Superior
Superior, Wisconsin

Roya Hosseini
Junction Avenue K-8
Livermore, California

Cynthia Alexander Kirk
Classroom Teacher, Learning Specialist
West Creek Academy
Valencia, California

Marie LaCross
Fair Oaks Ranch Community School
Santa Clarita, California

Emily Miller
Science Specialist
Madison Metropolitan School District
Madison, Wisconsin

Monica Murray, EdD
Principal
Bassett Unified School District
La Puente, California

Carolyn Quigley
Elementary Teacher
Ironia
Randolph, New Jersey

Wendy Savaske
Director of Instructional Services
School District of Holmen
Holmen, Wisconsin

Tina Topoleski
District Science Supervisor
Jackson School District
Jackson, New Jersey

Educator Advisory Panel Members

Dr. C. Alex Alvarez
Director of STEM and Curriculum
Valdosta City Schools
Valdosta, Georgia

Kerri Angel
Science Teacher
Department Chair
Churchill County School District
Churchill County Middle School
Fallon, Nevada

Maria Blue
Teacher
Emblem Academy, Saugus Union
    School District
Saugus, California

Regina Brinker
STEM Coordinator
Livermore Valley Joint Unified School
    District
Livermore, California

Andrea Brown
*District Science and STEAM Curriculum
    TOSA*
Hacienda La Puente Unified School
    District
Hacienda Heights, California

Conni Crittenden
4th and 5th Grade Classroom Teacher
Williamston Community Schools
Williamston, Michigan

Ronald M. Durso, Ed.S.
District Science Supervisor
Fair Lawn Public Schools
Fair Lawn, New Jersey

Cheryl Frye
NGSS/STEM Coordinator
Menifee Union School District
Menifee, California

Brandon A. Gillette, Ph.D
Middle School Science
The Pembroke Hill School
Kansas City, Missouri

**Susan L. Kallewaard, M.A. Ed.,
NBCT**
Fifth Grade Teacher
Haverhill Elementary School
Portage, Michigan

John Labriola
*Middle School Science Teacher, Science
    Content Coordinator*
Charities Middle School
Wood River Junction, Rhode Island

Gilbert J. Luna
K-12 Science Curriculum Specialist
Vancouver Public Schools
Vancouver, Washington

Jennifer Su Mataele
PreK-12 Technology, STEAM TOSA
Hacienda La Puente Unified School
    District
Hacienda Heights, California

Shawna Metcalf
Science Teacher Specialist
Glendale Unified School District
Glendale, California

Erica Rose Motamed
Science Teacher
Lake Center Middle School
Santa Fe Springs, California

Monica Murray, EdD
Principal
Bassett Unified School District
La Puente, California

Stefanie Pechan
*5th Grade Teacher, STEM Coordinator,
    PAEMST*
Robert Down Elementary
Pacific Grove, California

Christie Purdon
K-12 Science Coordinator
Blue Valley School District
Overland Park, Kansas

Stephen J. Rapa
Science Department Chair
Worcester Public Schools
Worcester, Massachusetts

Alison L. Riordan
Science Curriculum Coordinator, K-12
Plymouth Public Schools
Plymouth, Massachusetts

Greta Trittin Smith
Academic Coach--Science
Garvey School District
Rosemead, California

Marsha Veninga
8th Grade Science Teacher
Bloomington Junior High School,
    Bloomington District 87
Bloomington, Illinois

HMH SCIENCE DIMENSIONS™
ENGINEERED for the NEXT GENERATION

Program Overview

GRADES K–5

NEXT GENERATION
SCIENCE
STANDARDS

HMH SCIENCE DIMENSIONS™

Spark your Students' Curiosity in Science

Kids are born scientists. They want to know **WHY**: Is the sun a star? How do magnets work? It's our job to encourage their curiosity, creativity, and exploration while preparing them for careers in science, technology, engineering, and math.

At **Houghton Mifflin Harcourt**® we've created a brand new K–12 science curriculum based off of the Next Generation Science Standards (NGSS)* to raise the level of science literacy and achievement in our students.

A brand-new K–12 program, built from the ground up specifically for NGSS that:

- engages students
- promotes active learning and deeper thinking
- sparks an interest in science and science-related careers

- creates enduring understanding
- builds problem-solving skills
- creates lifelong learners

…better than any other program.

An **all-new**, complete solution for NGSS: Digital, print, and hands-on

HMH Science Dimensions™ is thoughtfully crafted to incorporate the Three Dimensions of Learning and Performance Expectations (PEs) of NGSS* into every lesson, every activity, every video—every piece!

What sets **HMH Science Dimensions** apart?

Three-Dimensional Learning. Designed—not aligned—around the Three Dimensions of Science Learning: Disciplinary Core Ideas (DCIs), Crosscutting Concepts (CCCs), and Science and Engineering Practices (SEPs)

Professional Support from HMH®. Simplifying your transition to an NGSS curriculum every step of the way

Active Learning. Activities, investigation, and evidence-gathering at the foundation of every lesson

Integrated Engineering & STEM. Developing students who are experts in the engineering design process

Digital-First Flexibility. Immersive learning experiences that engage students in doing science

Embedded Assessment. Preparing students to succeed on high-stakes performance-based assessments

*Next Generation Science Standards and logo are registered trademarks of Achieve. Neither Achieve nor the lead states and partners that developed the Next Generation Science Standards was involved in the production of, and does not endorse, this product.

Three-Dimensional Learning Made Simple

HMH Science Dimensions expertly weaves the Three Dimensions of Learning into each lesson in order to meet the Performance Expectations (PEs). This braided approach takes the burden off of you while ensuring a **quality 3D learning experience** for your students.

Grade 2 Teacher Edition

3D Learning Objectives

Each lesson has unique interrelated 3D Learning Objectives that can be found in the Teacher Edition. The objective is generated from the Science and Engineering Practices, Crosscutting Concepts, and Disciplinary Core Ideas associated with the Performance Expectations correlated to the unit. These **custom stepping-stone objectives** ensure that the lessons cover 100% of the NGSS* material associated with the PEs.

Clearly Labeled NGSS References

- The NGSS labeling in the Teacher Edition clearly identifies all the PEs, SEPs, DCIs, and CCCs of NGSS, including the math and ELA connections. This helps educators **identify the standards** that are being covered in any given lesson.

- Additionally, throughout the **HMH Science Dimensions** Teacher Edition, you will find features to help you orient toward the critical dimensions of the **EQuIP Rubric**. These features will demonstrate the best practices of NGSS summarized by this evaluation instrument.

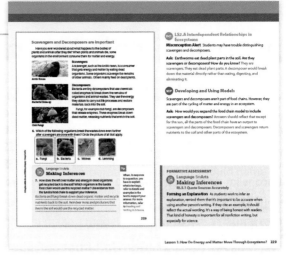

Grade 5 Teacher Edition

Follow the NGSS Story Through the Entire Curriculum!

- The **HMH Science Dimensions** Trace Tool to the NGSS helps you make sense of the standards, understand how they connect and spiral from one grade to another, and **identify HMH resources** to support your NGSS-based instruction.

- You can **trace the standards** by PEs, SEPs, CCCs, or DCIs. When you click on a standard, you can view where in the program that standard is covered.

- But the **Trace Tool** is more powerful than a typical correlation—it also shows you **how each standard** and **dimension spirals** throughout the entire K–12 sequence. It's a snap to see what students should know already, and what you're preparing them for.

Grade 5 Print Student Edition "Do the Math"

English Language Arts and Math Connections

Strong math and reading skills are essential to ensuring STEM learning and science literacy. **HMH Science Dimensions** offers Common Core **Math and ELA connections** throughout the curriculum.

Unmatched Professional Support to Help You Transition with Ease

HMH Science Dimensions invests as much in teachers as it does in students. With a thoughtfully structured Teacher Edition, professional development courses focused on NGSS* best practices, and professional learning videos built directly into the core curriculum, teachers have more support than ever. An NGSS curriculum requires a significantly different approach to teaching science, and although this new approach may be challenging, its **rewards** are immediate. HMH provides the support you need to make the transition to a **student-centered**, NGSS style of teaching.

Grade 2
Teacher Edition

Integrating the Three Dimensions of Learning

This lesson focuses on how heating and cooling change matter (DCI Structure and Properties of Matter and DCI Chemical Reactions). The lesson begins with children exploring how heat by melting, cooking, and burning causes changes to various materials (SEP Science Models, Laws, Mechanisms, and Theories Explain Natural Phenomena) and continues with children exploring how cooling causes changes to various materials. As they explore, children will observe patterns in changes caused by heating and cooling (CCC Cause and Effect). Finally, children will construct an argument using evidence from the lesson to support their claim of how heating and cooling cause changes to matter (SEP Engaging in Argument from Evidence).

Professional Development Go online to view **Professional Development videos** with strategies to integrate CCCs and SEPs, including the ones used in this lesson.

Build on Prior Knowledge

Children should already know and be prepared to build on the following concepts:
- A state of matter is an observable property of matter.
- Matter can be a solid. A solid keeps its shape. It will not change its shape unless you do something like cut, bend, or break it.
- Matter can be a liquid. A liquid does not have its own shape. A liquid takes the shape of its container.

Differentiate Instruction

Lesson Vocabulary
- melt
- freeze

Reinforcing Vocabulary To help children remember each vocabulary term, have them draw an illustration of each word. Then, have them write the word beneath the illustration, define it, and use it in a sentence. Remind children to look for these highlighted terms as they proceed through the lesson.

Extra Support Supply children with additional images of examples of solids and liquids and how these materials change from solid to liquid or from liquid to solid. Provide children with context of how these changes take place. For example, a solid ice pop melting into a puddle on a sunny day, or a pond freezing to ice in the winter.

Extension Children who want to find out more can do research on gases and how liquids change to gases by heating. Children should use their data to make a poster that illustrates the three states of matter of one material (e.g. water) and how it changes states.

ELL Strategy Be sure to point out all labels, pictures, captions, and headings throughout lesson to assist children with strategies to summarize chunks of content. Discuss with children real-life connections to content and provide hands-on examples of materials when possible to best support the needs of these learners.

Understand Where Your Instruction Fits

- The **Teacher Edition** (online and print) is organized around the familiar **5E instructional model**. This helps to lower the learning curve and provide a solid foundation upon which to build an NGSS curriculum.

- Additional Collaboration, Differentiate Instruction, Formative Assessment, and Claims, Evidence, and Reasoning suggestions provide a wealth of support and resources to help you **enrich the learning experience** for everyone.

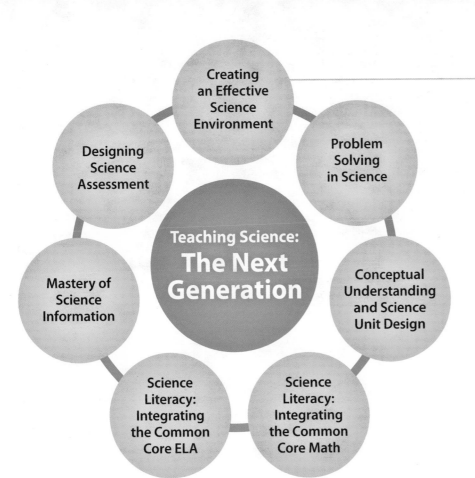

Creating an Effective Science Environment

Problem Solving in Science

Designing Science Assessment

Teaching Science: **The Next Generation**

Conceptual Understanding and Science Unit Design

Mastery of Science Information

Science Literacy: Integrating the Common Core ELA

Science Literacy: Integrating the Common Core Math

Professional Development to Build Your Confidence

- HMH offers 8 separate **best practices** courses that can help you transition to an NGSS curriculum with or without *HMH Science Dimensions*.

- Start with *Teaching Science: The Next Generation*, and follow it up with one or more additional modules as either a preparation to or support for your adoption of NGSS. Our expert consultant staff will introduce you to the new science standards, and explain how they have been designed and organized across disciplines and grades to provide all students an internationally benchmarked science education.

See NGSS in Action

Embedded professional development videos help teachers better prepare for this new approach to science education. Just-in-time videos featuring our **dynamic consulting authors** guide teachers through the key approaches that ensure NGSS success.

» **FOUNDATION** videos help educators and parents better understand the NGSS, as well as the background that led up to their development.

» **ENGINEERING** videos support educators as they incorporate the design process into their classrooms.

» **CHALLENGING** Content videos for Grades 4–12 help educators know how to address specific content areas that students tend to struggle with in an NGSS curriculum.

» **HANDS-ON Activity** videos for Grades K–2 model what the hands-on activities within the curriculum should look like when implemented. These help ensure a more successful implementation of an NGSS solution.

Michael DiSpezio, Author

Professional Development Video

*Next Generation Science Standards and logo are registered trademarks of Achieve. Neither Achieve nor the lead states and partners that developed the Next Generation Science Standards was involved in the production of, and does not endorse, this product. **T13**

Build Student Confidence with Authentic Investigations

Students are more engaged and learn more meaningfully through investigative inquiry. *HMH Science Dimensions* is built on this approach. Your students will learn to conduct hands-on investigations, define questions and objectives, make claims, and identify evidence—in short, to **take charge** and **fully engage** in their learning!

Every Lesson Is an Activity

- Each lesson begins with **Can You Explain It?**— a **problem to solve or discrepant event to explain.** This lesson-leading feature provides intrinsic motivation to spark curiosity and serves as the context for the three-dimensional learning and hands-on activities throughout the lessons. Students are motivated to think critically and construct explanations of *how* and *why*.

- The program is built around **active learning**. Rather than receive content passively, students are asked to **solve problems** or explain phenomena, by stating **claims**, gathering **evidence**, and providing explanations through **reasoning**.

CAN YOU EXPLAIN IT?

How might this island have appeared overnight?

In November 2013 off the coast of Japan, an island formed virtually overnight. The view quickly changed from calm Pacific waters to violent eruptions. By the next morning, an entirely new island had appeared. Now named Niijima, the island has been growing in size

How might this island have appeared overnight?

Grade 5 Online Student Edition

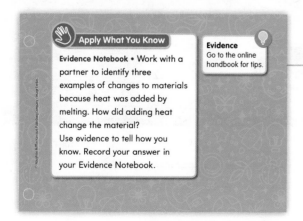

Apply What You Know

Evidence Notebook • Work with a partner to identify three examples of changes to materials because heat was added by melting. How did adding heat change the material? Use evidence to tell how you know. Record your answer in your Evidence Notebook.

Evidence
Go to the online handbook for tips.

Grade 2 Print Student Edition

Science Notebooking to Strengthen Writing Skills

Many of the lessons in *HMH Science Dimensions* support the use of **Evidence Notebooks. Helpful prompts** have been inserted throughout the lessons to guide students on when to use these notebooks. Students will love creating their own study guides that can be taken into the next grade, and teachers will love the extra writing practice!

Hands On Activity
Explore Cooling

Name_____

Materials
• solid • ice cube tray • liquid

Ask a Question
_____

Test and Record Data · Explore online. ▶

Step 1
Observe the solid and the liquid. Draw a picture to record your observations.

Flower	Juice

Step 2
Pour the liquid into the ice cube tray. Put the solid and the liquid in the freezer. Wait until the next day to take them out.

Lesson 2 • How Do Heating and Cooling Change Matter?   69

Grade 2 Print Student Edition

Drive Student Learning with Hands-On Investigations

- **Hands-On Activities** are integrated into many of the lessons. These are built with teachers' busy schedules in mind. Each activity uses **easily sourced materials**.

- Students get to actively "do science;" they **think critically** about their observations, practice gathering evidence, and defend their claims.

Cultivate Collaboration

Working as a team is an essential part of developing **21st-century skills**. *HMH Science Dimensions* provides ample opportunities for students to participate in groups to complete activities and partner with their peers to discuss their findings.

HANDS-ON ACTIVITY
Modeling Matter Moving within an Ecosystem

Objective
Collaborate with a partner to choose and model an ecosystem. Use this model to show how matter moves among organisms and their environment.

What question will you investigate to meet this objective?

Materials
• materials to model
• scissors
• index cards
• markers
• paste
• stapler

Objective
Collaborate with a partner to choose and model an ecosystem. Use this model to show how matter moves among organisms and their environment.

Procedure
STEP 1 ... an ecosystem to model. Research the organisms you will include in your model ecosystem.

Which ecosystem are you researching?
_____

Use your research to complete the table below.

Ecosystem	
Energy Source	
Producers	Consumers
Decomposers	

234

Grade 5 Print Student Edition

Save Prep Time with Equipment Kits

- **Equipment Kits** provide the **consumable** and **non-consumable** materials you need to complete most of the hands-on activities so you have all the materials you need right at your fingertips.

- The **Safety Kit** provides the materials you need to address **classroom safety** while performing the program activities.

The Students of Today Will Solve the Technology Challenges of Tomorrow!

NGSS* has raised the engineering design process to the same level as scientific inquiry. In *HMH Science Dimensions*, science, technology, engineering, and math are considered an **integral** part of the curriculum. Lessons are designed for students to explore science the same way real-life scientists do. Watch your students' eyes **light up** as they brainstorm solutions, share their ideas, and experiment to find solutions.

Elevate Engineering

In **HMH Science Dimensions,** engineering and STEM are carried throughout every unit and not just treated as an ancillary. This approach elevates engineering design to the same level as scientific literacy. Each Unit includes a **Performance Task**, offering students multiple opportunities throughout the program to apply the **engineering design process** by defining a problem and designing a solution.

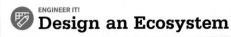

ENGINEER IT!
Design an Ecosystem

You work for company that is building an animal theme park. After studying the animals in their natural ecosystem, your team needs to choose an animal to bring back to live in the park. Your team has access to an empty room with a sprinkler for precipitation and temperature control. There are skylights in the ceiling to allow sunlight in. There is no floor, so the ground is covered in soil.

This reptile terrarium has everything the lizard needs to survive.

FIND A PROBLEM: What problem do you need to solve?

Before beginning, look at the checklist at the end of this project to be sure you are meeting all the requirements.

RESEARCH: Study the animal you plan to bring to the lab and write down your observations. Use online or library resources for research. Use multiple sources and cite them.

BRAINSTORM: Brainstorm three or more ideas with your team to solve the problem. Keep in mind the criteria and constraints.

Criteria	Constraints
☐ Animal must survive	☐ Your animal will not have access to the natural outdoors
☐ The landscape must mimic the animals natural ecosystem	☐ Limited to one room to build your ecosystem
☐ A food web must be present to meet your animal's nutrition needs	☐ Room is about the size of your classroom
☐ The animal needs enough room to exercise and move freely	☐ Room is 6 meters by 6 meters

270

Grade 5 Print Student Edition

Provide Extra Support for Students Who Need It

The **Science and Engineering Practices Online Handbook** will help students achieve a higher level of understanding and skill as they build their experience applying the **Science and Engineering Practices** of NGSS.

Build Literacy and Science Content Knowledge

- The program includes print and online access to **Science and Engineering Leveled Readers** for Grades K–5. These colorful, fun, and interesting Readers provide three levels of readability for students: **On-Level, Extra Support,** and **Enrichment**.

- The accompanying **Teacher Guide** provides **activities** and **support** for before reading, during reading, and during response to reading.

*Next Generation Science Standards and logo are registered trademarks of Achieve. Neither Achieve nor the lead states and partners that developed the Next Generation Science Standards was involved in the production of, and does not endorse, this product.

Engage with Meaningful Technology

HMH Science Dimensions is a truly digital-first program. The curriculum leverages the advantages of technology while prioritizing a **student-centered learning model**. Students can view videos and animations, interact with instructional images and text, enter responses, pursue their intellectual interests by choosing lesson paths, and enjoy simulation-based learning. All of these features help you maintain an **integrated three-dimensional approach** to learning science.

Grade 2 Online
Student Edition

Immersive Digital Curriculum

Online lessons are enriched above and beyond the print lessons with educational videos, learning interactivities, and places to save student work as **responses** and **technology-enhanced item choices**. Vocabulary is highlighted and clickable, with point-of-use pop-up definitions.

Maximize Student Choice

The **Take It Further** feature at the end of each lesson maximizes the opportunity for students to elaborate further on what they have learned so far. By leveraging the power of technology, students can continue to go in depth on **topics of their choice**, to learn more and create stronger, more personal links to their learning.

Grade 5
Online Student Edition

Deepen Understanding with Open-Ended Simulations

Unique **You Solve It** simulations provide completely **open-ended opportunities** for students to demonstrate their ability to problem solve and perform at the level described by the NGSS* Performance Expectations. The program encourages students to explore multiple answers to a problem and learn to develop explanations and defend their answers.

Grade 5 *You Solve It*

Explore Immersive Virtual Worlds

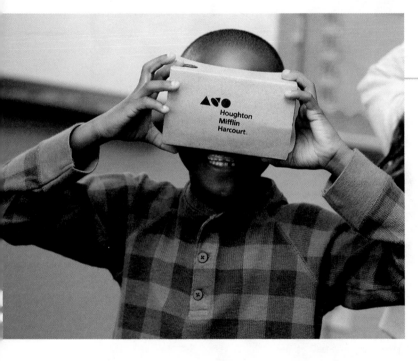

- As a Google® content partner, HMH has developed field trips for Google Expeditions.

HMH Field Trips
powered by
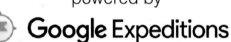 **Google** Expeditions

Using a simple Google Cardboard™ device and a smartphone, students are swept away into **3D, 360-degree experiences** in fascinating locations, directly tied to science content!

- An HMH **Teacher Guide** provides ideas for incorporating the Expeditions into your lessons, as well as tips on how to **guide** and **customize** the experience.

The Ultimate Online and Offline Program Experience

- Teachers can look forward to accessing **HMH Science Dimensions** through a new online learning system that supports integration with LMS solutions. This **flexible system** allows teachers to seamlessly embed the program's resources into their instruction.

- Additionally, program content can be accessed offline through the **HMH Player®** app. This allows for **maximum compatibility** in 1:1 or **Bring Your Own Device** learning environments and with the wide variety of technology that students have at home. No matter what, **HMH Science Dimensions** will be accessible.

HMH**PLAYER**®
Making 1:1 Learning a Reality

*Next Generation Science Standards and logo are registered trademarks of Achieve. Neither Achieve nor the lead states and partners that developed the Next Generation Science Standards was involved in the production of, and does not endorse, this product. **T19**

Let Students Show What They Know

For the first time ever, through NGSS,* science standards now include specific **measureable learning outcomes**. These Performance Expectations guide test developers and teachers in understanding how to measure student learning. **HMH Science Dimensions** offers flexible assessment tools in a variety of formats to help you assess both formative and summative student learning according to NGSS.

wax pictures.
ged from liquid

Name _____ Date _____

Twinkle, Twinkle, Different Stars

In this task, you will use a model to explore the brightness of different stars. You will organize your data into a table and graph.

OBJECTIVE
- Investigate apparent brightness.

PROCEDURE

Make the photometer.

1. Fold the aluminum foil, shiny side out, to be the same size as the wax blocks.
2. Place the aluminum foil between the two wax blocks.
3. Place the rubber band around the wax blocks to hold them together.
4. Check that the 60 watt bulb is in the electric socket setup A and the 25 watt bulb is in electric socket setup B.

Compare the brightness of different watts of light bulbs.

5. Place the photometer in between the electric socket setups A and B. Each bulb should be 60 centimters, cm, away from the aluminum foil in the photometer.

6. Notice that the side of photometer facing A is brighter than side facing B.

MATERIALS
- 1 calculator
- 1 electric light setup, 60 watt light bulb
- 1 electric light setup, 25 watt light bulb
- 1 meter stick
- 1 rubber band
- 1 safety goggles
- 1 piece aluminum foil
- 40 watt light bulb
- 100 watt light bulb
- 2 wax blocks

Photometer

rubber band
paraffin blocks
aluminum foil

60 cm   60 cm
60 watt light bulb   25 watt light bulb

Grade 5 Performance-Based Assessment

Authentic Performance Assessment

Performance-Based Assessments help you ensure that your students can perform the science and engineering practices called for by NGSS. And they also guide students toward making connections across Performance Expectations.

Assess on All Dimensions

- Formal assessment questions **aligned to multiple dimensions** provide you with a complete picture of student understanding.

- A unique **3D Evaluation Rubric** helps you evaluate open-ended student responses and identify the underlying cause of student misunderstanding so that you can target remediation where it's most needed.

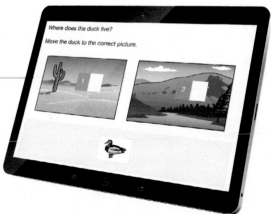

Performance-Based
Assessment
Teacher Resources

Task 1 Performance Rubric

Rating Scale	
3 Outstanding	1 Needs Improvement
2 Satisfactory	0 Did Not Demonstrate Skill

Skills	Rating
DCI.5-ESS1.A.1 The Universe and Its Stars The student demonstrates differences in apparent brightness of the sun and other stars.	
SEP.3-5.G.1 Engaging in Argument from Evidence The student uses data to explain that the sun appears to be larger and brighter than other stars because of its distance from Earth.	
CCC.3-5.C.1 Scale, Proportion, and Quantity The student demonstrates that stars vary in size and distance from the Earth.	
Additional: SEP.3-5.C.1 Planning and Carrying Out Investigations The student conducts an investigation to show that the difference in apparent brightness of stars is due to their relative distances from Earth.	
Additional SEP.3-5.C.2 Planning and Carrying Out Investigations The student makes measurements demonstrating the differences in apparent brightness of the sun and stars.	
Total	

LESSON SELF-CHECK

Lesson Check

CAN YOU EXPLAIN IT?

Why do you think the owls have left the area?

Now that you've learned more about food chains, explain what has happened in the video. Be sure to:
- Identify what has happened to the owls' ecosystem.
- Describe why the changes have caused the owls to leave.
- Identify what the city can do to try to get the owls to come back.

Grade 5 Online Student Edition

Reflect on Evidence Gathered

At the end of a lesson, the **Lesson Self-Check** encourages students to reflect on the evidence they gathered throughout the lesson. They have another chance to respond to the discrepant phenomenon or central question of the lesson with **open-ended response** questions.

Prepare for High-Stakes Tests

Technology-enhanced assessment items prepare your students for modern **computer-based high-stakes tests**. Parallel print assessments ensure that your students are challenged in the same way both on- and offline.

Where does the duck live?
Move the duck to the correct picture.

Kindergarten Online Assessment

*Next Generation Science Standards and logo are registered trademarks of Achieve. Neither Achieve nor the lead states and partners that developed the Next Generation Science Standards was involved in the production of, and does not endorse, this product. **T21**

1-PS4 Waves and their Applications in Technologies for Information Transfer

	Print and Digital Resources	
	Supporting Learning Experiences	**Assessment & Performance**

Performance Expectation
 	
1-PS4-1
 	
Plan and conduct investigations to provide evidence that vibrating materials can make sound and that sound can make materials vibrate.
	Unit 2
	Lesson 1 and **Hands-On Activity**
		Unit 2
		Unit Project
		You Solve It (digital only)
		Unit Performance Task
		Assessment Guide and Online
		   Lesson Quizzes
		   Unit Test
		Performance-Based Assessment
		   End-of-Year Test (or End-of Module Test)

Disciplinary Core Idea	**PS4.A Wave Properties** Sound can make matter vibrate, and vibrating matter can make sound.
Science and Engineering Practices	**Planning and Carrying Out Investigations** Plan and conduct investigations collaboratively to produce data to serve as the basis for evidence to answer a question. **Scientific Investigations Use a Variety of Methods** Science investigations begin with a question. Scientists use different ways to study the world.
Crosscutting Concept	**Cause and Effect** Simple tests can be designed to gather evidence to support or refute student ideas about causes.

1-PS4 Waves and their Applications in Technologies for Information Transfer
continued

	Print and Digital Resources	
	Supporting Learning Experiences	**Assessment & Performance**
Performance Expectation **1-PS4-2** Make observations to construct an evidence-based account that objects can be seen only when illuminated.	Unit 3 Lesson 1 and **Hands-On Activity**	Unit 3 Unit Project You Solve It (digital only) **Unit Performance Task** Assessment Guide and Online 　　Lesson Quizzes 　　Unit Test **Performance-Based Assessment** End-of-Year Test (or End-of Module Test)

Disciplinary Core Idea	**PS4.B Electromagnetic Radiation** Objects can be seen if light is available to illuminate them or if they give off their own light.
Science and Engineering Practice	**Constructing Explanations and Designing Solutions** Make observations (firsthand or from media) to construct an evidence-based account for natural phenomena.
Crosscutting Concept	**Cause and Effect** Simple tests can be designed to gather evidence to support or refute student ideas about causes.

1-PS4 Waves and their Applications in Technologies for Information Transfer
continued

	Print and Digital Resources	
	Supporting Learning Experiences	**Assessment & Performance**

Performance Expectation
 	
1-PS4-3
 	
Plan and conduct an investigation to determine the effect of placing objects made with different materials in the path of a beam of light.
	Unit 3
	Lesson 2 and **Hands-On Activity**
	Lesson 3 and **Hands-On Activity**
		Unit 3
		Unit Project
		You Solve It (digital only)
		Unit Performance Task
		Assessment Guide and Online
		   Lesson Quizzes
		   Unit Test
		Performance-Based Assessment
		End-of-Year Test (or End-of Module Test)

Disciplinary Core Idea	**PS4.B Electromagnetic Radiation** Some materials allow light to pass through them, others allow only some light through and others block all the light and create a dark shadow on any surface beyond them, where the light cannot reach. Mirrors can be used to redirect a light beam.
Science and Engineering Practice	**Planning and Carrying Out Investigations** Plan and conduct investigations collaboratively to produce data to serve as the basis for evidence to answer a question.
Crosscutting Concept	**Cause and Effect** Simple tests can be designed to gather evidence to support or refute student ideas about causes.

1-PS4 Waves and their Applications in Technologies for Information Transfer
continued

	Print and Digital Resources	
	Supporting Learning Experiences	**Assessment & Performance**
Performance Expectation **1-PS4-4** Use tools and materials to design and build a device that uses light or sound to solve the problem of communicating over a distance.*	Unit 2 Lesson 2 and **Hands-On Activity** Unit 3 Lesson 3 and **Hands-On Activity**	Unit 2 Unit Project You Solve It (digital only) **Unit Performance Task** Assessment Guide and Online 　Lesson Quizzes 　Unit Test 　**Performance-Based Assessment** 　End-of-Year Test (or End-of Module Test) Unit 3 Unit Project You Solve It (digital only) Unit Performance Task Assessment Guide and Online 　Lesson Quizzes 　Unit Test 　**Performance-Based Assessment** 　End-of-Year Test (or End-of Module Test)
Disciplinary Core Idea	**PS4.C Information Technologies and Instrumentation** People also use a variety of devices to communicate (send and receive information) over long distances.	
Science and Engineering Practice	**Constructing Explanations and Designing Solutions** Use tools and materials provided to design a device that solves a specific problem.	
Crosscutting Concept	**Influence of Engineering, Technology, and Science, on Society and the Natural World** People depend on various technologies in their lives; human life would be very different without technology.	

1-LS1 From Molecules to Organisms: Structures and Processes

	Print and Digital Resources	
	Supporting Learning Experiences	**Assessment & Performance**

Performance Expectation
 	
1-LS1-1
 	
Use materials to design a solution to a human problem by mimicking how plants and/or animals use their external parts to help them survive, grow, and meet their needs.
	Unit 4
	Lesson 1 and **Hands-On Activity**
	Lesson 2 and **Hands-On Activity**
	Lesson 3 and **Hands-On Activity**
	Lesson 4 and **Hands-On Activity**
		Unit 4
		Unit Project
		You Solve It (digital only)
		Unit Performance Task
		Assessment Guide and Online
		    Lesson Quizzes
		    Unit Test
		Performance-Based Assessment
		    End-of-Year Test (or End-of Module Test)

Disciplinary Core Ideas	**LS1.A Structure and Function** All organisms have external parts. Different animals use their body parts in different ways to see, hear, grasp objects, protect themselves, move from place to place, and seek, find, and take in food, water and air. Plants also have different parts (roots, stems, leaves, flowers, fruits) that help them survive and grow. **LS1.D Information Processing** Animals have body parts that capture and convey different kinds of information needed for growth and survival. Animals respond to these inputs with behaviors that help them survive. Plants also respond to some external inputs.	
Science and Engineering Practice	**Constructing Explanations and Designing Solutions** Use materials to design a device that solves a specific problem or a solution to a specific problem.	
Crosscutting Concepts	**Structure and Function** The shape and stability of structures in natural and designed objects are related to their function(s). **Influence of Engineering, Technology, and Science on Society and the Natural World** Every human-made product is designed by applying some knowledge of the natural world and is built using materials derived from the natural world.	

1-LS1 From Molecules to Organisms: Structures and Processes continued

	Print and Digital Resources	
	Supporting Learning Experiences	**Assessment & Performance**
Performance Expectation **1-LS1-2** Read texts and use media to determine patterns in behavior of parents and offspring that help offspring survive.	Unit 5 Lesson 3 and **Hands-On Activity**	Unit 5 Unit Project You Solve It (digital only) **Unit Performance Task** Assessment Guide and Online 　　Lesson Quizzes 　　Unit Test **Performance-Based Assessment** End-of-Year Test (or End-of Module Test)

Disciplinary Core Idea	**LS1.B Growth and Development of Organisms** Adult plants and animals can have young. In many kinds of animals, parents and the offspring themselves engage in behaviors that help the offspring to survive.
Science and Engineering Practices	**Obtaining, Evaluating, and Communicating Information** Read grade-appropriate texts and use media to obtain scientific information to determine patterns in the natural world. **Scientific Knowledge is Based on Empirical Evidence** Scientists look for patterns and order when making observations about the world.
Crosscutting Concept	**Patterns** Patterns in the natural world can be observed, used to describe phenomena, and used as evidence.

1-LS3 Heredity: Inheritance and Variation of Traits

	Print and Digital Resources	
	Supporting Learning Experiences	**Assessment & Performance**

Performance Expectation
 	
1-LS3-1
 	
Make observations to construct an evidence-based account that young plants and animals are like, but not exactly like, their parents.
	Unit 5
	
	Lesson 1 and **Hands-On Activity**
	
	Lesson 2 and **Hands-On Activity**
		Unit 5
		
		Unit Project
		
		You Solve It (digital only)
		
		Unit Performance Task
		
		Assessment Guide and Online
		
		    Lesson Quizzes
		
		    Unit Test
		
		Performance-Based Assessment
		
		    End-of-Year Test (or End-of Module Test)

Disciplinary Core Ideas	**LS3.A Inheritance of Traits** Young animals are very much, but not exactly like, their parents. Plants also are very much, but not exactly, like their parents. **LS3.B Variation of Traits** Individuals of the same kind of plant or animal are recognizable as similar but can also vary in many ways.
Science and Engineering Practice	**Constructing Explanations and Designing Solutions** Make observations (firsthand or from media) to construct an evidence-based account for natural phenomena.
Crosscutting Concept	**Patterns** Patterns in the natural world can be observed, used to describe phenomena, and used as evidence.

1-ESS1 Earth's Place in the Universe

	Print and Digital Resources	
	Supporting Learning Experiences	**Assessment & Performance**
Performance Expectation **1-ESS1-1** Use observations of the sun, moon, and stars to describe patterns that can be predicted.	Unit 6 Lesson 1 and **Hands-On Activity**	Unit 6 Unit Project You Solve It (digital only) **Unit Performance Task** Assessment Guide and Online 　Lesson Quizzes 　Unit Test **Performance-Based Assessment** 　End-of-Year Test (or End-of Module Test)
Disciplinary Core Idea	**ESS1.A The Universe and its Stars** Patterns of the motion of the sun, moon, and stars in the sky can be observed, described, and predicted.	
Science and Engineering Practice	**Analyzing and Interpreting Data** Use observations (firsthand or from media) to describe patterns in the natural world in order to answer scientific questions.	
Crosscutting Concepts	**Patterns** Patterns in the natural world can be observed, used to describe phenomena, and used as evidence. **Scientific Knowledge Assumes an Order and Consistency in Natural Systems** Science assumes natural events happen today as they happened in the past. Many events are repeated.	

Performance Expectation **1-ESS1-2** Make observations at different times of year to relate the amount of daylight to the time of year.	Unit 6 Lesson 2 and **Hands-On Activity**	Unit 6 Unit Project You Solve It (digital only) **Unit Performance Task** Assessment Guide and Online 　Lesson Quizzes 　Unit Test **Performance-Based Assessment** 　End-of-Year Test (or End-of Module Test)
Disciplinary Core Idea	**ESS1.B Earth and the Solar System** Seasonal patterns of sunrise and sunset can be observed, described, and predicted.	
Science and Engineering Practice	**Planning and Carrying Out Investigations** Make observations (firsthand or from media) to collect data that can be used to make comparisons.	
Crosscutting Concept	**Patterns** Patterns in the natural world can be observed, used to describe phenomena, and used as evidence.	

K-2-ETS1 Engineering Design

	Print and Digital Resources	
	Supporting Learning Experiences	**Assessment & Performance**

Performance Expectation
K-2-ETS1-1
Ask questions, make observations, and gather information about a situation people want to change to define a simple problem that can be solved through the development of a new or improved object or tool.
	Unit 1
	Lesson 1 and **Hands-On Activity**
	Lesson 2 and **Hands-On Activity**
		Unit 1
		Unit Project
		You Solve It (digital only)
		Unit Performance Task
		Assessment Guide and Online
		    Lesson Quizzes
		    Unit Test
		Performance-Based Assessment
		    End-of-Year Test (or End-of Module Test)

Disciplinary Core Ideas	**ETS1.A Defining and Delimiting Engineering Problems** A situation that people want to change or create can be approached as a problem to be solved through engineering. Asking questions, making observations, and gathering information are helpful in thinking about problems. Before beginning to design a solution, it is important to clearly understand the problem.
Science and Engineering Practices	**Asking Questions and Defining Problems** Ask questions based on observations to find more information about the natural and/or designed world(s). Define a simple problem that can be solved through the development of a new or improved object or tool.

	Print and Digital Resources	

Performance Expectation
K-2-ETS1-2
Develop a simple sketch, drawing, or physical model to illustrate how the shape of an object helps it function as needed to solve a given problem.
	Unit 1
	Lesson 2 and **Hands-On Activity**
		Unit 1
		Unit Project
		You Solve It (digital only)
		Unit Performance Task
		Assessment Guide and Online
		    Lesson Quizzes
		    Unit Test
		Performance-Based Assessment
		    End-of-Year Test (or End-of Module Test)

Disciplinary Core Idea	**ETS1.B Developing Possible Solutions** Designs can be conveyed through sketches, drawings, or physical models. These representations are useful in communicating ideas for a problem's solutions to other people.
Science and Engineering Practice	**Developing and Using Models** Develop a simple model based on evidence to represent a proposed object or tool.
Crosscutting Concept	**Structure and Function** The shape and stability of structures of natural and designed objects are related to their function(s).

K-2-ETS1 Engineering Design continued

	Print and Digital Resources	
	Supporting Learning Experiences	**Assessment & Performance**

Performance Expectation
 K-2-ETS1-3
 Analyze data from tests of two objects designed to solve the same problem to compare the strengths and weaknesses of how each performs.
	Unit 1
	 Lesson 2 and **Hands-On Activity**
		Unit 1
		 Unit Project
		 You Solve It (digital only)
		 Unit Performance Task
		 Assessment Guide and Online
		     Lesson Quizzes
		     Unit Test
		 Performance-Based Assessment
		     End-of-Year Test (or End-of Module Test)

Disciplinary Core Idea	**ETS1.C Optimizing the Design Solution** Because there is always more than one possible solution to a problem, it is useful to compare and test designs.	
Science and Engineering Practice	**Analyzing and Interpreting Data** Analyze data from tests of an object or tool to determine if it works as intended.	

Program Scope and Sequence

	Grade K-2	Grade 3-5
Engineering and Design	**GK Unit 1** Engineering and Technology* **G1 Unit 1** Engineering and Technology* **G2 Unit 1** Engineering Design Process*	**G3 Unit 1** Engineering * **G4 Unit 1** Engineering and Technology* **G5 Unit 1** Engineering and Technology*

Physical Science	**GK Unit 2** Forces and Motion
	G1 Unit 2 Sound
	    Unit 3 Light
	G2 Unit 2 Matter
		G3 Unit 2 Forces
		    Unit 3 Motion
		G4 Unit 2 Energy
		    Unit 3 Waves and Information Transfer
		G5 Unit 2 Matter

Life Science	**GK Unit 3** Plants and Animals
	G1 Unit 4 Plant and Animal Structures
	    Unit 5 Living Things and Their Young
	G2 Unit 3 Environments for Living Things
		G3 Unit 4 Life Cycles and Inherited Traits
		    Unit 5 Organisms and Their Environment
		    Unit 6 Fossils
		G4 Unit 4 Plant Structure and Function
		    Unit 5 Animal Structure and Function
		G5 Unit 3 Energy and Matter in Organisms
		    Unit 4 Energy and Matter in Ecosystems

Earth and Space Sciences	**GK Unit 4** Sun Warms Earth
	    Unit 5 Weather
	    Unit 6 Earth's Resources
	G1 Unit 6 Objects and Patterns in the Sky
	G2 Unit 4 Earth's Surface
	    Unit 5 Changes to Earth's Surface
		G3 Unit 7 Weather and Patterns
		G4 Unit 6 Changes to Earth's Surface
		    Unit 7 Rocks and Fossils
		    Unit 8 Natural Resources and Hazards
		G5 Unit 5 Systems in Space
		    Unit 6 Earth's Systems
		    Unit 7 Earth and Human Activities

*Engineering strand is embedded throughout other units and strands.   Included in this Teacher Edition

Grade 6-8

Engineering and Design

Module A Engineering and Science*
Unit 1 Introduction to Engineering and Science
Unit 2 The Practices of Engineering

Physical Science

Module I Energy and Energy Transfer
Unit 1 Energy and Matter
Unit 2 Energy Transfer

Module J Chemistry
Unit 1 The Structure of Matter
Unit 2 States of Matter and Changes of State
Unit 3 Chemical Processes and Equations
Unit 4 The Chemistry of Materials

Module K Forces, Motion, and Fields
Unit 1 Forces and Motion
Unit 2 Electric and Magnetic Forces

Module L Waves and Their Applications
Unit 1 Waves
Unit 2 Information Transfer

Life Science

Module B Cells and Heredity
Unit 1 Cells
Unit 2 Organisms as Systems
Unit 3 Reproduction, Heredity, and Growth

Module C Ecology and the Environment
Unit 1 Matter and Energy in Living Systems
Unit 2 Relationships in Ecosystems
Unit 3 Ecosystem Dynamics

Module D The Diversity of Living Things
Unit 1 The History of Life on Earth
Unit 2 Evolution
Unit 3 Human Influence on Inheritance

Earth and Space Sciences

Module E Earth's Water and Atmosphere
Unit 1 Circulation of Earth's Air and Water
Unit 2 Weather and Climate

Module F Geologic Processes and History
Unit 1 The Dynamic Earth
Unit 2 Earth Through Time

Module G Earth and Human Activity
Unit 1 Earth's Natural Hazards
Unit 2 Resources in Earth's Systems
Unit 3 Using Resources
Unit 4 Human Impacts on Earth Systems

Module H Space Science
Unit 1 Patterns in the Solar System
Unit 2 The Solar System and Universe

Pacing Guide

The following Pacing Guide recommends days for the core instructional elements of each unit. You have options for covering lesson materials: you may choose to follow the traditional path or you may choose the core path. You may also customize your Pacing Guide based on your classroom schedule and needs.

[handwritten: ✓ Require] *[handwritten: comprehensive 30 men.]*

Pressed for time? Follow the faster-paced core path.

	Core	Traditional 45 minute class	Customize Your Pacing Guide
Unit 1 Engineering and Technology			
Unit 1 Project		3 days	
Lesson 1 **Engineer It** · How Do Engineers Use Technology?	5 days	7 days	
Lesson 2 **Engineer It** · How Can We Solve a Problem?	5 days	7 days	
You Solve It		1 day	
Unit 1 Performance Task		2 days	
Performance-Based Assessment		2 days	
Unit 1 Review and Unit 1 Test	2 days	2 days	
Total Days for Unit 1	12 days	24 days	
Unit 2 Sound			
Unit 2 Project		3 days	
Lesson 1 What Is Sound?	5 days	7 days	
Lesson 2 **Engineer It** · How Can We Communicate With Sound?	5 days	7 days	
You Solve It		1 day	

	Core	Traditional 45 minute class	Customize Your Pacing Guide
Unit 2 Sound continued			
Unit 2 Performance Task		2 days	
Performance-Based Assessment		2 days	
Unit 2 Review and Unit 2 Test	2 days	2 days	
Total Days for Unit 2	12 days	24 days	
Unit 3 Light			
Unit 3 Project		3 days	
Lesson 1 How Does Light Help Us See?	5 days	7 days	
Lesson 2 How Do Materials Block Light?	5 days	7 days	
Lesson 3 How Does Light Travel?	5 days	7 days	
You Solve It		1 day	
Unit 3 Performance Task		2 days	
Performance-Based Assessment		2 days	
Unit 3 Review and Unit 3 Test	2 days	2 days	
Total Days for Unit 3	17 days	31 days	
Unit 4 Plant and Animal Structures			
Unit 4 Project		3 days	
Lesson 1 **Engineer It** · What Parts Help Plants Live?	5 days	7 days	

	Traditional 45 minute class	Customize Your Pacing Guide
Unit 4 Plant and Animal Structures continued		
Lesson 2 **Engineer It** • What Body Parts Help Animals Stay Safe?	5 days · 7 days	
Lesson 3 **Engineer It** • What Body Parts Help Animals Meet Their Needs?	5 days · 7 days	
Lesson 4 How Do Plants and Animals Respond to Their Environment?	5 days · 7 days	
You Solve It	1 day	
Unit 4 Performance Task	2 days	
Performance-Based Assessment	2 days	
Unit 4 Review and Unit 4 Test	2 days · 2 days	
Total Days for Unit 4	22 days · 38 days	
Unit 5 Living Things and Their Young		
Unit 5 Project	3 days	
Lesson 1 How Do Plants Look Like Their Parents?	5 days · 7 days	
Lesson 2 How Do Animals Look Like Their Parents?	5 days · 7 days	
Lesson 3 How Do Animals Take Care of Their Young?	5 days · 7 days	
You Solve It	1 day	
Unit 5 Performance Task	2 days	
Performance-Based Assessment	2 days	

	Core	Traditional 45 minute class	Customize Your Pacing Guide
Unit 5 Living Things and Their Young continued			
Unit 5 Review and Unit 5 Test	2 days	2 days	
Total Days for Unit 5	17 days	31 days	
Unit 6 Objects and Patterns in the Sky			
Unit 6 Project		3 days	
Lesson 1 How Do Objects in the Sky Seem to Change?	5 days	7 days	
Lesson 2 What Are Patterns of Daylight?	5 days	7 days	
You Solve It		1 day	
Unit 6 Performance Task		2 days	
Performance-Based Assessment		2 days	
Unit 6 Review and Unit 6 Test	2 days	2 days	
Total Days for Unit 6	12 days	24 days	

Cary I. Sneider, Ph.D.

Change is rarely welcomed with open arms. A few weeks ago I was helping a colleague facilitate a team of teacher-leaders develop a district plan to implement the Next Generation Science Standards (NGSS). During a break two of the teachers asked to speak with me. They were upset and nearly in tears. One of the teachers explained that they had spent the past 20 years developing the best possible science program for their school. The kids and parents loved it. The principal was proud of what they had accomplished. But now they would be asked to start all over because they would be assigned to teach science units they had never taught before.

It helped that the district leaders were listening and willing to consider some changes that these teachers recommended, although the leaders were quite firm about implementing the NGSS. It was also helpful for these teachers to learn that they would be helping other teachers by sharing the great ideas and resources that they had developed for their own students, so their creativity and hard work wouldn't be wasted. Even more important, I believe, was the gradual realization, over the next couple of days, that the profound changes called for by the NGSS

were not simply a change in when different science topics would be taught but rather a change in how they would be taught—in ways that these excellent teacher-leaders valued and had established with their own students.

> **"...the profound changes called for by the NGSS were not simply a change in when different science topics would be taught but rather a change in how they would be taught."**

What follows is a brief summary of the ways that the NGSS is similar to but also different from science as it has been taught for the past 20 years. I won't compare it with "traditional" science education, because the method of having students read and answer questions at the end of the chapter is (thankfully) rarely done these days. But the changes called for by the NGSS can be surprising even for teachers who are comfortable with a hands-on inquiry approach that has come to characterize the best of science teaching. And I'll admit some of these changes have been hard for me to get used to, after nearly 50 years as a science educator and as a member of the NGSS writing team.

Disciplinary Core Ideas

With respect to the disciplinary core ideas (what we used to call the "content") of the new standards, at least 80% are unchanged. Students still need to learn about Newton's Laws of Motion and the Periodic Table of Elements. Some topics in the Earth and space sciences have been updated—such as by the addition of a greater focus on human impacts on the environment—so that topics that many teachers introduced as a way to enrich the curriculum with contemporary issues are now mainstream.

Crosscutting concepts

Crosscutting concepts should also be familiar to teachers who appreciate the nature of scientific thinking. The purpose of these seven concepts is to help students see the commonalities among the science and engineering fields. They include the idea that patterns we observe in nature are clues to some underlying process. For example, the monthly pattern of moon phases can best be understood in terms of systems and system models by manipulating a model of the Earth-sun-moon system. The crosscutting concept of cause and effect grows from our human instinct to know why things occur as they do, and the concepts of energy and matter are fundamental to all fields of science and engineering. The crosscutting concept of structure and function is useful in understanding how the structure of molecules affect the macroscopic behavior of a substance, as well as understanding how the structure of an organ enables it to carry out its function in the body. As students mature they are more able to study the world by applying the concepts of scale, proportion, and quantity. And finally, the need to explain stability and change is at the

> **"Technology in the NGSS is portrayed as the application of science to the development of various products, processes, and systems to meet human needs..."**

root of our conservation laws in physics, chemical reactions in chemistry, and the theory of evolution in biology. By introducing these crosscutting concepts at appropriate times, teachers can help their students gain perspective on the study of various topics in science and see how they all—in a very important sense—reflect the same scientific way of thinking.

Emphasizing Technology and Engineering

Despite these similarities, the NGSS is very different from what has come before. One way it differs from prior standards is in the prominent role of technology and engineering. Although the idea that students should learn about technology and engineering has been around since the beginning of the standards movement[1], they have rarely been woven into the natural sciences as they are in the NGSS. Technology in

[1] American Association for the Advancement of Science. (1990). *Project 2061: Science for all Americans.* London: Oxford University Press.

the NGSS is portrayed as the application of science to the development of various products, processes, and systems to meet human needs, such as the application of wave phenomena to communication technologies. Engineering is positioned both as a core idea about defining and solving problems and as a means of applying the natural sciences to a wide variety of issues of both societal and environmental importance. And along with engineering comes a new set of skills for students to learn, such as defining problems by identifying criteria and constraints, applying tradeoffs to find the best acceptable solution, and learning to appreciate failure as a valuable aspect of the iterative design process.

Science and Engineering Practices

Some of the practices of science and engineering in the NGSS will be familiar to teachers, and some will seem quite different. What is especially different is that all of these practices are useful for scientific inquiry and engineering design. Table 1 illustrates why they are called practices of science and engineering.

It has taken me some time to fully appreciate what it means to help students develop skills in using these practices, since most of my career has focused on teaching concepts. I empathized with the two teachers whom I referred to in my opening paragraph because I've been in a similar position. My favorite subject is astronomy, and I've developed some really effective ways for students to use models so they can understand phenomena such as moon phases and seasons. I hated to give those methods up! But if students are to learn to develop and use models, then they are the ones who need to figure out how to use models to explain the phenomena. Telling them how to use the models just doesn't cut it. I should add that it's fine to illustrate how to use a model so they can learn how it's done, but at some point the students need to pick up the pieces as a means for figuring out why the moon goes through phases and how phases are different from eclipses. Another way to think about this is to consider who is doing the science. If the teacher is doing all of the explaining and asking all of the questions, the teacher—not the student—is doing the science.

Performance Expectations

Perhaps the most unusual aspect of the NGSS is the way these three dimensions are assembled—in single statements called Performance Expectations (PEs). They are called that because the NGSS is a set of assessment

> **"Perhaps the most unusual aspect of the NGSS is the way these three dimensions are assembled—in single statements called Performance Expectations."**

Table 1. Science and Engineering Practices

Practices	Science	Engineering
1. Asking Questions and Defining Problems	A basic practice of science is to ask questions about the world that can be answered by gathering data.	Engineering begins by defining a problem in terms of criteria for a successful solution, and constraints or limits.
2. Developing and Using Models	Science often involves the construction and use of models to help answer questions about natural phenomena.	Engineering makes use of models to analyze existing systems or to test possible solutions to a new problem.
3. Planning and Carrying Out Investigations	Scientific investigation can be controlled experiments to test predictions, attempts to identify correlations, or taxonomic identifications of species.	Engineers use investigations both to gain data essential for their design and to test the designs they develop.
4. Analyzing and Interpreting Data	Scientific investigations generally produce data that must be analyzed in order to derive meaning.	Engineers analyze and interpret data to determine how well each meets specific design criteria.
5. Using Mathematics and Computational Thinking	In science, mathematics and computers are used for a range of tasks from constructing models to analyzing data, and expressing relationship between variables.	In engineering, mathematics and computers are integral parts of the engineering design process.
6. Constructing Explanations and Designing Solutions	The goal of science is to explain phenomena in the natural world.	The goal of engineering is to solve meaningful problems.
7. Engaging in Argument From Evidence	In science, reasoning, argument, and participating actively in a community of peers is essential for finding explanations for natural phenomena.	In engineering, reasoning and argument are essential for finding the best possible solutions to problems.
8. Obtaining, Communicating and Presenting Information	A major practice of science is to communicate ideas and results of scientific inquiry and to obtain and evaluate findings reported by others.	Engineering needs to start by finding out how similar problems have been solved in the past and communicating ideas clearly and persuasively.

> **"The NGSS describes which practices students of various ages are expected to use in order to demonstrate their understanding of a specific core idea and crosscutting concept."**

standards. That is, they describe what students should be able to do at the end of instruction—not just what they know, but what they can do with what they know. That means achievement of these standards cannot be assessed with a multiple-choice test alone. Performance assessments of some sort will be necessary. The challenge for curriculum developers and teachers is to figure out what experiences they can provide so that their students will be able to meet these Performance Expectations not just at the end of class, but several months or even years later.

If all this seems daunting, keep in mind that the NGSS requires students to learn fewer core ideas than prior standards do so that teachers have time to teach those standards that remain in depth. When our writing team circulated drafts for public comment, we were told that there were too many standards to reasonably expect students to learn; so in the final round we cut the number of standards by one third. We did not "cheat" by combining standards—we actually cut the number of core ideas.

Another major advantage of the NGSS is that the standards are specific. I recall a project a few years ago, when I was helping to facilitate a team of teachers and other instructional leaders in the state of Washington to revise the state's standards. The Director of Science and I were meeting groups at various locations in the state to gather feedback on a draft. I recall one teacher who stood up to complain that the state test had questions that were impossible to anticipate because the standards were too vague. "Just tell us what the tests will be about," he said, "and we can help our students succeed!" The Next Generation Science Standards will not be subject to that objection. The NGSS describes which practices students of various ages are expected to use in order to demonstrate their understanding of a specific core idea and crosscutting concept. Each PE is followed by an additional clarification of the specific experiences that are referred to in the PE and also a list of performances that would not be assessed at that grade level.

So, to sum up: The great majority of core ideas in the NGSS are the same core ideas we've been teaching for years, with the addition of a few updates, especially related to societal and environmental issues. Although crosscutting concepts may sound new, they represent well-known features of scientific thinking. A new feature of the NGSS is that technology and engineering are woven deeply into the fabric of the document so that students are expected to develop skills that are quite new to most science teachers. And finally, the core ideas are fewer in number than prior standards in order to allow teachers more time to teach to mastery. The standards are also more specific to enable students to have greater success on tests by making it easier to align curriculum, instruction, and assessment. These last qualities alone are a reason for science teachers to cheer the NGSS.

Building an NGSS Curriculum

It's especially important for curriculum developers to keep in mind that the NGSS is sparse for a reason and to avoid including lessons just because they were there before and teachers expected to see them. Studies that have attempted to explain why U.S. students do poorly on international examinations have faulted textbooks in this country for being "a mile wide and an inch deep."[2] In light of that finding, I've been very impressed with the new **HMH Science Dimensions** textbook series. As a consulting author I've been pleased to see it develop as an entirely new curriculum that sticks to the PEs at each grade level, with rich science content and activities involving practices and core ideas but without extraneous material that would take up valuable instructional time.

It's hard to say what impact the NGSS will have, but I'm hopeful. For the past two years I've worked with middle school teachers in one school district in Oregon, which was one of the first states to adopt the NGSS. The teachers were given the task of designing units to match the sequence of PEs that their state recommended. I asked the teachers who had the most experience teaching a unit to design it for the district, even if they were not going to be teaching it in the fall. Initially some of the teachers protested having to spend a week during the summer preparing lessons they would not be teaching. One veteran teacher saved the day by saying, "Let's think of this as a barn raising. We'll all pitch in to help one group of teachers, and later they'll pitch in to help us."

Change is rarely embraced, but in the long run it has the advantage of keeping us on our toes. Science teachers are among the most creative people I know. With the support of their school and district leaders I know they will rise to the challenge, even if it means giving up some of their most treasured lessons. Their students will certainly be the beneficiaries of renewed instructional ideas and materials, especially as those students become the ones doing the science in the classroom.

> **"Science teachers are among the most creative people I know. With the support of their school and district leaders I know they will rise to the challenge."**

[2] Schmidt, W. H., McKnight, C., & Raizen, S. (Eds.). (1997). A splintered vision: An investigation of U.S. science and mathematics education (Vol. 1). Dordrecht, The Netherlands: Kluwer Academic Publishers.

Evidence Notebooks

by Michael A. DiSpezio

In **HMH Science Dimensions** you'll discover references to a brand-new type of tool—the evidence notebook—designed to support and reinforce the three-dimensional learning so central to NGSS pedagogy. Evidence notebook may be a new term to you. So what is it and how does it differ from a traditional lab notebook or science journal? Great questions. As you are about to discover, the evidence notebook is a critical part of an NGSS approach to effective science education.

Think back to science notebooks that you maintained throughout your student experience. There's a good chance that these were a linear chronology of your learning accomplishments. In the earlier grades, they were bound records of classroom experience. For the most part, these entries were limited to lab observations; data collection tables; and answers to specific, prepackaged questions. By the time you reached middle school, the role of the lab notebook often segued into worksheet-and-lab-report repository.

Typically, all notebooks were organized in the same manner. There was little opportunity for individuality, personal voice, or indication of a student's interests. Often, they were used as summative assessment based on the expected homogenization of entries.

With the Next Generation Science Standards' revolutionary approach to pedagogy, the role and organization of what had been a record-keeping device has evolved. No longer a landscape on which to record prescriptive responses, the evidence notebook assumes the role of conceptual "scratch-pad." Like computer RAM, this is where the higher processing occurs.

With this evolution to a much more interactive role for the evidence notebook, let's examine the nuts and bolts of creating and maintaining it. The first thing to consider is that the notebook is student directed. Remember, it's primarily for the students—not for you! With that in mind, it is organized according to each student's learning style, personal interests, questions, observations, and interaction with the three dimensions of science.

Using evidence notebooks, students can

- assume an increased role and responsibility for their own learning

- direct or create their own learning path by recording, selecting, and pursuing questions of interest

- organize their thinking

- record and analyze observations

- compare/contrast passive information to higher-level thinking and critical analysis

- better commit ideas to long-term memory through the writing process

- perfect language skills in an authentic learning experience

- communicate understanding and competency

- record and evaluate evidence both from within the classroom and outside of the classroom in a Claims/Evidence/Reasoning model

EVIDENCE NOTEBOOK

Beyond the Classroom Walls

The evidence notebook travels both literally and figuratively beyond the physical school boundary. Not limited to recording classroom experiences and prescribed assignments, it assumes the role of interactive diary. Students record relevant thoughts and observations of the world around them in their notebooks. For example, if studying runoff, they might write about or photograph neighborhood gullies or storm-drainage systems. Entries can then be examined in a context of active learning using these meaningful examples from students' immediate world.

Spreading It Out

One way in which students might organize their notebooks is based upon right- and left-side pages of a spread. The left side of the page spread might incorporate the higher-level thinking process associated with an investigation. The posed question, evolving thoughts, and critical-thinking analysis would form this page's content. The facing right-hand page might include more of the prescribed and quantitative thought processes, such as the steps, data collection, and observations.

Claims/Evidence/Reasoning Connection

Claims/Evidence/Reasoning, or CER for short, is a strategy for getting students to go beyond memorization and construct explanations. The evidence notebook is the ideal landscape on which to address all three of the CER components. First, students can record and further distill their claims into testable hypotheses. Then, based upon a student-directed investigation, they can collect and record data as evidence. Finally, the students can illustrate the logic they used in arriving at a reasoned explanation.

Evidence for Assessment

Don't overlook the role that the evidence notebook can play in formative assessment. By reviewing student notebooks, the instructor gains insight into each student's qualitative thinking. The instructor can then offer targeted feedback to help students improve their evidence notebook's organization and entries.

> **"The evidence notebook travels both literally and figuratively beyond the physical school boundary."**

From Data to Thinking About Data

As you know, "thinking about one's thinking" is a key element to successful learning. However, prior to evidence notebooks, students lacked a classroom tool adapted to metacognition. Now, within evidence notebooks, students can record and analyze their thinking processes. By reflecting on how best they learn, they can assume more control of personal learning. Not only does this awareness result in richer understanding, but it also evolves the organization and content of the evidence notebook to its most effective design.

Organizing the Evidence Notebook

By now, perhaps you are wondering what makes up the specific content and organization of an effective evidence notebook? The definitive answer is "it depends." That's because it varies from student to student. Although all notebooks should have a sequential format, the nature of each notebook's specific content and organization depends upon individual learning styles.

That said, effective evidence notebooks may include

- student interests and related questions

- a record of prior knowledge

- evidence collected from student-directed explorations

- short essays that address concepts and a student's personal thinking process

- graphic organizers such as concept maps and Venn diagrams

- drawings and embedded digital photographs

- observations that go beyond the classroom's physical boundaries

- reflections on understanding

- thinking and processes that address claims, evidence, and reasoning

21st Century Tools

Exploit the technology! As the installed base of tablets and PCs broadens, there are increasing opportunities for creating electronic evidence notebooks. Strategies in *HMH Science Dimensions* print and electronic student editions offer the opportunity for open-ended student input. Students can also construct an evidence notebook using appropriate apps and software. In addition to accepting written input, electronic versions can include embedded media such as digital photos, video clips, and sound files.

Dynamic, Not Static

Unlike its traditional counterpart, the evidence notebook is not a static record. It is a work in progress on which understanding is continually constructed. Students update its content on a daily basis, not just around investigations and lab reports. So remind students to keep it current and use it as a foundation on which to construct understanding.

How *HMH Science Dimensions* Supports an Evidence Notebook

Throughout both the Electronic Student Edition and the student text of *HMH Science Dimensions* are evidence-notebook writing prompts. They are designed to introduce and reinforce the skills that you've just read about. But these should be considered only the beginning. Let your imagination run wild, but most of all, encourage your students to use this important tool in ways that foster their own learning and understanding of science and engineering and their connections to everyday life.

By Marjorie Frank

As educators, we often think in terms of disciplines: I teach English. I'm a science teacher. I'm a math coach. While these may be useful distinctions, they obscure an important consideration: Our brain has no such distinctions.

The Brain and Learning

No special region is active during science class and inactive during English or math. Or, vice versa. Yet, we often operate as if it were. Most science teachers don't focus deeply on reading or writing skills; English and math teachers aren't greatly concerned with science concepts. Yet, the cognitive processes in all these—and other—disciplines are pretty much the same. We just talk about them differently . . . and sometimes, we don't even do that. For example, citing evidence to support a claim is central to science. Explaining how an author uses evidence to support particular points is central to English language study. How different are these phenomena, really?

Which Standards?

Here's a short activity to test this idea. The sentences below are from science and English language arts standards. Except for giveaway words such as science and nonfiction, which I've deleted, the standards are reproduced here verbatim. See if you can tell which are science standards and which are ELA standards. [Answers are at the end of this article.]

1. Obtain information using various texts, text features (e.g. headings, tables of contents, glossaries, electronic menus, icons), and other media that will be useful in answering a question.

2. Ask questions based on observations to find more information. . . .

3. Write arguments to support claims . . . using valid reasoning and relevant and sufficient evidence.

4. Construct an argument with evidence to support a claim.

5. Ask questions to clear up any confusion. . . .

6. Know and use various text features (e.g. headings, tables of contents, glossaries, electronic menus, icons) to locate key facts or information. . . .

7. Obtain and combine information from books and/or other reliable media to explain phenomena or solutions . . . to a design problem.

8. Integrate information from several texts on the same topic. . . .

This confluence of interdisciplinary realities is embodied in the Next Generation Science Standards.

Curriculum Crossover in NGSS

Released in April 2013, the Next Generation Science Standards are, I believe, the only standards to date that recognize and embrace the natural crossover of disciplines. If you were to print the standards, each page would include a set of Science and Engineering Practices, a set of Disciplinary Core Ideas, a set of Crosscutting Concepts, and sets of ELA and Mathematics standards—formalizing what is true naturally: they all work together.

> **"Much of the time, you may be engaging in cross-disciplinary practices without even realizing it."**

Much of the time, you may be engaging in cross-disciplinary practices without even realizing it. In English class, your students participate in exchanges that require close reading of a text. They cite evidence from the reading to support their responses to questions. Is this really different from asking students to cite evidence in support of a science claim? In science class, your students communicate solutions to a design problem via posters or verbal presentations. Is this all that different from reporting on a topic or engaging in collaborative discussions? Perhaps the expression a distinction without a difference applies here.

If your students are doing science, and I do mean doing science, they are likely to be engaging in crossover English language arts skills coincidentally.

HMH Science Dimensions takes the coincidence out of the crossover.

HMH Science Dimensions and Integrated Learning

The instructional design and lesson plans of the student-facing materials for all levels of *HMH Science Dimensions* facilitate English language arts in ways that are both subtle and explicit. Prompts throughout a lesson lead learners to collaborate, ask questions, summarize, explain, analyze. Frequent opportunities connected to students' Evidence Notebooks integrate writing into the process. You need only scroll through a digital lesson or page through the print to find evidence of these approaches.

Something else you'll find in the student-facing materials for young learners is a system of light-bulb icons and headings that identify an extensive structure of online handbooks containing tips and strategies for developing science, math, and language arts skills. Some of the language skills that receive attention include asking and answering questions, doing research, collaborating, using visuals, and describing problems.

For the youngest learners is a robust feature in the student-facing materials called Read, Write, Share! Here, children are guided to practice asking and answering questions, collaborating, drawing, writing, and presenting ideas to others. And throughout the teacher-facing materials you will find suggestions for collaboration, a quintessentially language-based endeavor.

For older learners you'll find a lesson feature called Language SmArts. These are activities that integrate language arts skills into the science learning process. Some Language SmArts activities appear in the student-facing materials; others appear only in the teacher-facing components. Examples of activities include those connected to making inferences, conducting research, and using visuals in multimedia displays among others. In all cases, they represent another way in which **HMH Science Dimensions** helps facilitate the alignment of English language arts and the Next Generation Science Standards.

In the end, if your goal is to help learners draw upon their full complement of natural abilities to gain ownership of science, you can relax knowing that you've come to the right place: **HMH Science Dimensions**.

Read, Write, Share!

Language SmArts

> **"...all levels of *HMH Science Dimensions* facilitate English language arts in ways that are both subtle and explicit."**

Answers:

1. NGSS standard; **2.** NGSS standard; **3.** English language arts standard; **4.** NGSS standard; **5.** English language arts standard; **6.** English language arts standard; **7.** NGSS standard; **8.** English language arts standard.

NGSS and College and Career Readiness

by Michael R. Heithaus, Ph.D.

Improving STEM education at every level—from K–12 through university—is a national priority. Distinction in STEM fields is critical to ensuring the ability of the United States to compete in international markets and to actualize intellectual goals, and jobs in STEM fields are projected to grow at higher rates than in other professions. Yet at the university and career levels, there is seemingly not enough interest or achievement in STEM fields. How we prepare students for college and career is a growing concern. The Next Generation Science Standards are built to ensure readiness.

What is college and career readiness?

At the simplest level, being college ready means that students are able to succeed in college classes without remediation. Being career ready means that graduates are prepared to obtain and succeed in entry-level positions. Sounds simple, but as STEM fields evolve and change, so do requirements

related to content-area knowledge. For that reason, NGSS and **HMH Science Dimensions** focus on students demonstrating that they have mastered important skills more than specific knowledge or facts. Through formative assessments, evidence notebooks, and summative assessments, including critical performance-based assessments, teachers are supplied with the tools they need to understand student performance. Strategies throughout this Teacher Edition provide means of addressing many deficiencies.

When students have mastered skills and understand the underlying connections between STEM fields and other curriculum areas, they will not only have the background knowledge they need but also be prepared to fill in gaps in their understanding independently, without the need for remediation or extensive on-the-job training. And although college and career readiness might seem like qualities for students to master in high school, NGSS brings a greater coherence across grade levels: students from primary grades through high school have the opportunity to work on these skills and learn to apply them in everyday life.

According to the NGSS, career and college-ready students should be able to

- make sense of the world and approach novel problems, phenomena, and information using a blend of science and engineering practices, disciplinary core ideas, and crosscutting concepts

- use valid research strategies

- be self-directed in planning, monitoring, and evaluation

- flexibly apply knowledge across disciplines (through continued exploration of Science and Engineering Practices, crosscutting concepts, and Disciplinary Core Ideas)

Not included in this list are some other skills that students should master to succeed in today's college classroom and workplace. First, students need to be

- comfortable working in diverse groups and with peers with different perspectives

- able to support their claims with logical arguments while being respectful and constructive in dealing with those who don't agree

- able to think critically and creatively

- able to communicate effectively in multiple settings and via diverse media

New teaching methods and a new role for teachers

The new focus on skills rather than content knowledge alone has led to big changes, backed by research, in how we teach science at universities and in K–12 classrooms. We know that active learning from student-centered activities that include group work and problem solving enhance student success.

There is no question that implementing NGSS requires teachers to shift both what and how they teach. For much of the instruction, the teacher's role in the classroom is different. Because NGSS integrates the practices of science and engineering with content-area knowledge, there is an increasing focus on students being scientists in the discovery process and leading their own investigations. Does this mean teachers are less important? Not by a long shot. In fact, teachers are probably more important than ever! It will take a bit of work to adapt your course to active learning and to integrate NGSS-style learning, but believe me, it will be worth it for you and your students.

Some things to keep in mind:

- Think about questions. Asking the right questions can be critical to getting students on—or back to— the right track to discovering material for themselves and making connections between concepts that are critical to NGSS. Pose questions to get students to think deeply about the nature and strength of evidence used to support a claim.

- Facilitate team learning. Science and engineering are all about teams, and students need to be comfortable working in groups with peers. Team learning can help students at very different levels benefit from the same course of investigation. I have found that strong students gain better mastery of concepts when they help students who are having trouble. On the flip side, some students actually learn better from a peer than a teacher! Pay attention to group dynamics, but facilitate cooperative teams wherever you can.

- Moderate discussions and peer critiques purposefully.

- Remember that NGSS can help improve math skills. Throughout **HMH Science Dimensions**, you'll find opportunities to practice age- and discipline-appropriate math practices to support science investigations and learning. Find ways to bring

> **"There is no question that implementing NGSS requires teachers to shift both what and how they teach. For much of the instruction, the teacher's role in the classroom is different."**

math into investigations. Math is critical to science and engineering, and science and engineering can make math more accessible and exciting to students!

- Help students make connections continuously. The **HMH Science Dimensions** Teacher Edition provides many strategies to assist students in making those connections. There is plenty of evidence that multiple opportunities to associate pieces of information in different contexts facilitate retention. NGSS is built so that particular standards can be blended with others and integrated throughout a year and across grade levels. Online resources facilitate this blending—and you will find them already integrated in HMH Science Dimensions!

- Collaborate! Whether you teach kindergarten or college, you are not alone in applying NGSS innovations in science education. When you talk to your colleagues and look online for best ideas and practices, you are serving as a role model for your students.

As you move into teaching NGSS and preparing students for college and career, look for the many strategies and opportunities for assessment embedded in both the student-facing materials and the Teacher materials of your **HMH Science Dimensions** program. These will facilitate implementation of best practices in NGSS pedagogy. Even if your students won't be entering STEM fields, solid science education at this point will help students prepare for the coming years by inculcating the critical thinking skills necessary for science literacy and making informed, reasonable, evidence-backed decisions in all facets of life.

❝Whether you teach kindergarten or college, you are not alone in applying NGSS innovations in science education.❞

NGSS has a sharp emphasis on teaching all standards to all students. One of the challenges of teaching using NGSS pedagogy is reteaching. The three dimensions of science would seem to present challenges that you haven't encountered before. But there is good news: two of the dimensions are self-reteaching!

Both the Science and Engineering Practices and the Crosscutting Concepts are revisited time and again throughout the year. Strategies for teaching these occur within the teacher margin materials.

While you may need to remind children (about CCCs) or monitor closely (for SEPs), multiple exposures to a concept in different contexts have been shown to be the most effective reteaching possible.

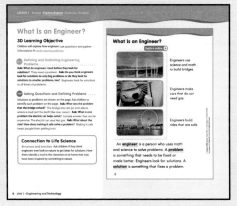

And for reteaching Disciplinary Core Ideas, **HMH Science Dimensions™** has you covered.

Key Science concepts are recontextualized in the *Science and Engineering Readers*. These readers present the same concepts at two different levels and provide additional concepts and advanced reading for children who are easily mastering the concepts.

Sciencesaurus provides a quick, in depth, visual reference at suitable readabilities for students. The engaging writing and illustrations help to present the content in another context and in slightly different ways so as to reinforce key DCIs and recontextualize the Science Dimensions student-facing materials. Recontextualization and easier reading are both shown to improve comprehension of difficult, but important, science concepts.

The *Interactive Worktext* and the *Interactive Online Student Edition* present the same content in different ways. The *Interactive Online Student Edition* provides additional interactions and voice over to reinforce and reteach the content in ways that enable children with reading deficits to learn the core science concepts. It also provides children with immediate feedback on many interactivities to reinforce learning.

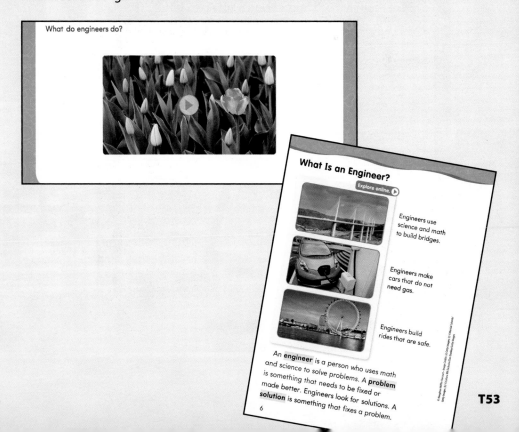

HMH Science Dimensions™ and the EQuIP Rubric

The **EQuIP Rubric** is an instrument for evaluating a curriculum's conformance with the contours of an authentic NGSS program. As such, one needs to bear in mind the known limitations and proper usages of the rubric:

• The rubric is intended to be applied to lessons or units, not to entire curricula.

• The rubric itself indicates that it is unlikely that a single lesson will lead to mastery of a Performance Expectation. High-Quality Units may do so.

• The evaluation process is intended to be done in a group, not by an individual.

• The rubric requires familiarity with the Performance Expectation and its supporting Dimensions of Learning. The **HMH Science Dimensions™ Trace Tool to the NGSS** can help provide this orientation.

Throughout the **HMH Science Dimensions Teacher Edition**, you will find features to help you orient toward the critical dimensions of the EQuIP Rubric. Using the book, you are well beyond the evaluation phase of considering a program, but these features will demonstrate the best practices of NGSS summarized by the evaluation instrument. Highlights of critical EQuIP Rubric evaluation points are summarized in the reduced pages you see here.

Unit Planning Pages

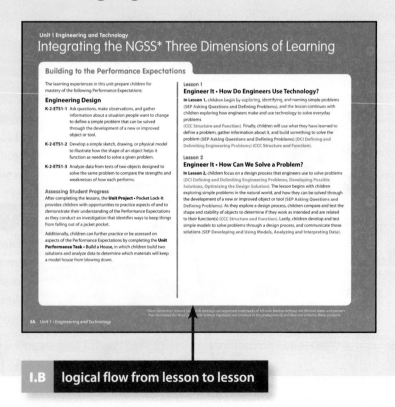

I.B logical flow from lesson to lesson

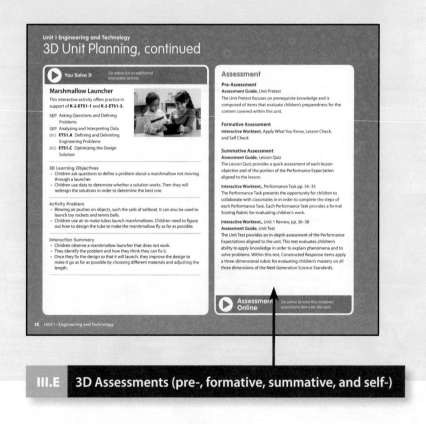

III.E 3D Assessments (pre-, formative, summative, and self-)

Lesson Planning Pages

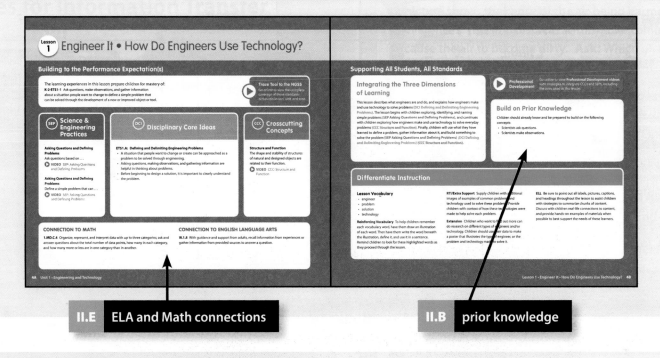

II.E ELA and Math connections

II.B prior knowledge

Lesson Opener Pages

II.A authentic and meaningful scenarios

II.D collaborative opportunities to express ideas and respond

HMH Science Dimensions™ and the EQuIP Rubric

Lesson Pages

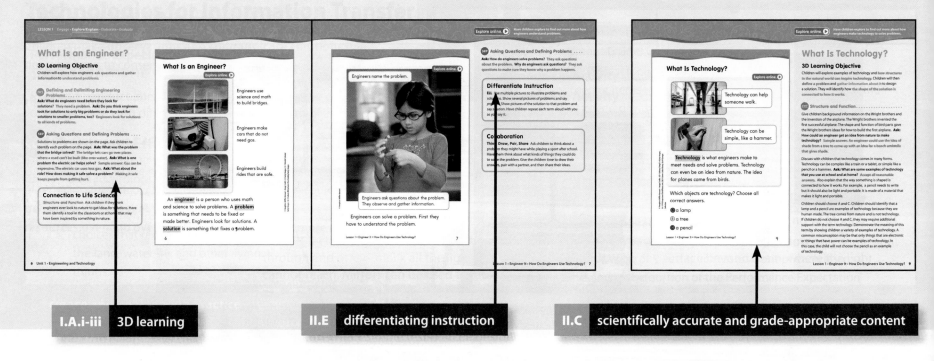

I.A.i-iii	3D learning
II.E	differentiating instruction
II.C	scientifically accurate and grade-appropriate content

Lesson Pages

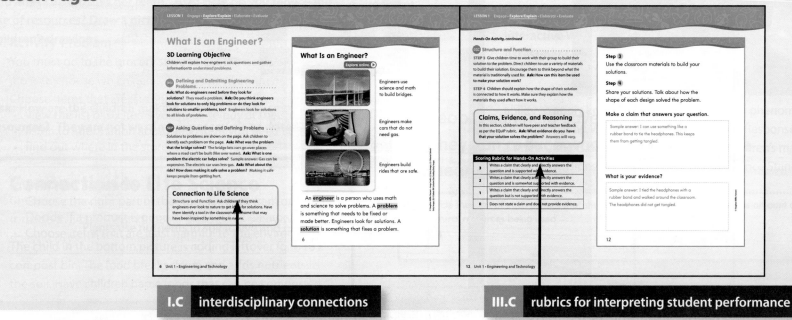

I.C	interdisciplinary connections
III.C	rubrics for interpreting student performance

Lesson Closer Pages

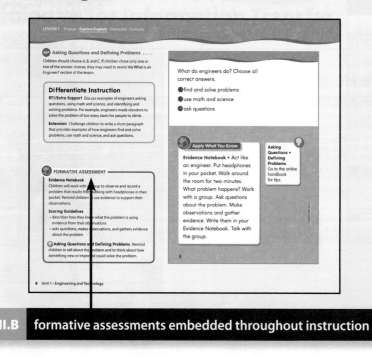

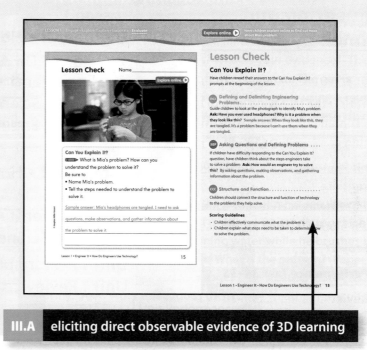

III.B formative assessments embedded throughout instruction

III.A eliciting direct observable evidence of 3D learning

Unit Interleaf Pages

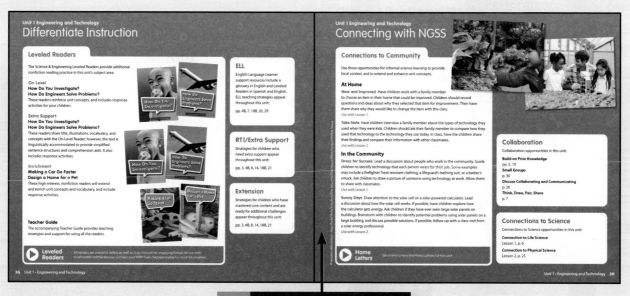

I.D developing connections

Unit 3 • Light...79

Unit 3
Light

© Houghton Mifflin Harcourt

xi

Unit 5 • Living Things and Their Young 217

Unit 6
Objects and Patterns in the Sky

Earth and Space Sciences
Unit 6 • Objects and Patterns in the Sky 275

© Houghton Mifflin Harcourt

Safety in Science

Doing science is fun. But a science lab can be dangerous. Know the safety rules and listen to your teacher.

⊘ Do not eat or drink anything.

⊘ Do not touch sharp things.

✔ Wash your hands.

✔ Wear goggles to keep your eyes safe.

✔ Be neat and clean up spills.

✔ Tell your teacher if something breaks.

✔ Show good behavior.

xv

Use the following discussion points to emphasize key safety rules for science hands-on activities.

Ask: What safety gear are the children in the picture using? They are wearing goggles and gloves. **Ask:** How does the gear keep them safer? The goggles protect their eyes from harmful things. The gloves protect their skin.

Show children an ordinary pair of glasses (or sunglasses). Then show them safety goggles. **Ask:** What is different about the safety goggles? The safety goggles are made of sturdy material and have protection all around the sides of the lenses.

Ask: What would you do if you spilled some water? Tell the teacher, and help clean up the spill. **Ask:** What could happen if the spill wasn't cleaned up? Water could make the floor slippery and increase the risk of falls.

Ask: Why is it important to wash your hands when you're done? Washing hands helps keep you from getting sick, and keeps you from rubbing things into your eyes.

Ask for a volunteer. Tell him or her to walk up to and point at a piece of safety equipment in the classroom. Then tell the class when and how to use it.

Safety in Science

Children should circle the pictures of hands being washed, and gloves and goggles being worn. Remind students that following these rules can help them stay safe. If children chose the picture of the child pouring water without wearing goggles, look at the lab safety rules again and remind them that wearing goggles is a rule that helps keep eyes safe. **Ask: Why is it important to wear goggles?** Goggles keep things from getting into your eyes.

Children should place an x on the children not wearing goggles and the child using scissors the wrong way. If children didn't choose those pictures, remind them that one of the safety rules is to not touch sharp things.

Circle the pictures where a safety rule is being followed. Place an X on the pictures where a safety rule is not being followed.

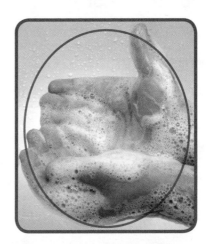

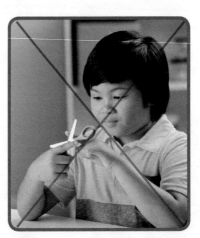

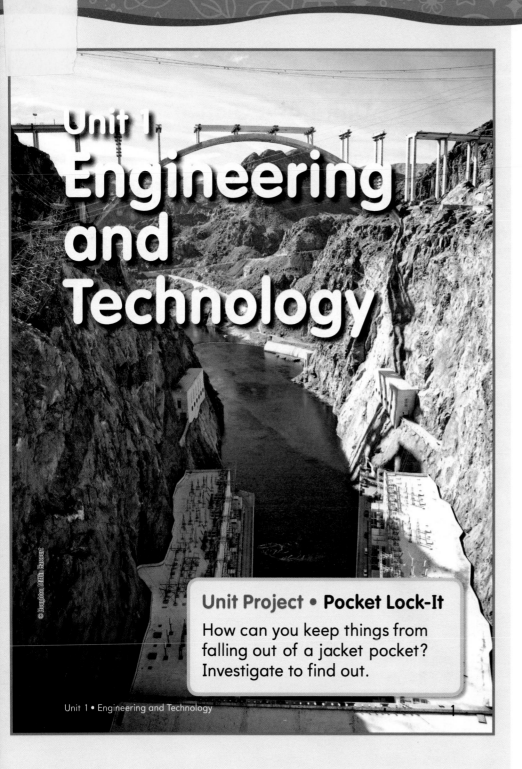

Unit 1
Engineering and Technology

Unit Project • Pocket Lock-It
How can you keep things from falling out of a jacket pocket? Investigate to find out.

Unit 1 • Engineering and Technology

Unit Overview

In this unit, children will…
- define and identify problems.
- define and identify examples of technology.
- describe how people understand problems and use technology to solve problems.
- explore and apply a design process.

About This Image

Guide children in a discussion about the picture on this page. **Ask: Did you ever ride over a bridge? What problem does a bridge solve?** Sample answer: It lets you cross over water. It also lets you cross over land that would be too hard to drive over. **Ask: What types of technology do you think were used to make this bridge?** Machines and other tools were used to build the bridge, and computers might have been used to design it.

Unit Project • Pocket Lock-It

Have children plan and conduct an investigation that identifies ways to keep things from falling out of a jacket pocket. Encourage children to collect various objects such as cups, bags, and books. Have children describe if each object could be used to contain and secure an item, and why or why not. Brainstorm characteristics of objects that could be used to contain and secure an item.

More support for the Unit Project can be found on pp. 3I–3L.

Unit 1 At a Glance

The learning experiences in this unit prepare children for mastery of:

Performance Expectations

K-2-ETS1-1 Ask questions, make observations, and gather information about a situation people want to change to define a simple problem that can be solved through the development of a new or improved object or tool.

K-2-ETS1-2 Develop a simple sketch, drawing, or physical model to illustrate how the shape of an object helps it function as needed to solve a given problem.

K-2-ETS1-3 Analyze data from tests of two objects designed to solve the same problem to compare the strengths and weaknesses of how each performs.

Explore online. ▶

In addition to the print resources, the following resources are available online to support this unit:

Unit Pretest
Lesson 1   Engineer It • How Do Engineers Use Technology?
- Interactive Online Student Edition
- Lesson Quiz
Lesson 2   Engineer It • How Can We Solve a Problem?
- Interactive Online Student Edition
- Lesson Quiz
You Solve It Marshmallow Launcher
Unit Performance Task
Unit Test

© Houghton Mifflin Harcourt

Unit Vocabulary

engineer a person who uses math and science to solve everyday problems (p. 6)

problem something that needs to be fixed or made better (p. 6)

solution something that fixes a problem (p. 6)

technology what engineers make to meet needs and solve problems (p. 9)

design process a plan with steps used to find solutions to problems (p. 20)

Vocabulary Game • Guess the Word

Materials
• 1 set of word cards

How to Play
1. Work with a partner to make word cards.
2. Place the cards face down in a pile.
3. One player picks the top card but does not show it.
4. The second player asks questions until they guess the word correctly.
5. Then the second player takes a card.

Unit Vocabulary

The Next Generation Science Standards emphasize explanation and demonstration of understanding versus rote memorization of science vocabulary words. Keep in mind that these vocabulary words are tools for clear communication. Use these words as a starting point, not an end goal, for children to build deeper understanding of science concepts.

Children can explore all vocabulary words in the **Online Glossary**.

Vocabulary Strategies

- Have children review the vocabulary words. Then have children work in pairs to make sentences using the vocabulary words. Challenge them to use two words in each sentence. Give children the opportunity to revise their sentences as they explore the unit.
- Have children think about how each word relates to engineering and technology. Have children work in pairs and share their ideas with a partner.

Differentiate Instruction

RTI/Extra Support Pronounce each word, and have children repeat it after you. Have children find each highlighted word within the unit content. Have children work in pairs and explain to a partner what they think each word means based on the surrounding context of imagery and text.

Extension Have children select two vocabulary words and work in small groups to illustrate and explain the words to a kindergarten child.

Vocabulary Game • Guess the Word

Preparation Assign children to pairs. Distribute five cards to each pair. Establish a time limit or a set number of words per partner.

Integrating the NGSS* Three Dimensions of Learning

Building to the Performance Expectations

The learning experiences in this unit prepare children for mastery of the following Performance Expectations:

Engineering Design

K-2-ETS1-1 Ask questions, make observations, and gather information about a situation people want to change to define a simple problem that can be solved through the development of a new or improved object or tool.

K-2-ETS1-2 Develop a simple sketch, drawing, or physical model to illustrate how the shape of an object helps it function as needed to solve a given problem.

K-2-ETS1-3 Analyze data from tests of two objects designed to solve the same problem to compare the strengths and weaknesses of how each performs.

Assessing Student Progress

After completing the lessons, the **Unit Project • Pocket Lock-It** provides children with opportunities to practice aspects of and to demonstrate their understanding of the Performance Expectations as they conduct an investigation that identifies ways to keep things from falling out of a jacket pocket.

Additionally, children can further practice or be assessed on aspects of the Performance Expectations by completing the **Unit Performance Task • Build a House,** in which children build two solutions and analyze data to determine which materials will keep a model house from blowing down.

Lesson 1
Engineer It • How Do Engineers Use Technology?

In Lesson 1, children begin by exploring, identifying, and naming simple problems **(SEP Asking Questions and Defining Problems)**, and the lesson continues with children exploring how engineers make and use technology to solve everyday problems **(CCC Structure and Function)**. Finally, children will use what they have learned to define a problem, gather information about it, and build something to solve the problem **(SEP Asking Questions and Defining Problems) (DCI Defining and Delimiting Engineering Problems) (CCC Structure and Function)**.

Lesson 2
Engineer It • How Can We Solve a Problem?

In Lesson 2, children focus on a design process that engineers use to solve problems **(DCI Defining and Delimiting Engineering Problems, Developing Possible Solutions, Optimizing the Design Solution)**. The lesson begins with children exploring simple problems in the natural world, and how they can be solved through the development of a new or improved object or tool **(SEP Asking Questions and Defining Problems)**. As they explore a design process, children compare and test the shape and stability of objects to determine if they work as intended and are related to their function(s) **(CCC Structure and Function)**. Lastly, children develop and test simple models to solve problems through a design process, and communicate those solutions **(SEP Developing and Using Models, Analyzing and Interpreting Data)**.

Standards Supported by This Unit

Explore online. Online only.

Next Generation Science Standards	Unit Project	Lesson 1	Lesson 2			Unit Performance Task	You Solve It
SEP Asking Questions and Defining Problems	•	•	•			•	•
SEP Analyzing and Interpreting Data	•		•			•	•
SEP Developing and Using Models	•		•			•	•
DCI **ETS1.A** Defining and Delimiting Engineering Problems	•	•	•			•	•
DCI **ETS1.B** Developing Possible Solutions	•		•			•	•
DCI **ETS1.C** Optimizing the Design Solution	•		•			•	•
CCC Structure and Function	•	•	•			•	•

NGSS* Across the Grades

Before	Grade 1	After
Engineering Design	**Engineering Design**	**Engineering Design**
K-2-ETS1-1	**K-2-ETS1-1**	**K-2-ETS1-1**
K-2-ETS1-2	**K-2-ETS1-2**	**K-2-ETS1-2**
K-2-ETS1-3	**K-2-ETS1-3**	**K-2-ETS1-3**

Trace Tool to the NGSS™ Go online to view the complete coverage of these standards across this grade level and time.

3D Unit Planning

Lesson 1 Engineer It • How Do Engineers Use Technology? pp. 4–17

Overview

Objective Explore how engineers make and use technology to solve problems.

SEP Asking Questions and Defining Problems
DCI **ETS1.A** Defining and Delimiting Engineering Problems
CCC Structure and Function

Math and **English Language Arts** standards and features are detailed on lesson planning pages.

	Print and Online Student Editions	Explore online.
ENGAGE	**Lesson Phenomenon** pp. 4–5 **Can You Explain It?** What is the problem?	**▶ Can You Explain It?** Video
EXPLORE/ EXPLAIN	**What Is an Engineer?** **What is Technology?** **Hands-On Activity Engineer It • Solve the Headphones Problem** pp. 11–12	**Hands-On** Worksheet You Solve It Marshmallow Launcher
ELABORATE	**Take It Further** pp. 13–14 **Careers in Science & Engineering • Packaging Engineer**	**Take It Further** Transportation Timeline
EVALUATE	**Lesson Check** p. 15 **Self Check** pp. 16–17	**Lesson Quiz**

Hands-On Activity Planning

Engineer It • Solve the Headphones Problem

Objective Children work collaboratively to define a problem, gather information about it, and build something to solve the problem.

👥 small groups
🕐 1 class period

Suggested Materials
• headphones
• classroom materials

Preparation/Tip
Preassemble materials bundles for pairs or groups. Alternatively, children may do this activity at home.

Lesson 2 Engineer It • How Can We Solve a Problem? pp. 18–33

Overview

Objective Develop and test simple models to solve problems through a design process and communicate those solutions.

SEP Asking Questions and Defining Problems
SEP Developing and Using Models
SEP Analyzing and Interpreting Data
DCI **ETS1.A** Defining and Delimiting Engineering Problems
DCI **ETS1.B** Developing Possible Solutions
DCI **ETS1.C** Optimizing the Design Solution
CCC Structure and Function

Math and **English Language Arts** standards and features are detailed on lesson planning pages.

	Print and Online Student Editions	Explore online. ▶
ENGAGE	**Lesson Problem** pp. 18–19 **Can You Solve It?** The Pulling Dog Problem	▶ **Can** You Solve It? Video
EXPLORE/ EXPLAIN	**A Design Process** **Step 1–Define a Problem** **Step 2–Plan and Build** **Step 3–Test and Improve** **Step 4–Redesign** **Step 5–Communicate** **Hands-On Activity Engineer It •** **Protect the Legs!** pp. 27–28	Hands-On Worksheet
ELABORATE	**Take It Further** pp. 29–30 **People in Science & Engineering •** **Mary Delaney**	Take It Further Solve a Paw-blem
EVALUATE	**Lesson Check** p. 31 **Self Check** pp. 32–33	Lesson Quiz

Hands-On Activity Planning

Engineer It • Protect the Legs!

Objective Children make observations, ask questions, and follow a design process to develop solutions in order to prevent a cat from scratching the furniture. 👥 small groups ⏱ 1 class period	**Suggested Materials** • a fork • a small chair • classroom materials

Preparation/Tip
Preassemble material bundles for pairs or groups.

▶ You Solve It

Go online for an additional interactive activity.

Marshmallow Launcher

This interactive activity offers practice in support of **K-2-ETS1-1** and **K-2-ETS1-3.**

SEP Asking Questions and Defining Problems

SEP Analyzing and Interpreting Data

DCI **ETS1.A** Defining and Delimiting Engineering Problems

DCI **ETS1.C** Optimizing the Design Solution

3D Learning Objectives

- Children ask questions to define a problem about a marshmallow not moving through a launcher.
- Children use data to determine whether a solution works. Then they will redesign the solutions in order to determine the best one.

Activity Problem

- Blowing air pushes on objects, such the sails of sailboat. It can also be used to launch toy rockets and tennis balls.
- Children use air to make tubes launch marshmallows. Children need to figure out how to design the tube to make the marshmallow fly as far as possible.

Interaction Summary

- Children observe a marshmallow launcher that does not work.
- They identify the problem and how they think they can fix it.
- Once they fix the design so that it will launch, they improve the design to make it go as far as possible by choosing different materials and adjusting the length.

Assessment

Pre-Assessment

Assessment Guide, Unit Pretest

The Unit Pretest focuses on prerequisite knowledge and is composed of items that evaluate children's preparedness for the content covered within this unit.

Formative Assessment

Interactive Worktext, Apply What You Know, Lesson Check, and Self Check

Summative Assessment

Assessment Guide, Lesson Quiz

The Lesson Quiz provides a quick assessment of each lesson objective and of the portion of the Performance Expectation aligned to the lesson.

Interactive Worktext,, Performance Task pp. 34–35

The Performance Task presents the opportunity for children to collaborate with classmates in in order to complete the steps of each Performance Task. Each Performance Task provides a formal Scoring Rubric for evaluating children's work.

Interactive Worktext,, Unit 1 Review, pp. 36–38
Assessment Guide, Unit Test

The Unit Test provides an in-depth assessment of the Performance Expectations aligned to the unit. This test evaluates children's ability to apply knowledge in order to explain phenomena and to solve problems. Within this test, Constructed Response items apply a three-dimensional rubric for evaluating children's mastery on all three dimensions of the Next Generation Science Standards.

▶ Assessment Online

Go online to view the complete assessment items for this unit.

Teacher Notes

_____

_____

_____

_____

_____

_____

_____

_____

_____

_____

_____

_____

_____

_____

Differentiate Instruction

Leveled Readers

The Science & Engineering Leveled Readers provide additional nonfiction reading practice in this unit's subject area.

On Level
How Do You Investigate?
How Do Engineers Solve Problems?
These readers reinforce unit concepts, and includes response activities for your children.

Extra Support
How Do You Investigate?
How Do Engineers Solve Problems?
These readers share title, illustrations, vocabulary, and concepts with the On-Level Reader; however, the text is linguistically accommodated to provide simplified sentence structures and comprehension aids. It also includes response activities.

Enrichment
Making a Car Go Faster
Design a Home for a Pet
These high-interest, nonfiction readers will extend and enrich unit concepts and vocabulary, and include response activities.

Teacher Guide
The accompanying Teacher Guide provides teaching strategies and support for using all the readers.

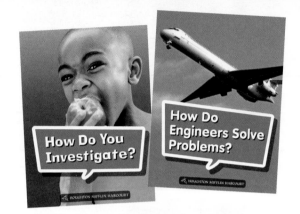

ELL

English Language Learner support resources include a glossary in English and Leveled Readers in Spanish and English. ELL teaching strategies appear throughout this unit:

pp. 4B, 7, 18B, 20, 29

RTI/Extra Support

Strategies for children who need extra support appear throughout this unit:

pp. 3, 4B, 8, 14, 18B, 21

Extension

Strategies for children who have mastered core content and are ready for additional challenges appear throughout this unit:

pp. 3, 4B, 8, 14, 18B, 21

Leveled Readers All readers are available online as well as in an innovative, engaging format for use with touchscreen mobile devices. Contact your HMH Sales Representative for more information.

Connecting with NGSS

Connections to Community

Use these opportunities for informal science learning to provide local context, and to extend and enhance unit concepts.

At Home

New and Improved Have children work with a family member to choose an item in their home that could be improved. Children should record questions and ideas about why they selected that item for improvement. Then have them share why they would like to change the item with the class.
Use with Lesson 1.

Take Note Have children interview a family member about the types of technology they used when they were kids. Children should ask their family member to compare how they used that technology to the technology they use today. In class, have the children share their findings and compare their information with other classmates.
Use with Lesson 2.

In the Community

Dress for Success Lead a discussion about people who work in the community. Guide children to identify technology that each person wears for their job. Some examples may include a firefighter' heat resistant clothing, a lifeguard's bathing suit, or a barber's smock. Ask children to draw a picture of someone using technology at work. Allow them to share with classmates.
Use with Lesson 1.

Sunny Days Draw attention to the solar cell on a solar-powered calculator. Lead a discussion about how the solar cell works. If possible, have children explore how the calculator gets energy. Ask children if they have ever seen large solar panels on buildings. Brainstorm with children to identify potential problems using solar panels on a large building, and discuss possible solutions. If possible, follow up with a class visit from a solar energy professional.
Use with Lesson 2.

Home Letters Go online to view the Home Letters for this unit.

Collaboration

Collaboration opportunities in this unit:

Build on Prior Knowledge
pp. 5, 19
Small Groups
p. 30
Discuss Collaborating and Communicating
p. 26
Think, Draw, Pair, Share
p. 7

Connections to Science

Connections to Science opportunities in this unit:

Connection to Life Science
Lesson 1, p. 6

Connection to Physical Science
Lesson 2, p. 25

Unit Project 👥 small groups 🕐 1 class period

Pocket Lock-It

There are many ways to complete this Unit Project. The steps and Suggested Materials indicate one way to complete the investigation. Encourage children to come up with their own ideas for how to investigate a design to secure things in a pocket. If children decide to follow another process to complete their investigation, be sure to review each group's plans before the children begin. Provide guidance for groups that may have strayed off topic.

3D Learning Objective

SEP Asking Questions and Defining Problems
Ask questions learn more information about why things fall out of a pocket. Describe the characteristics of a tool or object that would solve the problem. Plan and conduct an investigation to identify possible solutions to keep an object from falling out of a pocket.

Skills and Standards Focus

This project supports building children's mastery of **Performance Expectation K-2-ETS1-1.**

SEP Asking Questions and Defining Problems
SEP Developing and Using Models
DCI Defining and Delimiting Engineering Problems
DCI Developing Possible Solutions
DCI Optimizing the Design Solution
CCC Structure and Function

Suggested Materials

- a jacket with a pocket
- objects to carry in the pocket, such as fruit or coins
- an assortment of cups and bags

Preparation

Review the steps in a design process. Before beginning the project, identify or provide objects in the classroom that may be carried in a pocket. Encourage them to select objects with which they can test pockets or models. Allow children to experiment with their own jackets or with a jacket provided for this purpose.

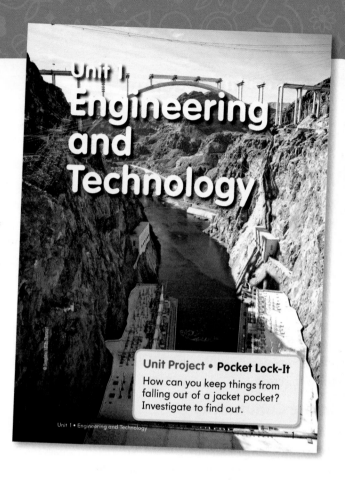

Unit Project • Pocket Lock-It
How can you keep things from falling out of a jacket pocket? Investigate to find out.

Unit 1 • Engineering and Technology

Differentiate Instruction

RTI/Extra Support Children can be provided with two to four objects that may help secure items in a pocket. They can then investigate to determine if one or more of those objects have characteristics that will help make a design.

Extension Challenge children to design a way to secure items in a pocket of someone has to take off the jacket and hang it up or lay it flat.

Name _____

Unit 1 Project

Pocket Lock-It

How can you keep objects from falling out of a pocket? Can you think of two different designs to solve this problem? Write your ideas on the lines below. Then choose one. Plan and conduct an investigation to choose the best idea for a design.

Children should write two ideas they have for a design to keep objects

from falling out of a pocket.

_____

_____

Materials
Draw and label the materials you will need.

Children should draw and label materials. The following are possible materials children can use for this investigation: cups, bags, books, other items found in the classroom.

Unit 1 Project • Page 1 of 3

Unit 1 Project
Pocket Lock-It

SEP **Asking Questions and Defining Problems** . . . .

Pose the unit project question to children. Encourage them to think about how a design process can help them to solve the problem. Discuss all of the ideas as a class. Have children identify a design process to carry out this investigation.

In the sample investigation shown, children ask questions about how objects can fall out of a jacket pocket, collect various objects, and describe why each object may or may not be useful to contain and secure an item.

Children will explore a variety of pockets and objects to learn more about the problem. They will examine materials that can be used to keep objects in a pocket. **Ask: How will you decide which objects can help you to design a possible solution?** I will find out more about the problem and look for objects that solve similar problems.

ESSENTIAL QUESTIONS Prepare children for their project by asking the following questions.

- What are some ways to keep an object in place?
- How can examining the way one object is made help to solve a different problem?
- What evidence can be collected to show a problem has been solved?

Ask: **What is a pocket? Why do people use pockets in clothing? How do you use a pocket?** A pocket is a place to keep things. People use them to keep items safe and to carry them without using their hands. Sometimes people use pockets to keep their hands warm. You put an item inside of a pocket until you need it.

Steps

Encourage children to think about the steps in a design process. Then have them write the steps they will follow to solve the problem of objects falling out of pockets.

CCC Structure and Function. . . . .

Before beginning the investigation, have children select one jacket with a pocket.

Ask: Is a pocket technology? Why or why not? **Yes, people make them.** Challenge children to identify what kind of objects would be likely to fall out of this pocket. Refer children to Lesson 1 Engineer It • What Is Technology?

At the end of the investigation, children will need to be able to tell what characteristics a design should have to best solve the problem. Children should record their observations using words and pictures.

Data

Children should make observations about the original problem, as well as observations about characteristics that keep objects secure in a pocket.

DCI Defining and Delimiting Engineering Problems

Challenge children to think of an object that would fall out of the pocket they chose. Encourage children to define or demonstrate the problem. Have them record their observations using words and pictures.

DCI Developing Possible Solutions. . . . .

Have children identify and collect objects in the classroom that would keep their item in place. Children may choose cups, books, backpacks, or other types of bags. **Ask: Why would this object keep my item from falling out?** Sample answers: It is bigger and has a zipper. It buttons at the top so my coins won't bounce out. **How can you use this observation to change your pocket?** I can make something like it to add to my pocket.

Steps Write the steps you will do.

Answers may vary but should reflect a logical order of steps in the investigation. Sample steps listed:

1. Find out more about why things fall out of pockets.

2. Think of ideas for two solutions.

3. Build and test both solutions.

4. Record observations.

5. Change the solutions to make them work better.

6. Share the solutions.

Data
Record your data.

Answers and drawings may vary but should observations about characteristics that keep objects secure in a pocket.

Analyze Your Result

Look for patterns in your data.

Restate Your Question

Write the question you investigated.

Answers should identify the question children initially chose at the

beginning of the investigation.

_____

Claims, Evidence, and Reasoning

Make a claim that answers your question.

Answers should identify the best idea to solve the problem.

_____

Review the data. What evidence from the investigation supports your claim?

Answer should cite evidence from the investigation to support which

idea will work best.

_____

Discuss your reasoning with a partner.

Analyze Your Result

Have children analyze their data. Elicit from them any patterns they noticed. Encourage them to compare test results. **Ask: What are the characteristics that keep the item contained?** Sample answers: It has a way to close up the opening. It is deeper so my fruit doesn't hang out.

Claims, Evidence, and Reasoning

Children should understand how to follow a design process to develop a solution using characteristics that keep items from falling out of a pocket. They should cite evidence to support their claim by using their drawings and written notations.

Ask: What claim can you make? I can use characteristics from other objects that hold things to design a solution to stop something from falling out of a pocket. **How does your evidence support your claim?** My evidence supports this because my model kept things in my pocket when I tested it. Encourage children to discuss their reasoning.

SEP Developing and Using Models . . . .

Review with children what it means to make a claim. Guide them to understand that the data they collected while using their models will be used as evidence to support their claim. **Ask: What can you use as evidence from your investigation?** The data collected, such as the drawings and writings, is evidence of my claim.

Scoring Rubric for Unit Project	
3	States a claim supported with evidence that their solution keeps an object from falling out of a pocket
2	States a claim somewhat supported with evidence that their solution keeps an object from falling out of a pocket
1	States a claim that is not supported by evidence
0	Does not state a claim, and does not provide evidence

Building to the Performance Expectation(s)

The learning experiences in this lesson prepare children for mastery of:

K-2-ETS1-1 Ask questions, make observations, and gather information about a situation people want to change to define a simple problem that can be solved through the development of a new or improved object or tool.

Trace Tool to the NGSS
Go online to view the complete coverage of these standards across this lesson, unit, and time.

SEP Science & Engineering Practices

Asking Questions and Defining Problems

Ask questions based on . . .

 **VIDEO** SEP: Asking Questions and Defining Problems

Asking Questions and Defining Problems

Define a simple problem that can . . .

VIDEO SEP: Asking Questions and Defining Problems

DCI Disciplinary Core Ideas

ETS1.A: Defining and Delimiting Engineering Problems

• A situation that people want to change or create can be approached as a problem to be solved through engineering.

• Asking questions, making observations, and gathering information are helpful in thinking about problems.

• Before beginning to design a solution, it is important to clearly understand the problem.

CCC Crosscutting Concepts

Structure and Function

The shape and stability of structures of natural and designed objects are related to their function.

 VIDEO CCC: Structure and Function

CONNECTION TO MATH

1.MD.C.4 Organize, represent, and interpret data with up to three categories; ask and answer questions about the total number of data points, how many in each category, and how many more or less are in one category than in another.

CONNECTION TO ENGLISH LANGUAGE ARTS

W.1.8 With guidance and support from adults, recall information from experiences or gather information from provided sources to answer a question.

Supporting All Students, All Standards

Integrating the Three Dimensions of Learning

This lesson describes what engineers are and do, and explains how engineers make and use technology to solve problems **(DCI Defining and Delimiting Engineering Problems)**. The lesson begins with children exploring, identifying, and naming simple problems **(SEP Asking Questions and Defining Problems),** and continues with children exploring how engineers make and use technology to solve everyday problems **(CCC Structure and Function)**. Finally, children will use what they have learned to define a problem, gather information about it, and build something to solve the problem **(SEP Asking Questions and Defining Problems) (DCI Defining and Delimiting Engineering Problems) (CCC Structure and Function)**.

Professional Development

Go online to view **Professional Development videos** with strategies to integrate CCCs and SEPs, including the ones used in this lesson.

Build on Prior Knowledge

Children should already know and be prepared to build on the following concepts:

- Scientists ask questions.
- Scientists make observations.

Differentiate Instruction

Lesson Vocabulary
- engineer
- problem
- solution
- technology

Reinforcing Vocabulary To help children remember each vocabulary word, have them draw an illustration of each word. Then have them write the word beneath the illustration, define it, and use it in a sentence. Remind children to look for these highlighted words as they proceed through the lesson.

RTI/Extra Support Supply children with additional images of examples of common problems and technology used to solve these problems. Provide children with context of how these technologies were made to help solve each problem.

Extension Children who want to find out more can do research on different types of engineers and/or technology. Children should use their data to make a poster that illustrates the type of engineer, or the problem and technology made to solve it.

ELL Be sure to point out all labels, pictures, captions, and headings throughout the lesson to assist children with strategies to summarize chunks of content. Discuss with children real-life connections to content, and provide hands-on examples of materials when possible to best support the needs of these learners.

Lesson Phenomenon

Lesson Objective

Through a variety of opportunities, children explore how engineers make and use technology to solve problems.

About This Image

Ask: Can you find the objects in this garden built by people? Who do you think built them? What problems do the objects solve? As you explore, you'll find out how and why people make and use things to solve problems.

 Defining and Delimiting Engineering Problems

Alternative Engage Strategy

Everyday Technology	small groups 15–25 minutes

Begin with a discussion about the technology that children use in their everyday lives. List the problems that the technology addresses. Remind children that examples of technology do not necessarily need to be electronic. Examples of everyday technology could be small kitchen tools, backpacks, lunchboxes, or items of clothing. Allow 5 minutes for children to discuss.

Then have children work in small groups to list a way they would make one of the technologies better. Allow 10 minutes for children to brainstorm and discuss.

Lesson 1   **Engineer It • How Do Engineers Use Technology?**

People make things to solve problems.

By the End of This Lesson
I will be able to describe how people understand problems and make technology.

4

Understand the Problem

Mia uses headphones to listen to music. She keeps them in her pocket.

Explore online. ▶

Can You Explain It?
✎ What is Mia's problem? How can you understand the problem to solve it?

Accept all reasonable answers.

_____

_____

_____

© Houghton Mifflin Harcourt

Can You Explain It?

Understand the Problem Ask children to record their initial thoughts about what happened and what problem Mia had in the video. If the video is not available, discuss the image on the page.

Collaboration

Build on Prior Knowledge You may want children to view and discuss the video as a whole class activity. In this way, you can assess their prior knowledge of problems, solutions, and technology.

Think about what you saw in the video. In your classroom, you may encounter problems like this everyday. Think about what kinds of problems come up in the classroom and how they might be solved.

What Is an Engineer?

3D Learning Objective

Children will explore how engineers **ask questions and gather information** to understand problems.

DCI Defining and Delimiting Engineering Problems . . . .

Ask: What do engineers need before they look for solutions? They need a problem. **Ask:** Do you think engineers look for solutions to only big problems or do they look for solutions to smaller problems, too? Engineers look for solutions to all kinds of problems.

SEP Asking Questions and Defining Problems . . . .

Solutions to problems are shown on the page. Ask children to identify each problem on the page. **Ask: What was the problem that the bridge solved?** The bridge lets cars go over places where a road can't be built (like over water). **Ask: What is one problem the electric car helps solve?** Sample answer: Gas can be expensive. The electric car uses less gas. **Ask: What about the ride? How does making it safe solve a problem?** Making it safe keeps people from getting hurt.

Connection to Life Science

Structure and Function Ask children if they think engineers ever look to nature to get ideas for solutions. Have them identify a tool in the classroom or at home that may have been inspired by something in nature.

What Is an Engineer?

Explore online. ▶

Engineers use science and math to build bridges.

Engineers make cars that do not need gas.

Engineers build rides that are safe.

An **engineer** is a person who uses math and science to solve problems. A **problem** is something that needs to be fixed or made better. Engineers look for solutions. A **solution** is something that fixes a problem.

6

Explore online. ▶

Engineers name the problem.

Engineers ask questions about the problem. They observe and gather information.

© Houghton Mifflin Harcourt

Engineers can solve a problem. First they have to understand the problem.

Lesson 1 • Engineer It • How Do Engineers Use Technology?

7

SEP Asking Questions and Defining Problems . . . .

Ask: How do engineers solve problems? They ask questions about the problem. **Why do engineers ask questions?** They ask questions to make sure they know why a problem happens.

Differentiate Instruction

ELL Use multiple pictures to illustrate problems and solutions. Show several pictures of problems and say *problem*. Show pictures of the solution to that problem and say *solution*. Have children repeat each term aloud with you as you say it.

Collaboration

Think, Draw, Pair, Share Ask children to think about a problem they might have while playing a sport after school. Have them think about what kinds of things they could do to solve the problem. Give the children time to draw their answers, pair with a partner, and then share their ideas.

SEP **Asking Questions and Defining Problems** . . . .

Children should choose A, B, and C. If children chose only one or two of the answer choices, they may need to revisit the What Is an Engineer? section of the lesson.

Differentiate Instruction

RTI/Extra Support Discuss examples of engineers asking questions, using math and science, and identifying and solving problems. For example, engineers made elevators to solve the problem of too many stairs for people to climb.

Extension Challenge children to write a short paragraph that provides examples of how engineers find and solve problems, use math and science, and ask questions.

 FORMATIVE ASSESSMENT

Evidence Notebook

Children will work with a group to observe and record a problem that results from walking with headphones in their pocket. Remind children to use evidence to support their observations.

Scoring Guidelines

- describes how they know what the problem is using evidence from their observations
- asks questions, makes observations, and gathers evidence about the problem

💡 **Asking Questions and Defining Problems** Remind children to tell about the problem and to think about how something new or improved could solve the problem.

What do engineers do? Choose all correct answers.

Ⓐ find and solve problems

Ⓑ use math and science

Ⓒ ask questions

 Apply What You Know

Evidence Notebook • Act like an engineer. Put headphones in your pocket. Walk around the room for two minutes. What problem happens? Work with a group. Ask questions about the problem. Make observations and gather evidence. Write them in your Evidence Notebook. Talk with the group.

Asking Questions • Defining Problems
Go to the online handbook for tips.

8

© Houghton Mifflin Harcourt

What Is Technology?

Explore online. ▶

Technology can help someone walk.

Technology can be simple, like a hammer.

Technology is what engineers make to meet needs and solve problems. Technology can even be an idea from nature. The idea for planes came from birds.

Which objects are technology? Choose all correct answers.

Ⓐ a lamp

Ⓑ a tree

Ⓒ a pencil

What Is Technology?

3D Learning Objective

Children will explore examples of technology and **how structures in the natural world can inspire technology**. Children will then **define a problem** and **gather information about it** to design a solution. They will identify how **the shape of the solution is connected to how it works**.

CCC Structure and Function. . . . .

Give children background information on the Wright brothers and the invention of the airplane. The Wright brothers invented the first successful airplane. The shape and function of bird parts gave the Wright brothers ideas for how to build the first airplane. **Ask: How could an engineer get an idea from nature to make technology?** Sample answer: An engineer could use the idea of shade from a tree to come up with an idea for a beach umbrella that gives shade.

Discuss with children that technology comes in many forms. Technology can be complex like a train or a tablet, or simple like a pencil or a hammer. **Ask: What are some examples of technology that you use at school and at home?** Accept all reasonable answers. Also explain that the way something is shaped is connected to how it works. For example, a pencil needs to write but it should also be light and portable. It is made of a material that makes it light and portable.

Children should choose A and C. Children should identify that a lamp and a pencil are examples of technology because they are human made. The tree comes from nature and is not technology. If children do not choose A and C, they may require additional support with the term *technology*. Demonstrate the meaning of this term by showing children a variety of examples of technology. A common misconception may be that only things that are electronic or things that have power can be examples of technology. In this case, the child will not choose the pencil as an example of technology.

Do The Math! • Interpret Data

Discuss how children use technology every day. Explain that the tally chart shows how many children in one class use different kinds of technology each day. **Ask: What does each mark on this chart stand for?** Each mark stands for one child. **Ask: How many children use a tablet each day?** 9 **Ask: How many children use a cell phone?** 6 **Ask: How many more children use a tablet than a cell phone each day?** 3

Explain to children who don't give 3 as the answer that they can subtract the number of children who use a cell phone from the number of children who use a tablet to find how many more.

 Interpret Data Remind children to study the data in a chart or a graph to gather information. Count to find out how many are in each group.

FORMATIVE ASSESSMENT

Read, Write, Share! • Evidence Notebook

Children will identify three kinds of technology, explain how they know each one is technology, and tell what problems they solve.

Scoring Guidelines

- identifies three kinds of technology
- explains how they know each one is technology
- writes to explain what problems each technology solves

 Recall Information Remind children to listen carefully to the question. Tell them to ask themselves, *What information is this question asking about?* Encourage children to review the reading to find answers. Look in books and on the Internet.

Do the Math! • This tally chart shows how children in one class use technology each day.

Classroom Technology	
pencil	IIIII
tablet	IIIII IIII
cell phone	IIIII I

Interpret Data Go to the online handbook for tips.

 How many more children use a tablet than a cell phone each day?

___3___ more children

Apply What You Know

Read, Write, Share! • Evidence Notebook • Find three kinds of technology. How do you know each one is technology? What problems do they solve? Use evidence to answer the questions. Write your answers in your Evidence Notebook.

Recall Information Go to the online handbook for tips.

10

© Houghton Mifflin Harcourt

Hands-On Activity 👥 small groups ⏱ 1 class period

Engineer It • Solve the Headphones Problem

SEP **Asking Questions and Defining Problems** . . . .

Children will work collaboratively to define a problem, gather information about it, and build something to solve the problem.

Suggested Materials headphones and classroom materials such as string, rubber bands, tape, and chenille sticks.

Preparation

Preassemble materials bundles for pairs or groups. Alternatively, children may do this activity at home.

Activity

As a class, view the video. Then discuss the question that will need to be answered. Have children record the question.

DCI **Defining and Delimiting Engineering Problems** . . . .

STEP 1 To help children gather information, use probing questions.

Ask: What is the problem? Why is it a problem? Where can you go to get some ideas of how to solve the problem? What are some ideas for a possible solution?

STEP 2 Have chidren plan two solutions to the problem. Have them describe how to make these solutions and what materials and steps they will use.

Name_____

Hands-On Activity

Engineer It • Solve the Headphones Problem

Materials • headphones • classroom materials

Ask a Question

How can you keep the headphones from looking like this in the future?

Test and Record Data Explore online. ▶

Step 1

Explain the problem. Gather information about the problem.

Step 2

Plan two solutions to the problem.

Check children's work.

_____

© Houghton Mifflin Harcourt

Lesson 1 • Engineer It • How Do Engineers Use Technology?   11

Hands-On Activity, continued

CCC Structure and Function . . . .

STEP 3 Give children time to work with their group to build their solution to the problem. Direct children to use a variety of materials to build their solution. Encourage them to think beyond what the material is traditionally used for. **Ask: How can this item be used to make your solution work?**

STEP 4 Children should explain how the shape of their solution is connected to how it works. Make sure they explain how the materials they used affect how it works.

Claims, Evidence, and Reasoning

In this section, children will have peer and teacher feedback as per the EQuIP rubric. **Ask: What evidence do you have that your solution solves the problem?** Answers will vary.

Scoring Rubric for Hands-On Activities	
3	Writes a claim that clearly and directly answers the question and is supported with evidence.
2	Writes a claim that clearly and directly answers the question and is somewhat supported with evidence.
1	Writes a claim that clearly and directly answers the question but is not supported with evidence.
0	Does not state a claim and does not provide evidence.

Step 3

Use the classroom materials to build your solutions.

Step 4

Share your solutions. Talk about how the shape of each design solved the problem.

Make a claim that answers your question.

Sample answer: I can use something like a rubber band to tie the headphones. This keeps them from getting tangled.

What is your evidence?

Sample answer: I tied the headphones with a rubber band and walked around the classroom. The headphones did not get tangled.

12

© Houghton Mifflin Harcourt

Explore online. ▶ Guide children to the Interactive Online Student Edition where they can choose from and explore both paths.

Take It Further

Careers in Science & Engineering • Packaging Engineer

Explore more online.

Transportation Timeline

Explore online. ▶

What do packaging engineers do? Here's a hint. You see their work on store shelves every day.

They design boxes and other packages. They use computers to plan their ideas.

Then they test their ideas. They drop and crush the packages! They make sure what is inside is protected.

A factory builds the final packages.

Take It Further

Careers in Science & Engineering • Packaging Engineer

Children investigate how packaging engineers design boxes, bottles, and other packages. The work of packaging engineers can be seen every day on store shelves. Explain to children that the packages you use every day started with an idea and a plan. Packaging engineers use computers to plan their ideas. Then they have to test their ideas to make sure that they work.

DCI Defining and Delimiting Engineering Problems. . . . .

Ask: Why do engineers need to design different types of packaging for different items? Engineers design different packages so that the items inside are easy to move and keep safe.

Take It Further, *continued*

Children should draw a line from the eggs to the egg carton, from the picture frame to the bubble wrap, and from the cereal to the box.

Ask: Why are these packages good for the item that goes inside them?

CCC **Structure and Function** . . . .

Ask: What are some other types of packaging you can think of that help protect something? Accept all reasonable answers. How does the shape of the package make it easier to carry the item that is inside? Accept all reasonable answers.

Differentiate Instruction

Extension Challenge children to come up with new or improved packaging ideas for items they use at home or at school. Children can share in small groups what their new packaging would look like and how or why it is improved.

RTI/Extra Support Show children additional pictures of items and their packaging to provide more examples and deepen understanding.

Explore more online. ▶

Transportation Timeline

Children investigate the order of four key transportation technology inventions.

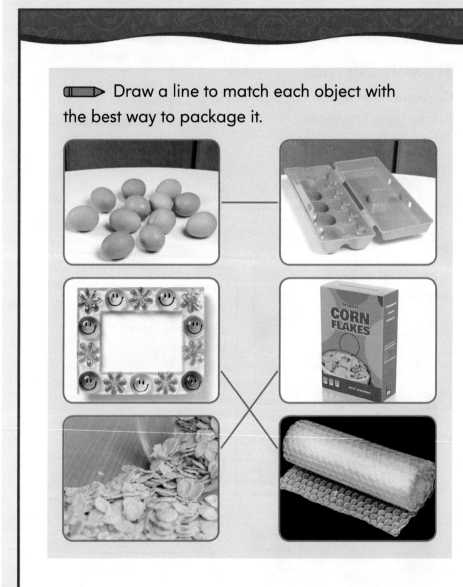

✏️ Draw a line to match each object with the best way to package it.

14

© Houghton Mifflin Harcourt • Image Credits: (d) ©Dorling Kindersley/Getty Images; (br) ©Peter Burnett/iStockPhoto.com; (bl) ©Akkalak/iStockPhoto.com; (cr) ©Gts/Shutterstock

Explore online. ▶ Have children explore online to find out more about Mia's problem.

Lesson Check

Lesson Check   Name_____

Explore online. ▶

Can You Explain It?

✏️▷ What is Mia's problem? How can you understand the problem to solve it?

Be sure to

• Name Mia's problem.

• Tell the steps needed to understand the problem to solve it.

Sample answer: Mia's headphones are tangled. I need to ask

questions, make observations, and gather information about

the problem to solve it.

_____

© Houghton Mifflin Harcourt

Lesson 1 • Engineer It • How Do Engineers Use Technology?   15

Can You Explain It?

Have children reread their answers to the Can You Explain It? prompts at the beginning of the lesson.

DCI **Defining and Delimiting Engineering Problems**. . . . .

Guide children to look at the photograph to identify Mia's problem. **Ask: Have you ever used headphones? Why is it a problem when they look like this?** Sample answer: When they look like this, they are tangled. It's a problem because I can't use them when they are tangled.

SEP **Asking Questions and Defining Problems** . . . .

If children have difficulty responding to the Can You Explain It? question, have children think about the steps engineers take to solve a problem **Ask: How would an engineer try to solve this?** By asking questions, making observations, and gathering information about the problem.

CCC **Structure and Function**. . . . .

Children should connect the structure and function of technology to the problems they help solve.

Scoring Guidelines

• Children effectively communicate what the problem is.
• Children explain what steps need to be taken to determine how to solve the problem.

Lesson Check, continued

SUMMATIVE ASSESSMENT
Self Check

1. Children should choose C—name a problem. If children choose A or B, reinforce that before an engineer can solve a problem, he or she must name the problem.

2. Children should circle the screwdriver and the boat. If children circle the flower or the rock, review the difference between natural objects and technology. Reinforce the concept that technology is what people make and use to solve problems to meet their needs.

Self Check

1. What does an engineer do first?

Ⓐ gather information about a problem

Ⓑ find a solution to a problem

Ⓒ name a problem

2. Which objects are examples of technology? Circle all correct answers.

16

3. Which is a problem technology could solve?

Ⓐ Maya lost a letter in her house.

Ⓑ Hector does not agree with his sister.

Ⓒ Theo's backpack straps are hard to wear.

4. What does the picture show?

Ⓐ an engineer

Ⓑ a problem

Ⓒ technology

5. How do engineers understand a problem? Choose all correct answers.

Ⓐ They ask questions.

Ⓑ They observe things.

Ⓒ They gather information.

3. Children should choose C—Theo's backpack straps are hard to wear. If children choose A or B, direct them to reread the What is Technology? section of the lesson. Ask guiding questions as children read to ensure understanding. Some children may need to review the vocabulary words *technology, problem,* and *solution*.

4. Children should choose C—technology. If children choose A or B, direct them to review the What is Technology? section of the lesson. Some children may require additional review of the vocabulary words *engineer, problem,* and *technology* in the lesson

5. Children should choose A—They ask questions. B—They observe things. C—They gather information. If children choose either A or B or C, but not all three, remind them to read the question carefully. Then direct children to the What Is An Engineer? section of the lesson.

Engineer It • How Can We Solve a Problem?

Building to the Performance Expectations

The learning experiences in this lesson prepare children for mastery of:

K-2-ETS1-1 Ask questions, make observations, and gather information about a situation people want to change to define a simple problem that can be solved through the development of a new or improved object or tool.

K-2-ETS1-2 Develop a simple sketch, drawing, or physical model to illustrate how the shape of an object helps it function as needed to solve a given problem.

K-2-ETS1-3 Analyze data from tests of two objects designed to solve the same problem to compare the strengths and weaknesses of how each performs.

 Trace Tool to the NGSS
Go online to view the complete coverage of these standards across this lesson, unit, and time.

 **Science & Engineering Practices**

Asking Questions and Defining Problems

Ask questions based on observations to find more information about the natural and/or designed world(s).

Define a simple problem that can be solved through the development of a new or improved object or tool.

 **VIDEO** SEP: Asking Questions and Defining Problems

Developing and Using Models

Develop a simple model based on evidence…

▶ **VIDEO** SEP: Developing and Using Models

Analyzing and Interpreting Data

Analyze data from tests of an object or tool…

▶ **VIDEO** SEPs: Analyzing and Interpreting Data / Using Mathematics and Computational Thinking

 **Disciplinary Core Ideas**

ETS1.A: Defining and Delimiting Engineering Problems

Before beginning to design a solution, it is important to clearly understand the problem.

ETS1.B: Developing Possible Solutions

Designs can be conveyed through sketches, drawings, or physical models. These representations are useful in communicating ideas for a problem's solutions to other people.

ETS1.C: Optimizing the Design Solution

Because there is always more than one possible solution to a problem, it is useful to compare and test designs.

 **Crosscutting Concepts**

Structure and Function

The shape and stability of structures of natural and designed objects are related to their function(s).

▶ **VIDEO** CCC: Structure and Function

CONNECTION TO MATH

1.MD.C.4 Organize, represent, and interpret data with up to three categories; ask and answer questions about the total number of data points, how many in each . . .

CONNECTION TO ENGLISH LANGUAGE ARTS

W.1.2 Write informative/explanatory texts in which they name a topic, supply some facts about the topic, and provide some sense of closure.

Supporting All Students, All Standards

Integrating the Three Dimensions of Learning

This lesson focuses on a design process that engineers use to solve problems (**DCI Defining and Delimiting Engineering Problems, Developing Possible Solutions, Optimizing the Design Solution**). The lesson begins with children exploring simple problems in the natural world and how they can be solved through the development of a new or improved object or tool (**SEP Asking Questions and Defining Problems**). As they explore a design process, children compare and test the shape and stability of objects to determine if they work as intended and are related to their function(s) (**CCC Structure and Function**). Lastly, children develop and test simple models to solve problems through a design process, and communicate those solutions (**SEP Developing and Using Models, Analyzing and Interpreting Data**).

Professional Development
Go online to view **Professional Development videos** with strategies to integrate CCCs and SEPs, including the ones used in this lesson.

Build on Prior Knowledge

Children should already know and be prepared to build on the following concepts:
- Objects are often designed to solve a problem.
- Problems can occur naturally and they are often solved with a simple solution.
- Solutions don't always work properly the first time, and they need to be redesigned and retested.

Differentiate Instruction

Lesson Vocabulary
- design process

Reinforcing Vocabulary To help children remember the vocabulary word, support them in forming real-life connections. Help children connect the idea of a process to their daily routine in the classroom. Discuss the steps of the daily routine; for example, 1. unpack, 2. take out homework, 3. sharpen pencils, etc. Guide children to recognize that if the steps are done out of order, they would not be prepared because their pencils would still be in their backpacks when they went to sharpen them.

RTI/Extra Support Provide additional opportunity for hands-on discovery. Allow children to explore other problems in the classroom and how they are solved with objects or tools. Discuss how the design process might have been used to make the solution, or how the design process could be used to make a better solution.

Extension Children who want to find out more can do research on other types of problem and solution relationships. Children can share their findings with the class by making a poster or other display, or with a demonstration of the specifically designed objects made to solve the problem.

ELL Be sure to point out all labels, pictures, captions, and headings throughout the lesson to assist children with strategies to summarize chunks of content. Discuss with children real-life connections to content, and provide hands-on examples of materials when possible to best support the needs of these learners.

Lesson Problem

Lesson Objective

Develop and test simple models to solve problems through a design process and communicate those solutions.

About This Image

Have children look at the picture of the dog walker and the dogs. **Ask: Have you ever walked a dog? What problems can happen during a walk? Do you see a problem that needs to be solved?** Accept all reasonable answers. Remind children that they will explore how they can solve problems such as these in this lesson.

 Asking Questions and Defining Problems

Alternative Engage Strategy

Solving Problems in the Classroom	pairs
	⏱ 15–20 minutes

Hold up a pair of scissors. **Ask: What is this? What problem does it solve? How does it work? Why is it shaped this way? What types of materials were used to make it?**

Allow children to brainstorm answers. Record these for the class to see. Then have children work in pairs to choose any object in the classroom and brainstorm what the object is and how its design helps solve a problem. Allow each pair to present their object to the class. Allow 10 minutes to brainstorm and discuss.

Lesson 2 **Engineer It • How Can We Solve a Problem?**

Engineers solve big and small problems.

By the End of This Lesson
I will be able to describe and use a design process to solve a problem.

18

© Houghton Mifflin Harcourt • Image Credits: ©Big Cheese Photo LLC/Alamy

Can You Solve It?

The Pulling Dog Problem Max has a problem when he walks his dog. Play the video to find out more about his problem. If the video is not available, discuss the photograph on the page.

Ask children to record their initial leash design to solve this problem. Accept all reasonable answers. At the end of this lesson in the Lesson Check, children should be able to pose a design solution to Max's problem.

Collaboration

Build on Prior Knowledge You may want to discuss the picture and the problem as a whole-class activity. In small groups, have children discuss their experiences with walking dogs. Guide children in a discussion about different materials they could use to allow the dog to move freely without pulling too hard on the leash.

The Pulling Dog Problem

Explore online. ▶

Everyday problems need solutions.
Max's dog keeps pulling on its leash.

Can You Solve It?

✏️ How would you design a leash to solve the problem of a dog pulling during a walk?

Accept all reasonable answers.

© Houghton Mifflin Harcourt

A Design Process

3D Learning Objective

Children **ask questions** to define a problem about crumbled dog treats. They **gather information** in order to find solutions to the problem.

DCI **Defining and Delimiting Engineering Problems**. . . . .

Ask: What does an engineer do? Engineers use a design process to solve many kinds of problems. **Ask: What types of things do engineers build?** Engineers build things like bridges, planes, robots, and computers.

SEP **Asking Questions and Defining Problems** . . . .

Ask children to identify each step of the design process referred to in the text. Guide children to summarize the five-step design process. **Ask: Why do you think it's a good idea to plan before you build?** You need to make sure you have the materials, and that you have thought about all the parts. **Ask: Do you think engineers stop after one try? Why or why not?** No, because there might be more than one way to solve a problem.

Differentiate Instruction

ELL Children may be familiar with the words *design* and *process*; however, children may require additional support to understand how these words are used together in this context. Explain that in everyday conversation, the word *design* can mean a drawing, but in engineering it has a special meaning. **Ask: What is a design?** A design is a plan. **Ask: What is a process?** A process is the steps you follow to do something. **Ask: What is a design process?** The steps you follow to build something that solves a problem.

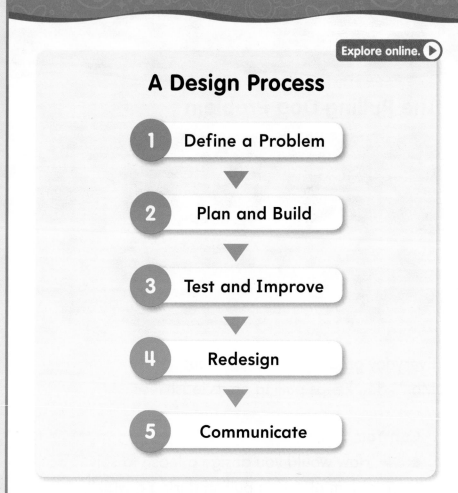

Explore online.

A Design Process

1. Define a Problem
2. Plan and Build
3. Test and Improve
4. Redesign
5. Communicate

How can we solve problems? One way is to follow a design process. A **design process** is a plan with steps that helps engineers find good solutions.

20

© Houghton Mifflin Harcourt

Step 1–Define a Problem

Look at the picture.
What is Tara's problem?

The treats for Tara's dog keep crumbling. Tara defines her problem. She asks questions about it. She gathers information about the problem.

Explore online.

 What is Step 1 of a design process?

Define a problem.

Apply What You Know

Define a problem in your classroom. Ask questions about it. Make observations and gather information. Write in your Evidence Notebook. Talk with others about the problem. Tell what you know about it.

Asking Questions • Defining Problems
Go to the online handbook for tips.

© Houghton Mifflin Harcourt

Step 1–Define a Problem

SEP Asking Questions and Defining Problems . . . .

Discuss with children why it is important to define the problem first. Guide children to understand that asking questions is necessary in order to understand the problem fully. **Ask: How does asking questions about the problem help us understand the problem?** Sample answer: Learning as much as possible about the problem helps us develop the best solution.

Differentiate Instruction

RTI/Extra Support Discuss with children that a problem is something that needs to be improved or solved. Provide multiple real-life examples, such as a water bottle that leaks and gets your notebook wet.

Extension Ask children if they have ever solved a problem. Discuss the types of problems they have solved and ask how they discovered the problem.

 FORMATIVE ASSESSMENT

Children may use words or pictures to describe a problem that needs to be solved in the classroom. Children should use evidence to support why the situation is a problem.

Scoring Guidelines
- describes a reasonable problem within the classroom
- asks questions about the problem
- makes observations and gathers information about the problem

Asking Questions • Defining Problems Remind children that as they explore, they should stop to ask themselves questions about important details and things that are not clear. Have children tell about a problem and how something new or better can solve the problem.

Lesson 2 • Engineer It • How Can We Solve a Problem?   **21**

LESSON 2   Engage • **Explore/Explain** • Elaborate • Evaluate

Explore online.   Have children explore to find out more about Step 2 of the design process.

Step 2–Plan and Build

3D Learning Objective

Children **plan and build multiple solutions** to the problem. They **build models of the solutions** to test.

DCI **Optimizing the Design Solution** . . . .

Reinforce with children that developing more than one solution is necessary when solving a problem. **Ask: Why should you think of more than one idea?** Your first idea might not be the best idea.

SEP **Developing and Using Models** . . . .

Discuss with children that a model can be a drawing or something they build. Engineers make models first in order to test their solutions and make any necessary improvements.

 FORMATIVE ASSESSMENT

Children work in pairs or small groups to plan and build a model. Remind children they need to plan and build more than one solution.

Scoring Guidelines
• designs more than one solution to the problem
• makes a model of the possible solutions

💡 **Developing and Using Models • Structure and Function** Remind children that models can show how something works. A model can be a drawing or something you build. Remind children that the shape and stability of something can affect how it functions. Brainstorm a variety of materials that the children could use for their solutions.

Step 2–Plan and Build

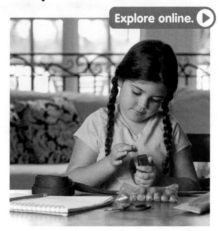

Explore online. What does Tara do next? She thinks of an idea for two solutions. Tara makes models of her solutions. She chooses materials and builds the solutions.

✏️ You want to plan a solution. What is the first thing you should do?

Think of an idea.

Apply What You Know

Think about the classroom problem you found. Think of an idea for two solutions. Make models of your solutions. Then, choose materials and build your solutions. Follow your models.

💡 **Developing and Using Models • Structure and Function** Go to the online handbook for tips.

22

Step 3–Test and Improve

Explore online.

Tara tests her solutions. They both work. But the baggy is hard to use, and the long paper roll is tricky to tip over. Can she make her solutions better?

✏️ What do you do after you build your solutions?

Test and improve the solutions.

✋ **Apply What You Know**

Evidence Notebook • Test your solutions for solving the classroom problem. Which one works best? Show your evidence to explain. Compare your results and improve.

💡 **Analyzing and Interpreting Data** Go to the online handbook for tips.

© Houghton Mifflin Harcourt

Step 3–Test and Improve

3D Learning Objective

Children use **observations as data** to determine the successfulness of their designs. They analyze the **shape and stability of each solution related to its function.**

SEP Analyzing and Interpreting Data . . . .

When testing their solutions, children should make observations. Have children discuss what they observed. **Ask: How will you know if your solutions are successful?** The dog treats will remain whole and not fall out.

CCC Structure and Function . . . .

Allow children to discuss the materials they used and how that affected their results. Hold a class discussion about how the shape and stability of their solutions affected the results.

✋ **FORMATIVE ASSESSMENT**

Evidence Notebook
Children work in pairs or small groups to test their models. Make sure that children use evidence to support their evaluations of their solutions.

Scoring Guidelines
• tests solutions
• collects data and uses evidence to explain results

💡 **Analyzing and Interpreting Data** Remind children that before testing their solution, they need to determine what would be considered a successful test. Share that making observations is a form of data collection.

Step 4–Redesign

3D Learning Objective

Children **redesign their solutions** and **collect data to determine how successful their redesign was.** They will analyze **how the shape and stability** of their redesigned solutions affected their results.

DCI **Optimizing the Design Solution** . . . .

Ask: What does it mean to redesign? How is this different from the first design step? You take what worked well from your test and improve based on that. You change what didn't work well.

SEP **Analyzing and Interpreting Data** . . . .

Ask: How do you use your results from your redesigned model? You compare them to the first results, and decide if the new idea works better.

CCC **Structure and Function** . . . .

After children complete the Apply What You Know, **Ask:** Did your classroom model work the way you expected? Is there a way to improve your solution? Answers will vary according to the problem selected by the children.

 FORMATIVE ASSESSMENT

Evidence Notebook
Children will redesign and test their solutions. They will use evidence to support their analysis of their designs.

Scoring Guidelines
• redesigns their solution and tests it
• collects data and uses evidence to explain results

Step 4–Redesign

Look at the picture. How does Tara redesign her paper towel roll solution?

She thinks a short roll will work better, so she cuts it in half. Then she tests the solution again. It works!

Explore online. ▶

✏ What happens at Step 4 of a design process?

Redesign the solution and test it again.

 Apply What You Know

Evidence Notebook • Now redesign your solution for the classroom problem. Test the solution. Record the results in your Evidence Notebook. Does the new solution work better? Use evidence to tell how you know.

24

Step 5–Communicate

Explore online. ▶

Tara takes a picture to show what she did. You can draw, take photos, or write notes to tell about a solution. Why is this step important? People may want to use your idea. They may try to make it better.

How can you communicate the solution to a problem? Choose all correct answers.

Ⓐ Make drawings.

Ⓑ Take photos.

Ⓒ Write notes.

© Houghton Mifflin Harcourt

Step 5–Communicate

3D Learning Objective

Children identify ways **to communicate ideas for a problem's solution.** They **use the data they collected** to communicate about solving a problem.

DCI Developing Possible Solutions. . . . .

Ask: Why is it important to communicate your solution to a problem? By sharing your ideas, other people can use your solution, and you can get suggestions from others to make your solution even better.

SEP Analyzing and Interpreting Data . . . .

Discuss with children the answers to the question "How can you communicate the solution to a problem?" **Ask: Why should you use more than one way to communicate a solution to a problem?** Drawings, photographs, and written notes can make it easier to understand your ideas.

Connection to Physical Science

Electromagnetic Radiation Light helps us see things. Brainstorm with children the different times of day a person may take their pet for a walk. Explain that during the winter months, it gets darker earlier in the evening. **Ask: What problem would someone have if they plan on taking their pet for a walk in the evening?** If it is dark, the person won't be able to see where they are walking. Discuss with children how they could use a design process to develop a solution. Possible solutions could be taping a flashlight to the leash or taping a flashlight to a hat the person wears. Have children draw possible solutions that could be used for walking a pet in the evening. Have children share their ideas.

Do the Math! • Represent Data

Children represent data in a tally chart. They should show six tally marks for Solution 2. Discuss with children why it is important to collect data when testing their solutions. **Ask: What does each tally mark show?** The number of times Tara tested each solution. **Ask: Which design did she test more times?** Solution 2 **Ask: How do tally marks make it easier to count?** Tally marks are grouped by fives, so you can skip count by fives and ones to find the total.

💡 **Represent Data** Children can organize, or sort, data into groups so it is easier to understand. Show the data in a chart or a graph. Use tally marks or pictures to show the amount in each group. Each tally mark stands for one thing.

Collaboration

Discuss Collaborating and Communicating Anticipate children not wanting to share their ideas because of someone taking their idea. Refer to famous inventions such as the light bulb, the automobile, or the airplane. Emphasize how important it was for the inventors to share their ideas because of how they changed the world. Without communicating your ideas, you might be missing out on help you could get from others.

 FORMATIVE ASSESSMENT

Children work in pairs or small groups to prepare their results and present them to the rest of the class.

Scoring Guidelines
- describes the problem and the solution
- communicates results by drawing, taking photographs, and writing notes

Do the Math! • Tara builds two solutions to stop her cat from scratching a chair. She tests Solution 1 three times. She tests Solution 2 six times. Add tally marks to the chart to show how many times Tara tests Solution 2.

💡 **Represent Data** Go to the online handbook for tips.

Number of Times Scratched	
Solution 1	III
Solution 2	ⷘⷮ I

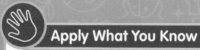 **Apply What You Know**

You found a solution to your classroom problem. Now tell others about it. Draw a picture of the solution. Write notes to tell what you did. Take some photographs.

26

Name_____

Hands-On Activity
Engineer It • Protect the Legs!

| Materials | • a fork • classroom materials |
| | • a small chair |

Ask a Question

How do you prevent a cat from scratching furniture?

Test and Record Data   **Explore online.** ▶

Step 1

Define the problem.

I need to prevent a cat from

scratching furniture.

Step 2

Plan two solutions.
Choose the materials
you will use.

> Children should draw or write to show their solutions.

Step 3

Build your solutions. Follow your plan.

© Houghton Mifflin Harcourt

Hands-On Activity   👥 small groups   ⏱ 1 class period
Engineer It • Protect the Legs!

3D Learning Objective

SEP **Asking Questions and Defining Problems** . . . .

Children make observations, ask questions, and follow a design process to develop solutions in order to prevent a cat from scratching the furniture.

Suggested Materials fork, classroom materials, a small chair

Preparation
Pre-assemble materials bundles for pairs or groups.

Activity
In order for children to record their question, they need to observe the photograph in Step 1. It may be easier for children to define the problem and then rephrase it in the form of a question.

STEP 1 Guide children in a discussion about the photograph. Have children make observations about what is wrong with the chair leg. Remind children that the scratches on the leg aren't the problem, but preventing the cat from making the scratches is.

STEP 2 Ask children to draw a plan to show how they would solve the problem as well as identify the materials they may need. Monitor children as they draw their plan. Guide the children to include labels in their design.

CCC **Structure and Function** . . . .

Discuss with children the types of materials they might use to prevent the scratches. Have children use evidence when explaining why they chose the materials they did. **Ask: Why does the type of materials you use matter?** Sample answer: Cat claws are sharp, so the material needs to be very strong.

STEP 3 Allow children time to build their solutions. Make sure that they build at least two solutions.

Hands-On Activity, continued

STEP 4 Demonstrate for the children how to gently use the fork to simulate the claws of a cat. Make sure to monitor children closely while they test their solutions.

SEP **Analyzing and Interpreting Data** . . . .

Have children discuss the things that worked well with their designs and things that did not work well. Share with the children that this is a form of data collection. **Ask: What problems do you see with your design? How could you change your design to fix that problem?** Answers will vary.

STEP 5 Guide children to record their designs in the workspace to show how they would improve their designs. Monitor children as they share information and record their designs.

Claims, Evidence, and Reasoning

Children should write a claim, supported with evidence, that describes how they can build something to stop a cat from scratching furniture. **Ask: What is something you can change about this design that will make it better? How would you design your change?** Sample answer: The material I used at first was not very strong, so a cat might be able to scratch through it.

Scoring Rubric for Hands-On Activity	
3	Writes a solution for how to stop a cat from scratching furniture and provides evidence to support their solution
2	Writes a solution for how to stop a cat from scratching furniture that is supported with weak evidence
1	Writes a solution for how to how to stop a cat from scratching furniture but is not supported with evidence
0	Does not state a claim and does not provide evidence

Step 4

Test your solutions. Look for ways to improve your designs.

Step 5

Think of a way you could redesign your solutions. Share your solutions.

Children should show how they redesigned their solutions.

Make a claim that answers your question.

Sample answer: I can add padding to the chair to keep a cat from scratching it.

What is your evidence?

Sample answer: I added padding to the chair and tested it. When I scratched the padding, the chair was protected.

28

© Houghton Mifflin Harcourt

Explore online. ▶ Guide children to the Interactive Online Student Edition where they can choose from and explore both paths.

Take It Further

People in Science & Engineering •
Mary Delaney

Mary Delaney lived in Manhattan, New York. When she walked her dog she would get frustrated with the constant rearranging of the leash in her hand because the dog would walk around a lamp post or pedestrian. Many times, the leash would fall out of her hand and the dog would run away. This problem led her to design a better working leash. Her design had a box with a spring in it. When the dog moved away from her, the leash would extend out. Then when the dog moved closer to her, the leash would retract. This helped her manage the dog, and reduced the number of times the leash would become entangled or dropped. Mary had to submit her design plans in order to get a patent on her invention. Mary's design is still used today.

SEP Developing and Using Models . . . .

Ask: How did Mary Delaney use a design process to invent her leash? Sample answer: Mary Delaney looked at leashes that already existed and improved the design.

Differentiate Instruction

ELL For children who have never owned a pet dog, it may be helpful to bring in a retractable leash as well as a nonretractable leash for the children to compare. It also may be helpful to demonstrate what the word retractable means. Show how the leash moves in and out, where as the other leash does not.

Take It Further

People in Science & Engineering •
Mary Delaney

Explore more online. ▶
Solve a Paw-blem

Explore online. ▶

Did you know that a leash we use today was invented a long time ago?

New York City in 1908

Mary Delaney lived in New York City in 1908. She saw a problem. Dogs ran all over. People needed a way to keep them close.

Delaney made a leash that could pull out and back. Over time, people made the idea better.

Delaney's leash today

© Houghton Mifflin Harcourt • Image Credits: (t) ©Everett Collection Historical/Alamy; (b) ©Lynne Carpenter/Getty Images

Take It Further, continued

Read, Write, Share! • Write to Inform and Explain

Children research dog leash designs. Encourage them to make a plan for their online research to help them stay focused on the topic. Children make a report to explain what they found out about dog leash designs.

CCC Structure and Function

Ask: How does the structure of the dog leash help it work?
Answers will vary.

💡 **Write to Inform and Explain** Remind children to write a topic sentence. A topic sentence tells what all the other sentences are about. Write detail sentences that tell facts about the topic. Include words that tell how, when, or where.

Collaboration

Small Groups You may choose to have children work in small groups to research a dog leash design. Encourage group members to brainstorm and discuss research questions. Have each group member research the answer to a particular question, and then have that group member share his or her findings.

Explore more online. ▶

Solve a Paw-blem

Children use a design process to solve a muddy paw problem.

Take It Further

Read, Write, Share! • Go online. Research a dog leash design. How does it work? What problem does it solve? Make a report to share what you learned. You can use a computer or a tablet. Add pictures to show the leash design.

💡 **Write to Inform and Explain**
Go to the online handbook for tips.

✏️ Draw and write to tell about the leash.

Accept all reasonable answers.

30

Explore online. ▶ Have children explore online to find out more about Max's problem.

Lesson Check

Lesson Check   Name_____

Explore online. ▶

Can You Solve It?

✏️ How would you design a leash to solve the problem of a dog pulling during a walk? Be sure to

• Name the steps in a design process.

• Tell how you would use the steps to solve the problem.

Sample answer: I would define the problem. Then, I would plan

and build two solutions. Next, I would test the solutions.

Then, I would redesign one of my solutions to make it better.

Last, I would communicate my solution.

_____

© Houghton Mifflin Harcourt

Lesson Check

Can You Solve It?

Have children reread their answers to the Can You Solve It? prompts at the beginning of the lesson.

DCI **Defining and Delimiting Engineering Problems.** . . . .

Review the photograph and discuss the problem. Discuss with children who don't mention making more than one solution how important that step is in a design process. Explain that multiple solutions help ensure an engineer is designing the best solution to the problem. If a child does not mention redesigning their solutions, explain that many times engineers must redesign their solution in order to get to a working solution. **Ask: Why is it a problem if a dog pulls during a walk?** Sample answer: The dog or the person holding the leash could get hurt. **How can you use a design process to solve the problem?** Sample answer: I could design a leash that the dog wouldn't pull.

Scoring Guidelines

• Children should name the steps in a design process.
• Children should write how they use the steps to develop a solution to the problem.

Lesson Check, continued

SUMMATIVE ASSESSMENT
Lesson Check

1. Children should choose A—Ask questions; B—Make observations; and C—Gather information. Remind children that in order to fully understand a problem, it is necessary to make observations and ask questions to gather enough information about the problem. If children do not choose all three, direct them to the A Design Process—Step 1 section.

2. Children should choose B—Plan and Build. If children choose A or C, discuss what is happening in the picture. Ask children to think about which step includes making a model. Remind children that planning and building is necessary in order to test their solutions. If children do not choose B, direct them to the Step 2—Plan and Build section.

3. Children should choose B—Find ways to improve it. If children choose A or C, direct them to the Step 3—Test and Improve section. Point out that Gabriel is using a design process, so he is trying to solve a problem. When he tested his solution, it did not work, so he needs to redesign it and test again.

Self Check

1. How do you understand a problem in Step 1 of a design process? Choose all correct answers.

   Ⓐ Ask questions.
   Ⓑ Make observations.
   Ⓒ Gather information.

2. Which step of a design process does this photo show?

   Ⓐ Define a Problem
   Ⓑ Plan and Build
   Ⓒ Communicate

3. Gabriel uses a design process to build a back scratcher. He tests the back scratcher. It is not long enough. What should he do next?

   Ⓐ Throw out the back scratcher.
   Ⓑ Find ways to improve it.
   Ⓒ Communicate his solution.

32

4. Kim builds a clay boat. The boat needs to be strong enough to hold a few pennies. How will Kim know her boat works?

  Ⓐ She will test to find out if the boat floats.

  Ⓑ She will test to find out if the pennies float.

  Ⓒ She will test to find out if the water is high enough.

5. Juan builds a shelf for his books. The shelf keeps falling over. He finds new materials and rebuilds it. What problem is he solving?

  Ⓐ Juan's books are not light enough.

  Ⓑ Juan's shelf is not strong enough.

  Ⓒ Juan does not have enough books.

4. Children should choose A—She will test to find out if the boat floats. If children choose B or C, have them reread the question and think about the goal of Kim's design. Also, guide children back to the A Design Process—Step 1 section. Have children make observations about the picture to have a better understanding of what the problem is.

5. Children should choose B—Juan's shelf is not strong enough. If children choose A or C, have them reread the question and think about the object that Juan is trying to improve. Guide children back to the Step 4—Redesign section. Remind children that Juan had to observe the shape and stability of his design in order to improve it. Using stronger materials will help his bookshelf stay upright.

Unit 1 Performance Task

Engineer It • Build a House

👥 small groups 🕐 2 class periods

Objective

Children will **build two solutions** and **analyze data** to **determine which materials** will keep a model house from blowing down.

Suggested Materials

cardboard, paper, craft sticks, tape, scissors, fan or blow dryer, other classroom materials

Preparation

Collect and assemble materials for children. You may want to have children bring in materials from home in advance of this activity. Bring in a fan or blow dryer.

SEP **Asking Questions and Defining Problems.** . . . . .

Ask: Why is it important to define the problem? Sample answer: It is important to understand the problem so that I can begin thinking about solutions.

STEPS

Step 1 • Define a Problem

Guide children in a discussion about the problem they will solve.

Step 2 • Plan and Build

Ask: How can you explore which materials are best for your house? Sample answer: I can make the houses in similar shapes, but use different materials.

CCC **Structure and Function.** . . . .

Ask: What types of materials do you think would help keep a house from being blown down by wind? Why? Sample answer: Heavy cardboard and craft sticks would make the house strong.

 Unit 1 Performance Task

Engineer It • **Build a House**

Materials
- cardboard
- paper
- craft sticks
- tape
- scissors
- fan or blow dryer
- other classroom materials

STEPS

Step 1

Define a Problem You want to build a house that can not be blown down by wind.

Step 2

Plan and Build Plan at least two solutions. Think about the materials you will need. Build your solutions.

Step 3

Test and Improve Test your solutions. How can you improve your solutions?

34

Step 4

Redesign Make changes to the materials or how you put the materials together. Test your new solutions.

Step 5

Communicate Share your solutions. Explain which materials you used and why you chose them. Use evidence to tell how your solutions solve the problem.

 Check

_____ I built two solutions.
_____ I tested my solutions.
_____ I redesigned my solutions.
_____ I shared my solutions with others.

Step 3 • Test and Improve

 Analyzing and Interpreting Data. . . . .

Have children compare their solutions to help them identify what parts of each house were successful. Children could make a T-chart listing the materials and characteristics of each house to help them with the comparison. **Ask: What materials did you use in the first house, but not the second? How did you arrange the materials in each house? How do you think the different materials and arrangements affected the stability of each house?**

Step 4 • Redesign

CCC **Structure and Function. . . . .**

Prompt children to implement one improvement to each house based on their comparisons in Step 3. Children should retest their houses in order to evaluate the houses' performance with the improvements in place. **Ask: How did the improvements help to make the house stand up against the wind?**

Step 5 • Communicate

Children should communicate their results, and include an explanation for each step of a design process that they followed. Children should explain, based on their test results, which materials and arrangement of materials are most effective for building a house that will not get blown down by wind.

Scoring Rubric for Performance Task	
3	Builds, tests, and redesigns at least two model houses that are not blown down by wind. Communicates results.
2	Builds and tests two model houses, but does not redesign them; or builds, tests, and redesigns one model. Communicates results for one model.
1	Builds two model houses, but does not test or redesign them. Does not communicate results.
0	Does not build, test, or redesign a model house.

Unit 1 Review

1. Children should choose A—uses math and science to solve problems; B—follows a design process; and C—makes new technology. If children do not choose all three answers, remind them to read the question carefully. By completing What Is an Engineer in Lesson 1, children explored what an engineer does.

2. Children should choose C—build a solution. If children choose A or B, reinforce that gathering information and defining the problem must come before planning and building the solution. By completing Step 1–Define a Problem and Step 2–Plan and Build in Lesson 2, children explored the first two steps of a design process.

3. Children should choose A—fishing pole; and B—dock. If children choose C, reinforce that lakes occur in nature and are not made by engineers. By completing What Is Technology in Lesson 1, children explored what technology is.

4. Children should choose C—training wheels. If children choose A or B, explain that while a helmet and sneakers are both important for learning to ride a bike, they do not solve the problem of falling over. By completing What Is Technology in Lesson 1, children explored what technology is.

Unit 1 Review   Name _____

1. What does an engineer do? Choose all correct answers.
   - Ⓐ uses math and science to solve problems
   - Ⓑ follows a design process
   - Ⓒ makes new technology

2. What is the last thing an engineer does to solve a problem?
   - Ⓐ gather information
   - Ⓑ define the problem
   - Ⓒ build a solution

3. Which objects in the picture are examples of technology? Choose all correct answers.
   - Ⓐ fishing pole
   - Ⓑ dock
   - Ⓒ lake

4. Kayla is learning to ride a bike. What technology solves the problem of her falling over?
   - Ⓐ a helmet
   - Ⓑ sneakers
   - Ⓒ training wheels

36

5. Which problem can Derek solve with technology?
   Ⓐ Derek can not find a piece of paper.
   Ⓑ Derek has a flat tire on his bike.
   Ⓒ Derek can not make up his mind about what snack he wants.

6. Draw a line to match each problem to the technology that can help solve it.

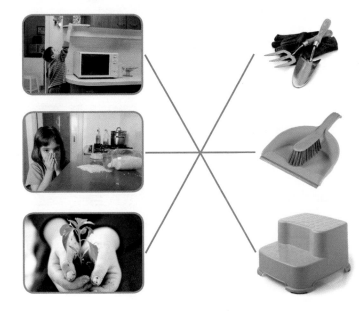

5. Children should choose B—Derek has a flat tire on his bike. If children choose A or C, reinforce that technology is something that engineers make. Discuss with children the technology that Derek can use to fix the flat tire on his bike. By completing What Is Technology in Lesson 1, children explored how technology is used to solve a problem.

6. Children should match the child reaching up with the step stool; the child and the mess with the dust pan and hand broom; and the plant with the garden tools. If children do not match the problems with the correct technologies, discuss the problem shown in each image on the left and the technology shown in each image on the right. By completing What Is Technology in Lesson 1, children explored how technology is used to solve a problem.

7. Children should choose B—Problems can have many solutions. If children choose A, remind them that they planned two solutions. If children choose C, reinforce that anyone can solve problems. By exploring Step 2–Plan and Build in Lesson 2, children explored the second step of a design process.

8. Children should choose A—Plan and Build. If children choose B or C, reinforce that plan and build comes before test, improve, or redesign. By completing Lesson 2, children explored the five steps of a design process.

9. Children should choose C—Test and Improve. If children choose A or B, discuss the picture. By completing Step 3–Test and Improve in Lesson 2, children explored that Test and Improve comes after Plan and Build.

10. Children should choose A—take photos or draw pictures; and B—write notes to tell about it. If they choose C, discuss that asking questions and making observations are part of Step 1, Define a Problem. By completing Step 5–Communicate in Lesson 2, children explored ways to communicate.

3D Item Analysis	1	2	3	4	5	6	7	8	9	10
SEP Asking Questions and Defining Problems	•				•	•		•		
SEP Developing and Using Models		•	•				•		•	
SEP Analyzing and Interpreting Data		•					•			•
DCI Defining and Delimiting Engineering Problems	•			•	•	•		•		
DCI Developing Possible Solutions		•					•	•		
DCI Optimizing the Design Solution									•	•
CCC Structure and Function		•								

7. Which is true about a problem?
   Ⓐ Problems only have one solution.
   Ⓑ Problems can have many solutions.
   Ⓒ Problems can only be solved by engineers.

8. Jacob finds a problem. He asks questions, makes observations, and gathers data. What should he do next?
   Ⓐ Plan and Build
   Ⓑ Test and Improve
   Ⓒ Redesign

9. What step of a design process does the picture show?
   Ⓐ Find a Problem
   Ⓑ Communicate
   Ⓒ Test and Improve

10. Which are ways to communicate a solution?
    Ⓐ take photos or draw pictures
    Ⓑ write notes to tell about it
    Ⓒ ask questions and make observations

38

Unit 2
Sound

Unit Project • Explore Sound
How do vibrations make sound?
Investigate to find out.

Unit 2 • Sound

39

Unit 2 • Sound

Unit Overview
In this unit, children will…
- explore the relationship between sound and vibration.
- compare the volume and the pitch of different sounds.
- investigate how sound makes materials move.
- identify ways people communicate using sound.
- explore how technology is used to help people communicate with sound over distances.

About This Image
Guide children in a discussion about the picture on this page. Explain that the picture shows splashes of paint bouncing from a surface into the air. **Ask: What do you think is making the paint bounce into the air?** Sample answer: Something is making the surface move, which bounces the paint into the air. After children have explored the relationship between sound and vibration, have them revisit the photo and offer a new answer. **Ask: Could sound make the paint bounce?** Accept all reasonable answers.

Unit Project • **Explore Sound**
Have children plan and conduct an investigation to determine how vibrations make sound. Have children feel the vibrations in their throats when they hum, and on their lips when they play kazoos. If available, play music through a speaker and allow children to place their hands on the speaker. Ask children to explain what they think the connection is between the vibrations and the sounds.

More support for the Unit Project can be found on pp. 41I–41L.

Unit 2 At a Glance

The learning experiences in this unit prepare children for mastery of:

Performance Expectations

PS4-1 Plan and conduct investigations to provide evidence that vibrating materials can make sound, and that sound can make materials vibrate.

PS4-4 Use tools and materials to design and build a device that uses sound to solve the problem of communicating over a distance.

Explore online.

In addition to the print resources, the following resources are available online to support this unit:

Unit Pretest

Lesson 1 What Is Sound?
- Interactive Online Student Edition
- Lesson Quiz

Lesson 2 Engineer It • How Can We Communicate with Sound?
- Interactive Online Student Edition
- Lesson Quiz

You Solve It Getting the Band Together

Unit Performance Task

Unit Test

Unit 2 At a Glance

© Houghton Mifflin Harcourt

40

Unit Vocabulary

sound a kind of energy you hear when something vibrates (p. 44)

vibrate to move quickly back and forth (p. 44)

volume how loud or soft a sound is (p. 46)

pitch how high or low a sound is (p. 47)

communicate to share information (p. 60)

Vocabulary Game • **Make a Match**

Materials
- 1 set of word cards
- 1 set of definition cards

How to Play
1. Work with a partner to make word and definition cards.
2. Place the cards face up on a table.
3. Pick a word card, read the word, and match it to a definition.
4. If you make a match, keep the cards and play again.
5. If not, your partner takes a turn.

© Houghton Mifflin Harcourt

Unit Vocabulary

The Next Generation Science Standards emphasize explanation and demonstration of understanding versus rote memorization of science vocabulary words. Keep in mind that these vocabulary words are tools for clear communication. Use these words as a starting point, not an end goal, for children to build deeper understanding of science concepts.

Children can explore all vocabulary words in the **Online Glossary**.

Vocabulary Strategies

- Have children review the vocabulary words. Then have children work in pairs to share an example of each word and explain why they think it's an example. Have pairs record their examples to refer back to during the unit.

- Have children think about how each word relates to sound. Have children work in pairs and share their ideas with a partner.

Differentiate Instruction

RTI/Extra Support Pronounce each word, and have children repeat it after you. Have children find each highlighted word within the unit content. Have children work in pairs and explain to a partner what they think each word means based on the surrounding context of imagery and text.

Extension Have children select two vocabulary words and work in small groups to illustrate and explain the words to a kindergarten child.

Vocabulary Game • **Make a Match**

Preparation Assign children to pairs. Give a set of cards to each pair. Establish a time limit or a set number of rounds for the game.

Integrating the NGSS* Three Dimensions of Learning

Building to the Performance Expectations

The learning experiences in this unit prepare children for mastery of the following Performance Expectations:

Waves and their Applications in Technologies for Information Transfer

1-PS4-1 Plan and conduct investigations to provide evidence that vibrating materials can make sound and that sound can make materials vibrate.

1-PS4-4 Use tools and materials to design and build a device that uses light or sound to solve the problem of communicating over a distance.

Assessing Student Progress

After completing the lessons, the **Unit Project • Explore Sound** provides children with opportunities to practice aspects of and to demonstrate their understanding of the Performance Expectations as they plan and conduct an investigation to determine how vibrations make sound.

Additionally, children can further practice or be assessed on aspects of the Performance Expectations by completing the **Unit Performance Task • Communicate with Sound,** in which children plan materials to test sound signals in order to communicate a message.

Lesson 1
What Is Sound?

In Lesson 1, children begin by observing that sound can cause materials to move and that vibrating materials can make sound (**DCI Wave Properties**). Children ask questions and explore the concepts of vibration, pitch, and volume (**SEP Scientific Investigations Use a Variety of Methods**). They also plan and conduct investigations to produce data about the relationship between sound and vibrations (**SEP Planning and Carrying Out Investigations**). Children use the results of their observations from their investigation to make claims about the cause-and-effect relationship between sound and vibration (**CCC Cause and Effect**).

Lesson 2
Engineer It • How Can We Communicate with Sound?

In Lesson 2, children explore the different ways people communicate with sound, including devices that allow people to communicate over long distances (**DCI Information Technologies and Instrumentation**). Children use tools and materials provided to build and modify a tool for making sound and communicating over a distance (**SEP Constructing Explanations and Designing Solutions, SEP Asking Questions and Defining Problems**) (**DCI Defining and Delimiting Engineering Problems**). Children investigate technologies people use to communicate with one another (**CCC Influence of Engineering, Technology, and Science on Society and the Natural World**) and how sound engineers and people in other careers make use of technology to study and modify sound.

Standards Supported by This Unit

 Explore online. Online only.

Next Generation Science Standards	Unit Project	Lesson 1	Lesson 2	Unit Performance Task	You Solve It
SEP Planning and Carrying Out Investigations	•	•		•	
SEP Scientific Investigations Use a Variety of Methods	•	•		•	•
SEP Constructing Explanations and Designing Solutions	•		•	•	•
DCI **PS4-A** Wave Properties	•	•		•	
DCI **PS4-C** Information Technologies and Instrumentation			•	•	•
CCC Cause and Effect	•	•		•	
CCC Influence of Engineering, Technology, and Science on Society and the Natural World			•	•	•

NGSS* Across the Grades

Before	Grade 1	After
Coverage of the **Performance Expectations** within this unit originates in Grade 1.	**Waves and their Applications in Technologies for Information Transfer** **1-PS4-1** **1-PS4-4**	**Waves and their Applications in Technologies for Information Transfer** **4-PS4-1** Develop a model of waves to describe patterns in terms of amplitude and wavelength and that waves can cause objects to move. **4-PS4-2** Develop a model to describe that light reflecting from objects and entering the eye allows objects to be seen. **4-PS4-3** Generate and compare multiple solutions that use patterns to transfer information.

 **Trace Tool to the NGSS™** Go online to view the complete coverage of these standards across this grade level and time.

3D Unit Planning

Lesson 1 What Is Sound? pp. 42–57

Overview

Objective Plan and conduct an investigation in order to gather evidence of how sound and vibration are related.

SEP Planning and Carrying Out Investigations
SEP Scientific Investigations Use a Variety of Methods
DCI **PS4-A** Wave Properties
CCC Cause and Effect

Math and **English Language Arts** standards and features are detailed on lesson planning pages.

	Print and Online Student Editions	Explore online.
ENGAGE	Lesson Phenomenon pp. 42–43 **Can You Explain It?** Why does the water move?	▶ Can You Explain It? Video
EXPLORE/ EXPLAIN	Make a Sound **Volume and Pitch** **What Makes It Move?** **Hands-On Activity** **Make Something Move with Sound** pp. 51–52	**Hands-On** Worksheet **You Solve It** Getting the Band Together
ELABORATE	Take It Further pp. 53–54 **People in Science & Engineering •** Ludwig van Beethoven	**Take It Further** Pitch In
EVALUATE	Lesson Check p. 55 Self Check pp. 56–57	Lesson Quiz

🔍 Hands-On Activity Planning

Make Something Move With Sound

Objective Children work in small groups to answer the question, "Can sound make rice move?" 👥 small groups ⏱ 1 class period	**Suggested Materials** • a metal can • cling wrap • a rubber band • rice • a pot • a wooden spoon

Preparation/Tip

Pre-assemble materials bundles for groups, including all materials except rice. Allow children to place a handful of rice on their drum once they have assembled the drum.

Overview

Objective Design a solution to the problem of communicating over a distance.

SEP Constructing Explanations and Designing Solutions
DCI **PS4-C** Information Technologies and Instrumentation
CCC Influence of Engineering, Technology, and Science on Society and the Natural World

Math and **English Language Arts** standards and features are detailed on lesson planning pages.

	Print and Online Student Editions	Explore online. ⏵
ENGAGE	**Lesson Problem** pp. 58–59 **Can You Solve It?** Sound Signals	⏵ **Can You Solve It?** Video
EXPLORE/ EXPLAIN	**Communicate with Sound** **Communicate Over Distances** **Send a Message** **Hands-On Activity** **Engineer It •** **Communicate Over Distance** pp. 63–64	**Hands-On** Worksheet
ELABORATE	**Take It Further** pp. 69–70 **Careers in Science & Engineering •** **Sound Engineer**	**Take It Further** Morse Code
EVALUATE	**Lesson Check** p. 71 **Self Check** pp. 72–73	**Lesson Quiz**

🔍 Hands-On Activity Planning

Engineer It • Communicate Over Distance

Objective Children make sound to communicate over a distance. They then use materials to design something that will make the sound louder. Children use evidence from their investigation to support a claim about how they can communicate with sound over a distance.

👥 small groups
🕐 1 class period

Suggested Materials
- an object that makes noise
- craft materials

Preparation/Tip
Provide the materials children need for the activity.

3D Unit Planning, continued

 You Solve It   Go online for an additional interactive opportunity.

Getting the Band Together

This virtual lab offers practice in support of **1-PS4-1** and **1-PS4-4.**

SEP Constructing Explanations and Designing Solutions

SEP Scientific Investigations Use a Variety of Methods

DCI **PS4-C** Information Technologies and Instrumentation

CCC Influence of Engineering, Technology, and Science on Society and the Natural World

3D Learning Objectives

- Children see a video of a person playing a xylophone and answer onscreen questions to put one together for a child in the band.
- Children see a video of a real drum in action. They will then be given a set of tools to build, test, and modify the design for a drum for a child in the band.
- Children see a video of a real guitar in action. They will then be given a set of tools to build, test, and modify the design for a guitar for a child in the band.

Activity Problem

You apply what you learned about sound to make homemade musical instruments to play as a band in the school talent show.

Interaction Summary

- Explores different parts of instruments to observe how vibration creates sound.
- Uses homemade materials to build instruments to be used by children.
- Observes the instruments being played by children at the school talent show.
- Explains how vibrations produce the sounds they hear from the instruments.
- Explains how tools made to produce sounds help us to communicate.

Assessment

Pre-Assessment

Assessment Guide, Unit Pretest

The Unit Pretest focuses on prerequisite knowledge and is composed of items that evaluate children's preparedness for the content covered within this unit.

Formative Assessment

Interactive Worktext, Apply What You Know, Lesson Check, and Self Check

Summative Assessment

Assessment Guide, Lesson Quiz

The Lesson Quiz provides a quick assessment of each lesson objective and of the portion of the Performance Expectation aligned to the lesson.

Interactive Worktext, Performance Task pp. 74–75

The Performance Task presents the opportunity for children to collaborate with classmates in in order to complete the steps of each Performance Task. Each Performance Task provides a formal Scoring Rubric for evaluating children's work.

Interactive Worktext, Unit 2 Review, pp. 76–78
Assessment Guide, Unit Test

The Unit Test provides an in-depth assessment of the Performance Expectations aligned to the unit. This test evaluates children's ability to apply knowledge in order to explain phenomena and to solve problems. Within this test, Constructed Response items apply a three-dimensional rubric for evaluating children's mastery on all three dimensions of the Next Generation Science Standards.

 **Assessment Online**   Go online to view the complete assessment items for this unit.

Teacher Notes

_____

_____

_____

_____

_____

_____

_____

_____

_____

_____

_____

_____

_____

Differentiate Instruction

Leveled Readers

The Science & Engineering Leveled Readers provide additional nonfiction reading practice in this unit's subject area.

On Level • **What Are Forces and Energy?**
This reader reinforces unit concepts, and includes response activities for your children.

Extra Support • **What Are Forces and Energy?**
This reader shares title, illustrations, vocabulary, and concepts with the On-Level Reader; however, the text is linguistically accommodated to provide simplified sentence structures and comprehension aids. It also includes response activities.

Enrichment • **Soccer Moves!**
This high-interest, nonfiction reader will extend and enrich unit concepts and vocabulary, and includes response activities.

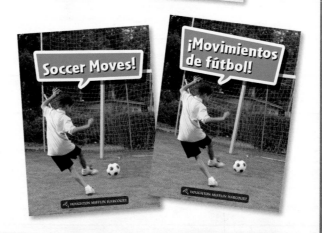

Teacher Guide
The accompanying Teacher Guide provides teaching strategies and support for using all the readers.

ELL

English Language Learner support resources include a glossary and Leveled Readers in Spanish and English. ELL teaching strategies appear throughout this unit:

pp. 42B, 48, 58B, 61

RTI/Extra Support

Strategies for children who need extra support appear throughout this unit:

pp. 41, 42B, 47, 58B, 62

Extension

Strategies for children who have mastered core content and are ready for additional challenges appear throughout this unit:

pp. 41, 42B, 47, 58B, 62

Leveled Readers

All readers are available online as well as in an innovative, engaging format for use with touchscreen mobile devices. Contact your HMH Sales Representative for more information.

Connecting with NGSS

Connections to Community

Use these opportunities for informal science learning to provide local context, and to extend and enhance unit concepts.

At Home

Play a Game Have children invite a family member to play a listening game. They will sit quietly, listen to sounds around them, and take turns describing the sounds to each other. They should try to include words such as "high pitch," "low pitch," 'loud," and "soft"in their descriptions. The other person should try to identify the source of the sound. If neither person can identify the sound, they can investigate to find the source together before moving on. Children can keep a list or draw pictures to share.
Use with Lesson 1.

Sound Effects Ask children to think about what movies were like when this technology was new. Discuss how early movies were silent. Ask children to watch part of a television show or movie at home with the volume turned off. Have them draw something they saw happen that would normally make a sound. They can share the picture with the class or a partner and recreate how it may have sounded with the volume turned up.
Use with Lesson 2.

In the Community

Guest Speaker Invite a singer or band member to speak to the class about how they use their voice or an instrument to make sound. Have children prepare questions for him or her to answer. Encourage children to ask questions about how they learned to recognize and create a variety of sounds.   *Use with Lesson 1.*

Have You Heard? Guide children to think about the way places in their community sound. Ask them to think of places that often have loud sounds. Examples may include a store, a factory, or a construction site. Discuss places that may have unsafe levels of noise and guide children to consider technology that may keep workers and visitors safe. Next, have children to think of places that are most often quiet. Examples may include the public library, a hiking trail, or a nursing home. Discuss why these places are quiet.
Use with Lesson 1 or 2.

Home Letters   Go online to view the Home Letters for this unit.

Collaboration

Collaboration opportunities in this unit:

Build on Prior Knowledge
pp. 43, 59

Think, Pair, Share
pp. 48, 55, 71

Small Groups
p. 66

Connections to Science

Connections to Science opportunities in this unit:

Connection to Engineering Design
Lesson 1, p. 54

Connection to Earth and Space Science
Lesson 2, p. 60

Unit Project

Unit Project 👥 small groups ⏱ 1 class period

Explore Sound

There are many ways to complete this Unit Project. The steps and Suggested Materials indicate one way to complete the investigation. Encourage children to come up with their own ideas to observe how sound and vibration are related. If children decide to follow another process to complete their investigation, be sure to review each group's plans before the children begin. Provide guidance for groups that may have strayed off topic.

3D Learning Objective

SEP Constructing Explanations and Designing Solutions
Explore the relationship between sound and vibration by planning and conducting an investigation. Collect data to use as evidence to answer a question. Explain a problem and construct a solution based on a claim.

Skills and Standards Focus

This project supports building children's mastery of **Performance Expectation 1-PS4-1.**

SEP Planning and Carrying Out Investigations
SEP Scientific Investigations Use a Variety of Methods
SEP Constructing Explanations and Designing Solutions
DCI Wave Properties
CCC Cause and Effect

Suggested Materials

- kazoo
- speaker
- alternatively, an electric pencil sharpener and pencil

Preparation

Before beginning the project, ask children to explain what they think the connection between vibration and sound is. Explain that this activity has the potential to be loud. Discuss with children that loud noises can damage hearing. Instruct the children to never put their ears near loud noises.

Unit 2
Sound

Unit Project • Explore Sound
How do vibrations make sound? Investigate to find out.

Unit 2 • Sound   39

Differentiate Instruction

RTI/Extra Support Children can be provided with two to four different, predetermined ways to observe the relationship between sound and vibration. They can then choose their method to investigate.

Extension Challenge children to investigate whether the type of sound affects the way an object vibrates. Challenge them to make observations about sounds with different pitch and/or volume as they sing or hum. They may want to extend the investigation to include observations about vibrations produced by speaking, in addition to vibrations produced by music.

Name _____

Unit 2 Project
Explore Sound

How do vibrations make sound? Can you think of two different ways to test this? Write your ideas on the lines below. Then choose one. Plan and conduct an investigation to find out.

Children should write two ideas they have for investigating how

vibrations make sound.

_____

Materials
Draw and label the materials you will need.

Children should draw and label materials. The following are possible materials children can use for this investigation: kazoos, speakers

© Houghton Mifflin Harcourt Publishing Company

Unit 2 Project • Page 1 of 3

Unit 2 Project
Explore Sound

SEP **Planning and Carrying Out Investigations . . . .**

Pose the unit project question to children. Encourage them to think of two ways to investigate how vibrations make sound. Discuss all of the ideas as a class. Have children choose one to investigate.

In the sample investigation shown, children investigate three familiar sources of sound to explore the relationship between vibration and sound.

Children will place a hand on their throat while they hum. They will make observations about how a kazoo feels as they use it to make sound. Children will observe how a speaker feels as it plays music or other sound. **Ask: Do you think you can make sound without vibration? Why or why not?** No, I think vibration makes sound.

ESSENTIAL QUESTIONS Prepare children for their project by asking the following questions.

- How does sound affect materials?
- What does a material do when it makes sound?

Ask: What happens when an object makes a sound? What happens to the materials around that object as it is making sound? The object vibrates when it makes sound. The sound makes the materials around it vibrate.

Steps

Have children think about the steps they follow to make a plan or to carry out an investigation. Discuss with the children the importance of following steps in order to get the most accurate results.

SEP **Planning and Carrying Out Investigations . . . .**

Prior to the investigation, have children observe how their throat, the kazoo and the speaker feel when they are not producing sound.

Ask: If you were wearing ear plugs and could not hear anything, how might you be able to tell an object is making sound? I could touch it to feel for vibrations. Challenge children to consider how the vibration might feel if the volume or pitch of a sound changes. Have children observe each source of sound. At the end of the investigation, children should be able to identify how each source of sound vibrates and causes materials around it to also vibrate also. Observations can be recorded using words and pictures.

Data

Children should record data that reflects what happens when sound is produced and when sound is absent.

DCI **Wave Properties . . . .**

Ask: How can you describe the volume of a sound? loud or soft **How can you describe the pitch of a sound?** high or low Refer children to Lesson 1 What Is Sound? Have them record their observations using words and pictures.

CCC **Cause and Effect . . . .**

Remind children that a cause is why something happens and an effect is what actually happens. **Ask: As the kazoo vibrates and makes sound, what happens to your mouth and hand that touches the kazoo?** They are also vibrating. **How does the sound of your hum change when you hum into a kazoo?** It sounds louder than my hum without the kazoo. The sound has a higher pitch, like a buzz. **What do you think causes the kazoo to change the sound you make?** It vibrates in a different way. Refer children to Lesson 1 What Is Sound?

Steps Write the steps you will do.

Answers may vary but should reflect a logical order of steps in the

investigation. Sample steps listed:

1. Place hand lightly on throat.

2. Hum a song. Stop. Hum again.

3. Record observations.

4. Play a kazoo. Stop. Play again.

5. Record observations.

6. Place hands on a speaker with sound on and off.

7. Record observations.

Data
Record your data.

> Answers and drawings may vary but should reflect that a person's throat, a kazoo, and a speaker vibrates when making sound.
>
> Throat _____
> Kazoo _____
> Speaker _____

Analyze Your Result

Look for patterns in your data.

Restate Your Question

Write the question you investigated.

Answers should identify the idea children initially chose at the

beginning of the investigation.

Claims, Evidence, and Reasoning

Make a claim that answers your question.

Answers should connect the vibrations of the throat, kazoo, and

speaker with sound.

Review the data. What evidence from the investigation supports your claim?

Answer should cite evidence from the investigation to support a

connection between sound and vibration.

Discuss your reasoning with a partner.

Analyze Your Result

Have children analyze their data. Elicit from them any patterns they noticed. Then have them share their data with the other groups in order to compare test results. **Ask: When does a throat, a kazoo, or a speaker vibrate?** when it is making sound **Can you feel these things vibrate when they are not making sound?** no.

Claims, Evidence, and Reasoning

Children should make the connection that when a material vibrates, it can make sound. An object that makes sound can make the materials around it also vibrate. Review what it means to make a claim. Explain that the observations they recorded will be used as evidence to support their claim. **Ask: What claim can you make?** Sound causes vibration. **How does your evidence support your claim?** The objects vibrated when they made sound and were still present when there was no sound. Encourage children to discuss their reasoning.

SEP **Constructing Explanations and Designing Solutions** . . . .

Discuss with children how their claim can help them to explain a problem and then design a solution. **Ask: How can you explain why a cup of loose coins placed on a speaker makes sound?** The sound of the speaker makes the coins vibrate and make noise. **How could you stop the sound of the coins?** I could turn off the speaker or move the cup.

Scoring Rubric for Unit Project	
3	States a claim supported with evidence that sound causes materials to move and vibrating materials can make sound
2	States a claim and somewhat supported with evidence that sound and vibration are related
1	States a claim that is not supported by evidence
0	Does not state a claim, and does not provide evidence

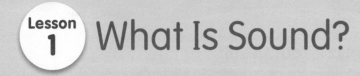

Lesson 1: What Is Sound?

Building to the Performance Expectation

The learning experiences in this lesson prepare children for mastery of:

1-PS4-1 Plan and conduct investigations to provide evidence that vibrating materials can make sound and that sound can make materials vibrate.

Trace Tool to the NGSS
Go online to view the complete coverage of these standards across this lesson, unit, and time.

 **Science & Engineering Practices**

Planning and Carrying Out Investigations
Plan and conduct investigations collaboratively to produce data to serve as the basis for evidence to answer a question.

 **VIDEO** SEP: Planning and Carrying Out Investigations

Scientific Investigations Use a Variety of Methods
- Science investigations begin with a question.
- Scientists use different ways to study the world.

 Disciplinary Core Ideas

PS4.A: Wave Properties
Sound can make matter vibrate, and vibrating matter can make sound.

 Crosscutting Concepts

Cause and Effect
Simple tests can be designed to gather evidence to support or refute student ideas about causes.

CONNECTIONS TO MATH

1.NBT.B.3 Compare two two-digit numbers based on the meanings of the tens and ones digits, recording the results of comparisons with the symbols >, =, and <.

CONNECTIONS TO ENGLISH LANGUAGE ARTS

SL.1.1 Participate in collaborative conversations with diverse partners about grade 1 topics and texts with peers and adults in small and larger groups.

Supporting All Students, All Standards

Integrating the Three Dimensions of Learning

This lesson focuses on exploring sound and vibration. Children begin by observing that sound can cause materials to move and that vibrating materials can make sound **(DCI Wave Properties)**. Children ask questions and explore the concepts of vibration, pitch, and volume **(SEP Scientific Investigations Use a Variety of Methods)**. They plan and conduct investigations to produce data about the relationship between sound and vibrations **(SEP Planning and Carrying Out Investigations)**. Children use the results of their observations from their investigation to make claims about the cause-and-effect relationship between sound and vibration **(CCC Cause and Effect)**.

 Professional Development Go online to view **Professional Development videos** with strategies to integrate CCCs and SEPs, including the ones used in this lesson.

Build on Prior Knowledge

Children should already know and be prepared to build on the following concepts:

- We can hear sounds.
- Sound is an important part of everyday life.
- We can identify loud sounds and soft sounds.
- We can identify high sounds and low sounds.

Differentiate Instruction

Lesson Vocabulary

- sound
- vibrate
- volume
- pitch

Reinforcing Vocabulary Help children connect the word *vibrate* to real-life experiences by inviting them to place their hand on a vibrating phone or think about what it feels like to touch a purring cat. Reinforce the difference between volume and pitch by having one child make a sound and having another child give an instruction to change the pitch or to change the volume. The first child makes the change and the second child identifies whether the change was correct.

RTI/Extra Support Provide additional opportunities for hands-on discovery. Allow children to explore vibration, pitch, and volume using simple musical instruments such as drums, kazoos, bells, and chimes. If these instruments are not available, have children make a simple instrument with a shoebox and a couple of rubber bands.

Extension Children who want to find out more can research how the human ear detects the vibrations that make sound. Provide resources, such as books or the Internet, in order to help children gather information. Have children share their findings with the class.

ELL Help children identify the key words in captions and headings throughout the lesson, and encourage children to refer to those key words as they explore the activities in the lesson. Provide hands-on examples of important concepts such as volume, pitch, sound, and vibration whenever possible to support the needs of these learners.

Lesson Phenomenon

Lesson Objective

Plan and conduct an investigation in order to gather evidence of how sound and vibration are related.

About This Image

Have children observe the drops of water in the picture. **Ask: What do you see happening?** Drops of water are jumping or bouncing. **Ask: What do you think might be making the drops move?** Water is sitting on an object that is making a loud noise. The noise made them move. Lead children in a discussion about what is causing the movement in the picture. Explain that sound can make materials move. Tell children that they will observe examples of sound making things move in this lesson.

 **Wave Patterns**

Alternative Engage Strategy

Humming and Buzzing	👥 partners 🕐 10–15 minutes

Have children place two fingers on their throats and hum softly. **Ask: What do you hear?** a humming sound **Ask: What do you feel?** My throat is vibrating a little bit.

Have pairs discuss questions they have about sound and vibrations as well as ways to go about getting answers to their questions. Have children share their questions by contributing to a class list that can later be used for additional investigations.

Lesson 1 **What Is Sound?**

Sound can make materials move.

By the End of This Lesson
I will be able to explain that materials that vibrate make sound, and that sound can make materials vibrate.

42

Sound Makes Objects Move

A speaker makes sound. Look at what happens when water is placed over the speaker.

Explore online. ▶

Can You Explain It?

🖍️➔ Why does the water move?

Accept all reasonable answers.

_____

_____

_____

© Houghton Mifflin Harcourt

Can You Explain It?

Sound Makes Objects Move Sound has some interesting effects. Play the video to see how placing the water over the speaker can make the water move. If the video is not available, have children observe and discuss the picture on the page.

Ask children to record their initial thoughts about what is making the water move. At the end of the lesson children will revisit this video as part of the Lesson Check. At this point, they should be able to explain that sound made the water move.

Collaboration

Build on Prior Knowledge Have children work in pairs to describe sounds they are familiar with. Encourage them to describe a variety of sounds, from soft to loud and from sudden to constant. Invite children to share some of their ideas with the class. **Ask: How do you think these different sounds might make water move in different ways?** I think quiet sounds might make the water move a little bit and loud sounds might make it move a lot. I think sudden sounds might make the water bounce up a bit and constant sounds might make gentle waves in the water.

Make a Sound

3D Learning Objective

Children **investigate to answer a question about the nature of sound.** They explore the relationship between sound and vibration and **perform simple tests to support or refute their ideas.**

SEP Scientific Investigations Use a Variety of Methods . . . .

Invite a few children to share their thoughts about what sound might be or what it might be caused by. After children have viewed the pictures or videos that show a piano string being hit with a hammer to produce sound, have them talk with a classmate about how their observations helped them understand what sound is or what causes it. Then, volunteers can share their ideas with the class. **Ask: What other questions do you have about sound?** Accept reasonable answers. **Ask: What is another way to find answers to your questions?** We can do an investigation.

DCI Wave Properties . . . .

As children view the pictures on the pages or the video of the piano string being hit, guide them to see what is making the sound. Help children understand that the sound is a result of a series of events. **Ask: What causes the sound?** The hammer hits the string. **Ask: What happens as a result of that?** The string vibrates. **Ask: What happens when the string vibrates?** The vibrations make a sound.

Make a Sound

Sounds are all around you, but what is sound? **Sound** is a kind of energy that you hear when something vibrates. To **vibrate** is to move quickly back and forth.

Explore online. ▶

A hammer in the piano hits a string.

The string vibrates, or moves. It makes a sound you can hear.

44

When does a piano string make sound?

Ⓐ when it stretches

Ⓑ when it vibrates

Ⓒ when it curls

Apply What You Know

Work with a group. Hold a metal ruler down on a table. Let half of the ruler hang over the edge of the table. Pluck the part of the ruler sticking out. What do you hear? Do tests to make different sounds. What causes the sound to change?

Cause and Effect Go to the online handbook for tips.

DCI **Wave Properties** . . . .

Children should choose—B when it vibrates—to demonstrate their understanding of the relationship between sound and vibration. Have children who choose A or C view the video or pictures again of the piano string being hit. **Ask: What does the piano string do when it is hit?** The piano string vibrates. **Ask: What causes the sound?** The vibrating string causes the sound.

FORMATIVE ASSESSMENT

Children work with a group to perform a simple test to gather evidence about the effect of causing a metal ruler to vibrate and to answer questions about what causes the sound to change. Remind children that everyone in the group should have a turn holding and plucking the ruler.

Scoring Guidelines
- describes the sound made by plucking a metal ruler hanging over the edge of a desk
- makes different sounds by changing how much of the ruler hangs over the edge of the desk
- makes a claim about why the sound changes

 Cause and Effect Remind children that a cause is why something happens and the effect is what actually happens. Instruct them to think carefully about everything they did and describe the one thing they did that caused the sound to change.

Volume and Pitch

3D Learning Objective

Children **gather evidence** that helps them **answer questions about** volume and pitch.

DCI Wave Properties. . . . .

Remind children that vibrations cause sound. Have children describe what is happening in both pictures. Encourage children to share experiences they have had with loud and soft sounds. **Ask:** **What are some loud sounds you have heard? What are some soft sounds you have heard?** Accept reasonable answers. Guide children to think about how the vibrations that cause loud sounds might differ from the vibrations that cause soft sounds. Have children think about the amount of force that is required in order to make a loud sound versus a soft sound. **Ask:** **How might the vibrations that cause a fire engine's siren sound be different from the vibrations that cause a soft whisper?** The vibrations that cause a loud sound like a siren are stronger than vibrations used to produce soft sounds like whispers.

CCC Cause and Effect . . . .

Ask: **How can you gather evidence about how vibrations that cause loud sounds are different from vibrations that cause soft sounds?** Have children discuss ideas with a classmate. Once pairs have formulated some ideas, such as observing or conducting investigations, invite volunteers to share some of them with the class. As a class, pick one of the ideas and test it in order to gather evidence to answer questions about vibrations in relation to loud and soft sounds.

Volume

Explore online. ▶

A siren makes a loud sound.

A whisper is a soft sound.

What is the difference between a siren and a whisper? They have different volumes. One is loud and one is soft. **Volume** is how loud or soft a sound is.

46

Pitch

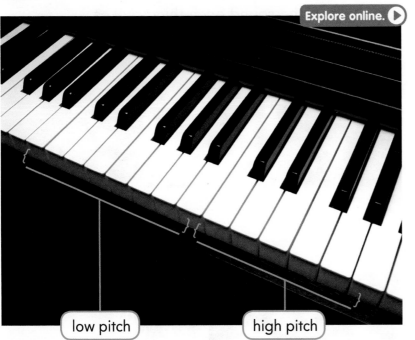

low pitch   high pitch

Sounds can also be high or low. **Pitch** is how high or low a sound is. You can hear a high pitch and a low pitch on a piano. The keys on one side of a piano make low sounds. The keys on the other side of a piano make high sounds.

© Houghton Mifflin Harcourt • Image Credits: dymax/Shutterstock, Inc.

Lesson 1 • What Is Sound?   47

SEP Scientific Investigations Use a Variety of Methods . . . .

Review with children all of the information they have gathered so far about sound. Encourage them to share questions they still have about vibration, volume, or pitch. Post their list of questions, and draw children's attention to one of the questions when it relates to an activity they are doing or an idea they are investigating.

DCI Wave Properties . . . .

Explain to children that piano strings differ in length and thickness as well as tension. Shorter, thinner strings under more tension will produce a high pitch because they vibrate faster. Longer, thicker strings under less tension will produce a low pitch because they vibrate slower. **Ask: How is the sound that keys at one end of a piano make different from the sound keys at the other end make?** Keys at one end make sounds with a high pitch and keys at the other end make sounds with a low pitch. **Ask: Why do you think the sounds are different?** Strings that vibrate fast have a high pitch, and strings that vibrate slower have a low pitch.

Differentiate Instruction

RTI/Extra Support Children might have trouble remembering the difference between high pitch and low pitch because high and low have different meanings when they describe pitch than they do when they describe position. Help children remember by having them try to make both kinds of sounds when they look down low and when they look up high. **Ask: Is it easier to make a sound with a high pitch or a low pitch when you look down?** A low pitch. **Ask: Is it easier to make a high pitch or a low pitch when you look up?** A high pitch.

Extension Have children research to find how other musical instruments make sounds with different pitches. Provide resources, such as books or the Internet. Have them share some examples of what they find with the class.

DCI Wave Properties . . . .

Highlight the fact that each of the sounds shown is made by vibrations. **Ask: What do you think causes the sound the wind chimes make?** The wind moves the metal tubes. As the tubes collide, they produce vibrations. The vibrations make sound.

Tell children that wind chimes make high-pitched sounds and low-pitched sounds, or demonstrate with a set of wind chimes. Remind children to think back about what they discovered regarding high pitches and low pitches in piano strings. **Ask: Why do you think the wind chimes make some high sounds and some low sounds?** They have metal tubes that are different lengths and widths. These cause different vibrations that make the different sounds.

Differentiate Instruction

ELL Divide a poster board in half. Have children cut pictures out of magazines to make a collage that has pictures of things that make loud sounds on one side and things that make soft sounds on the other side. Have children label and say the name of each item they included in the collage.

Collaboration

Think, Pair, Share Have children think of ways they might measure the volume of sounds. Then have them work with a partner to expand upon their ideas. Encourage them to think about what nonstandard unit they might measure volume with. Invite children to share some of their ideas with the class.

✏️ Look at the pictures. Write **loud** or **soft** to tell about the sound each thing makes.

 **Explore online.** ▶

loud

_____

soft

_____

loud

_____

soft

_____

✏️ Write **high** or **low** to complete the sentence. The sound of thunder has a ____low____ pitch.

48

Do the Math! • Pitch is measured with hertz. Hertz is a measurement for sound. A tuba can play a note with a pitch of 32 hertz. A cello can play a note with a pitch of 65 hertz.

 Compare Numbers Go to the online handbook for tips.

Compare the numbers. Write **<, >,** or **=.**

32   (<)   62

 Apply What You Know

Read, Write, Share! • Explore pitch in your classroom. Find objects that make sounds with a high pitch. Find objects that make sounds with a low pitch. List the objects. Talk with others about your list.

Participate in Discussions Go to the online handbook for tips.

 © Houghton Mifflin Harcourt

Lesson 1 • What Is Sound?   49

Do the Math! • Compare Numbers

Children should indicate that 32 is less than (<) 62. If children indicate that 32 is equal to 62 or is greater than 62, have them use base-ten blocks (tens rods and ones cubes) or counters (grouped in tens and ones) to represent the numbers and compare them.

💡 **Compare Numbers** If necessary, model grouping the counters by tens. Guide children to see that both numbers have the same number of ones, but 32 has 3 tens and 62 has 6 tens.

✋ **FORMATIVE ASSESSMENT**

Read, Write, Share! • Participate in Discussions
Children will work with a partner to list objects in the classroom that make sounds with a high pitch and objects that make sounds with a low pitch. Have each pair of children compare their list with another pair. Have them provide evidence of why they organized objects the way they did.

Scoring Guidelines
- lists objects in the classroom that make sounds with a high pitch
- lists objects in the classroom that make sounds with a low pitch
- participates respectfully in group discussion
- provides evidence for objects on each list

💡 **Participate in Discussions** Remind children to ensure that everyone in the group has a turn listening and a turn speaking while others listen.

LESSON 1 Engage • **Explore/Explain** • Elaborate • Evaluate

Explore online. ▶ Have children explore to find out more about how sound can make objects move.

What Makes It Move?

3D Learning Objective

Children **ask questions and observe pictures** to find out more about **how sound makes the balloon move.** They make claims about why the balloon moved and **use evidence from their observations to support their claim**.

 Cause and Effect . . . .

Ask: How could you use a balloon and a speaker to find out whether sound makes objects move? You could put a balloon near a speaker, turn the speaker on, and watch to see whether the balloon starts to move. **Ask:** What happened when the speaker was turned off? The balloon did not move. **Ask:** What happened when the speaker was turned on? The balloon moved. **Ask:** What caused the balloon to move? The sound coming out of the speaker.

 FORMATIVE ASSESSMENT ━━━━━

Evidence Notebook
Children should write a plan with a list of steps and materials. They should include their observations, conclusions, and evidence to support their findings in their Evidence Notebook.

Scoring Guidelines
• plans a simple investigation to show that sound can make water vibrate
• gathers data as evidence to explain what happened

💡 **Cause and Effect • Planning and Carrying Out Investigations** If children plan an investigation that does not produce useful data, encourage them to modify their plan as necessary.

What Makes It Move?

 **Explore online.** ▶

Look at the pictures. When the speaker is off, there is no sound. The balloon does not move. What happens when the speaker is on and sound begins to play? Vibrations from the speaker hit the balloon. The balloon moves.

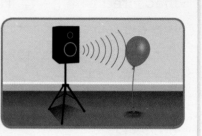 **Apply What You Know**

Evidence Notebook • Work with a partner. Use a tuning fork and a glass of water to explore sound. Plan a test to show that sound can make materials vibrate. Use evidence to tell what happened.

💡 **Cause and Effect • Planning and Carrying Out Investigations** Go to the online handbook for tips.

© Houghton Mifflin Harcourt

50

Name _____

Hands-On Activity
Make Something Move with Sound

Materials
- a metal can
- cling wrap
- a rubber band
- rice
- a pot
- a wooden spoon

Ask a Question

Can sound make rice move?

Test and Record Data Explore online. ▶

Step 1

Make a drum. Now put a handful of rice on top of the drum.

Step 2

Do the test. Bang a pot loudly very close to the drum.

Step 3

Record what you observe. Did the sound from the pot move the rice?

Children should record their observations.

© Houghton Mifflin Harcourt

Lesson 1 • What Is Sound?

51

Hands-On Activity 👥 small groups 🕐 1 class period

Make Something Move with Sound

3D Learning Objective

SEP **Planning and Carrying Out Investigations** . . . .

Children work in small groups to answer the question, Can sound make rice move?

Suggested Materials metal can, cling wrap, rubber band, rice, pot, wooden spoon

Preparation

Pre-assemble materials bundles for groups, including all materials except rice. Allow children to place a handful of rice on their drum once they have assembled the drum.

Activity

STEP 1 Model pulling the cling wrap tightly over the top of the can and securing it with a rubber band. Children might need assistance handling the rice. Only a small amount is needed.

SEP **Scientific Investigations Use a Variety of Methods** . . . .

Ask: What do you think will happen when you bang a pot near your drum? Vibrations from the pot will make the rice jump.

STEP 2 Remind children to take turns banging the pot.

STEP 3 If children observe that the sound from the pot did not move the rice, encourage them to check that their cling wrap is secured tightly to the top of their drum, to try banging the pot closer to the drum, or to try banging the pot a bit harder to make a louder sound.

Hands-On Activity, continued

 Cause and Effect . . . .

STEP 4   Ask: What did you find out about sound making the rice move when you tightened your drum (or moved the pot closer or banged the pot louder)? I found out that a sound has to be very loud in order to make the rice move.

If children did not modify their investigation, **Ask: How could you change this investigation a bit to figure out whether loud or soft sounds make rice move more?** I could bang the pot loudly or quietly and see how much the rice moves each time.

Claims, Evidence, and Reasoning

Children should make a claim that states that a loud sound close to a drum will cause rice on the drum to move. They should cite evidence to support their claim, based on their observations, specifically, that they banged a pot near their drum, and the rice on the drum began to move. **Ask: How do you know the rice moved because you banged the pot and not because the pot came near the drum?** The rice did not move when we held the pot near the drum, just when we banged the drum.

	Scoring Rubric for Hands-On Activity
3	States a claim supported with evidence about whether sound can make rice move on a drum
2	States a claim somewhat supported with evidence about whether sound can make rice move on a drum
1	States a claim that is not supported by evidence
0	Does not state a claim and does not provide evidence

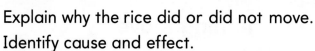

Step 4

Explain why the rice did or did not move. Identify cause and effect.

> Accept reasonable answers. Children should identify cause and effect.

Make a claim that answers your question.

> Sample answer: Sound can make rice move.

What is your evidence?

> Sample answer: The sound from the pot made the rice move.

52

© Houghton Mifflin Harcourt

Explore online. ▶   Guide children to the Interactive Online Student Edition where they can choose from and explore both paths.

Take It Further

People in Science & Engineering • Ludwig van Beethoven

Explore more online.

Pitch In

Explore online. ▶

sheet music

Ludwig van Beethoven wrote music all of his life. He gave his first concert at age 7. He had a problem as he got older. He started to lose his hearing. Still, he found ways to write music. He felt the piano vibrate. He used sounds with low pitch because he could feel them better.

Take It Further

People in Science & Engineering • Ludwig van Beethoven

Children explore the life of composer Ludwig van Beethoven and how he used vibrations to continue to experience and compose music after he lost his hearing.

Beethoven was born in 1770 in Germany. He was the eldest of seven children in his family. Beethoven was a child prodigy and for a short time studied with Mozart. He is considered one of the greatest composers of his time. Much of his work was produced during the transitional period between the Classical and Romantic Eras. His *Ninth Symphony* was his final composed piece that combined both vocals and instrumental music. Beethoven was not only a pianist but could play the viola and violin as well.

DCI **Wave Properties** . . . .

Discuss with children the relationship between sound and vibration. **Ask: Why was Ludwig van Beethoven's piano vibrating?** The sounds in the music he played made the piano vibrate. The piano strings vibrated, and that made sound. The sound made the rest of the piano vibrate.

Take It Further, continued

Children will identify strategies Beethoven used to keep writing music when he could no longer hear it. Children should choose A—He used low-pitch sounds and C—He felt his piano vibrate. If children choose B or do not choose A or C, have them review the information about Beethoven on the previous page and underline the ways Beethoven felt or heard music after he lost his hearing.

Connection to Engineering Design

Defining and Delimiting Engineering Problems A situation that people want to change or create can be approached as a problem to be solved through engineering. Such problems may have many acceptable solutions.

Have children work with a partner to design a doorbell for people who have lost their hearing. Tell children to think about what they know about sound and movement and to incorporate what they have explored into their designs. Children should draw and label their designs and explain how a person would know when someone was at the door. Invite volunteers to explain their design to the class. **Ask: In what ways were some of the designs similar?** Most of the designs used sound to make something move. **Ask: In what ways were the designs different?** Accept all reasonable answers.

Explore more online. ▶

Pitch In

Children explore how putting different amounts of water into bottles affects the sound that occurs when they blow on the bottles.

Beethoven wrote some of the most famous music in the world. Students study him. Orchestras play his music.

How did Beethoven keep writing music after he lost his hearing? Choose all correct answers.

Ⓐ He used low-pitch sounds.

Ⓑ He played music more loudly.

Ⓒ He felt his piano vibrate.

54

Explore online. ▶   Have children review how sound can make objects move.

Lesson Check

Name _____

Explore online. ▶

Can You Explain It?

✏️▶ Why does the water move?

Be sure to

• Describe how sound can affect materials.

• Explain what causes the water to move.

Sample answer: Sound can make materials vibrate. The sound

from the speaker makes the water vibrate.

_____

_____

© Houghton Mifflin Harcourt

Lesson 1 • What Is Sound?   55

Lesson Check

Can You Explain It?

Have children reread their answers to the Can You Explain It? prompt at the beginning of the lesson.

DCI Wave Properties . . . .

Guide children to observe the picture. Remind them of what causes sound and how sound can make things move. **Ask: What is happening to the water?** The water vibrates when it is placed over the speaker.

CCC Cause and Effect . . . .

Remind children of the cause-and-effect relationship between sound and vibrations. Have them think back to the information about the piano strings and the evidence they gathered during the Hands-On Activity. Vibrating materials can make sound, and sound can make materials vibrate. **Ask: What caused the water to vibrate?** The sound from the speaker caused it to vibrate.

Collaboration

Think, Pair, Share After children have thought about the Can You Explain It? question, have them discuss the question with a partner. Direct children to discuss what makes sound, what causes the water to move, and how sound affects materials such as the water. Children can record their responses in sentences or in a labeled diagram.

Scoring Guidelines

• Children should describe how sound affects materials.
• Children should explain what caused the water to move.

Lesson Check, continued

SUMMATIVE ASSESSMENT
Self Check

1. Children should choose B—vibrations. If children choose A or C, have them look at the Make a Sound section of the lesson and review what happens when a hammer hits a piano string. **Ask: When does a piano string make sound?** It makes sound when a hammer hits it and makes it vibrate.

2. Children should choose C—volume. If children choose A or B, ensure they understand what a jackhammer is and what it sounds like. Refer children to the Volume and Pitch section of the lesson. **Ask: What does a whisper sound like?** It is a soft sound. **Ask: Does soft describe pitch, vibration, or volume?** volume

3. Children should circle the guitar strings and the bell. If children circle the boiling water, remind them that to vibrate is to move quickly back and forth. Have children think about the movement of boiling water and if boiling water makes a sound.

Self Check
1. What causes sound?

Ⓐ pitch

Ⓑ vibrations

Ⓒ volume

_____

2. What is the main way the sounds of a jackhammer and a whisper are different?

Ⓐ pitch

Ⓑ vibration

Ⓒ volume

_____

3. Which pictures show that vibrations can make sound? Circle all correct answers.

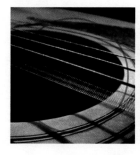  

56

4. Nicole wants to answer this question,
   Can sound make materials move? Which
   test should she do to answer the question?

   Ⓐ She should pluck a guitar string.

   Ⓑ She should bang a pot near a pile of rice.

   Ⓒ She should blow across the top of a
   water bottle.

5. Tim does the test shown in this photo. What
   does this tuning fork test tell Tim?

   Ⓐ Sound can make materials move.

   Ⓑ Sound is vibrations you can hear.

   Ⓒ Sounds can be loud or soft.

4. Children should choose B—She should bang a pot near a pile of rice. If children choose A or C, guide them to understand that Nicole needs to include materials that can move in her test. **Ask: What does Nicole need to have in order to conduct her test and answer her question?** She needs something that makes sound, and she needs a material that can move.

5. Children should choose A—Sound can make materials move. If children choose B or C, guide them to recognize that Tim's test does not provide data that can be used as evidence to show B or C. Ask guiding questions to help children understand that Tim's observation provides evidence that sound can make the water move, but it does not provide evidence that sound is a vibration you can hear or that sounds can be loud or soft.

Engineer It • How Can We Communicate with Sound?

Building to the Performance Expectation

The learning experiences in this lesson prepare children for mastery of:

1-PS4-4 Use tools and materials to design and build a device that uses light or sound to solve the problem of communicating over a distance.

Trace Tool to the NGSS
Go online to view the complete coverage of these standards across this lesson, unit, and time.

SEP **Science & Engineering Practices**

Constructing Explanations and Designing Solutions
Use tools and materials provided to design a device that solves a specific problem.

 VIDEO SEPs: Constructing Explanations and Designing Solutions/ Engaging in Argument from Evidence

Asking Questions and Defining Problems
Define a simple problem that can be solved through the development of a new and improved object or tool.

 VIDEO SEP: Asking Questions and Defining Problems

DCI **Disciplinary Core Ideas**

PS4.C: Information Technologies and Instrumentation
People also use a variety of devices to communicate (send and receive information) over long distances.

ETS1.A: Defining and Delimiting Engineering Problems
A situation that people want to change or create can be approached as a problem to be solved through engineering.

CCC **Crosscutting Concepts**

Influence of Engineering, Technology, and Science on Society and the Natural World
People depend on various technologies in their lives; human life would be very different without technology.

CONNECTION TO MATH

1.MD.A.2 Express the length of an object as a whole number of length units, by layering multiple copies of a shorter object (the length unit) end to end; understand that the length measurement of an object is the number of same-size length units that span it with no gaps or overlaps.

CONNECTION TO ENGLISH LANGUAGE ARTS

W.1.7 Participate in shared research and writing projects (e.g., explore a number of "how-to" books on a given topic and use them to write a sequence of instructions).

Supporting All Students, All Standards

Integrating the Three Dimensions of Learning

 Professional Development Go online to view **Professional Development videos** with strategies to integrate CCCs and SEPs, including the ones used in this lesson.

In this lesson, children explore the different ways people communicate with sound, including devices that allow people to communicate over long distances (DCI Information Technologies and Instrumentation). Children use tools and materials provided to build and modify a tool for making sound and communicating over a distance (SEP Constructing Explanations and Designing Solutions, SEP Asking Questions and Defining Problems) (DCI Defining and Delimiting Engineering Problems). Children investigate technologies people use to communicate with one another (CCC Influence of Engineering, Technology, and Science on Society and the Natural World) and how sound engineers and people in other careers make use of technology to study and modify sound.

Build on Prior Knowledge

Children should already know and be prepared to build on the following concepts:

- People share information with one another by talking and by writing.
- We recognize sounds with different volumes, including loud sounds and soft sounds.
- We recognize sounds with different pitches, including low pitches and high pitches.
- Sound is a kind of energy that we hear when something vibrates.

Differentiate Instruction

Lesson Vocabulary
- communicate

Reinforcing Vocabulary Take opportunities throughout the day when children are communicating with one another to point out that this is what they are doing — communicating, or sharing information. Have children make a list of all the ways they communicate with each other during the week. At the end of the week, have children review the ways they have communicated and discuss any other ways they can share information through sound.

RTI/Extra Support It may help provide children with additional opportunities to communicate at a distance with each other. Arrange for children to talk to one another using cell phones or video calling, send emails to children or teachers in other classrooms, and listen to radio broadcasts.

Extension Children who want to find out more can explore technologies that allow people who speak different languages to communicate over distances, for example, translation software. Alternatively, children could explore software that converts speech to text or text to speech. Have children suggest situations in which these types of communication technologies might be useful.

ELL Be sure to point out all labels, pictures, captions, and headings throughout the lesson to assist children with strategies to summarize chunks of content. In particular, highlight the names of technologies used to communicate. Have children make a bank of these words or make a class word wall to refer to throughout the lesson.

Lesson Problem

Lesson Objective

Design a solution to the problem of communicating a message over a distance.

About This Image

Direct children's attention to what the children in the photograph are doing. Discuss how people use sound to communicate. **Ask: What kinds of messages do people communicate with music?** Music can communicate happiness or sadness. It can communicate information, as the alphabet song does. **Ask: In what other ways do people use sound to communicate?** People talk to each other. A bell tells us when it is time to come into the school. Babies cry to tell their parents that they need something.

 **Information Technologies and Instrumentation**

Alternative Engage Strategy

The Silent Treatment	small groups 15–20 minutes

Have children work in groups to do a short task without making any sound. For example, they could make a pattern with blocks or put themselves in order by height. Allow 10 minutes to complete the task. Then, as a class, discuss how sound would have made the task easier. **Ask: How could you have used sound to make your task easier?** We could have planned what we would do together and we could have told people when they were doing something right.

Lesson 2 **Engineer It • How Can We Communicate with Sound?**

Music is one way to send messages with sound.

By the End of This Lesson

I will be able to explain how people use sound to send messages over a distance.

58

Sound Signals

Explore online. ▶

Dolphins use sound to send each other messages.

Can You Solve It?

✏️➤ How could you use sound to send a message over a distance?

Accept all reasonable answers.

_____

_____

© Houghton Mifflin Harcourt • Image Credits: ©ken Kiefer 2/Cultura/Getty Images

Lesson 2 • Engineer It • How Can We Communicate with Sound?
    59

Can You Solve It?

Sound Signals Animals use sound to communicate. Play the video to see how dolphins communicate using sound. If the video is not available, discuss with children the picture of the dolphins on the page.

Ask children to record their initial thoughts about how they could send a message over a distance using sound. At the end of this lesson, children will revisit this section as part of the Lesson Check. At this point, children should be able to explain a way to send a message over a distance.

Collaboration

Build on Prior Knowledge You may want children to view the video and then discuss it in pairs before they share their ideas with the class. In this way, children have opportunities to engage directly in a review of what they already know about sound.

Think about the activities you have already done that relate to sound. How is sound made? How do you think sound travels from one dolphin to another? Use evidence to support your answer.

Communicate with Sound

3D Learning Objective

Children **explore the ways people communicate with sound** and identify several ways people send and receive information using sound.

 **Information Technologies and Instrumentation** . . . .

Ask: What tools or devices are the people using to help them communicate? **guitars, a whistle, and a cell phone** Have children work with a partner to list as many devices as they can that help people communicate with sound. Invite pairs to share their ideas and work with children to make a class list.

CCC **Influence of Engineering, Technology, and Science on Society and the Natural World.** . . .

Ask: Think about the guitars the people in the picture are playing. How would life be different if we did not have guitars? We would not be able to share information with others through song or music played on a guitar.

Connection to Life Science

Information Processing This picture shows different ways people can communicate. Animals use sound to communicate, too. They have body parts that capture and convey information. Have pairs or small groups of children use books or the Internet to find two different animals that use sound to communicate. Have each pair or group make a poster and share their findings with the class.

What is a way to communicate with sound? Choose all correct answers.

Ⓐ drawing

Ⓑ singing

Ⓒ talking

 Apply What You Know

✏ Work with a partner or small group. Take turns showing a way to communicate with sound. Name each way you communicate with sound.

Accept reasonable answers.

_____

_____

_____

_____

Lesson 2 • Engineer It • How Can We Communicate with Sound?　61

DCI Information Technologies and Instrumentation . . . .

Children should choose B—singing; and C—talking. If children choose A, explain that drawing is not a way to communicate using sound. Guide them to understand that different methods of communication—and different communication technologies—might suit different purposes. **Ask: When might you communicate by singing instead of by talking?** I might sing when I want to show that I am really happy. **Ask: When might you talk on the phone instead of talking in person?** I might talk on the phone when I need to talk to someone who is far away.

Differentiate Instruction

ELL Ensure children understand the meanings of the verbs in the answer choices for this question and throughout the lesson. Invite volunteers to demonstrate drawing, singing, and talking. Also, reinforce the names of what children are doing in the Apply What You Know.

FORMATIVE ASSESSMENT

Children will work with a partner or a small group to role play different ways they could communicate with sound and to name each one. Encourage children to include several different methods of communication. Discuss some of the methods children identify as a class.

Scoring Guidelines
- takes part in group role play of ways to communicate with sound
- names a variety of ways to communicate with sound

Communicate Over Distances

3D Learning Objective

Children observe how people **use devices to help them communicate with sound over distances.** Children **explore the important role technology plays in enabling communication.**

DCI   **Information Technologies and Instrumentation** ·

As a class, discuss how a megaphone and a cell phone can help people communicate over distance. **Ask: How are these devices alike?** They both help people communicate using sound when people are far apart. **How are they different?** The megaphone makes a person's voice louder so many people can hear. The cell phone carries the sound to another place so someone there can hear it. People use a cell phone to speak with one other person.

CCC   **Influence of Engineering, Technology, and Science on Society and the Natural World.** · · · ·

Ask: Think about cell phones and telephones. How would life be different if these devices were not around? We would not be able to communicate with people that are far away from us.

Differentiate Instruction

RTI/Extra Support Have children construct a simple megaphone with paper and tape. Have partners see how far apart they can stand and still hear one another when they speak at a normal volume through the megaphone.

Extension Have children explore different megaphone designs. **Ask: Which helps your partner hear you from farther away, a wide megaphone or a narrow megaphone?** A narrow megaphone that isn't too narrow.

Communicate Over Distances

Explore online. ▶

A megaphone makes a voice louder. People can hear the voice from farther away.

A cell phone sends out sound. It also receives sound from other cell phones.

Technology helps people communicate with sound over long distances.

© Houghton Mifflin Harcourt • Image Credits: (t) DAJ/Getty IMages; (b) ©123RF ltd

62

Hands-On Activity

Engineer It • Communicate Over Distance

Name _____

Materials
• an object that makes noise
• craft materials

Ask a Question

How can you communicate with sound?

Test and Record Data Explore online. ▶

Step 1

Go outside with your object. Have your partner walk 50 steps away.

Step 2

Make sound with your object. Try to communicate different things to your partner. Use different volumes and patterns with the sound.

© Houghton Mifflin Harcourt

Hands-On Activity 👥 small groups ⏱ 1 class period

Engineer It • Communicate Over Distance

3D Learning Objective

 SEP **Constructing Explanations and Designing Solutions** . . . .

Children design and construct a device to enhance communication with sound over a distance. They will use evidence from their investigation to support their claims.

Suggested Materials an object that makes noise, such as a whistle or a bell, and craft materials such as posterboard, cardboard tubes, glue, and scissors

Preparation

Pre-assemble materials bundles for each group. Reserve an area around the school where they have enough room to test their devices.

Activity

As a class, view the video and then discuss the question. Have children record their question.

STEP 1 Discuss with children a way to make sure the steps they take are roughly the same size. Children might suggest placing the heel of one step right against the toe of the previous step so every step will be one shoe length. Encourage children to mark their locations so they can return to them.

DCI **Information Technologies and Instrumentation** . . . .

STEP 2 Have children experiment with different volumes and with different patterns of sound. **Ask: How did you use patterns or volume to communicate different things?** We decided a loud sound would mean "Stand up" and a soft sound would mean "Sit down." When I heard a sound pattern, I stood up or sat down in the same pattern.

Hands-On Activity, continued

DCI **Defining and Delimiting Engineering Problems** . . . .

STEP 3 **Ask: How could you use the materials you have to make your sound louder?** We can think about how a megaphone makes a person's voice louder and try to design a similar object.

SEP **Constructing Explanations and Designing Solutions** . . . .

STEP 4 Together, make a list of the materials children used in the activity. In pairs, have children discuss how each material helped them make sound or communicate the sound over 50 shoe lengths. Then, ask volunteers to share some ideas with the class.

Claims, Evidence, and Reasoning

Children should make a claim that explains how they used the materials provided in this activity to help them communicate with sound. They should cite their observations in the activity as evidence. **Ask: How do you think someone could use the results of this activity to solve a problem about communicating over a distance?** A coach could use the objects we built to communicate better with the players.

Scoring Rubric for Hands-On Activity	
3	States a claim supported with evidence about how the materials provided can help them communicate with sound
2	States a claim somewhat supported with evidence about how the materials provided can help them communicate with sound
1	States a claim that is not supported by evidence
0	Does not state a claim and does not provide evidence

Step 3

Plan and build something that makes your sound louder. Repeat Steps 1 and 2 to test your design.

Step 4

Record what you observed. Tell how you used sound to communicate over a distance. Tell how your design made your sound louder.

Make a claim that answers your question.

Sample answer: I can communicate with sound by using different patterns and volumes of sound.

What is your evidence?

Sample answer: I used different patterns and volumes of sound to communicate to my partner. My partner understood my message.

64

© Houghton Mifflin Harcourt

 Circle each kind of technology that helps people communicate with sound over distances.

Apply What You Know

Do the Math! • Work with a small group. Make a sound. How far away can you hear it? Use your feet to measure the distance.

Use Nonstandard Units to Measure Length Go to the online handbook for tips.

CCC Influence of Engineering, Technology, and Science on Society and the Natural World. . . .

Children should circle the radio and the cell phone. **Ask:** What problems do you think people would have if there were no radios? They might not be able to hear traffic reports in the car, and they might not be able to hear news about storms that are coming. **Ask:** What problems do you think people might have if there were no cell phones? Children might not be able to let their parents know if they needed help, and people might not be able to keep in touch with their families in other countries.

FORMATIVE ASSESSMENT

Do the Math! • Use Nonstandard Units to Measure Length

Children could estimate the distance they think the sound will travel, and then check by measuring with their feet. Or, children could measure a distance with their feet, and then compare how well two or more objects allow them to communicate over that distance.

 Use Nonstandard Units to Measure Length Discuss ways to ensure measuring with shoe lengths is fair. For example, children might suggest using shoes of a similar length for each measurement and always placing the heel of one step against the toe of the previous step. Children might also suggest that the same person always does the measuring.

Send a Message

3D Learning Objective

Children observe the differences between older communication technologies versus newer communication technologies. They explore what life would be like without key technologies. Children use what they know about communications technologies to design a solution to a problem involving communication from one classroom to another.

💡 **Influence of Engineering, Technology, and Science on Society and the Natural World** Discuss with children how people depend on various technologies in their lives.

DCI **Information Technologies and Instrumentation** . . . .

Ask: How does a letter carry information from one person to another? Someone writes information on a piece of paper, places it in an envelope with an address and a stamp, and the postal service delivers that envelope to another person. **Ask: How does an email carry information from one person to the another?** Someone types information on a computer or a phone and the information is carried through wires or through the air to another computer or phone. **Ask: Which form of communication do you think is better and why?** Accept all reasonable answers.

Collaboration

Small Groups Have groups of children write letters to children in another class and place the the letters in a box for you to deliver the next morning. Have the same groups write emails to the children in another class, using a school email address. **Ask: What was similar about receiving an email and receiving a letter?** They both told us what the other class was doing. **Ask: What was different?** It took the letter longer to arrive than the email.

Send a Message

You use technology to communicate. How would your life be different without technology?

💡 **Influence of Engineering, Technology, and Science on Society and the Natural World** Go to online handbook for tips.

Explore online. ▶

You can use email to send messages. Without email, you might have to send letters. Letters take more time to send.

66

© Houghton Mifflin Harcourt • Image Credits: (t) © EIRG Photography / Alamy Stock Photo; (b) © Frank Sanchez / Alamy Stock Photo

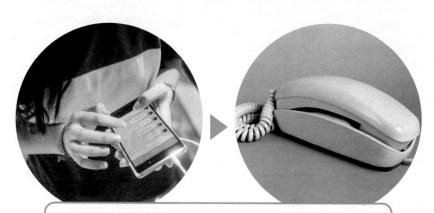

You can take a cell phone anywhere. Before cell phones, people used different kinds of phones. People had to be in a place that had a phone.

What would life be like without email and cell phones?

(A) Life would be the same.

(B) People would have to use different technology.

(C) There would be no technology at all.

CCC Influence of Engineering, Technology, and Science on Society and the Natural World. . . .

Encourage children to consider how life might be different without cell phones. **Ask: What do people use their cell phones for?** People use their cell phones for talking to other people, sending text messages, storing phone numbers, playing games, taking pictures, and watching videos. **Ask: What do people use the older type of phone for?** People use it just for talking to other people.

Have children work in small groups to discuss how they think life would have been different when people could not do the things they now do on cell phones. Invite groups to share some of their ideas. Ask guiding questions such as, "Where did people store other people's phone numbers?" "Where did people play games?" and "Where did people watch movies?"

DCI Information Technologies and Instrumentation . . . .

Children should choose B—People would have to use different technology. If children choose C—There would be no technology at all, ask them what other technologies they know of that people use to communicate. Guide them to understand that radio, television, and landlines are also types of technology. Remind them that people have developed and used a wide variety of technology to communicate with one another. If children choose A—Life would be the same, remind children how much technology has changed over the years, and direct them back to the two pictures of the phones at the top of the page.

FORMATIVE ASSESSMENT

Evidence Notebook

Children will work in small groups to list ideas to solve a problem by communicating with sound over a distance. They will draw and label one of their solutions on paper or with a drawing program on the computer. Have children use evidence to tell why they think their solution will work.

Scoring Guidelines

• proposes a solution that solves the problem of communicating with the classroom next door using sound
• draws and labels their proposed solution
• provides sufficient evidence to support the claim that their solution will work

Designing Solutions Encourage children to accept a variety of ideas for a solution to this problem in their groups. Help children understand that even ideas that seem impossible are valuable in the design process because they can help improve other solutions.

Apply What You Know

Evidence Notebook • The clock in the next classroom is broken. You want to tell that class what time it is, but you cannot leave your room. List ideas for solutions in your Evidence Notebook.

Designing Solutions Go to the online handbook for tips.

> ✏️ Draw one of your solutions. Use evidence to tell why you think it will work.

Accept reasonable answers.

_____

_____

_____

© Houghton Mifflin Harcourt

68

Explore online. ▶   Guide children to the Interactive Online Student Edition where they can choose from and explore both paths.

Take It Further

Careers in Science & Engineering •
Sound Engineer

Explore more online.

Morse Code

Explore online. ▶

Sound engineers study sound and how sound is made. They find ways to change sound to make it better.

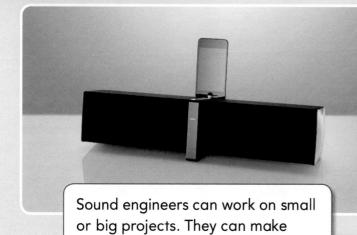

Sound engineers can work on small or big projects. They can make headphones or speakers, or they may do the sound for a big theater.

© Houghton Mifflin Harcourt • Image Credits: (tl) Juanmonino/ Getty Images; (b) © Gavin Roberts/Tap Magazine via Getty Images

Lesson 2 • Engineer It • How Can We Communicate with Sound?   69

Take It Further

Careers in Science & Engineering •
Sound Engineer

Children explore the variety of work done by sound engineers, including both large- and small-scale projects. Sound, or audio engineers, perform many different tasks, such as recording and mixing music for artists, films, and television. They can also perform sound checks for various equipment such as microphones and speakers. It is important for sound engineers to stay current on the latest technology. Digital audio workstations, mixing consoles, amplifiers, and loudspeakers are a few of the many types of technology they work with. Their main goal is to ensure that the quality of sound is as crisp and clear as possible.

CCC **Influence of Engineering, Technology, and Science on Society and the Natural World. . . .** Discuss with children some examples of what a sound engineer might do. Encourage them to recognize the types of projects a sound engineer can be involved in. For example, music production, movies, computer speakers, and school public address systems. **Ask: How might sound engineers help in each of these kinds of project?** They could make sure the music or movie sound is the right volume at the right time. They could make sure the speakers in the computer or the public address system make the sound clear.

Take It Further, continued

Read, Write, Share! • Participate in a Writing Project

Children will work with a group to research other careers in which people use sound or study sound. Have suitable books available. You could also bookmark websites that present relevant information at an appropriate reading level.

💡 **Participate in a Writing Project** Remind children to brainstorm ideas and decide what to draw or write together as a group. Work as a team to write a topic sentence and sentences that tell details.

DCI **Defining and Delimiting Engineering Problems** . . . .

Discuss what children found in their research. **Ask: What other careers use sound?** Accept all reasonable answers. **Ask: Do you think sound engineers solve problems? Why?** I do think they solve problems, because if something does not sound right, they can make it sound better. **Ask: Do you think sound engineers use a design process to help them? Why or why not?** Yes, I think they have to draw their ideas and test them many times before they have a working product.

Explore more online. ▶

Morse Code

Children view a video of a telegraph in action and develop their own code to send messages.

Read, Write, Share! • Work with a group. Do research. Find another career where people use sound or study sound.

Participate in a Writing Project Go to the online handbook for tips. 💡

✏️➤ Draw or write about what you found.

Accept reasonable answers.

_____

_____

© Houghton Mifflin Harcourt

70

Lesson Check

Name _____

Explore online. ▶

Can You Solve It?

✐ How could you use sound to send a message over a distance?

Be sure to

• Describe how people use technology to communicate.

• Explain how life would be different without this technology.

Sample answer: I can use technology, such as a cell phone, to

send a message with sound over a distance. Without a cell phone,

I would have to find a place with a phone to send my message.

Lesson 2 • Engineer It • How Can We Communicate with Sound?   71

© Houghton Mifflin Harcourt • Image Credits: ©ken Kiefer 2/Cultura/Getty Images

Lesson Check

Can You Solve It?

Have children reread their answers to the Can You Solve It? prompt at the beginning of the lesson.

DCI   Information Technologies and Instrumentation . . . .

Guide children to think about the many tools and technologies people use to communicate over a distance. **Ask: What technology might someone use to ask a friend to come and visit?** a cell phone **Ask: What technology might someone use to hear what the weather will be like tomorrow?** a radio **Ask: What technology might someone use to invite a lot of people to an event?** email on a computer or cell phone **Ask: How would life be different if you could not email a large group of people to tell them about an event?** It would make it harder because I would have to either call each person or write them a message individually.

Collaboration

Think, Pair, Share After children have thought about the Can You Solve It? question, have them discuss the question with a partner. Guide children to discuss the variety of ways people use technology to communicate over a distance and how life would be different without each of these communication technologies.

Scoring Guidelines

• Children should describe how people use technology to communicate over a distance.

• Children should explain how they think life would be different without the technology they describe.

Lesson Check, continued

SUMMATIVE ASSESSMENT
Self Check

1. Children should choose A—They communicate. If children choose B or C, guide them to the Communicate with Sound section of the lesson. Have them point to the word *communicate* on the page and tell what it means. Have children identify examples of communicating that they see in the picture on that page.

2. Children should choose B—Sound can be used to communicate over distances. If children choose A or C, ask them guiding questions. **Ask: Are John and his sister close together or far apart?** They are far apart. His sister is in the next room. **When John rings the bell, is he communicating with his sister?** Yes

3. Children should choose A—They wrote letters; and B—They used different kinds of phones. If children choose C, guide them to the Send a Message section of the lesson. Have children look at the pictures to identify types of technology people used before they had cell phones.

Self Check

1. What do people do when they share information with others?

   Ⓐ They communicate.

   Ⓑ They measure.

   Ⓒ They vibrate.

2. John rings a bell to wake his sister in another room. What does this show?

   Ⓐ Life would be different without technology.

   Ⓑ Sound can be used to communicate over distances.

   Ⓒ People need many tools to communicate.

3. What did people do before they had cell phones? Choose all correct answers.

   Ⓐ They wrote letters.

   Ⓑ They used different kinds of phones.

   Ⓒ They did not communicate.

© Houghton Mifflin Harcourt

72

4. Circle all of the photos that show people using sound to communicate over distances.

5. If people no longer had email, what would they most likely do?

Ⓐ Give up on technology.

Ⓑ Stop communicating.

Ⓒ Write letters.

© Houghton Mifflin Harcourt • Image Credits: (l) ©Peter Dazeley/Photographer's Choice/Getty Images; (c) © ai/Digital Vision/ Getty Images; (r) Marco Garcia/Getty Image News/Getty Images

4. Children should circle the person talking on the phone and the person using a megaphone. If children circle the person writing a letter, remind them that the question is asking about using sound to communicate. Have them point to each picture and identify how sound is being used or if it is being used. If children do not circle the person talking on the phone or the person using the megaphone, ask guiding questions about each picture, such as "Is this person sharing information?" and "Is this person using sound to convey information?"

5. Children should choose C—Write letters. If children choose A or B, ask guiding questions to help children recognize that there are many communication and technology options available to people. **Ask: What kinds of technology, other than email, help people communicate?** Megaphones help people communicate because they make the person's voice louder, cell phones help people talk to each other when they are far apart, and fire alarms warn people when there is a fire.

Unit 2 Performance Task

Communicate with Sound

 individuals   ⏱ 1 class period

Objective
Children **plan materials** to **test sound signals** in order to **communicate a message**.

Suggested Materials
musical instruments

Preparation
Collect and assemble musical instruments for children.

 Scientific Investigations Use a Variety of Methods . . . .

Ask: Why does your school use sounds to communicate messages? Sample answer: Sounds can communicate a message to the whole school, like a bell that rings to start the day.

STEPS

Step 1
Allow children five minutes to make a list before sharing ideas.

Step 2
 Constructing Explanations and Designing Solutions . . . .

Ask: How can you use your materials to make sound? Sample answer: When I bang the cymbals together, they vibrate.

Step 3
Ask: Why is it important to decide what the different sounds and patterns will mean? Sample answer: If people don't know what the sounds mean, I won't be able to communicate with them.

 Unit 2 Performance Task
Communicate with Sound

> **Materials**
> • musical instruments

STEPS

Step 1
Does your school have a bell that rings at the start of the day? Make a list of the sounds your school uses to communicate messages. Talk about the list with others.

Step 2
Think of ways you can use sounds to communicate with another class. Plan what materials you will use.

Step 3
Decide what different sounds and patterns of sound will mean. Make a list to help people learn the sounds and their meanings.

© Houghton Mifflin Harcourt

74

Step 4

Test your sound signals. Can others understand your message?

Step 5

Compare your plan with the plans of your classmates. Talk about how they are alike and different.

✔ Check

_____ I talked about the sounds my school uses to communicate.

_____ I planned which materials I would use to communicate with sound.

_____ I made a list of what my different sounds mean.

_____ I tested my sound signals with others.

_____ I compared my plan to other plans.

Step 4

 Cause and Effect . . . .

Have children work in pairs to test their sound signals. Encourage children to discuss whether they understand the message. If they cannot understand the message, encourage them to discuss how the volume or pattern of the sound could be changed to make the message clearer.

Step 5

Have children work in small groups to discuss their communication plans. Ask groups to share their observations about the similarities and differences among the plans. **Ask: In what ways were many of the plans alike? Why do you think so many of you chose to design your plans this way?**

Scoring Rubric for Performance Task	
3	Describes sounds used by the school, and designs and tests a communication system, including materials and meanings of sounds. Compares plan with others.
2	Describes sounds used by the school, and designs a communication system, including materials and meanings of sounds, but does not test the system. Compares plan with others.
1	Describes sounds used by the school OR designs a communication system, including materials and meanings of sounds, but does not test the system. Does not compare plan with others.
0	Does not describe sounds used by the school, or design a communication system.

Unit 2 Review

SUMMATIVE ASSESSMENT

1. Children should choose A—It moves back and forth quickly;
   B—It can make sound; and C—It can make materials move.
   If children do not choose all three answers, remind them to
   read the question carefully. By completing Make a Sound in
   Lesson 1, children explored how vibrations make sound. By
   completing What Makes It Move? in Lesson 1, children explored
   how vibrations can make things move.

2. Children should choose C—She should pluck a guitar string. If
   children choose A, reinforce that vibrations are observed using
   the sense of sight. If children choose B, reinforce that to vibrate
   is to move quickly back and forth. By completing Make a Sound
   in Lesson 1, children explored the cause-and-effect relationship
   between vibration and sound.

3. Children should write loud for the top-left image of the
   girl with the megaphone; soft for the top-right image of
   whispering; soft for the bottom-left image of the music box,
   and loud for the bottom-right image of children cheering. If
   children answer incorrectly, discuss the activity in each image
   to ensure their understanding. By completing Volume in Lesson
   1, children learned that volume is how loud or soft a sound is.

Unit 2 Review   Name _____

1. **What happens when something vibrates?
   Choose all correct answers.**
   - (A) It moves back and forth quickly.
   - (B) It can make sound.
   - (C) It can make materials move.

---

2. **Beth thinks that vibrating materials can make
   sound. Which test should she do to see this?**
   - (A) She should listen to sounds in
     her neighborhood.
   - (B) She should boil a pot of water.
   - (C) She should pluck a guitar string.

---

3. **Write loud or soft to tell the volume of the
   sound in each picture.**

loud

soft

soft

loud

4. Which sound has a high pitch?
   Ⓐ growling dog
   Ⓑ squeaky wheel
   Ⓒ purring cat

5. Which pictures show how vibrations from sound can move materials?

Ⓐ  Ⓑ  Ⓒ

6. Gerard wants to do a test to show that sound can move materials. Which test should he do?
   Ⓐ Place sand on a drum and bang a pot next to it.
   Ⓑ Pour a cup of sand into a large pot.
   Ⓒ Put sand in a shaker and shake it.

7. What would happen if you plucked the string of the guitar in the picture? Choose all correct answers.
   Ⓐ It would vibrate.
   Ⓑ It would make a sound.
   Ⓒ It would make other materials in the room move.

4. Children should choose B—squeaky wheel. If children choose A or C, provide additional examples of high- and low-pitched sounds. By completing Pitch in Lesson 1, children learned that pitch is how high or low a sound is.

5. Children should choose A—the tuning fork; and B—the rice on the speaker. If children choose C, reinforce that to vibrate is to move quickly back and forth, and explain that the balloons are moving because of wind, which does not vibrate. By completing What Makes it Move in Lesson 1, children explored how vibrations can move objects.

6. Children should choose A—Place sand on a drum and bang a pot next to it. If children choose B or C, explain that if Gerard pours the sand into a pot or shakes the sand in a shaker, he is moving it with his hands. By completing What Makes it Move in Lesson 1, children explored how vibrations can move objects.

7. Children should choose A—It would vibrate; and B—It would make a sound. If children choose A or B but not both, reinforce that when the string is plucked it moves quickly back and forth, causing it to vibrate and make a sound. If children choose C, explain that the sound waves from the vibrating string would not be strong enough to move other materials in the room. By completing What Makes it Move in Lesson 1, children explored how vibrations can move objects.

3D Item Analysis	1	2	3	4	5	6	7
SEP Planning and Carrying Out Investigations		•				•	
SEP Scientific Investigations Use a Variety of Methods		•			•		
DCI Wave Properties	•	•	•	•	•	•	•
CCC Cause and Effect	•	•			•	•	•

8. Children should choose C—They share information. If children choose A, explain that vibration produces sound, but sound itself is not communication. If children choose B, explain that recorded data is not always shared with others. By completing Communicate with Sound in Lesson 2, children explored different ways people communicate with sound.

9. Children should choose A—the microphone; and C—the smart phone. If children choose B, explain that light can be used to communicate, but light is not a form of sound. By completing Communicate Over Distances in Lesson 2, children explored technology that can be used to communicate with sound over distances.

10. Children should choose B—Ava uses a sound to communicate over a distance. If children choose A, explain that a dog whistle is only one tool. If children choose C, explain that while the dog whistle is a form of technology, Ava could use her voice or clap her hands to call her dog. By completing Send a Message in Lesson 2, children explored ways to communicate without technology.

3D Item Analysis	8	9	10
SEP Constructing Explanations and Designing Solutions	•	•	•
DCI Information Technologies and Instrumentation	•	•	•
CCC Influence of Engineering, Technology, and Science on Society and the Natural World			•

8. What do people do when they communicate with sound?
   Ⓐ They vibrate.
   Ⓑ They record data.
   Ⓒ They share information.

9. Which are kinds of technology that help people use sound to communicate over a distance? Choose all correct answers.

Ⓐ   Ⓑ   Ⓒ

10. Ava's dog runs across a field. She uses a whistle to call the dog back to her. What does this show?
   Ⓐ Ava needs many tools to communicate.
   Ⓑ Ava uses a sound to communicate over a distance.
   Ⓒ Ava could not call her dog without technology.

© Houghton Mifflin Harcourt • Image Credits: (l) ©AndreyTTL/E+/Getty Images; (c) ©Juanmonino/E+/Getty Images; (r) ©hudiemm/DigitalVision Vectors/Getty Images

Unit 3
Light

Unit Project • Make a Rainbow

How can you make a rainbow?
Investigate to find out.

Unit 3 • Light

Unit Overview

In this unit, children will…

- provide evidence, based on observations, of the relationship between the amount of light and how an object is seen.
- explain, using evidence based on observations, why objects that give off their own light can be seen in the dark.
- explain and demonstrate how different materials can allow different amounts of light to pass through.
- explain how shadows are made.
- observe that light shines in a straight line until it hits an object.
- explore how reflection can be used to redirect light.
- explore how technology is used to send and receive information using light.

About This Image

Guide children in a discussion about the picture on this page. **Ask: What allows you to see the buildings?** Light from the sun is shining on the buildings.

Unit Project • **Make a Rainbow**

Have children plan and conduct an investigation to determine how to make a rainbow. Show children images of rainbows. Have children brainstorm questions such as; "What is a rainbow?", "Where do you see rainbows?", "When do rainbows occur?" Children record their answers and ideas.

More support for the Unit Project can be found on pp. 81I–81L.

Unit 3 At a Glance

The learning experiences in this unit prepare children for mastery of:

Performance Expectations

PS4-2 Make observations to construct an evidence-based account that objects can be seen only when illuminated.

PS4-3 Plan and conduct an investigation to determine the effect of placing objects made with different materials in the path of a beam of light.

PS4-4 Use tools and materials to design and build a device that uses light or sound to solve the problem of communicating over a distance.

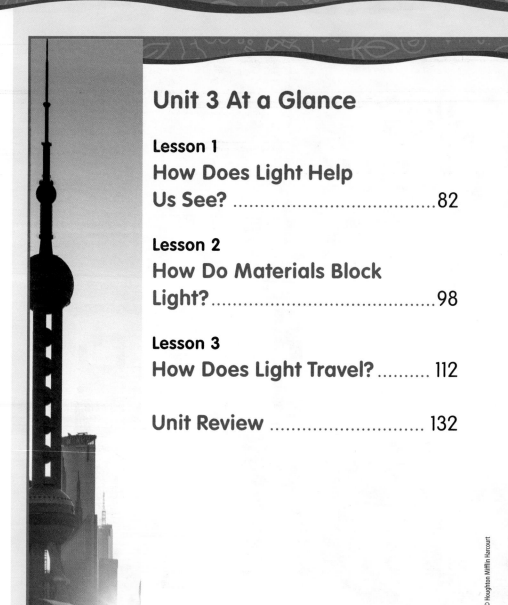

Explore online. ▶

In addition to the print resources, the following resources are available online to support this unit:

Unit Pretest
Lesson 1 How Does Light Help Us See?
- Interactive Online Student Edition
- Lesson Quiz

Lesson 2 How Do Materials Block Light?
- Interactive Online Student Edition
- Lesson Quiz

Lesson 3 How Does Light Travel?
- Interactive Online Student Edition
- Lesson Quiz

You Solve It Message Projector
Unit Performance Task
Unit Test

80

Unit Vocabulary

light a kind of energy that lets you see (p. 84)

shadow a dark spot made when an object blocks light (p. 104)

reflect to bounce back from a surface (p. 118)

Vocabulary Game • Guess the Word

Materials
• 1 set of word cards

How to Play
1. Work with a partner to make word cards.
2. Place the cards face down in a pile.
3. One player picks the top card but does not show it.
4. The second player asks questions until they guess the word correctly.
5. Then the second player takes a card.

© Houghton Mifflin Harcourt

81

Unit Vocabulary

The Next Generation Science Standards emphasize explanation and demonstration of understanding versus rote memorization of science vocabulary words. Keep in mind that these vocabulary words are tools for clear communication. Use these words as a starting point, not an end goal, for children to build deeper understanding of science concepts.

Children can explore all vocabulary words in the **Online Glossary**.

Vocabulary Strategies

• Have children review the vocabulary words. Then have children work in pairs to share an example of each word and explain why they think it's an example. Have pairs record their examples to refer back to during the unit.
• Have children think about how each word relates to light. Have children work in pairs and share their ideas with a partner.

Differentiate Instruction

RTI/Extra Support Pronounce each word, and have children repeat it after you. Have children find each highlighted word within the unit content. Have children work in pairs and explain to a partner what they think each word means based on the surrounding context of imagery and text.

Extension Have children select two vocabulary words and work in small groups to illustrate and explain the words to a kindergarten child.

Vocabulary Game • Guess the Word

Preparation Assign partners. Consider having children make two cards for each word for a total of six cards in the game. Establish a time limit or a set number of rounds for the game.

Integrating the NGSS* Three Dimensions of Learning

Building to the Performance Expectations

The learning experiences in this unit prepare children for mastery of the following Performance Expectations:

Waves and their Applications in Technologies for Information Transfer

PS4-2 Make observations to construct an evidence-based account that objects can be seen only when illuminated.

PS4-3 Plan and conduct an investigation to determine the effect of placing objects made with different materials in the path of a beam of light.

PS4-4 Use tools and materials to design and build a device that uses light to solve the problem of communicating over a distance.

Assessing Student Progress

After completing the lessons, the **Unit Project** Make a Rainbow provides children with opportunities to practice aspects of and to demonstrate their understanding of the Performance Expectations as they plan and conduct an investigation to determine how to make a rainbow.

Additionally, children can further practice or be assessed on aspects of the Performance Expectations by completing the **Unit Performance Task** Observe Reflections, in which children observe reflections in a mirror and use their observations to predict where their partner should stand in order to be visible in the mirror. Children will observe the cause-and-effect relationship between where they stand and whether they are visible in the mirror.

Lesson 1
How Does Light Help Us See?

In Lesson 1, children will observe how light is necessary to see an object. They will explore how the amount of light affects how much can be seen **(CCC Cause and Effect).** As the lesson progresses, they will observe objects that give off their own light **(DCI Electromagnetic Radiation).** During a Hands-On activity, children will record observations and compare how much they can see in different amounts of light. **(SEP Constructing Explanations and Designing Solutions).** Finally, children will discuss how Thomas Edison's invention of the light bulb helped bring electricity to people's homes.

Lesson 2
How Do Materials Block Light?

In Lesson 2, children will observe how light passes through objects **(DCI Electromagnetic Radiation)** and develop an understanding of transparent, translucent, and opaque objects **(SEP Constructing Explanations and Designing Solutions).** Children will also explore how shadows are made **(CCC Cause and Effect).**

Lesson 3
How Does Light Travel?

In Lesson 3, children explore how light travels, including how it can be reflected or redirected **(DCI Electromagnetic Radiation).** They also explore how people use light to communicate **(DCI Information Technologies and Instrumentation) (CCC Influence of Engineering, Technology, and Science, on Society and the Natural World).** Children gather observations how light travels and what causes light to be redirected **(CCC Cause and Effect).** They carry out an investigation to test how smooth, shiny surfaces affect a beam of light **(SEP Planning and Carrying Out Investigations).** Finally, children design a way communicate with light **(SEP Constructing Explanations and Designing Solutions).**

Standards Supported by This Unit

 Explore online.
Online only.

Next Generation Science Standards	Unit Project	Lesson 1	Lesson 2	Lesson 3		Unit Performance Task	You Solve It
SEP Constructing Explanations and Designing Solutions	•	•	•	•		•	•
SEP Planning and Carrying Out Investigations	•			•		•	•
DCI **PS4.B** Electromagnetic Radiation	•	•	•	•		•	•
DCI **PS4.C** Information Technologies and Instrumentation				•		•	
CCC Cause and Effect	•	•	•	•		•	•
CCC Influence of Engineering, Technology, and Science on Society and the Natural World			•			•	

NGSS* Across the Grades

Before	**Grade 1**	**After**
Coverage of the **Performance Expectations** within this unit originates in Grade 1.	**Waves and their Applications in Technologies for Information Transfer** **1-PS4-2** **1-PS4-3** **1-PS4-4**	**Waves and their Applications in Technologies for Information Transfer** **4-PS4-1** Develop a model of waves to describe patterns in terms of amplitude and wavelength and that waves can cause objects to move. **4-PS4-2** Develop a model to describe that light reflecting from objects and entering the eye allows objects to be seen. **4-PS4-3** Generate and compare multiple solutions that use patterns to transfer information.

 **Trace Tool to the NGSS™** Go online to view the complete coverage of these standards across this grade level and time.

3D Unit Planning

Lesson 1 How Does Light Help Us See? pp. 82–97

Overview

Objective Make observations to explain how objects can be seen if the objects give off their own light or if light is available to shine on them.

SEP Constructing Explanations and Designing Solutions
DCI **PS4.B** Electromagnetic Radiation
CCC Cause and Effect

Math and **English Language Arts** standards and features are detailed on lesson planning pages.

	Print and Online Student Editions	**Explore online.** ▶
ENGAGE	**Lesson Phenomenon** pp. 82–83 **Can You Explain It?** How can you see fireworks in a dark sky?	▶ Can You Explain It? Video
EXPLORE/ EXPLAIN	**Let There Be Light!** **Different Amounts of Light** **See In The Dark** 🔍 **Hands-On Activity** Make Observations in Different Light pp. 87–88	**Hands-On** Worksheet
ELABORATE	**Take It Further** pp. 93–94 People in Science & Engineering • Thomas Edisom	**Take It Further** Animals That Glow
EVALUATE	**Lesson Check** p. 95 **Self Check** pp. 96–97	**Lesson Quiz**

Hands-On Activity Planning

Make Observations in Different Light

Objective Children will make observations in different amounts of light. Children will record observations under bright, limited, and low light conditions. They will then make a claim and support that claim using evidence from their observations during the exploration.

👥 small groups ⏱ 1 class period	**Suggested Materials** • drawing paper • pencils

Preparation/Tip

Identify strategies to achieve different levels of light in the classroom. If necessary, gather items to help to make the room darker, such as a piece of dark fabric or paper to block light from entering. If changing the amount of light is not possible, find a room that you can control the light. Take three different pictures of the room, one with a lot of light, one with some light, and one with no light. Use the pictures for each step of the hands on activity.

Lesson 2 How Do Materials Block Light? pp. 98–111

Overview

Objective Ask questions, make observations, and gather information to describe how light passes through objects.

SEP Constructing Explanations and Designing Solutions
DCI **PS4.B.2** Electromagnetic Radiation
CCC Cause and Effect

Math and **English Language Arts** standards and features are detailed on lesson planning pages.

	Print and Online **Student Editions**	Explore online. ▶
ENGAGE	**Lesson Phenomenon** pp. 98–99 **Can You Explain It?** How does the artist make the shapes?	▶ Can You Explain It? Video
EXPLORE/ EXPLAIN	**How Much Light?** **Shadows** **Big Shadow, Little Shadow**	**Hands-On** Worksheet
	Hands-On Activity Test How Light Passes Through Materials pp. 101–103	
ELABORATE	**Take It Further** pp. 107–108 Prisms	**Take It Further** Make a Sundial
EVALUATE	**Lesson Check** p. 109 **Self Check** pp. 110–111	**Lesson Quiz**

Hands-On Activity Planning

Test How Light Passes Through Materials

Objective Children will investigate beams of light and discover what happens when different materials are placed in the path of the light.

Suggested Materials
- a flashlight
- clear plastic
- frosted plastic
- plywood

👥 small groups
🕐 1 class period

Preparation/Tip
Gather materials for each group.

3D Unit Planning, continued

Lesson 3 How Does Light Travel? pp. 112–131

Overview

Objective Gather evidence to support or refute ideas about causes relating to how light travels and explore how people use light devices to communicate over distances.

SEP Planning and Carrying Out Investigations
SEP Constructing Explanations and Designing Solutions
DCI **PS4.B** Electromagnetic Radiation
DCI **PS4.C** Information Technologies and Instrumentation
CCC Cause and Effect
CCC Influence of Engineering, Technology, and Science on Society and the Natural World

Math and **English Language Arts** standards and features are detailed on lesson planning pages.

	Print and Online **Student Editions**	Explore online.
ENGAGE	**Lesson Problem** pp. 112–113 **Can You Solve It?** How could you point light away from your eyes?	Can **You Solve It?** Animation
EXPLORE/ EXPLAIN	**Straight On** **In the Way** **What Reflects Light?** **A New Direction** **Communicate with Light** **Hands-On Activity** Test What Happens to Light pp. 121–123	**Hands-On** Worksheet **You Solve It** Message Projector
ELABORATE	**Take It Further** pp. 127–128 Careers in Science & Engineering • Camera Engineer	**Take It Further** Art with Light
EVALUATE	**Lesson Check** p. 129 **Self Check** pp. 130–131	Lesson Quiz

Hands-On Activity Planning

Test What Happens to Light

Objective Children will make a claim about how smooth, shiny surfaces affect a beam of light. They will support their claim with evidence and data from their observations during the exploration.

small groups
1 class period

Suggested Materials
- a flashlight
- a mirror
- a metal spoon
- tin foil
- tin pan

Preparation/Tip
Make sure all flashlights have batteries and give off a strong light. If the light is too dim, children will have a difficult time observing reflections.

3D Unit Planning, continued

You Solve It   Go online for an additional interactive opportunity.

Message Projector

This virtual lab offers practice in support of **1-PS4-2, 1-PS4-3,** and **1-PS4-4.**

SEP Planning and Carrying Out Investigations

SEP Constructing Explanations and Designing Solutions

DCI **PS4.B** Electromagnetic Radiation

CCC Cause and Effect

3D Learning Objectives

- Children use a homemade slide projector to send a message using light.
- Children will use the data to explain which materials block light, reflect light, and take in more light after wall color is selected.

Activity Problem

You need to find two ways to send messages to a friend using light. Consider which materials block light and which ones do not. Then, determine how to combine the materials to make a message.

- You will make a slide projector to show your message on the wall.
- You need to choose materials to make two messages on slides in different ways.
- You will test your projector to see how well your messages work.

Interaction Summary

- Make two simple messages, choosing the background and message materials.
- Choose two combinations of materials to make the slides.
- Choose location for slide and the flashlight in the projector box. Test.
- Choose material for the lens. Determine if gray wall should be lighter or darker.
- Analyze data to explain which materials block light, reflect, or take in light.

Assessment

Pre-Assessment

Assessment Guide, Unit Pretest

The Unit Pretest focuses on prerequisite knowledge and is composed of items that evaluate children's preparedness for the content covered within this unit.

Formative Assessment

Interactive Worktext, Apply What You Know, Lesson Check, and Self Check

Summative Assessment

Assessment Guide, Lesson Quiz

The Lesson Quiz provides a quick assessment of each lesson objective and of the portion of the Performance Expectation aligned to the lesson.

Interactive Worktext, Performance Task pp. 132–133

The Performance Task presents the opportunity for children to collaborate with classmates in in order to complete the steps of each Performance Task. Each Performance Task provides a formal Scoring Rubric for evaluating children's work.

Interactive Worktext, Unit 3 Review, pp. 134–136

Assessment Guide, Unit Test

The Unit Test provides an in-depth assessment of the Performance Expectations aligned to the unit. This test evaluates children's ability to apply knowledge in order to explain phenomena and to solve problems. Within this test Constructed Response items apply a three-dimensional rubric for evaluating children's mastery on all three dimensions of the Next Generation Science Standards.

Assessment Online   Go online to view the complete assessment items for this unit.

Differentiate Instruction

Leveled Readers

The Science & Engineering Leveled Readers provide additional nonfiction reading practice in this unit's subject area.

On Level • **What Are Forces and Energy?**
This reader reinforces unit concepts and includes response activities for your children

Extra Support • **What Are Forces and Energy?**
This reader shares title, illustrations, vocabulary, and concepts with the On-Level Reader; however, the text is linguistically accommodated to provide simplified sentence structures and comprehension aids. It also includes response activities.

Enrichment • **Soccer Moves!**
This high-interest, nonfiction reader will extend and enrich unit concepts and vocabulary and includes response activities.

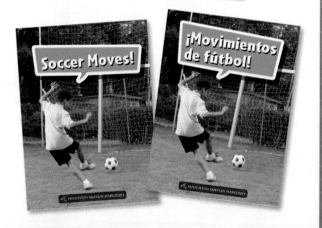

Teacher Guide
The accompanying Teacher Guide provides teaching strategies and support for using all the readers.

ELL

English Language Learner support resources include a glossary in Spanish and Leveled Readers in Spanish and English. ELL teaching strategies appear throughout this unit:

pp. 82B, 91, 98B, 112B, 119

RTI/Extra Support

Strategies for children who need extra support appear throughout this unit:

pp. 81, 82B, 90, 98B, 102, 105, 107, 112B, 118

Extension

Strategies for children who have mastered core content and are ready for additional challenges appear throughout this unit:

pp. 81, 82B, 90, 98B, 102, 105, 107, 112B, 118

Leveled Readers

All readers are available online as well as in an innovative, engaging format for use with touchscreen mobile devices. Contact your HMH Sales Representative for more information.

Connecting with NGSS

Connections to Community

Use these opportunities for informal science learning to provide local context and to extend and enhance unit concepts.

At Home

Giving off Light Encourage children to find items in their home that give off their own light (for example, bulbs, phones, televisions, clocks, and flashlights). Create a class list and have children add to it as they discover more items that give off their own light in their homes.
Use with Lesson 1.

Blocking Light Have children work with a parent or guardian to investigate how different materials in the home block light. Have children record their results in a table, listing each item in one column and whether the item blocks all light, blocks some light, or blocks no light in another column. As children share their results in class, encourage them to suggest why it might be important for an item to block light or let light through. (2)
Use with Lesson 2.

In the Community

Lights for Safety Invite a police officer to discuss how lights on vehicles help drivers to see and keep people safe, and how darkness affects drivers' ability to see pedestrians. If possible arrange for a demonstration of headlights and bicycle lights.
Use with Lesson 1.

Light Walk Walk around the community looking for examples of objects that light passes through, objects that take light in, and objects that light bounces off. Stop periodically and ask children "Where do you see light hitting an object here? Does the light pass through the object? Does it reflect? Describe what you see." (For example, a vehicle can provide examples of all three types.)
Use with Lesson 3.

Home Letters Go online to view the Home Letters for this unit.

Collaboration

Collaboration opportunities in this unit:

Build on Prior Knowledge pp. 83, 99, 108, 113, 114

Small Groups p. 127

Think, Write, Pair, Share pp. 84, 128

Connections to Science

Connections to Science opportunities in this unit:

Connection to Earth Science
Lesson 1, p. 89

Connection to Earth and Space Sciences
Lesson 2, p. 104

Connection to Engineering and Design
Lesson 3, p. 125

Unit Project

Unit Project   👥 small groups   🕐 1 class period

Make a Rainbow

Have children plan and conduct an investigation to determine how to make a rainbow. Show children images of rainbows. Discuss rainbows. What is a rainbow? Where do you see rainbows? When do rainbows occur? Brainstorm a list of ideas and record them.

3D Learning Objective

SEP Constructing Explanations and Designing Solutions
Plan and conduct an investigation to explain how a rainbow forms.
Use tools and materials to carry out an investigation.
Make observations and draw conclusions.

Skills and Standards Focus

This project supports building children's mastery of **Performance Expectation 1-PS4-3.**

SEP	Planning and Carrying Out Investigations
SEP	Constructing Explanations and Designing Solutions
DCI	**PS4.B** Electromagnetic Radiation
CCC	Cause and Effect

Suggested Materials

- photos of rainbows
- tall drinking glasses (preferably with flat bottoms)
- water
- white paper
- light source, such as a bright window

Preparation

Clear a spot near a bright window or another light source large enough for children to make their observations. Have enough drinking glasses with relatively flat bottoms for each pair or group of children. Fill each glass to near the top with water. Children will probably find they need to hold the glass two or three feet directly above the paper to see an image of a rainbow on the paper. Caution children to be careful not to spill the water, but be prepared to mop up spills if they do occur.

Unit 3
Light

© Houghton Mifflin Harcourt

Unit Project • Make a Rainbow
How can you make a rainbow?
Investigate to find out.

79

Differentiate Instruction

RTI/Extra Support Ask guiding questions: What do you think will happen to the light when it passes through the water? Where do you think we should we put the paper?

Extension Have children experiment with the materials to change the rainbow they created and explain what may have caused the rainbow to change the way it did.

Name _____

Unit 3 Project
Make a Rainbow

How can you make a rainbow? Write your ideas on the lines below. Plan and conduct an investigation to make a rainbow.

Children should write ideas for what they could do to make a rainbow.

_____

_____

Materials

• water   • a drinking glass   • white paper   • bright light

Draw how you could use these materials to make a rainbow.

Children should draw and label a possible arrangement of the materials. Drawings should show light passing through water in the glass.

Unit 3 Project • Page 1 of 3

Unit 3 Project
Make a Rainbow

SEP Constructing Explanations and Designing Solutions . . . .

Show children images of rainbows and ask them if they have ever seen a rainbow. Where did they see it? When did they see it? Ask children what a rainbow is made of. How do they think a rainbow forms? Guide children to see that light passing through water forms a rainbow.

Ask children how they might arrange light and water to make their own rainbow.

In the sample investigation below, children observe the effects of light passing through a glass of water to form a rainbow on a white sheet of paper.

Children will place a piece of white paper near a bright light source and hold a glass of water over the paper to create the image of a rainbow on the paper. **Ask: Do you think the light that goes into the water will be the same as the light that comes out the other side?** I think the light that comes out the other side will be colored like a rainbow.

ESSENTIAL QUESTIONS Prepare children for their project by asking the following questions.

• What is light?
• How can we tell that light is shining on something? What do we observe?
• How does light travel?
• What happens to light when you put something in its path?

Ask: What happens to light when it hits water? Light passes through water. **What do you expect to see on the other side of if you shine light at a glass of water?** I think the light will move in a straight line on the other side of the water and I will see light shining on things on the other side of the water.

Steps

Engage children in a discussion that reflects the importance of making a plan while doing an investigation.

 **Electromagnetic Radiation**

Before beginning the investigation, have children look through a glass of water.

Ask: **What do you see through the water?** Sample answers: children, classroom. **Do they look the same as they do when you aren't looking through the glass of water?** Almost, but the shapes get a little wavy, especially at the edges. **What do you think happens to light as it passes through the glass of water?** I think it gets a little wiggly, and doesn't travel in a straight line. Refer children to Lesson 3 Straight On. **Ask:** **Could you make a rainbow through a glass of orange juice?** No. Have children move the glass of water over the paper until they see a rainbow on the paper, approximately 2-3 feet above the paper. Children should record their observations about what they saw and about the position of the light, the water, and the image using words and pictures.

Data

Children should record data that reflects what happens when light hits the glass of water.

DCI Electromagnetic Radiation . . . .

Ask: **What happened to the light when it hit the glass of water?** It passed through the water, but it added colors. **What evidence did you collect to show this?** We saw a rainbow of colored light falling on the white paper.

CCC Cause and Effect . . . .

Ask: **What do you think caused the rainbow to form?** The glass of water caused the light's straight path to bend and change color. Refer children to Lesson 3 How Does Light Travel?

Steps Write the steps you will use to make a rainbow.

Answers may vary but should reflect a logical order of

steps in the investigation. Sample steps listed:

1. Fill the glass with water.

2. Place the paper near the window.

3. Hold the glass of water over the paper.

4. Move the glass around until I see a rainbow on the paper.

5. Observe and record what the rainbow looks like.

Data
Record your data.

Answers and drawings may vary but should reflect that different colors of light appeared on the paper when light passed through the water.

Analyze Your Result

Look for patterns in your data.

Restate Your Question

Write the question you investigated.

Answers should identify the question children were asked at the

beginning of the investigation.

Claims, Evidence, and Reasoning

Make a claim that answers your question.

Answers should identify the arrangement of materials children used

to create a rainbow.

Review the data. What evidence from the investigation supports your claim?

Answer should cite evidence from the investigation to support

children's claim about how they can create a rainbow.

Discuss your reasoning with a partner.

Unit 3 Project • Page 3 of 3

Analyze Your Result

Have children analyze their data. Elicit from them any patterns they noticed. Encourage them to share their data with the other groups in order to compare test results. **Ask: What did you see when light passed through the glass of water?** a rainbow

Claims, Evidence, and Reasoning

Children should understand that the rainbow they observed was formed by the light as it passed through the glass of water. They should cite evidence to support their claim by using their drawings and written notes.

Ask: What claim can you make? Light can form a rainbow when it passes through water. **How does your evidence support your claim?** I held a glass of water near a window and saw a rainbow on a piece of paper under the glass of water. Encourage children to discuss their reasoning.

SEP **Engaging in Argument from Evidence** . . . .

Review with children what it means to make a claim. Guide them to understand that the data they collected will be used as evidence to support their claim. **Ask: What can you use as evidence from your investigation?** the rainbow I saw on the paper, and the drawing I made of it

Scoring Rubric for Unit Project	
3	States a claim supported with evidence that light can form a rainbow when it passes through water
2	States a claim and somewhat supported with evidence that light can form a rainbow when it passes through water
1	States a claim that is not supported by evidence
0	Does not state a claim and does not provide evidence

Lesson 1 · How Does Light Help Us See?

Building to the Performance Expectation

The learning experiences in this lesson prepare children for mastery of:

1-PS4-2 Make observations to construct an evidence-based account that objects can be seen only when illuminated.

 Trace Tool to the NGSS
Go online to view the complete coverage of these standards across this lesson, unit, and time.

 Science & Engineering Practices

Constructing Explanations and Designing Solutions
Make observations (firsthand or from media) to construct an evidence-based account for natural phenomena.

 VIDEO SEPs: Constructing Explanations and Designing Solutions / Engaging in Argument from Evidence

---

Disciplinary Core Ideas

PS4.B Electromagnetic Radiation
Objects can be seen if light is available to illuminate them or if they give off their own light.

 Crosscutting Concepts

Cause and Effect
Simple tests can be designed to gather evidence to support or refute student ideas about causes.

CONNECTION TO MATH

1.MD.B.3 Tell and write time in hours and half-hours using analog clocks.

CONNECTION TO ENGLISH LANGUAGE ARTS

SL.1.1 Participate in collaborative conversations with diverse partners about grade 1 topics and texts with peers and adults in small and larger groups.

Supporting All Students, All Standards

Integrating the Three Dimensions of Learning

This lesson focuses on how light helps us see (**DCI Electromagnetic Radiation**). Children will explore how light is necessary to see an object and how the amount of light affects how much can be seen (**CCC Cause and Effect**). They will use observations to provide evidence of a relationship between the amount of light and how an object is seen (**SEP Constructing Explanations and Designing Solutions**). As the lesson progresses, they will observe objects that give off their own light (**DCI Electromagnetic Radiation**).

 Professional Development Go online to view **Professional Development videos** with strategies to integrate CCCs and SEPs, including the ones used in this lesson.

Build on Prior Knowledge

Children should already know and be prepared to build on the following concepts:
- People and animals see with eyes.
- The sun shines light on Earth.

Differentiate Instruction

Lesson Vocabulary
- light

Reinforcing Vocabulary To help children remember this vocabulary term, ask them to think about what they do when they go into a dark room. Explain that when we talk about *light* in this lesson, we are talking about energy that helps you see. Ask the class to listen as you say three or four sentences. Have them raise their hands if they think the word *light* in the sentence means an *energy that helps you see*. Include one sentence in which the term *light* refers to weight. (e.g., The box of feathers felt light.) Challenge children to think of a sentence that uses *light* to mean energy that helps us see. Remind children to look for the highlighted term as they proceed through the lesson.

RTI/Extra Support Encourage children to explore a personal connection to light. Have them draw the room in their home that has the most light. Ask them to circle all of the ways light gets into the room (lamp, window, etc.). Allow them to share their drawings and tell why this room has more light than other rooms.

Extension Children who want to find out more can do research on how lights are used for different purposes. Provide children with both print and online resources. Ask them to write three examples of how people use light for different reasons (for safety/light in a stairway; for reading during the night; to get attention/police car lights).

ELL Be sure to point out all labels, pictures, captions, and headings throughout the lesson to assist children with strategies to summarize chunks of content. Discuss with children real-life connections to content and provide hands-on examples of materials, when possible, to best support the needs of these learners.

Lesson Phenomenon

Lesson Objective

Make observations to explain how objects can be seen if the objects give off their own light or if light is available to shine on them.

About This Image

Ask: What time of day was this picture taken? nighttime
What do you see? sky, buildings, water Which of these things can you see best? the buildings Where is light coming from in the photograph? the buildings Which is darker, the sky or the water? The sky is mostly dark. The water has some light.

Point out the water. **Ask: Why is it easier to see the water than the sky?** The water has light on it from the buildings. **How would this picture look different if it was taken during the day?** There would be more light. **Where does most of the light come from during the daytime?** the sun **Do you think we would notice the building lights as much during the day?** Answers will vary.

 Electromagnetic Radiation

Alternative Engage Strategy

Lights, Camera, Action!	👥 whole class 🕐 30 minutes

Use a digital camera or other device to take pictures of children for use with this activity. Take a picture of the class in a dimly lit room. Do not use a flash. Then, take a similar picture in the same room with all available lights turned on. If possible, display the pictures on an interactive whiteboard or have children look at them on the digital device's display. Have children work in small groups to compare what they can see in each photograph. Have them identify which photograph was taken with more light and explain how they know.

Lesson 1   How Does Light Help Us See?

Light helps you see things.

By the End of This Lesson

I will be able to explain why you can see an object if it gives off its own light or if light shines on it.

82

Light in Darkness

The sun has set. It is dark. But you can see fireworks in a dark sky.

Explore online. ▶

Can You Explain It?

✏️ How can you see fireworks in a dark sky?

Accept all reasonable answers.

_____

_____

_____

Lesson 1 • How Does Light Help Us See?

83

Can You Explain It?

Light in Darkness Some things are easier to see in the dark. Go online to watch a video showing fireworks. If the video is not available, review the two pictures on the page.

Ask children to record their initial thoughts about how it is possible to see fireworks when it is dark. Accept all reasonable answers. At the end of this lesson, children will revisit these pictures as part of the Lesson Check. At that point, children should be able to explain why some things can be seen in the dark.

Collaboration

Build on Prior Knowledge You may want children to view the video as a whole-class activity. In this way, you can assess their prior knowledge of light sources.

Ask: Think about how the sky looks before the fireworks start. What can you see? What do you see when the fireworks appear? How are you able to see them in the dark sky? Use details from the pictures to support your answers.

Let There Be Light!

3D Learning Objective

Children will **observe how light affects** whether an object can be seen and how that object looks. They will **use these observations to provide evidence** of a relationship between the amount of light and how an object is seen.

CCC Cause and Effect . . . .

Ask: **What would you see if you went into the cave without a lamp?** nothing, darkness If children suggest items seen in this photograph, remind them they would have no light without a lamp. Discuss with children how they could test to see whether or not the lamp is what allows the person in the photograph to see.

DCI Electromagnetic Radiation . . . .

Ask: **How does the lamp help the person in the cave?** It shines light to let him see the things inside the cave. **Ask:** **Where should this person shine the light to see where he will step?** toward the floor of the cave

SEP Constructing Explanations and Designing Solutions . . . .

Draw children's attention to the photograph of the stadium. Explain that the sun has gone down and a game will start soon. **Ask:** **How do these lights help the players?** They will be able to see the ball and the other players. **Ask:** **Would the people at the stadium be able to watch the game without lights? Why or why not?** No, they would not be able to watch because it would be dark.

Let There Be Light!

Explore online.

The cave is dark. The lamp shines light inside it. This helps a cave explorer see the walls and objects.

Lights in a stadium help players see.

How can you see in dark places? You can see objects if light shines on them. Light from lamps helps people see. **Light** is energy that lets you see.

© Houghton Mifflin Harcourt • Image Credits: (t) ©Mclein/Shutterstock; (b) ©Vasyl Syniuk/Creatas Video/Getty Images

84

When can you see objects in dark places?

Ⓐ all the time

Ⓑ if you look carefully

Ⓒ when light shines on them

Do the Math! • Emma sees the sun rise. Her clock shows the time. What time did the sun rise?

Tell and Write Time Go to the online handbook for tips.

© Houghton Mifflin Harcourt

Ⓐ 6:00

Ⓑ 12:00

Ⓒ 12:30

Lesson 1 • How Does Light Help Us See?   85

ᴅᴄɪ Electromagnetic Radiation . . . .

Guide children to discuss the question and answer choices. Ask children to choose an answer. **Ask: Can you see objects in dark places all the time?** No, I can't see them if there is no light to shine on them. **Ask: If you look carefully, can you see objects in the dark?** no **Ask: What happens to objects if light shines on them?** We can see them.

Do the Math! • Tell and Write Time

Guide children as they read and discuss the word problem. **Ask: What do you need to find out?** The time Emma sees the sun rise.

💡 **Tell and Write Time** Remind children that the parts of the clock that turn are called hands. When the minute hand points to the 12, the hour hand points to the number that names the hour. When the minute hand points to the 6, it means the time is 30 minutes after the hour.

Collaboration

Think, Write, Pair, Share Direct children to think about their neighborhood at night. Have them make a list of three or more objects that light shines on after dark. Ask them to pair with another child to share lists. Encourage them to discuss why they think each object has light on it at night.

Explore online. ▶ Have children explore to find out more about how the amount of light in a room affects what can be seen.

SEP **Constructing Explanations and Designing Solutions** . . . .

Hold a class discussion about the three pictures on the page. Have children share what they notice about all three pictures. Children should conclude that the three pictures are of the same place in the room, but the amount of light is different. Discuss the amount of detail that they can see in each photograph. **Ask: When can you see more details in the room?** when there is more light

 FORMATIVE ASSESSMENT

Read, Write, Share! • Collaborate with Groups

Make the classroom as dark as possible. Once the room is darkened, provide small groups of children with flashlights. Encourage children to make observations about certain objects with the light shining directly on them. Then tell them to turn the light off and make observations. Children can share their thoughts and observations within small groups. Remind children to compare how things looked when the flashlights were on and when they were off. Have children record their observations and remind them to add details to their writing.

Scoring Guidelines

• collaborates with classmates about observations
• records their detailed observations in writing

💡 **Collaborate with Groups** Tell children to think about the question on their own before sharing ideas with their group. Remind them to be active listeners when their classmates are sharing. Encourage them to ask questions of the speaker to engage in conversation.

Different Amounts of Light

Explore online. ▶

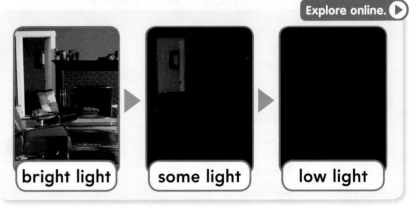

bright light → some light → low light

The amount of light affects how much you can see. You can see a lot in a room with bright light. You see less when there is only some light. You see very little in low light.

 Apply What You Know

Read, Write, Share! • How can you see objects in a dark room? Think about the answer. Turn on a flashlight in a dark classroom. Make observations. Talk with your classmates. Add details to your answer.

Collaborate with Groups
Go to the online handbook for tips.

© Houghton Mifflin Harcourt

86

Hands-On Activity

Make Observations in Different Light

Materials • drawing paper • a pencil

Ask a Question

What can you see in different amounts of light?

Test and Record Data Explore online. ▶

Step 1

Observe your classroom when there is a lot of light. How well can you see objects and details? Record your observations.

Children should record their observations.

Step 2

Now observe the same room when it has only some light. How well can you see the same objects and details? Record your observations.

Children should record their observations.

Lesson 1 • How Does Light Help Us See? 87

© Houghton Mifflin Harcourt

Hands-On Activity 👥 pairs ⏱ 1 class period

Make Observations in Different Light

SEP **Constructing Explanations and Designing Solutions** . . . .

Children will make observations in different amounts of light. Children will record observations under bright light, some light, and low light. They will then make a claim and support that claim using evidence from their observations during the exploration.

Suggested Materials drawing paper, pencils

Preparation

Identify strategies to achieve different levels of light in the classroom. If necessary, gather items to help to make the room darker, such as a piece of dark fabric or paper to block light from entering. If changing the amount of light is not possible, find a room where you can control the light. Take three different pictures of the room, one with a lot of light, one with some light, and one with no light. Use the pictures for each step of the activity.

Activity

Discuss as a class what you will be investigating. Have children brainstorm a question that will be answered as they work through the activity.

STEP 1 Remind children that when making observations it is important to pay close attention to detail. They should record how much of something they see, the color of each thing they see, or specific words they can read. **Ask: Why is it important to pay attention to details when making observations?** Paying attention to details is important because the amount of light may change what details we can see.

STEP 2 Discuss with children why it is important to observe the same objects in both steps. Explain that in order to determine how light affects what we can see, we must compare the same objects in different amounts of light. That way, we know that the only difference in what we see is the amount of light, not the objects.

Hands-On Activity, continued

STEP 3 Remind children to observe the same objects they observed in the first two steps.

STEP 4 Return the classroom to normal lighting conditions. Hold a class discussion about what the children observed. Remind children that observations are subjective and each person may have seen things differently.

CCC Cause and Effect . . . .

Have children think about what caused objects to look different in the room. **Ask: Do you think changing the amount of light in the room caused the objects to look different?** Sample answer: Yes, I think it did because I could see different things in different amounts of light.

Claims, Evidence, and Reasoning

Children should make a claim that relates to the amount of light shining on an object with the ability to see details about the object. They should cite evidence to support the claim. **Ask: Why is it important to have a light source when going someplace that is dark?** Having a light is important so that you can see all the details of the space. Being able to see things will keep you safe.

Scoring Rubric for Hands-On Activity	
3	States a claim supported with evidence about how the amount of light affects the ability to see an object
2	States a claim somewhat supported with evidence about how the amount of light affects the ability to see an object
1	States a claim that is not supported by evidence
0	Does not state a claim and does not provide evidence

Step 3

Finally, observe the room with very little light. What has changed? Record your observations.

Children should record their observations.

Step 4

Talk about your observations. What caused objects to look different?

Make a claim that answers your question.

Sample answer: Objects look different in different amounts of light. The more light in a room, the more details I can see.

What is your evidence?

Sample answer: I observed objects in a room in different amounts of light. I recorded what I saw.

88

© Houghton Mifflin Harcourt

See in the Dark

Explore online. ▶

A campfire gives off its own light. You can see it in the dark.

A glow stick gives off its own light. You can see it in the dark.

You can see an object in the dark if you shine light on it. You can also see an object in the dark if it gives off its own light.

Lesson 1 • How Does Light Help Us See?

89

See in the Dark

3D Learning Objective

Children will **observe** objects that give off their own light and **use their observations to explain** why these objects can be seen in the dark.

 Electromagnetic Radiation . . . .

Remind children that we can see objects when light shines on them. Direct their attention to the picture of the campfire. **Ask: How can we see the fire even though it is dark outside?** The fire gives off its own light. **Ask: Would you be able to see the area around the fire if the fire were out?** No, because the fire gives off the light that allows me to see the area around the fire.

 Constructing Explanations and Designing Solutions . . . .

Guide children to make observations about the second picture. Have children share a time they may have used or seen a glow stick. Ask them to share why the glow stick was being used. **Ask: How is the glow stick like the campfire?** Both give off their own light.

Connection to Earth and Space Sciences

The Universe and its Stars Discuss that the sun gives off its own light. That light allows us to see things during the day. This happens each day. Discuss with children things that can be seen in the night sky. Share with children that stars, such as the sun, give off their own light, which is why we can see stars in the night sky. Have children fold a sheet of paper in half. Tell them to draw the night sky on one side and the daytime sky on the other. Have children share the differences between the two images. Discuss how light changes what they see during the day and at night.

DCI Electromagnetic Radiation . . . .

Children should choose the night-light as something you could see in a dark room. Have children discuss why the stuffed bear and wooden block would be hard to see in a dark room. Discuss with children that the night-light gives off its own light, but the stuffed bear and wooden block do not. **Ask: How could you see the stuffed bear and wooden block in a dark room?** You could shine a light on them.

Differentiate Instruction

RTI/Extra Support Some children may have trouble differentiating between objects that can only be seen when light shines on them and objects that give off their own light. Place five stickers that glow and four stickers that do not glow in a grid on a piece of cardboard or poster board. Have children shine a flashlight onto each sticker in bright daylight. Then have them take the poster and the flashlight into a dark area to make additional observations. Alternatively, they could look at the poster under a cloth or blanket to observe it in the dark.

Extension Have children research how a lighthouse works. Children can use books or the Internet for research as well as draw on personal experience. Ask them to write an opinion about whether it is more important for a lighthouse to be seen or to help other objects be seen. They should include reasons for their opinion.

✏️ Circle the object you could see best in a dark room.

90

Explore online. ▶ Have children explore to find out more about what they can see in a cave when light shines in it.

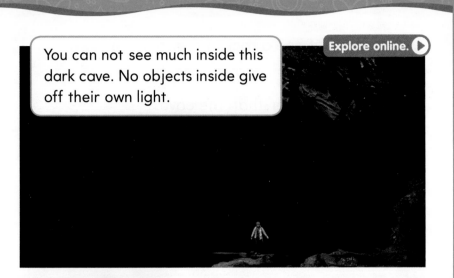

You can not see much inside this dark cave. No objects inside give off their own light.

Explore online. ▶

A spotlight lights up the cave. It shines on rocks and other objects. Then you can see them.

You can not see an object that does not give off light. You can not see an object that has no light shining on it.

© Houghton Mifflin Harcourt • Image Credits: (t) ©Alex Treadway/Getty Images; (b) ©John and Lisa Merrill/Getty Images

Lesson 1 • How Does Light Help Us See?

91

CCC Cause and Effect . . . .

Have children make observations about both pictures. Hold a class discussion about what the differences are between the two pictures. **Ask: Why is there a difference in what you can see in the top picture and bottom picture?** The top picture has no light so you can't see inside the cave. The bottom picture has a light shining so you can see inside the cave.

DCI Electromagnetic Radiation . . . .

Guide children in their understanding about the difference between an object that gives off its own light and an object that does not. Explain that the cave is dark because nothing inside the cave gives off light. **Ask: How could you make the top picture more like the bottom picture?** You could shine a light inside the cave in the top picture, and you would be able to see the details as you can in the bottom picture.

Differentiate Instruction

ELL Review the prepositions *on* and *off* as they are used in this lesson. Discuss the phrases *shines light on* and *gives off its own light* to be sure children understand the source of light.

DCI Electromagnetic Radiation . . . .

If children choose A, discuss that neither the rock nor the surrounding cave could be seen if the cave is dark. If children choose only B or only C, encourage them to think about all the ways an object can be seen. **Ask: What are the ways a hiker can see an object in a dark cave?** if there is light shining on the object or the object gives off its own light

 FORMATIVE ASSESSMENT

Evidence Notebook

Ask small groups of children to design a simple test that will answer the question, "How can we see some objects in the dark?" Turn off the classroom lights, and draw the blinds as needed to make the room as dark as possible. Encourage children to make observations and gather evidence to answer the question.

Scoring Guidelines

• identifies a strategy to collect facts
• designs a test that will provide evidence to support an explanation

💡 **Constructing Explanations and Designing Solutions** Encourage children to think of different ways they could design a test to answer the question. Remind them of what they have explored about light.

💡 **Cause and Effect** Children should use the facts they observe to describe what happens and look for the reason something happens. Have them study their test results. Do the results show their ideas are correct?

A hiker can not see a rock in a dark cave. Why not? Choose all correct answers.

Ⓐ The rock is darker than the cave.

Ⓑ There is no light shining on the rock.

Ⓒ The rock does not give off light.

✋ **Apply What You Know**

Evidence Notebook • Work with a small group. Make your classroom dark. Think about this question—How can you see some objects in the dark? Together, design a simple test to answer the question. Make observations. Use evidence to answer the question.

💡 **Constructing Explanations and Designing Solutions** • **Cause and Effect** Go to the online handbook for tips.

© Houghton Mifflin Harcourt

92

Explore online. 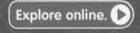   Guide children to the Interactive Online Student Edition where they can choose from and explore both paths.

Take It Further

People in Science & Engineering •
Thomas Edison

Explore more online.

Animals That Glow

Explore online. ▶

Thomas Edison

Thomas Edison made many important inventions. One of his most important inventions was the light bulb. He made one of the first light bulbs in 1879. Light bulbs need electricity to work. Edison helped bring electricity to people's homes.

early lamp

Take It Further

People in Science & Engineering •
Thomas Edison

Thomas Edison was an inventor. From an early age he was curious about how things worked. His mother was a school teacher who realized early on his eagerness to learn. He constantly tinkered with things and eventually built a laboratory to test his ideas. His most famous inventions include the light bulb, telegraph, and motion pictures.

DCI **Electromagnetic Radiation** . . . .

As a class, read the information about Thomas Edison. Discuss one of his most important inventions. **Ask: What was one of Edison's most important inventions? the light bulb Ask: What do light bulbs need to work? electricity**

CCC **Cause and Effect** . . . .

Encourage children to share their ideas about how electricity and light bulbs changed the way people did things. **Ask: How do you think people lit their homes before they had electricity and light bulbs? fire, candles Ask: What are some things people use light to do? read, eat, clean Ask: How do you think the invention of the light bulb made it easier to do these things? People could just turn on a light bulb to shine light on what they wanted to see. Ask: Why did Edison work to make it easier to use electricity? so people could use his inventions**

Take It Further, continued

Children should choose C, It gave off light. Have children discuss their answer to the question and use evidence from the lesson to support their answer. Explain that even though a light bulb is hooked up to wires and needs power, neither of those would show Edison that the light bulb worked. He needed to observe light coming from the bulb in order to know his design was successful. **Ask: What do you think Edison did to know his light bulb worked?** He tested it.

DCI **Electromagnetic Radiation** . . . .

Discuss with children that Thomas Edison didn't just make light bulbs, he also built switches to control them. Have children share real life examples of ways they control light bulbs. Discuss why a switch for a light bulb is so important.

Explore more online. ▶

Animals That Glow

Children investigate animals that give off light.

Edison also built switches and wires that made lights work.

How did Thomas Edison know that his light bulb worked?

Ⓐ It was hooked up to wires.

Ⓑ It needed power.

Ⓒ It gave off light.

94

Explore online. ▶ Have children review how fireworks can light up a dark sky.

Lesson Check

Name _____

Explore online. ▶

Can You Explain It?

🖍 How can you see fireworks in a dark sky?

Be sure to

• Explain when you can see objects in the dark.

• Tell why you can see fireworks in the dark.

Sample answer: To see an object in the dark, it must give off

its own light or have a light shine on it. You can see fireworks

in the dark because they give off their own light.

_____

© Houghton Mifflin Harcourt • Image Credits: (l) ©phaitoons/Creatas Video/Getty Images; (r) ©Kontent Real/Image Bank Film/Getty Images

Lesson 1 • How Does Light Help Us See?   95

Lesson Check

Can You Explain It?

Have children reread their answers to the Can You Explain It? prompt at the beginning of the lesson.

DCI **Electromagnetic Radiation** . . . .

Review the definition of the term *light*. **Ask: What part of our body do we use to see things?** eyes **Ask: What kind of energy helps us see?** light **Ask: Can our eyes see without light?** no

CCC **Cause and Effect** . . . .

Ask children to recall the discussion about the cave explorer earlier in this lesson. **Ask: Why was it dark in the cave?** Sunlight did not reach the inside the cave. **Ask: What did the explorer use to see?** a lamp **Ask: What could the explorer see in the cave with the lamp?** walls, floor, ceiling **Ask: What did the lamp do to help the explorer see these things?** It made light. The light helped the explorer see inside the cave.

Lead a discussion about other ways to see in a dark place. **Ask: What else could help you to see in a dark place?** a glow stick, a candle, a flashlight, a fire

SEP **Constructing Explanations and Designing Solutions** . . . .

Ask: What are the ways you can see an object in the dark? if it has light shining on it or if it gives off its own light **Ask: Why can you see fireworks in the dark?** They give off light.

Scoring Guidelines

• Children should describe how light helps us see.
• Children should identify fireworks as objects that give off light.
• Children should explain that fireworks can be seen in the dark because they give off light.

Lesson 1 • How Does Light Help Us See?   **95**

Lesson Check, continued

SUMMATIVE ASSESSMENT
Lesson Check

1. Children should choose B—when the object gives off light; and C—when light shines on the object. If children choose A or did not choose B and C, direct them to the See in the Dark section of the lesson. Guide children to look for clues in the text and photos.

2. Children should choose B—Try to see it in the dark. If children choose A or C, direct them to the See in the Dark section of the lesson. Have them think about objects they can see in the dark without any light shining on them.

3. Children should choose A, B, and C—the sun, glow sticks, and fires. These are all objects that give off their own light. If children do not choose all three answers, direct them to the See in the Dark section of the lesson. Have them look for photos and read the text to review objects that give off their own light.

Self Check

1. When can you see an object? Choose all correct answers.

   Ⓐ when it is dark

   🅱 when the object gives off light

   Ⓒ when light shines on the object

2. How could you test if an object gives off its own light?

   Ⓐ Put it under a lamp.

   🅱 Try to see it in the dark.

   Ⓒ Shine a flashlight on it.

3. Which objects give off their own light? Choose all correct answers.

   🅐 the sun

   🅑 glow sticks

   🅒 fires

96

4. You can see a few objects in this living room. Complete the sentence to tell why.

The living room is lit with _____.

Ⓐ many lamps

Ⓑ no lamps

Ⓒ one lamp

5. The campers see the fire. Why can they see it?

Ⓐ A light shines on the fire.

Ⓑ The space around the fire is dark.

Ⓒ The fire gives off its own light.

4. Children should choose C—one lamp. If children choose A or B, direct them to the section of the lesson that discusses how different amounts of light affect how objects can be seen. Have them think about what amount of light helps them see only a few objects.

5. Children should choose C—The fire gives off its own light. If children choose A or B, direct them to look closely at the photograph. Guide children to look for objects that have light shining on them and objects that are giving off light.

How Do Materials Block Light?

Building to the Performance Expectation

The learning experiences in this lesson prepare children for mastery of:

1-PS4-3 Plan and conduct an investigation to determine the effect of placing objects made with different materials in the path of a beam of light.

Trace Tool to the NGSS
Go online to view the complete coverage of these standards across this lesson, unit, and time.

 (SEP) Science & Engineering Practices

Planning and Carrying Out Investigations

Plan and conduct investigations collaboratively to produce data to serve as the basis for evidence to answer a question.

 VIDEO SEP: Planning and Carrying Out Investigations

(DCI) Disciplinary Core Ideas

PS4.B: Electromagnetic Radiation

Some materials allow light to pass through them, others allow only some light through and others block all the light and create a dark shadow on any surface beyond them, where the light cannot reach. Mirrors can be used to redirect a light beam.

(CCC) Crosscutting Concepts

Cause and Effect

Simple tests can be designed to gather evidence to support or refute student ideas about causes.

CONNECTION TO MATH

1.NBT.A.1 Count to 120, starting at any number less than 120. In this range, read and write numerals and represent a number of objects with a written numeral.

CONNECTION TO ENGLISH LANGUAGE ARTS

SL.1.1 Participate in collaborative conversations with diverse partners about grade one topics and texts with peers and adults in small and larger groups.

Supporting All Students, All Standards

Integrating the Three Dimensions of Learning

This lesson focuses on how different materials allow different amounts of light to pass through **(DCI Electromagnetic Radiation)**. Children investigate and gather evidence **(SEP Planning and Carrying Out Investigations)** of how light passes through objects in order to support their ideas about causes **(CCC Cause and Effect)**. They explore how shadows are made and how moving the light source can change a shadow's size.

 Professional Development

Go online to view **Professional Development videos** with strategies to integrate CCCs and SEPs, including the ones used in this lesson.

Build on Prior Knowledge

Children should already know and be prepared to build on the following concepts:
- Light helps us see.
- Objects can be seen only when illuminated.

Differentiate Instruction

Lesson Vocabulary
- shadow

Reinforcing Vocabulary Remind children to look for this highlighted word as they proceed through the lesson. Inform children that a *shadow* is a dark spot that is made when an object stops the light from passing through. Then, have a volunteer hold out his or her hand while you shine a light on it. Discuss what happens and how the shadow is made.

RTI/Extra Support Set up a light source large enough to cast a shadow of a child's profile onto a whiteboard or bulletin board covered with a large piece of construction paper. Draw around the child's profile shadow cast on the construction paper. Cut out the child's profile to form a silhouette and ask the class if they can tell who the child is by looking at the cutout. Discuss how you knew where to cut because you followed the line around the child's shadow.

Extension Prepare several cutouts of various object's shadows; for example, a pencil, a pair of scissors, an eraser, a teddy bear, and so on. Ask children to identify as many objects as possible based on their shadow.

ELL Be sure to point out all labels, pictures, captions, and headings throughout the lesson to assist children with strategies to summarize chunks of content. Discuss with children real-life connections to content and provide hands-on examples of materials when possible to best support the needs of these learners.

Lesson Phenomenon

Lesson Objective

Ask questions, make observations, and gather information to describe how light passes through objects and how shadows are made.

About This Image

Ask: Why do things look dark in this picture? There is less light in the sky because it is evening. Light helps us see things better. As you explore, you will find out how light passes through some materials and not others. Sometimes light can form shadows.

DCI Electromagnetic Radiation

Alternative Engage Strategy

Shadow Walk	👥 pairs ⏱ 15–25 minutes

Take children on a walk around the school grounds on a sunny day. Have them observe the shadows being made. After returning to class, have pairs brainstorm how and why the shadows for various objects were made. Have pairs share their ideas with the class.

Lesson 2

How Do Materials Block Light?

Materials block light in different ways.

By the End of This Lesson

I will be able to explain how shadows are made and that different materials allow different amounts of light to pass through.

98

Block the Light

This puppet show is in a dark room.
Even though it is dark, you can see
different shapes.

Explore online. ▶

Can You Explain It?

 How does the artist make the shapes?

Accept all reasonable answers.

Can You Explain It?

Block the Light Light is a type of energy that lets us see. When light is blocked, shadows are made. Have children watch the video of the shadow puppets. If the video is not available, have children observe the pictures on the page. As a class, discuss what is happening and how children think the shapes can be seen in a dark room. Then talk about how the artist is able to make the shapes.

Ask children to record their initial thoughts about how the shapes are made. At the end of this lesson, children will revisit this question as part of the Lesson Check. At this point, children should be able to explain how shadows are made.

Collaboration

Build on Prior Knowledge Allow children time to familiarize themselves with different hand puppets. Then guide children to write a short play that includes something about shadows to present to the class. The play could explain how shadows are formed, why shadows sometimes disappear, or how they can change size. Children can make up a story about an animal who is afraid of his shadow or even discover songs that include the word *shadow* and sing them.

LESSON 2   Engage • **Explore/Explain** • Elaborate • Evaluate

Explore online. ▶   Have children explore to find out more about how different materials allow different amounts of light to pass through them.

How Much Light?

3D Learning Objective

Children explore how different materials allow different amounts of light to pass through. They discuss investigations that can be done in order to support their ideas about causes.

DCI Electromagnetic Radiation . . . .

Ask: What are some differences you see in the objects in each picture? The door is made of wood, the glass is clear, and the waxed paper is not clear. **Ask: What happens when you shine a light source on these objects?** The door blocks the light, some light can go through the waxed paper, and all the light goes through the glass. These objects will not let the same amount of light through because they are made of different materials.

SEP Planning and Carrying Out Investigations . . . . .

CCC Cause and Effect . . . .

Ask: Suppose you wanted to find out how much light can pass through some objects in your classroom. What could you do? I could make a plan and then investigate using different materials and a light source. **Ask: What do you think would be the effect of using the light source?** Some objects would let light pass through, while others would block it.

Collaboration

Small Groups Provide children with clear plastic cups and challenge them to see if they can change how the light passes through them. Ask the following questions to get children thinking, "What if we stack several cups together?"; "What if we color the plastic?" Have children write a short summary of their ideas and share it with the class.

How Much Light?

Explore online. ▶

No light can pass through wood.

Some light can pass through waxed paper.

All light can pass through clear glass.

© Houghton Mifflin Harcourt

Different amounts of light can pass through different materials.

100

Hands-On Activity

Test How Light Passes Through Materials

Materials	• a flashlight	• clear plastic
	• frosted plastic	• plywood

Ask a Question

How much light passes through different materials?

Test and Record Data Explore online. ▶

Step 1

Turn on the flashlight. Shine light through the clear plastic. Observe how much light passes through the plastic.

clear plastic

Step 2

Test the rest of the materials. How much light passes through each material? How do you know?

frosted plastic	plywood

Lesson 2 • How Do Materials Block Light?

101

© Houghton Mifflin Harcourt

Hands-On Activity 👥 small groups 🕐 1 class period

Test How Light Passes Through Materials

3D Learning Objective

SEP Planning and Carrying Out Investigations . . . . .

Children investigate what happens when different materials are placed in the path of light. They will use data they gathered as evidence to answer their question and support or refute their ideas about causes.

Suggested Materials a flashlight, clear plastic, frosted plastic, and plywood.

Preparation

Pre-assemble materials bundles for each group. Remind children to not shine the flashlight into other children's eyes or faces.

Ask a Question

Guide children to brainstorm different questions for the activity. **Ask: What is the question we want to answer as we think about the lesson?** How much light passes through different materials?

CCC Cause and Effect . . . .

While completing Steps 1 and 2, have children think about the effects that happen each time light shines on each of the materials.

Activity

STEP 1 Guide children to shine the flashlight through the clear plastic object and observe how much light passes through the object. Ask children to draw a picture of what they find.

STEP 2 Guide children to shine the flashlight through the other objects and observe how much light passes through each object. Ask children to draw a picture of what they find in the boxes. Have children compare all three pictures.

Hands-On Activity, continued

 Cause and Effect . . . .

STEP 3 Allow children time to explain why different materials allow different amounts of light to pass through those materials. Guide children to identify the cause-and-effect relationship. **Ask: What causes light to pass through some objects, but not others?** the type of material the object is made of

Claims, Evidence, and Reasoning

Children should write a claim that describes how light travels through different objects. They should cite evidence to support their claims. **Ask: Did the flashlight shine through all of the objects in the same way? Why or why not?** No, different amounts of light passed through different objects depending on what they were made of.

	Scoring Rubric for Hands-On Activity
3	States a claim supported with evidence that different materials allow different amounts of light to pass through
2	States a claim somewhat supported by evidence that different materials allow different amounts of light to pass through
1	States a claim that is not supported by evidence
0	Does not state a claim and does not provide evidence

Step 3

Explain why different materials allow different amounts of light to pass through. Identify cause and effect.

Sample answer: Different materials are made of different things. Some materials are made of things that let all light through. Some materials are made of things that let no light through. When light shines on a material that lets all light through, you can see all the light pass through the material.

Make a claim that answers your question.

Sample answer: All light passes through clear plastic. Some light passes through frosted plastic. No light passes through plywood.

What is your evidence?

Sample answer: I tested the three materials. I saw that different amounts of light passed through each material.

© Houghton Mifflin Harcourt

102

How much light passes through a clear glass bowl?

(A) all light

(B) some light

(C) no light

Apply What You Know

Do the Math! • Explore your classroom. Make lists of objects that let all light pass through, some light pass through, and no light pass through. Count and write how many objects are in each group.

Count Objects Go to the online handbook for tips.

All Light	Some Light	No Light
_____	_____	_____

© Houghton Mifflin Harcourt

DCI **Electromagnetic Radiation** . . . .

Children should choose A—all light. If children choose B or C, have them return to the three pictures from the beginning of the lesson and review their results from the Hands-On Activity. **Ask: What happens when you shine light on clear objects?** All of the light will pass through.

Differentiate Instruction

ELL Demonstrate the words *all, some,* and *no* by placing your hand over a flashlight in varying positions to let all, some, and no light through. Repeat by shining the flashlight on objects and repeating the words *all, some,* and *no.*

FORMATIVE ASSESSMENT

Do the Math! • **Count Objects**
Monitor children as they locate objects and categorize them as All Light, Some Light, and No Light. Guide children to count the objects and finish the chart. Allow time at the end for groups to share their findings.

Count Objects Remind children to count objects by touching the object and saying the number name until all objects have been counted. The last number tells how many objects are in the group.

Scoring Guidelines
• categorizes objects and gives evidence for placement
• counts objects in each column accurately

Shadows

3D Learning Objective

Children explore how shadows are made. They **observe, investigate, and gather information** of the **causes and effects of shadows changing**.

DCI Electromagnetic Radiation . . . .

Have children think about what is needed in order to make a shadow. **Ask: What are shadows?** Shadows are the dark spots made when something blocks the light. **Ask: Why can't we see a shadow in the top picture?** The flashlight is turned off. Shadows can't be made without a light source.

CCC Cause and Effect . . . .

Guide children to look for the reason a shadow appears. Have them observe and describe what is happening in each picture. **Ask: What is the light source in these pictures?** The flashlight is the light source. **Ask: What is causing the shadow in these pictures?** The book is blocking the light from passing through and causes a shadow. **Ask: Where do we see the shadow?** The shadow appears on the wall behind the book.

Connection to Earth and Space Sciences

The Universe and its Stars The sun is a light source that can cause shadows when it shines on objects. Throughout the day, as Earth rotates, shadows change in size. Have children pick a stationary object, such as a small plant or sign on the school grounds. Have them observe their chosen object in the morning, at noon, and in the afternoon. Children should write a sentence describing the size of the object's shadow for each observation. Have children share and compare their observations.

Shadows

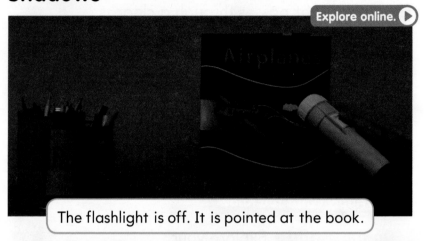

The flashlight is off. It is pointed at the book.

The flashlight is on. The book blocks the light and makes a shadow.

A **shadow** is a dark spot made when an object blocks light. The light does not pass through the object.

104

Big Shadow, Little Shadow

Explore online. ▶

The size of a shadow changes when the light shining on the object moves.

© Houghton Mifflin Harcourt

Lesson 2 • How Do Materials Block Light?

105

DCI Electromagnetic Radiation . . . .

Guide children to note the differences in the pictures. **Ask: How can we make a shadow look bigger?** Move the light source closer to the object. **Ask: How can we make a shadow look smaller?** Move the light source farther away from the object.

SEP Planning and Carrying Out Investigations . . . . .

CCC Cause and Effect . . . .

Have children test the concept of shadows changing in size. Pick two classroom objects, and have volunteers shine a light on both. Each time, they should move the light source closer to and farther away from the objects. Then discuss how the shadows were made to look larger or smaller. **Ask: What was the effect of moving the light source?** The size of the shadows changed.

Differentiate Instruction

RTI/Extra Support Take a picture of a small section of the playground in the morning and in the afternoon on a sunny day. Ask children to compare the two pictures. Guide the discussion to note differences in the shadows. **Ask: Why do the shadows seem different?** The sun appears to have moved, causing the shadows to change in size.

Extension Introduce the poem *Shadow Race* by Shel Silverstein. Guide children to discuss what is happening in the poem. Allow children time to make a presentation of the poem and interpret its meaning according to the information gained about how light passes through things.

DCI Electromagnetic Radiation . . . .

For the first question, children should choose A—An object blocks light. If children choose B or C, review how shadows are made by lowering the lights in the classroom. Use a flashlight to shine light on an object, and discuss what happens. For the second question, children should choose B—It will get bigger. If children choose A or C, continue with the demonstration mentioned for the first question, but this time move the flashlight closer to and farther away from the object.

 FORMATIVE ASSESSMENT

Evidence Notebook

Guide children to think about how an object's shape affects the way a shadow looks. Monitor children as they design and conduct an investigation using different shapes of paper to gather evidence that will answer the question. Children should record their results in their Evidence Notebook.

Scoring Guidelines

- describes how the shape of an object affects the shadow
- makes a claim to explain why the shape of objects has an effect on the shadow
- provides evidence to support the claim based on the findings of their investigation

💡 **Planning and Carrying Out Investigations • Cause and Effect** Guide children to work with others to plan and do an investigation. Collect data from the investigation to use as evidence to answer the question. Encourage children to look for the reason something happens.

What causes a shadow?

Ⓐ An object blocks light.

Ⓑ A dark spot behind an object blocks light.

Ⓒ Light shines on an object.

....

How will a book's shadow change if light moves closer to the book?

Ⓐ It will get smaller.

Ⓑ It will get bigger.

Ⓒ It will stay the same size.

 Apply What You Know

Evidence Notebook • Work with a group. How does the shape of an object affect the shadow? Design a test using paper and light to answer the question. Do your test. Gather evidence. Use evidence to answer the question.

Planning and Carrying Out Investigations • Cause and Effect Go to the online handbook for tips.

© Houghton Mifflin Harcourt

106

Explore online. ▶ Guide children to the Interactive Online Student Edition where they can choose from and explore both paths.

Take It Further

Prisms

Children explore what a prism is and how prisms affect light. The white light of sunlight is a mixture of colors. When sunlight hits a prism, colored light comes out. White light bends, or refracts, as it passes through a prism. Each color of light bends differently. Each color of light comes out of the prism separate from the other colors.

DCI **Electromagnetic Radiation** . . . .

Ask: What happens when white light goes through a prism? Different colors come out the other side. What are two examples of a prism? Glass and raindrops can both act like prisms.

Take It Further
Prisms

Explore more online.
Make a Sundial

Explore online. ▶

prism

A prism is a piece of glass. Light goes in one side of the glass. The light splits up. Colors come out the other side of the glass.

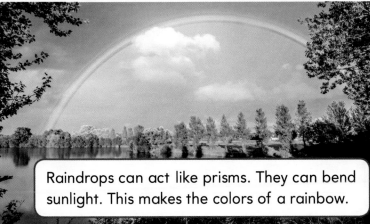

Raindrops can act like prisms. They can bend sunlight. This makes the colors of a rainbow.

Differentiate Instruction

RTI/Extra Support Demonstrate for children how a prism works. Cut a narrow slit in a sheet of black paper, and tape the paper to the bottom of a window. Close the blinds enough to make a narrow beam of light. Hold the prism in the light over a white sheet of paper. Slowly turn the prism until it makes a rainbow on the paper. Have children discuss what happened and draw and label a picture to share their observations with the class.

Extension Challenge children to research more information about prisms and light refraction. Provide resources, such as books or the Internet. Have children make a poster to describe their findings and share it with the class.

Take It Further, continued

Read, Write, Share! • Participate in Discussions

Have children discuss what they have learned about prisms and how this relates to rainbows. **Ask: What happens to light when it passes through drops of water?** Light splits up and comes out as different colors. Guide children to draw or write what they discussed with their classmates.

💡 **Participate in Discussions** Remember to follow these discussion rules. Be polite, look at the speaker, listen carefully, take turns talking, and talk only about the topic.

Collaboration

Build on Prior Knowledge Have children form groups and look in books or online for investigations on the following topics: shadows, prisms, or rainbows. Have children conduct the investigation and record their results. Host a Science Fair Exhibit where children can share their results with parents.

Explore more online. ▶

Make a Sundial

Have children go online to explore how to make a sundial.

Read, Write, Share! •
Discuss what you learned about prisms with classmates. Share whether you have ever seen a prism or a rainbow.

💡 **Participate in Discussions** Go to the online handbook for tips.

✏️➤ Draw or write to show what you talked about with your classmates.

Accept reasonable answers.

_____

_____

© Houghton Mifflin Harcourt

108

Lesson Check

Name _____

Explore online. ▶

Can You Explain It?

✏️ How does the artist make the shapes?

Be sure to

• Explain that different amounts of light can pass through different materials.

• Explain how shadows are made.

Sample answer: The artist places his/her hands in front of

light. The hands block all light. This makes the shadows in

the show.

Lesson 2 • How Do Materials Block Light?   109

Lesson Check

Can You Explain It?

Have children reread their answers to the Can You Explain It? prompt at the beginning of the lesson.

DCI **Electromagnetic Radiation** . . . .

Review both pictures, and discuss how light passes through different objects. **Ask: What is happening in these pictures?** Shadows are appearing where the light is being blocked by hands.

Ask: How does the artist make the shapes? The artist places his or her hands in front of a light to make the shadows. All of the light is blocked by the hands.

CCC **Cause and Effect** . . . .

The puppet show is in a dark room. Have children think about the light that is required when making shadow puppets. **Ask: What would be the effect of turning on all the lights in the room?** We would not be able to see the shadow puppets anymore.

Scoring Guidelines

• Children should describe how light passes through some objects, but not all objects.

• Children should explain that shadows are made when an object blocks light.

• Children should use evidence to support their ideas.

Lesson Check, continued

SUMMATIVE ASSESSMENT
Self Check

1. Children should circle the third glass. If children circle the first picture of the mug, guide children to observe that the mug is blocking all light from passing through. If children select the second picture of a frosted plastic cup, remind them that only some light would pass through this cup. Encourage children to review the information found in the How Much Light? section of the lesson.

2. Children should make the following three matches:

   1. the glass jar with the middle label (All light passes through.)

   2. the plastic cup with the last label (Some light passes through.)

   3. the aluminum bottle with the first label (No light passes through.)

   If children make incorrect matches, review the information found in the How Much Light? section of the lesson.

Self Check

1. Circle the glass that allows the most light to pass through.

2. Draw a line to match each object to the label that tells how much light passes through it.

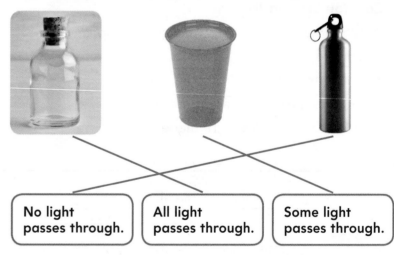

| No light passes through. | All light passes through. | Some light passes through. |

110

3. Eli thinks that all objects block all light. How can he test his idea?

Ⓐ Make a shadow on a wall.

Ⓑ Move a light closer to an object.

Ⓒ Shine light on different objects.

4. Where is the shadow in this picture? Circle it to show your answer.

5. You make a shadow of your hand on a wall with a flashlight. You want the shadow to be smaller. How should you move the flashlight?

Ⓐ Move it closer to your hand.

Ⓑ Move it farther from your hand.

Ⓒ Keep it in the same place.

3. Children should choose C—Shine light on different objects. If children choose A, remind them that using one object to make a shadow will not mean that the other objects block light. If children choose B, remind them that moving a light closer to an object would change the size of its shadow.

4. Children should circle the shadow on the green wall of the back of the chair. If children do not locate the shadow, review the Shadows section of the lesson. Remind children that shadows are the dark spots made when an object blocks light.

5. Children should choose B—Move it farther from your hand. If children choose A or C, guide children to review the Big Shadow, Little Shadow section of the lesson. Remind children that moving the flashlight closer to your hand will make the shadow bigger. If the flashlight stays in the same place, the shadow will not change in size.

Building to the Performance Expectations

The learning experiences in this lesson prepare children for mastery of:

1-PS4-3 Plan and conduct an investigation to determine the effect of placing objects made with different materials in the path of a beam of light.

1-PS4-4 Use tools and materials to design and build a device that uses light or sound to solve the problem of communicating over a distance.

Trace Tool to the NGSS
Go online to view the complete coverage of these standards across this lesson, unit, and time.

Science & Engineering Practices (SEP)

Planning and Carrying Out Investigations
Plan and conduct investigations collaboratively to produce data to serve as a basis for evidence to answer a question.

▶ **VIDEO** SEP: Planning and Carrying Out Investigations

Disciplinary Core Ideas (DCI)

PS4.B Electromagnetic Radiation
Some materials allow light to pass through them, others allow only some light through and others block all the light and create a dark shadow on any surface beyond them, where the light cannot reach. Mirrors can be used to redirect a light beam.

PS4.C Information Technologies and Instrumentation
People also use a variety of devices to communicate (send and receive information) over long distances.

Crosscutting Concepts (CCC)

Cause and Effect
Simple tests can be designed to gather evidence to support or refute student ideas about causes.

Influence of Engineering, Technology, and Science on Society and the Natural World
People depend on various technologies in their lives; human life would be very different without technology.

CONNECTIONS TO MATH

1.OA.A.2 Solve word problems that call for addition of three whole numbers whose sum is less than or equal to 20, e.g., by using objects, drawings, and equations with a symbol for the unknown number to represent the problem.

CONNECTIONS TO ENGLISH LANGUAGE ARTS

W.1.7 Participate in shared research and writing projects (e.g., explore a number of "how-to" books on a given topic and use them to write a sequence of instructions).

SL.1.1 Participate in collaborative conversations with diverse partners about grade 1 topics and texts with peers and adults in small and larger groups.

Supporting All Students, All Standards

Integrating the Three Dimensions of Learning

This lesson focuses on how light travels, including how it can be reflected and redirected (DCI Electromagnetic Radiation). It also explores how people use light to communicate (DCI Information Technologies and Instrumentation) (CCC Influence of Engineering, Technology, and Science on Society and the Natural World). Children observe how light travels and what causes light to be redirected (CCC Cause and Effect). They carry out an investigation to test how smooth, shiny surfaces affect a beam of light (SEP Planning and Carrying Out Investigations).

 Professional Development Go online to view **Professional Development videos** with strategies to integrate CCCs and SEPs, including the ones used in this lesson.

Build on Prior Knowledge

Children should already know and be prepared to build on the following concepts:

- Light is a type of energy that lets us see.
- Objects can be seen if light shines on them.
- Objects can be seen if they give off their own light.
- Different amounts of light can pass through different materials.
- Shadows are dark spots that are made when an object blocks light.

Differentiate Instruction

Lesson Vocabulary
- reflect

Reinforcing Vocabulary To help children remember the vocabulary word, help them form real-life connections. Demonstrate the meaning of *reflect* by using a mirror and explaining that you see your reflection when you look in the mirror. Remind children to look for the highlighted word and pictures that illustrate the word as they proceed through the lesson.

RTI/Extra Support Provide additional opportunity for hands-on discovery throughout the lesson. Allow children to explore how light reflects by letting them use a flashlight to recreate some of the pictures in the Interactive Worktext. Remind children to ask or write down any questions they have or concepts they do not understand.

Extension Children who want to find out more about reflection can do research on other types of mirrors. Suggest that children research reflections they see in mirrors that are curved and mirrors that are flat. Children can draw the reflections of an object from a curved mirror and from a flat mirror. Encourage them to list the differences in the reflections and to share their drawings with others.

ELL Be sure to point out all labels, pictures, captions, and headings throughout the lesson to assist children with strategies to summarize chunks of content. Discuss with children real-life connections to content, and provide hands-on examples of materials when possible to best support the needs of these learners.

Lesson Problem

Lesson Objective

Gather evidence to support or refute ideas about causes relating to how light travels, and explore how people use light devices to communicate over distances.

About This Image

Have children look at the cityscape of Chicago. Explain to children that the large sculpture in the photograph is The Cloud Gate Sculpture. However, it is commonly called The Chicago Bean. **Ask: What is something in your home that has a smooth, shiny surface like The Chicago Bean?** Sample answer: a mirror. **Ask: Suppose you were in front of The Chicago Bean. Would you see yourself and other objects more clearly in the day or at night? Why?** daytime, because there is more light Lead children in a discussion about how The Chicago Bean acts like a mirror they have seen.

 **Cause and Effect**

Alternative Engage Strategy

| **Smooth Seeing** | 👥 small groups |
| | ⏱ 15–20 minutes |

Have children work in pairs. Tell one partner to hold a hand-held mirror so that the other partner can see his or her reflection. The child in front of the mirror will write or draw his or her observations. Now tell the children to place the mirror in a clear plastic bag and repeat their observations. Encourage children to share their observations, and discuss what caused their reflections to look different when the mirror was in the plastic bag.

Lesson 3 **How Does Light Travel?**

Light can move from one place to another.

By the End of This Lesson

I will be able to explain how smooth surfaces reflect light and how to communicate with light.

112

© Houghton Mifflin Harcourt · Image Credits: ©Travelpix Ltd/Photographer's Choice/Getty Images

Light in Your Eyes

Explore online. ▶

The sun's light shines right in Jayden's eyes.
Light in your eyes can be a problem.

Can You Solve It?

✏️➤ How could you point light away
from your eyes?

Accept reasonable answers.

_____

_____

Can You Solve It?

Light in Your Eyes Sometimes light can shine in your eyes and be a problem. Play the animation to see how light can shine in someone's eyes. If the animation is unavailable, have children look at the picture on the page and discuss it.

Ask children to record their initial thoughts about how to point light away from their eyes. Accept all reasonable answers. At the end of this lesson, children will revisit this question and their answers as part of the Lesson Check. At this point, children should be able to describe a solution of how to point light away from their eyes.

Collaboration

Build on Prior Knowledge You may want children to view and discuss the animation as a whole class activity. This way, you can assess their prior knowledge of how light travels. Have children discuss how they would redirect light away from something. Ask children to use evidence from the animation or from their experiences to support their answers.

Straight On

3D Learning Objective

Children explore that light travels in a straight line and **gather evidence about what causes light to be redirected.**

DCI **Electromagnetic Radiation** . . . .

Discuss with children that light travels in a straight line. Then draw children's attention to the top picture. **Ask: How does the light travel?** in a straight line **Ask: What happens to the light when it is shined at the glass tank?** Since the tank and water are clear, the light does not stop. It goes through the glass and water.

Have children look at the children playing flashlight tag in the bottom picture. **Ask: What happens to the light from the flashlight when it hits the boy?** The light travels in a straight line until it hits the boy. Then the light stops.

Collaboration

Small Groups Have children recreate either the water tank demonstration or the flashlight demonstration. Ask them to write down their observations about how light travels and any questions they have about how light travels.

Straight On

Explore online. ▶

The light travels through the water in the tank. It travels in a straight line.

The children play tag with a light. The light travels in a straight line until it hits an object.

Light travels in a straight line until it hits an object.

© Houghton Mifflin Harcourt

114

In the Way

When light hits an object,
different things may happen.

Explore online. ▶

The light hits the glass.
What happens? All the light
passes through the object.

The light hits the foil.
Foil is smooth and shiny.
The light bounces back.

The light hits the cardboard.
Light is taken in by the
cardboard.

© Houghton Mifflin Harcourt

Lesson 3 • How Does Light Travel?

115

Discuss with children that not all materials allow light to pass
through them. Then have children look at each photograph of the
children investigating light and observe what happens when light
hits each object. **Ask: What evidence helps you explain that light
passes through the glass?** I can see the light from the flashlight
pass through the glass and onto the wall behind it. **Ask: What
evidence helps you explain that light doesn't pass through the
foil or the cardboard?** The light stops when it hits the foil and the
cardboard. It does not pass through the material onto the wall.
The light bounces back when it hits the foil.

Draw children's attention to the photograph of the light hitting the
foil. **Ask: What causes the light to bounce back?** smooth, shiny
surface of the foil **Ask: What is the effect when the light hits the
foil?** The light bounces back. **Ask: What evidence supports your
answer?** The light does not go through the foil; it bounces off
the shiny surface.

CCC **Cause and Effect** . . . .

Children should connect the clay vase to The light is taken in.; the glass to The light passes through.; and the smooth, shiny surface to The light bounces back. If children have difficulty connecting the photographs to the labels, have them review the section Straight On. Ask children to think about the materials they saw in that section and what happened when light hit those materials. Have them draw parallels between those materials and the materials they see here.

Discuss with children the cause-and-effect relationship between light and each material in the photographs. **Ask: What causes light to pass through, be taken in, or bounce back?** the type of material it hits **Ask: What is the effect when the light hits the clay pot?** It is taken in. Have children use evidence from their observations to support their answers.

DCI **Electromagnetic Radiation** . . . .

Discuss with children the material of each object in the photographs. **Ask: What material can light pass through?** clear glass **Ask: Why doesn't light bounce back when it hits the clay vase?** It isn't shiny and smooth.

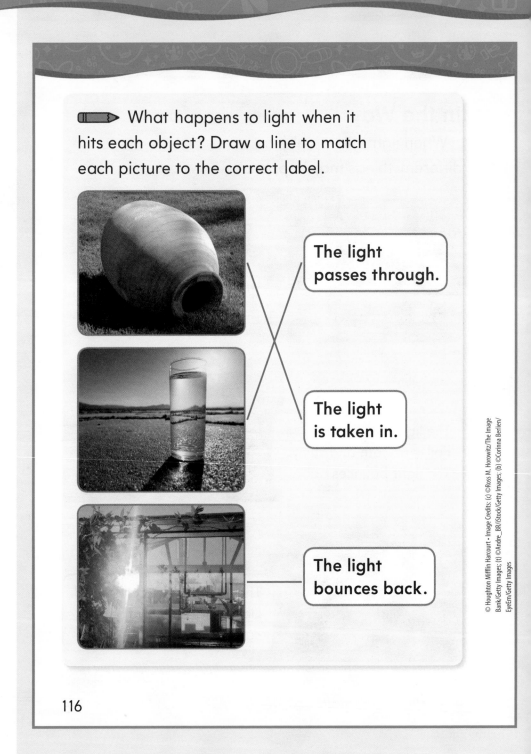

What happens to light when it hits each object? Draw a line to match each picture to the correct label.

The light passes through.

The light is taken in.

The light bounces back.

© Houghton Mifflin Harcourt • Image Credits: (c) ©Ross M. Horowitz/The Image Bank/Getty Images; (t) ©Andre_BR/iStock/Getty Images; (b) ©Corinna Berlien/EyeEm/Getty Images

116

What does the light in the water
tank show about light?

Ⓐ Light does not travel.

Ⓑ Light travels in a straight line.

Ⓒ Light never hits objects.

![hand icon] **Apply What You Know**

Evidence Notebook • Work with a group. Answer the question, How can we show that light travels in a straight line? Use cards and a flashlight. Do the activity. Gather evidence.

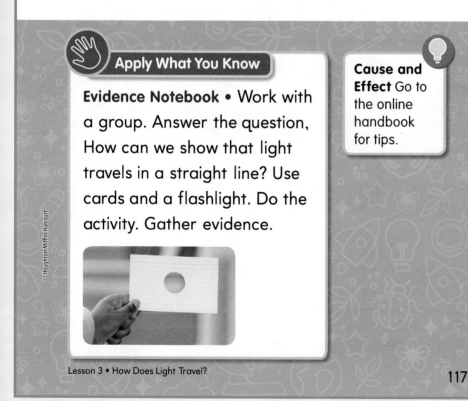

Cause and Effect Go to the online handbook for tips.

© Houghton Mifflin Harcourt

DCI **Electromagnetic Radiation** . . . .

Children should choose B—Light travels in a straight line. If children choose A or C, have them review the information in the section Straight On.

Have children look at the photograph of light shining through the water tank. **Ask: Why doesn't the light move in a different direction?** The tank and water are clear so the light passes through it. It is not shiny so light does not bounce off of it.

![hand icon] **FORMATIVE ASSESSMENT**

Evidence Notebook

Children work with a group to show how light travels in a straight line. In preparation, provide groups with three identical index cards with a 1-inch hole cut into the center of each card. After they complete the activity, tell them to provide evidence to support the claim that light travels in a straight line.

Scoring Guidelines

• uses tools and materials to prove the claim that light travels in a straight line

• provides sufficient evidence to support the claim that light travels in a straight line

 Cause and Effect Children should plan a way to show that light travels in a straight line and test their ideas. They should explain the reason something happens and whether their test shows that their ideas are correct.

A New Direction

3D Learning Objective

Children **gather evidence about what causes** light to reflect and be redirected.

DCI **Electromagnetic Radiation** . . . .

Ask children to make a connection between the tin foil they saw in the section Straight On and the mirror they see here. **Ask:** How **are the tin foil and the mirror alike?** They are both smooth, shiny surfaces. **Ask:** Do they both reflect light? How do you **know?** Yes, they both reflect light. I know because the light from the flashlight bounced back when it hit the foil. The light from the window bounces back when it hits the mirror.

Differentiate Instruction

RTI/Extra Support Display a mirror in the classroom, and direct at the mirror a light source such as a flashlight or light from the sun. Demonstrate how light is reflected by the mirror, and repeat the definition of *reflect* as you demonstrate.

Extension Have children use books or the Internet to research materials that reflect light. Challenge children to devise a way to display their findings.

What Reflects Light?

Explore online. ▶

Some windows reflect light and can make the light bounce back.

Smooth water can act like a mirror. You can see yourself and other things reflected in it.

Smooth and shiny surfaces can reflect light. **Reflect** means to bounce back from a surface.

118

A New Direction

Explore online. ▶

Light hits the mirror. It bounces off the mirror and moves in a new direction.

When the mirror moves, the light moves in a different direction.

Light can move in a new direction when it hits a smooth, shiny surface.

© Houghton Mifflin Harcourt

Lesson 3 • How Does Light Travel?

119

ccc Cause and Effect . . . .

Have children look at each picture. **Ask: What evidence helps you explain that the light bounces off the mirror?** I can see the light shine at the mirror. Then where it hits the mirror the light moves another way off the mirror. **Ask: What happens when the mirror moves?** The light bounces off the mirror in a different direction.

Remind children that the properties of objects determine whether light will reflect off the objects or not. **Ask: What causes the mirror to reflect the light?** The mirror has a shiny and smooth surface. **Ask: What do you think would happen if the mirror were covered with dark paper or cardboard? Would it still reflect the light?** Sample answer: No, dark paper and cardboard are not smooth, shiny surfaces. They would not reflect the light.

Differentiate Instruction

ELL Review the words *smooth* and *shiny*. Provide objects for children to explore that are smooth, rough, shiny, and dull. Have children describe the qualities of the objects. Then have them sort the objects into groups.

DCI Electromagnetic Radiation . . . .

Children should circle the sunglasses, the doors, and the platter. If children choose the bookshelf, have them review what kind of surfaces reflect light.

Some children may have the misconception that for light to reflect, the objects seen in the reflection must be recognizable. Show a sheet of foil and shine a light on it. **Ask: Does the light bounce off the foil? Why?** **Yes; the foil is shiny and smooth.**

Discuss with children that the foil is shiny and smooth, so light reflects off it. However, they may not see reflections in the foil as clearly as they see reflections in a mirror.

CCC Cause and Effect . . . .

Children should choose A—They change the direction of light. If children choose B or C, suggest they go back and review what happens when light hits a mirror.

Cause and Effect Children should think about the effect that smooth, shiny surfaces have on a beam of light.

✏️ **Circle each object that reflects light.**

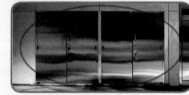

What does this picture show about smooth, shiny materials?

Ⓐ They change the direction of light.

Ⓑ They allow light to pass through.

Ⓒ They take in all light.

Cause and Effect Go to the online handbook for tips.

© Houghton Mifflin Harcourt • Image Credits: (tl) ©SVGiles/Moment/Getty Images; (tr) ©dimdimich/iStock/Getty Images; (cl) ©Alexis Gerard/Flickr Select/Getty Images; (cr) ©gilas/iStock/Getty Images; (b) ©MEEK, TORE/AFP/Staff/Getty Images

120

Name_____

Hands-On Activity
Test What Happens to Light

Materials	• a flashlight	• a mirror
• a metal spoon	• tin foil	• tin pan

Ask a Question

How do smooth, shiny surfaces affect a beam of light?

Test and Record Data   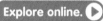 Explore online. ▶

Step 1

Plan a way to test how smooth, shiny surfaces affect a beam of light. Write your plan.

Step 2

Use the materials to do your test.
Record what happens.

Children should record the results of their test.

Lesson 3 • How Does Light Travel?   121

Hands-On Activity 👥 small groups ⏱ 1 class period
Test What Happens to Light

3D Learning Objective

SEP **Planning and Carrying Out Investigations . . . .**

Children will make a claim about how smooth, shiny surfaces affect a beam of light. They will support their claim with evidence and data from their observations during the exploration.

Suggested Materials a flashlight, a mirror, a metal spoon, tin foil, and a tin pan. You may want to also include a variety of different colored metallic paper that reflects light.

Preparation

Make sure all flashlights have batteries and give off a strong light. If the light is too dim, children will have a difficult time observing reflections.

Activity

As a class, view the video. Then, discuss the question that will need to be answered. Have children record the question.

STEP 1 Have children write their plan as a numbered list of steps that they will do. You may also suggest that children look at the materials they have to help them come up with a plan.

STEP 2 Children should follow their plan to do a test. Remind children that observations can be made with words, drawings, or both. **Ask: What do you observe about each shiny surface when you shine the light on it? The light reflects off the surface and bounces back.**

Hands-On Activity, continued

 Cause and Effect . . . .

STEP 3 Remind children that a cause is why something happens. Allow children to explain what caused the beam of light to behave the way it did. **Ask: How did the material that was placed in the beam of light affect the light?** The material caused the beam of light to move in a new direction.

Claims, Evidence, and Reasoning

Children should make a claim that shows their understanding that the object's type of material determines if light will reflect off the object. **Ask: What properties do all the objects you tested have in common?** They are all shiny and smooth.

	Scoring Rubric for Hands-On Activity
3	States a claim supported with evidence about the effect of light reflecting off objects that are shiny and smooth
2	States a claim somewhat supported with evidence about the effect of light reflecting off objects that are shiny and smooth
1	States a claim that is not supported by evidence
0	Does not state a claim and does not provide evidence

Step ③

Explain what happened to the beam of light. Identify cause and effect.

Cause	**Effect**
Children should write or draw to show a cause. Sample answer: A shiny surface was placed in the path of a beam of light.	Children should write or draw to show an effect. Sample answer: The light moved in a new direction when it hit the surface.

Make a claim that answers your question.

What is your evidence?

Sample answer: Light reflects when it hits a smooth, shiny surface.	Sample answer: I placed a smooth, shiny surface in the path of a beam of light. I saw the light reflect when it hit the surface.

122

© Houghton Mifflin Harcourt

Do the Math! • A beam of light travels 5 feet. A mirror reflects it. The light travels 6 feet more. Then it bounces off a metal door and travels 2 feet more. How many feet does the light travel in all?

 Solve Word Problems Go to the online handbook for tips.

Ⓐ 11 feet

Ⓑ 13 feet

Ⓒ 15 feet

✋ Apply What You Know

Evidence Notebook • Can you reflect light so it hits a spot you want? Work with a partner. Use a flashlight and three small mirrors to do a test. Then talk with your classmates. Collect evidence. Write and draw in your Evidence Notebook. Use evidence to explain if your test worked.

 Planning and Carrying Out Investigations Go to the online handbook for tips.

Do the Math! • Solve Word Problems

Children should choose B—13 feet. If children choose A, they are adding only the first two addends. If they choose C, they have mistakenly added the addend 2 twice. Suggest they use counters to model each part of the word problem to find the correct answer.

💡 **Solve Word Problems** Remind children to read word problems carefully to help them choose the correct operation to solve the problem.

✋ FORMATIVE ASSESSMENT

Evidence Notebook

Children work with a partner as they explore how to reflect light so it hits a certain spot. They will do a test and collect evidence.

Scoring Guidelines

• uses the flashlight and three mirrors to reflect light on a certain spot

• provides sufficient evidence to explain if their test worked

💡 **Planning and Carrying Out Investigations** Doing an investigation is a way for children to study something carefully. They should collect facts from the investigation to see if light can be reflected to hit a certain spot.

Communicate with Light

3D Learning Objective

Children explore how **people use technology to communicate with light over distances.** They design a simple way to send a message with light.

(DCI) Information Technologies and Instrumentation . . . .

Draw children's attention to the traffic light. **Ask: How does a driver know when to go when they look at the light?** when the light turns green **How does a driver know when to stop?** when the light turns red **What does it mean when the light turns yellow?** It warns a driver to slow down.

Have children discuss other ways lights communicate information to drivers. **Ask: What would you expect drivers to do if a fire truck with its lights on was coming down the street?** I would expect that drivers would move to the side so the fire truck could safely drive through traffic.

(CCC) Influence of Engineering, Technology, and Science on Society and the Natural World. . . .

Explain to children that before traffic lights were invented, traffic police would direct traffic. **Ask: What do think is better about having lights direct traffic instead of having people direct traffic?** Sample answer: It is probably safer for lights to direct traffic than for people to direct traffic. Traffic lights can work all day and all night, but people can't work this long.

Communicate with Light

Explore online. ▶

A traffic light communicates with colored lights. Green means go. Red says stop!

Flashing police lights communicate that the police car is moving fast.

124

Connection to Engineering and Design

Defining and Delimiting Engineering Problems
Discuss with children that each of the solutions they see on these pages were made because people saw problems they wanted to solve. **Ask: Why do you think people started building lighthouses? What problem did they see?** Sample answer: People started building lighthouses because they saw that boats were getting lost or crashing. They wanted to make something that would help boats find their way.

Collaboration

Small Groups Some children may not know how lighthouses work or the purpose of lighthouses. Research in small groups the history of how lights in lighthouses have been used to communicate messages. Note how lighthouses are used and how they have changed over the years. Children can make a "how-to" book to share their research. Suggest that children also choose one lighthouse for the cover of their book.

The light from a lighthouse helps boats find their way. It also warns them of danger.

People can use light to communicate.
Different lights send different messages.

© Houghton Mifflin Harcourt • Image Credits: ©Smithore/Creatas Video+/Getty Images Plus/Getty Images

Information Technologies and Instrumentation . . . .

Children should circle the fire truck and the lighthouse—If children circle the lamp, remind them that a lamp does give off light, but it doesn't communicate a message.

 Circle the pictures that show ways to communicate with light.

FORMATIVE ASSESSMENT

Children work with a partner or small group to plan and test a way to send a message with light. They use evidence to explain how they know the message was understood. If needed, they will redesign their plan and retest.

Scoring Guidelines
- describes the plan
- uses appropriate materials to test sending a message with light
- redesigns the plan if necessary
- provides sufficient evidence to support that the message was understood

💡 **Planning and Carrying Out Investigations** Children should work with others to make a plan for their design.

💡 **Constructing Explanations and Designing Solutions** Children should collect facts from the investigation to decide if the message is understood.

Apply What You Know

Work with a partner or small group. Find a way to send a message with light. Make a plan. Gather materials. Test your plan. How will you know your message is understood? Redesign your plan. Make any needed changes and test it again.

Planning and Carrying Out Investigations • Constructing Explanations and Designing Solutions Go to the online handbook for tips.

126

© Houghton Mifflin Harcourt • Image Credits: (l) ©slobo/E+/Getty Images; (c) ©Narvikk/Vetta/Getty Images; (r) ©Dvougao/iStock/Getty Images

Explore online. ▶ Guide children to the Interactive Online Student Edition where they can choose from and explore both paths.

Take It Further

Careers in Science & Engineering • Camera Engineer

Explore more online.
Art with Light

Explore online. ▶

camera engineer

What do camera engineers do? They help design and build cameras for photos, movies, and videos. They may make large cameras for movies. They may make small cameras that go inside cell phones.

movie camera

cell phone camera

Lesson 3 • How Does Light Travel?   127

Take It Further

Careers in Science & Engineering • Camera Engineer

Camera engineers design and build cameras to meet the needs of customers. They might build a camera for a movie, a new phone, or even a camera that attaches to a racing car! Camera engineers need to know how light behaves and how it reacts with materials in order to design cameras.

DCI **Information Technologies and Instrumentation** . . . .

Tell children that camera engineers need to know about how light travels when they are designing cameras. They need to know how light will react with the materials they use to build cameras. Prompt children to think about the lenses in cameras. **Ask: Do you think a material such as wood or cardboard would be a good material to use for a lens? Why or why not?** Sample answer: No, wood or cardboard would not be good materials for a lens because light does not pass through them. You would not be able to see through the lens.

Collaboration

Small Groups You may choose to show children a few photographs of different objects and settings. Have children discuss in small groups what each photograph communicates to them. Then have them decide the light source used in each photograph. Have groups compare observations.

Take It Further, continued

Read, Write, Share! • Participate in a Writing Project • Participate in Discussions

Children will write two questions they would like to ask a camera engineer. Suggest to children that one of their questions include something they want to know about how a camera engineer uses information about light.

💡 **Participate in a Writing Project** Children should work with their partner to brainstorm questions. Have partners read the questions to each other to make sure they make sense.

💡 **Participate in Discussions** Remind children that talking with others is one way to learn more. Asking questions is also a way to find out about a person and what they do.

Collaboration

Think, Write, Pair, Share! Children should brainstorm and write their questions together. They should check their questions before they begin researching. Children should share their questions and research with others and discuss any new questions they have.

Explore more online. ▶

Art with Light

Children use aluminum foil and other objects that reflect light to make art projects that incorporate reflected light.

Read, Write, Share! •
What would you like to ask a camera engineer? Write at least two questions. Work with a partner to research answers to your questions. Write about what you found. Share what you learned with others.

💡 **Participate in a Writing Project • Participate in Discussions**
Go to the online handbook for tips.

© Houghton Mifflin Harcourt • Image Credits: ©Huchen Lu/E+/Getty Images

128

Lesson Check

Name _____

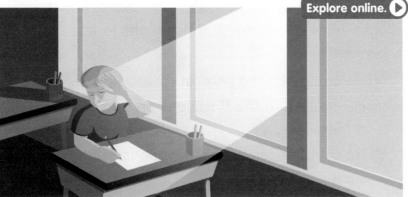

Explore online. ▶

Can You Solve It?

✏️ How could you point light away from your eyes?

Be sure to

• Explain what kind of surface can point light
  in a new direction.

• Describe how the surface points light
  in a new direction.

Sample answer: I could use a mirror to point light away from

my eyes. Mirrors have smooth, shiny surfaces that reflect

light. I could turn the mirror to bounce the light in the direction

I want.

© Houghton Mifflin Harcourt

Lesson Check

Can You Solve It?

Have children reread their answers to the Can You Solve It? prompt at the beginning of the lesson.

DCI **Electromagnetic Radiation** . . . .

Have children think about what they explored about how light travels and what causes light to be redirected. **Ask: What kind of surfaces can point light in a new direction?** Sample answer: smooth shiny surfaces such as tin foil and mirrors

SEP **Constructing Explanations and Designing Solutions** . . . .

Encourage children to think about how they could use something such as tin foil or mirrors to redirect a light beam. Remind children to construct their explanations by using evidence to formulate their answers.

Scoring Guidelines

• Children should explain what kind of surfaces reflect light.
• Children should describe how light can be pointed in a new direction.
• Children should effectively explain how to use a smooth, shiny surface to point the light away from their eyes.

Lesson Check, continued

SUMMATIVE ASSESSMENT
Self Check

1. Children should choose C—He could observe what happens when light shines at a mirror. If children choose A, remind them that a wood door may be smooth, but it is not shiny. If children choose B, direct them back to the question and what it is asking. The question asks about how to test a statement about reflection, not how to communicate with light.

2. Children should connect the shirt to Light is taken in.; the window to Light passes through.; and the mirror to Light reflects. If children have difficulty matching the pictures to the correct sentences, suggest that they first think of what object light can pass through. Then suggest that they next work on identifying the object that takes in light. Now they can confirm that the mirror reflects light.

Self Check

1. Ted thinks that smooth, shiny surfaces reflect light. How could he use a flashlight to test his idea?

Ⓐ He could aim the light at a wood door.

Ⓑ He could turn the flashlight on and off to send a message.

Ⓒ He could observe what happens when light shines at a mirror.

2. How does light act when it hits each material? Draw a line to match each picture to the words that tell what happens when light hits it.

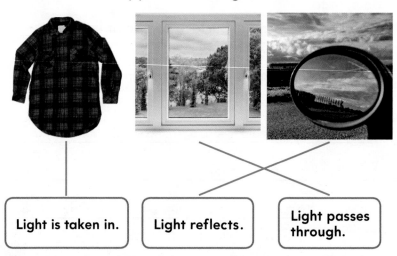

Light is taken in.   Light reflects.   Light passes through.

130

3. Anna builds a tool that uses light to communicate. How does Anna know if the tool works?

(A) Anna can send a message and find out if someone understands it.

(B) Anna can observe if light comes out of the tool.

(C) Anna can plan a message to send using her tool.

4. What happens to light when it hits a smooth, shiny piece of foil?

(A) It will be taken in.

(B) It will pass through.

(C) It will be reflected.

5. Circle all the pictures that show ways to communicate with light over distances.

© Houghton Mifflin Harcourt • Image Credits: (l) ©Kaitlyn Eckart/EyeEm/Getty Images; (c) ©Filipe Frazao/Shutterstock; (r) ©Pat LaCroix/The Image Bank/Getty Images

Lesson 3 • How Does Light Travel?   131

3. Children should choose A—Anna can send a message and find out if someone understands it. If children choose B, remind them that Anna is trying to communicate with her device, not to see if the device works. If children choose C, have them reread the question. It says that Anna wants to know if the tool works. Making a plan would not tell Anna if the tool works.

4. Children should choose C—It will be reflected. If children choose A or B, have them review what happens when light hits a shiny surface.

5. Children should circle the traffic light and the ambulance. If children have difficulty with this question, have them discuss whether the light in each picture sends a message.

Unit 3 Performance Task

Observe Reflections

👥 pairs   ⏱ 1 class period

Objective

Children observe reflections in a mirror and **use their observations to predict** where their partner should stand in order to be visible in the mirror. Children will **observe the cause-and-effect relationship** between where they stand and whether they are visible in the mirror.

Suggested Materials

mirror, masking tape, paper

Preparation

Assemble material bundles for children.

SEP **Planning and Carrying Out Investigations . . . .**

Ask: How can you and your partner find out where to stand in order to be seen in the mirror? Sample answer: We can make a plan and then investigate. We could make predictions about where to stand and then try them out.

STEPS

Step 1

DCI **Electromagnetic Radiation . . . .**

Ask: Could we perform this investigation in the dark? Why or why not? Sample answer: No, because there wouldn't be enough light to bounce off our faces.

Step 2

CCC **Cause and Effect . . . .**

Ask: Would you see the same parts of the room if you moved a step to the left or to the right? Why? Sample answer: No, because different objects would reflect light to the mirror.

 Unit 3 Performance Task
Observe Reflections

Materials
- mirror
- masking tape
- paper

STEPS

Step 1

Attach the mirror to the wall. Look into the mirror. You see your reflection because light bounces off your face.

Step 2

Stand to the side and look in the mirror. What parts of the room do you see? Write or draw your observations.

Step 3

Work with a partner to cover the mirror. Think about where you each need to stand to see each other in the mirror. Mark those places with tape.

© Houghton Mifflin Harcourt

132

Step 4

Take the paper off the mirror. Then stand on the tape. Can you see your partner? If not, try again. Write or draw to record your observations.

Step 5

Compare your results with others. Talk about how light traveled from your face and bounced off the mirror so your partner could see it.

✅ Check

_____ I observed my reflection in the mirror.
_____ I worked with a partner to guess where to stand.
_____ I recorded my observations.
_____ I compared my results with others.

© Houghton Mifflin Harcourt

Step 3

Ask: Why did you choose to stand there? Sample answer: I saw the bookcase in the reflection, so I stood in front of the bookcase.

Step 4

 Constructing Explanations and Designing Solutions . . . .

Ask: Why didn't you see your reflection the first time? The light reflecting from my face did not travel to the mirror. **Ask:** How did you use the results of your first try to help you decide where to stand for your second try? Sample answer: I saw the reflection of the bookcase next to me, so on the second try I moved in front of the bookcase.

Step 5

 Constructing Explanations and Designing Solutions . . . .

Discuss children's results as a class. **Ask: How do you think your reflection in the mirror would change as you moved farther from the wall in Step 2?** Sample answer: I would see more of the room in the reflection. **Ask: How would this affect your results in Steps 3 and 4?** Sample answer: There would be more places my partner could stand and still be in the reflection.

Scoring Rubric for Performance Task	
3	Records observations of reflection, and works with a partner to predict where to stand, recording the results. Compares results with others.
2	Works with a partner to predict where to stand and records the results. Compares results with others. Does not record observations of reflection.
1	Works with a partner to predict where to stand, but does not record observations or results. Does not compare results with others.
0	Does not observe, predict, or record results.

Unit 3 Review

1. Children should choose A—a room with bright light. If children choose B or C, reinforce that you can see objects if a light shines on them, and a bright light would shine on more objects. By completing Different Amounts of Light! in Lesson 1, children explored how the amount of light affects how much you can see.

2. Children should choose B—Fireworks give off their own light. If children choose A, reinforce that a dark sky would not provide light that would let you see the fireworks. If children choose C, explain that fireworks are explosions in the air. By completing See in the Dark in Lesson 1, children learned that you can see an object in the dark if you shine light on it, or if it gives off its own light.

3. Children should choose A—turn on more lamps. If children choose B or C, reinforce that you can see objects if a light shines on them, and turning off all lamps or making the light lower would provide less light. By completing Different Amounts of Light! in Lesson 1, children explored how the amount of light affects how much you can see.

Unit 3 Review

Name _____

1. In which room could you see the most objects?
   Ⓐ a room with bright light
   Ⓑ a room with some light
   Ⓒ a room with low light

---

2. Why can you see fireworks in the night sky?
   Ⓐ The sky around the fireworks is dark.
   Ⓑ Fireworks give off their own light.
   Ⓒ Light shines on the fireworks.

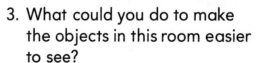

---

3. What could you do to make the objects in this room easier to see?
   Ⓐ turn on more lamps
   Ⓑ turn off all lamps
   Ⓒ make the light lower

134

4. Draw a line to match each window to the label that tells how much light can pass through it.

No light passes through.	All light passes through.	Some light passes through.

5. What causes a shadow?
   Ⓐ An object blocks light.
   Ⓑ An object gives off its own light.
   Ⓒ Light shines on an object.

6. You walk by a lamp and make a shadow on the wall. You want the shadow to be bigger. What should you do?
   Ⓐ Walk closer to the lamp.
   Ⓑ Step away from the lamp.
   Ⓒ Jump up and down in the same spot.

© Houghton Mifflin Harcourt

4. Children should connect the first window to All light passes through; the second window to Some light passes through; and the third window to No light passes through. If children answer incorrectly, discuss how the pictures show different amounts of light passing through each window. By completing How Much Light? and the Hands-On Activity Test How Light Passes Through Materials in Lesson 2, children explored how different amount of light can pass through different materials.

5. Children should choose A—An object blocks light. If children choose B or C, reinforce light is energy that lets you see, and you can see objects that give off their own light or have light shining on them. By completing Shadows in Lesson 2, children explored how shadows are formed when an object blocks light.

6. Children should choose A—Walk closer to the lamp. If children choose B or C, perform a demonstration by casting a shadow on a child as the child moves toward and away from the light and jumps up and down. By completing Big Shadow, Little Shadow in Lesson 2, children explored how the size of a shadow changes when the light shining on the object moves.

7. Children should choose B—Light travels in a straight line until it hits an object; and C—Light can reflect off an object. If children choose A, reinforce that light cannot move around objects by helping children connect this concept with shadows. By completing In the Way in Lesson 3, children explored the possible results when light hits an object.

8. Children should choose A—a piece of foil; and C—a mirror. If children choose B, have them describe the properties of a wooden spoon and reinforce that smooth and shiny surfaces can reflect light. By completing What Reflects Light? in Lesson 3, children learned that *reflect* means to bounce back.

9. Children should choose C—The light will reflect off the spoon. If children choose A or B, reinforce that smooth and shiny surfaces can reflect light. By completing What Reflects Light? in Lesson 3, children learned that *reflect* means to bounce back.

10. Children should choose A—They use light to warn about danger; and C—They use light to tell people to stop their cars. If children choose B, have them reread the question. If children choose A or C, but not both, discuss the types of lights used for each purpose. By completing Communicate with Light in Lesson 3, children explored how people can use light to communicate.

3D Item Analysis	1	2	3	4	5	6	7	8	9	10
SEP Planning and Carrying Out Investigations									•	
SEP Constructing Explanations and Designing Solutions						•				
DCI Electromagnetic Radiation	•	•	•	•	•	•	•	•	•	•
DCI Information Technologies and Instrumentation										•
CCC Cause and Effect	•	•	•	•	•	•			•	•

7. Which sentences are true about the way light travels? Choose all correct answers.
   Ⓐ Light can move around objects.
   Ⓑ Light travels in a straight line until it hits an object.
   Ⓒ Light can reflect off an object.

8. Which objects could you use to reflect light?
   Ⓐ a piece of foil
   Ⓑ a wooden spoon
   Ⓒ a mirror

9. Brad tests what happens when he places a metal spoon in the path of a beam of light. What will he most likely see?
   Ⓐ The light will pass through the spoon.
   Ⓑ The spoon will take in all the light.
   Ⓒ The light will reflect off the spoon.

10. How do people use light to communicate over distances?
    Ⓐ They use light to warn about danger.
    Ⓑ They use light to brighten a room.
    Ⓒ They use light to tell people to stop their cars.

136

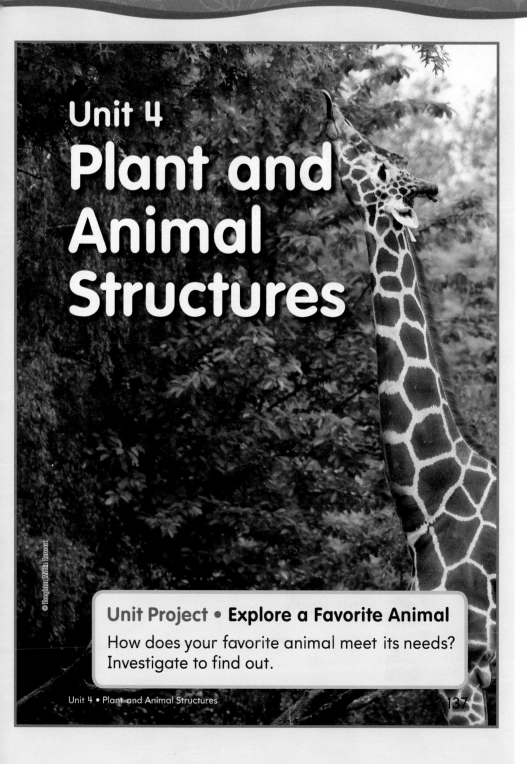

Unit 4
Plant and Animal Structures

© Houghton Mifflin Harcourt

Unit Project • Explore a Favorite Animal

How does your favorite animal meet its needs? Investigate to find out.

Unit 4 • Plant and Animal Structures

137

Unit 4 • Plant and Animal Structures

Unit Overview

In this unit, children will…

- describe how parts of a plant help it to survive and grow.
- explain how parts of an animal help it to survive and grow.
- relate the shape and stability of structures to their function(s).
- use evidence to describe how plants and animals process and respond to information.
- describe how human-made products are designed by applying knowledge of the natural world.
- use observations to design a solution to a human problem by mimicking how plants use their parts to survive.

About This Image

Guide children in a discussion about the picture on this page. **Ask: What kind of animal is this? What is it doing?** A giraffe is reaching up to eat leaves from a tree. **Ask: Which body parts help the giraffe get food?** long neck and tongue **Do you think a long neck can help a giraffe stay safe? How?** A long neck lets the giraffe see far away. They can run away when they see danger coming.

Unit Project • Explore a Favorite Animal

Have children plan and conduct an investigation about an animal they like. Discuss what the investigation should include. Have children brainstorm questions that should be answered, such as: "What does my animal need to live?" and "What are important traits for my animal to have?"

To begin, share details about an animal you have researched. Include traits that help explain how the animal meets its needs. More support for the Unit Project can be found on pp. 139K–139N.

Unit 4 At a Glance

The learning experiences in this unit prepare children for mastery of:

Performance Expectation

1-LS1-1 Use materials to design a solution to a human problem by mimicking how plants and/or animals use their external parts to help them survive, grow, and meet their needs.

Explore online. ▶

In addition to the print resources, the following resources are available online to support this unit:

Unit Pretest

Lesson 1 Engineer It • What Parts Help Plants Live?
- Interactive Online Student Edition
- Lesson Quiz

Lesson 2 Engineer It • What Body Parts Help Animals Stay Safe?
- Interactive Online Student Edition
- Lesson Quiz

You Solve It Build a Safety Helmet

Lesson 3 Engineer It • What Body Parts Help Animals Meet Their Needs?
- Interactive Online Student Edition
- Lesson Quiz

Lesson 4 How Do Plants and Animals Respond to Their Environment?
- Interactive Online Student Edition
- Lesson Quiz

Unit Performance Task

Unit Test

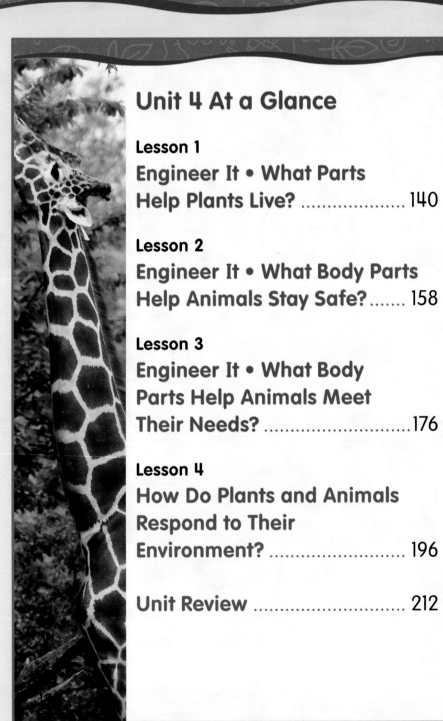

© Houghton Mifflin Harcourt

Unit Vocabulary

mimic to copy (p. 147)

gills body parts that take in oxygen from water (p. 183)

lungs body parts that take in air (p. 183)

adaptation something that helps a living thing survive in its environment (p. 198)

environment all the living and nonliving things in a place (p. 198)

Vocabulary Game • Make a Match

Materials
- 1 set of word cards
- 1 set of definition cards

How to Play
1. Work with your partner to make word and definition cards.
2. Place the cards face up on the table.
3. Pick a word card, read the word, and match it to a definition.
4. If you make a match, keep the cards and play again.
5. If not, your partner takes a turn.

©Houghton Mifflin Harcourt

Unit Vocabulary

The Next Generation Science Standards emphasize explanation and demonstration of understanding versus rote memorization of science vocabulary words. Keep in mind that these vocabulary words are tools for clear communication. Use these words as a starting point, not an end goal, for children to build deeper understanding of science concepts.

Children can explore all vocabulary words in the **Online Glossary**.

Vocabulary Strategies

- Have children review the vocabulary words. Then have children work in pairs to share an example of each word and explain why they think it's an example. Have pairs record their examples to refer back to during the unit.
- Have children think about how each word relates to plants or animals. Have children work in pairs and share their ideas with a partner.

Differentiate Instruction

RTI/Extra Support Pronounce each word, and have children repeat it after you. Have children find each highlighted word within the unit content. Have children work in pairs and explain to a partner what they think each word means based on the surrounding context of imagery and text.

Extension Have children select two vocabulary words and work in small groups to illustrate and explain the words to a kindergarten child.

Vocabulary Game • Make a Match

Preparation Assemble vocabulary game cards. Assign children to pairs. The player with the most matches wins. Establish a time limit or a set number of rounds for the game.

Integrating the NGSS* Three Dimensions of Learning

Building to the Performance Expectations

The learning experiences in this unit prepare children for mastery of the following Performance Expectations:

From Molecules to Organisms: Structures and Processes

1-LS1-1 Use materials to design a solution to a human problem by mimicking how plants and/or animals use their external parts to help them survive, grow, and meet their needs.

Assessing Student Progress

After completing the lessons, the **Unit Project** Explore a Favorite **Animal** provides children with opportunities to practice aspects of and to demonstrate their understanding of the Performance Expectations as they plan and conduct an investigation about an animal they like.

Additionally, children can further practice or be assessed on aspects of the Performance Expectations by completing the **Unit Performance Task** Design a House, in which children define a problem and design a solution by applying the structure and function of the parts of water plants.

Lesson 1
Engineer It • What Parts Help Plants Live?

In Lesson 1, children explore how the external parts of plants allow them to survive and grow (DCI Structure and Function). Children will explore how people design solutions by mimicking how plant parts function (CCC Influence of Engineering andTechnology...). Finally, children will build a solution to a human problem (DCI Defining and Delimiting...) (SEP Asking Questions and Defining Problems).

Lesson 2
Engineer It • What Body Parts Help Animals Stay Safe?

In Lesson 2, children mimic animal parts to construct a solution to a human problem (SEP Constructing Explanations and Designing Solutions) (DCI Optimizing the Design Solution). Children explore how the structure of animal parts is related to their function (CCC Structure and Function).

Lesson 3
Engineer It • What Body Parts Help Animals Meet Their Needs?

In Lesson 3, children will explore how the body parts of animals allow them to meet their needs (CCC Structure and Function). Children will explore how people design solutions to problems by mimicking animal parts (CCC Influence of Engineering and Technology...). Finally, children mimic animal body parts and function to build a solution. (DCI Defining and Delimiting...) (SEP Analyzing and Interpreting Data).

Lesson 4
How Do Plants and Animals Respond to Their Environment?

In Lesson 4, children will explore how plants and animals respond to their environments (CCC Cause and Effect), carry out an investigation about the effects of light on plant growth (SEP Constructing Explanations and Designing Solutions), and explore how animal senses help them process information (DCI Information Processing).

Standards Supported by This Unit

▶ Explore online.
Online only.

Next Generation Science Standards	Unit Project	Lesson 1	Lesson 2	Lesson 3	Lesson 4	Unit Performance Task	You Solve It
SEP Constructing Explanations and Designing Solutions	•	•	•	•	•	•	•
SEP Asking Questions and Defining Problems		•				•	
SEP Developing and Using Models			•		•	•	
SEP Analyzing and Interpreting Data				•		•	
DCI LS1.A Structure and Function	•	•	•	•	•	•	•
DCI ETS1.A Defining and Delimiting Engineering Problems		•	•	•		•	
DCI ETS1.C Optimizing the Design Solution		•				•	
DCI LS1.D Information Processing					•	•	
CCC Structure and Function	•	•	•	•		•	•
CCC Cause and Effect					•	•	
CCC Influence of Engineering, Technology, and Science on Society and the Natural World		•	•	•		•	

NGSS* Across the Grades

Before	**Grade 1**	**After**
From Molecules to Organisms: Structures and Processes	**From Molecules to Organisms: Structures and Processes**	**From Molecules to Organisms: Structures and Processes**
K-LS1-1 Use observations to describe patterns of what plants and animals (including humans) need to survive.	**1-LS1-1**	**4-LS1-1.** Construct an argument that plants and animals have internal and external structures that function to support survival, growth, behavior and reproduction.

 **Trace Tool to the NGSS™** Go online to view the complete coverage of these standards across this grade level and time.

3D Unit Planning

Lesson 1 Engineer It • What Parts Help Plants Live? pp. 140–157

Overview

Objective Design a solution to a human problem by mimicking how plants use their parts to survive and grow.

SEP Constructing Explanations and Designing Solutions
SEP Asking Questions and Defining Problems
DCI **LS1.A** Structure and Function
DCI **ETS1.A** Defining and Delimiting Engineering Problems
CCC Structure and Function
CCC Influence of Engineering, Technology, and Science on Society and the Natural World

Math and **English Language Arts** standards and features are detailed on lesson planning pages.

Print and Online Student Editions	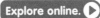 Explore online.
ENGAGE	**Lesson Problem** pp. 140–141 **Can You Solve It?** How did the maple seed give people ideas to make the helicopter blades?	▶ **Can You Solve It?** Video
EXPLORE/ EXPLAIN	**Plant Parts** **Shape Up** **Looking to Nature** **Plants Give Ideas**	**Hands-On** Worksheet
	Hands-On Activity Engineer It • Use Ideas from Plants to Design a Solution pp. 151–152	
ELABORATE	**Take It Further** pp. 153–154 People in Science & Engineering • Janine Benyus	**Take It Further** Plants We Eat
EVALUATE	**Lesson Check** p. 155 **Self Check** pp. 156–157	**Lesson Quiz**

Hands-On Activity Planning

Engineer It • Use Ideas from Plants to Design a Solution

Objective Children will use an idea from a plant to design and build something that would help keep them cool on hot days. They will use a design process to solve their problem.

👥 small groups

🕐 1 class period

Suggested Materials
• craft materials

Preparation/Tip

This activity can be an extension from the Apply What You Know exercise in the Plants Give Ideas section of the lesson. Children can look at the plant pictures in the Plants Give Ideas section or at pictures of plants for ideas.

Overview

Objective Design a solution to a human problem by mimicking how animals use parts of their body for protection.

SEP Constructing Explanations and Designing Solutions
SEP Developing and Using Models
DCI **LS1.A** Structure and Function
DCI **ETS1.A** Defining and Delimiting Engineering Problems
DCI **ETS1.C** Optimizing the Design Solution
CCC Structure and Function
CCC Influence of Engineering, Technology, and Science on Society and the Natural World

Math and **English Language Arts** standards and features are detailed on lesson planning pages.

	Print and Online Student Editions	Explore online.
ENGAGE	**Lesson Problem** pp. 158–159 **Can You Solve It?** What ideas can you get from a hedgehog to keep something safe?	▶ **Can You Solve It?** Video
EXPLORE/ EXPLAIN	**Moving Away from Danger** **Hiding from Danger** **Facing Danger** **Staying Safe in Weather** **Animals as Models** **Hands-On Activity Engineer It •** Design a Shoe pp. 169–170	**Hands-On** Worksheet **You Solve It** Build a Safety Helmet
ELABORATE	**Take It Further** pp. 171–172 Careers in Science & Engineering • Bioengineer	**Take It Further** New Body Parts for Animals
EVALUATE	**Lesson Check** p. 173 **Self Check** pp. 174–175	**Lesson Quiz**

 ## Hands-On Activity Planning

Engineer It • Design a Shoe

Objective Children identify a problem related to keeping feet safe and use ideas about animals body parts to develop a solution to the problem.

👥 small groups
🕐 1 class period

Suggested Materials
- ice
- scissors
- craft materials

Preparation/Tip
Gather a variety of craft materials and clean recyclable items that children may want to use in their shoe design.

3D Unit Planning, continued
Lesson 3 Engineer It • What Body Parts Help Animals Meet Their Needs?
pp. 176–195

Overview

Objective Design a solution to a human problem by mimicking how animals use their body parts to meet their needs.

SEP Constructing Explanations and Designing Solutions
SEP Analyzing and Interpreting Data
DCI **LS1.A** Structure and Function
DCI **ETS1.A** Defining and Delimiting Engineering Problems
CCC Structure and Function
CCC Influence of Engineering, Technology, and Science on Society and the Natural World

Math and **English Language Arts** standards and features are detailed on lesson planning pages.

	Print and Online Student Editions	Explore online. ▶
ENGAGE	**Lesson Problem** pp. 176–177 **Can You Solve It?** How can you get an idea from the giraffe to make a tool that reaches high places?	▶ **Can You Solve It?** Video
EXPLORE/ EXPLAIN	**Parts to Find Food** **Parts to Eat Food** **Parts to Breathe** **Parts to Take in Water** **Animals as Models** **Hands-On Activity Engineer It •** Use Ideas from Animals pp. 189–190	**Hands-On** Worksheet
ELABORATE	**Take It Further** pp. 191–192 Animals Can Use Tools!	**Take It Further** Hear Like a Bat
EVALUATE	**Lesson Check** p. 193 **Self Check** pp. 194–195	**Lesson Quiz**

Hands-On Activity Planning

Engineer It • Use Ideas from Animals

Objective Children will use an idea from an animal to design and build a tool that would help them pick up food. They will use the design process to solve their problem. Children will share their tool with a partner and talk about how it solves the problem.

Suggested Materials
- animal books
- craft materials

👥 small groups
🕐 1 class period

Preparation/Tip

Preassemble material bundles for groups. Children will need a variety of sources that show and describe different animals. Alternatively, children may do this activity as a whole class if materials are limited.

Lesson 4 How Do Plants and Animals Respond to Their Environment?

pp. 196–211

Overview

Objective Make observations to describe how behaviors of living things help them grow and survive.

SEP Constructing Explanations and Designing Solutions
DCI **LS1.D** Information Processing
CCC Cause and Effect

Math and **English Language Arts** standards and features are detailed on lesson planning pages.

	Print and Online **Student Editions**	Explore online.
ENGAGE	**Lesson Phenomenon** pp. 196–197 **Can You Explain It?** Why are the trees growing in unusual ways?	▶ Can You Explain It? Images
EXPLORE/ EXPLAIN	**Plant Places** **Plants and Seasons** **Animals Use Senses** **Animals on the Move** **Animals and Seasons** ⊙ **Hands-On Activity** Change How a Plant Grows pp. 199–200	**Hands-On** Worksheet
ELABORATE	**Take It Further** pp. 207–208 Careers in Science & Engineering • Forest Ranger	**Take It Further** Insects in Winter
EVALUATE	**Lesson Check** p. 209 **Self Check** pp. 210–211	**Lesson Quiz**

Hands-On Activity Planning

Change How a Plant Grows

Objective Children make observations from an investigation to construct an evidence-based account for a plant's growth pattern.

👫 pairs
⏱ 1 class period plus 10 minutes each day for 2 weeks

Suggested Materials
- a shoebox
- a bean plant
- scissors
- cup of water

Preparation/Tip
Provide bean plants, or other fast-growing seedlings, or plant seeds 10 days or more in advance to provide seedlings of an appropriate size. Have the shoeboxes cut in advance. Make sure the hole is about three inches in circumference. Allow children time to observe and water the plant each day for 2 weeks.

3D Unit Planning, continued

You Solve It Go online for an additional interactive opportunity.

Build a Safety Helmet

This virtual lab offers practice in support of **1-LS1-1.**

SEP Constructing Explanations and Designing Solutions

DCI **LS1.A** Structure and Function

CCC Structure and Function

3D Learning Objectives
- Children explore the structure and function of a variety of materials.
- Children use a design process to create helmets for the construction workers.

Activity Problem
- You will first explore the different tools that construction workers use and how they mimic certain animals.
- You will then use your understanding of how animals use different parts to protect themselves to design protective helmets for the construction workers.
- Lastly, you will use a desgin process to determine if your helmet is safe to use by the construction workers.

Interaction Summary
- When given tools/materials inspired by different animals children will choose the correct material, shape, and strap/no strap to make the safest helmet for the workers.
- Children will test the helmet to see if their helmet is safe for the workers to use.
- Children will successfully explain that engineering design is often inspired by animal structures and behavior. They will give examples of technologies or structures around the airport that have been inspired by animals.
- After the experiment, children will be able to connect different animals to the technologies that they have inspired.

Assessment

Pre-Assessment
Assessment Guide, Unit Pretest

The Unit Pretest focuses on prerequisite knowledge and is composed of items that evaluate children's preparedness for the content covered within this unit.

Formative Assessment
Interactive Worktext, Apply What You Know, Lesson Check, and Self Check

Summative Assessment
Assessment Guide, Lesson Quiz

The Lesson Quiz provides a quick assessment of each lesson objective and of the portion of the Performance Expectation aligned to the lesson.

Interactive Worktext, Performance Task pp. 212–213

The Performance Task presents the opportunity for children to collaborate with classmates in in order to complete the steps of each Performance Task. Each Performance Task provides a formal Scoring Rubric for evaluating children's work.

Interactive Worktext, Unit 4 Review, pp. 214–216
Assessment Guide, Unit Test

The Unit Test provides an in-depth assessment of the Performance Expectations aligned to the unit. This test evaluates children's ability to apply knowledge in order to explain phenomena and to solve problems. Within this test Constructed Response items apply a three-dimensional rubric for evaluating children's mastery on all three dimensions of the Next Generation Science Standards.

Assessment Online Go online to view the complete assessment items for this unit.

Teacher Notes

Differentiate Instruction

Leveled Readers

The Science & Engineering Leveled Readers provide additional nonfiction reading practice in this unit's subject area.

On Level
What Can We Learn About Animals?
What Is a Plant?
These readers reinforce unit concepts and include response activities for your children.

Extra Support
What Can We Learn About Animals?
What Is a Plant?
These readers share titles, illustrations, vocabulary, and concepts with the On-Level Reader; however, these texts are linguistically accommodated to provide simplified sentence structures and comprehension aids. They also include response activities.

Enrichment
Amazing Animals
Weird and Wacky Plants
These high-interest, nonfiction readers will extend and enrich unit concepts, vocabulary and include response activities.

Teacher Guide
The accompanying Teacher Guide provides teaching strategies and support for using all the readers.

All readers are available online as well as in an innovative, engaging format for use with touchscreen mobile devices. Contact your HMH Sales Representative for more information.

ELL

English Language Learner support resources include a glossary and Leveled Readers in Spanish and English. ELL teaching strategies appear throughout this unit:

pp. 140B, 142, 154, 158B, 160, 176B, 178, 188, 190, 196B, 202

RTI/Extra Support

Strategies for children who need extra support appear throughout this unit:

pp. 139, 140B, 143, 149, 150, 158B, 169, 176B, 179, 181, 186, 192, 196B, 205

Extension

Strategies for children who have mastered core content and are ready for additional challenges appear throughout this unit:

pp. 139, 140B, 143, 149, 150, 158B, 169, 176B, 179, 181, 186, 192, 196B, 205

Connecting with NGSS

Connections to Community

Use these opportunities for informal science learning to provide local context and to extend and enhance unit concepts.

At Home

Tools at Home Have children talk with a parent or guardian about a tool they use frequently at home, including what it is made of, what it is used for, and how its design helps it do its job. Invite children to share what they learned about the tools they examined with the class.
Use with Lesson 3.

Animal Journal Encourage children to observe a family pet or birds and squirrels in their local area several times over the course of a day and report on how the animal uses parts of its body to meet its needs. Children could record their observations in a table listing time of day, the body part used, and what it was used for.
Use with Lesson 4.

In the Community

Meet the Plants/Meet the Animals Take a trip to a local zoo, farm, nursery, or pet store, or just around the neighborhood. Encourage children to note each plant's or animal's unique characteristics and speculate about how each characteristic might help that plant or animal survive.
Use with Lesson 1, 2, 3, or 4.

Tools We Use Invite one or more visitors to share with the class the tools they use in their job or their craft, especially those that are similar in some way to the body part of a plant or an animal. For example, a nurse could show children types of bandages (like protective skin) and splints (like a tree trunk), a carpenter could show children files and clamps, and someone who sews could show children needles and thimbles. Encourage children to discuss with the visitor how some of those tools are similar in structure or function to a plant's or an animal's body parts.
Use with Lesson 3.

Collaboration

Collaboration opportunities in this unit:

Build on Prior Knowledge
pp. 141, 159, 177, 179, 182, 197

Partners
p. 208

Small Groups
pp. 147, 184, 191, 204

Think , Pair, Share
pp. 146, 172

Connections to Science

Connections to Science opportunities in this unit:

Connection to Engineering and Design
Lesson 2, p. 166

Connection to Physical Science
Lesson 4, p. 203

Unit Project

Unit Project 👥 small groups 🕐 1 class period

Explore a Favorite Animal

Have children plan and conduct an investigation about an animal they like. Discuss what the investigation should include. Have children brainstorm questions that should be answered, such as: What does my animal need to live? What are important traits for my animal to have?

To begin, share details about an animal you have researched. Include traits that help explain how the animal meets its needs.

3D Learning Objective

SEP Constructing Explanations and Designing Solutions …
Develop questions about how an animal meets its particular needs for survival. Conduct focused research to collect information that will help answer those questions. Construct a claim about how the animal meets its survival needs using evidence from the research.

Skills and Standards Focus

This project supports building children's mastery of **Performance Expectation LS1.A.**

SEP Constructing Explanations and Designing Solutions
DCI **LS1.A** Structure and Function
CCC Structure and Function

Suggested Materials

books and appropriate websites about animals including the characteristics of the environments they live in and how the animals meet their needs in that environment

Preparation

Arrange for a wide selection of books about animals to be available to children as they work on this project. In addition, you could bookmark or help children identify videos online that provide information about the particular animals children are interested in. Plan to allow time for the research and for children to share what they learned with the class.

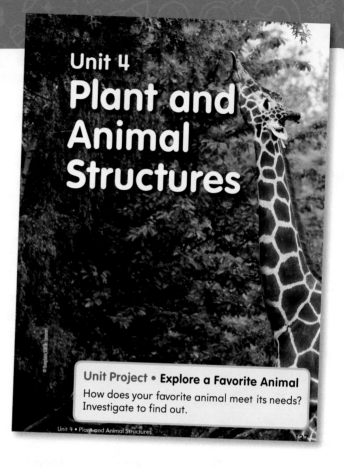

Unit 4
Plant and Animal Structures

Unit Project • Explore a Favorite Animal
How does your favorite animal meet its needs? Investigate to find out.

Unit 4 • Plant and Animal Structures

Differentiate Instruction

RTI/Extra Support Provide books at a variety of reading levels, including several picture books. Guide children to resources and sections of resources that are likely to include information related to the animal they are researching.

Extension Encourage children to identify tools or techniques that people use to stay healthy and safe that are similar to those used by the animal they investigated.

Name _____

Unit 4 Project

Explore a Favorite Animal

What animal is one of your favorites? What helps that animal survive? Write two questions you have about what the animal needs to survive and how it meets its needs. Plan and conduct an investigation to find answers.

Children should write two questions they have bout the animal they

chose and how it meets its particular needs to survive and grow.

_____

Materials

Where could you look for answers to your questions? Make a list.

Children should list possible sources of information, for example, classroom books, the school or public library, the internet, or staff at a local zoo.

Unit 4 Project • Page 1 of 3

Unit 4 Project
Explore a Favorite Animal

SEP **Constructing Explanations and Designing Solutions** . . . .

Pose the unit project question to children. **Ask: What do animals need to survive and grow?** Food, water, warmth, safety, and so on. Tell children that every animal has developed its own way to get the things it needs and to survive. For example, a giraffe has a long neck to help it reach high leaves. **Ask: What other animals do you know of that have special ways to survive?** Sample answer: Birds have wings that help them fly to new places.

In this investigation, children will pose questions about the survival needs of a particular animal and how that animal meets those needs. Then they will conduct research to find answers to their questions. Invite children to suggest questions they have about how different animals obtain food or water or stay safe. **Ask: How do you think you could find answers to your questions?** Sample answer: I could look in books, use the internet, or watch a video.

ESSENTIAL QUESTIONS Prepare children for their project by asking the following questions.

- What helps you stay healthy and grow?
- What helps you stay safe?
- How do you get the things you need to stay healthy and safe?

Ask: How do you think animals get what they need to stay healthy and safe? Sample answer: They need to get them themselves. They use parts of their body to get food and to protect themselves.

Steps

Discuss the value of following steps in a logical order as one way to allow their questions to be answered most accurately.

 Structure and Function . . . .

Ask: What animals can you think of that have specialized body parts? Sample answer: Elephants have long trunks, porcupines have sharp quills, and fish have scales. **How might those body parts help the animal?** A trunk might help an elephant pick up water to drink, quills might help a porcupine scare off an attacker, and scales might help protect a fish's skin from scratches or cuts.

Provide time for children to peruse books, videos, or websites and write and draw to record what they learn. Help them maintain focus by reminding them that they are researching to find information that will help them answer the questions they asked at the beginning of the investigation.

Data

Children should record data that includes information about the animal's specialized body parts.

 Structure and Function . . . .

Remind children that the shape of any object is related to the object's function. **Ask: What is special about the shape or structure one of your animal's body parts? How does that help the animal?** Sample answer: A stork has a really long bill. That helps it grab fish to eat when the fish are swimming in the water. Refer children to Lesson 3 Engineer It • **What Body Parts Help Animals Meet Their Needs?** Have them view the photographs of the bear and the frog and identify what is special about the shape of the bear's claws and the structure of the frog's tongue. **Ask: How do long sharp claws help the bear? How does a sticky tongue help the frog?** Long sharp claws help the bear catch slippery fish, and a sticky tongue helps the frog catch flies.

Steps Write the steps you will do to help you answer your questions.

Answers may vary but should reflect a logical order of steps in the investigation. Sample steps listed:

1. Find books about the animal.

2. Find information in the books.

3. Make notes and draw pictures to record what I learn about how the animal survives.

4. Answer the question and state the evidence I have.

Data
Record your data.

Answers and drawings may vary but should include information about the animal's specialized body parts, for example, ears, nose, fur, or fins, and the roles they play in helping the animal survive and grow.

Analyze Your Result

Look for patterns in your data.

Restate Your Question

Write the questions you investigated.

Answers should identify the questions children initially chose at the

beginning of the investigation.

Claims, Evidence, and Reasoning

Make a claim that answers your question.

Answers should describe how an animal uses its specialized body

parts to help it survive or grow.

Review the data. What evidence from the investigation supports your claim?

Answer should cite evidence from the research to support claims

about how the animal's specialized body parts help it survive.

Discuss your reasoning with a partner.

Unit 4 Project • Page 3 of 3

Analyze Your Result

 Structure and Function . . . .

Have children analyze their data. Encourage them to identify the connection between the structure of each body part and the function of that body part as it relates to the animal's survival.

Claims, Evidence, and Reasoning

Children should understand that all animals have developed special ways to survive and grow. They should use written notes or labeled drawings to explain how each adaptation helps the animal. Since this investigation involves research, encourage children to list the books or videos they consulted and include this list as evidence for their claims.

SEP **Constructing Explanations and Designing Solutions** . . . .

Review with children what it means to make observations. Point out that in this case, children made observations from media, such as books or videos. Guide them to understand that these observations can be used as evidence to support their claim. **Ask: What can you use as evidence from your investigation?** the facts and photographs in the books I looked at

Scoring Rubric for Unit Project	
3	States a claim supported with evidence about how animals use specialized characteristics to help them survive
2	States a claim and somewhat supported with evidence about how animals use specialized characteristics to help them survive
1	States a claim that is not supported by evidence
0	Does not state a claim and does not provide evidence

Engineer It • What Parts Help Plants Live?

Building to the Performance Expectation

The learning experiences in this lesson prepare children for mastery of:

1-LS1-1 Use materials to design a solution to a human problem by mimicking how plants and/or animals use their external parts to help them survive, grow, and meet their needs.

 Trace Tool to the NGSS
Go online to view the complete coverage of these standards across the lesson, unit, and time.

 SEP | **Science & Engineering Practices**

Constructing Explanations and Designing Solutions
Use materials to design a device that solves a specific problem . . .

 VIDEO SEPs: Constructing Explanations and Designing Solutions / Engaging in Argument from Evidence

Asking Questions and Defining Problems
Define a simple problem that can be solved . . .

 VIDEO SEP: Asking Questions and Defining Problems

DCI | **Disciplinary Core Ideas**

LS1.A: Structure and Function
All organisms have external parts. Different animals use their body parts in different ways to see, hear, grasp objects, protect themselves, move from place to place, and seek, find, and take in food, water, and air. Plants also have different parts (roots, stems, leaves, flowers, fruits) that help them survive and grow.

ETS1.A: Defining and Delimiting Engineering Problems
Before beginning to design a solution, it is important to clearly understand the problem.

 CCC | **Crosscutting Concepts**

Structure and Function
The shape and stability of structures of natural and designed objects are related to their function(s).

 VIDEO CCC: Structure and Function

Influence of Engineering, Technology, and Science on Society and the Natural World
Every human-made product is designed by applying some knowledge of the natural world and is built using materials derived from the natural world.

CONNECTION TO MATH

1.MD.C.4 Organize, represent, and interpret data with up to three categories; ask and answer questions about the total number of data points, how many in each category, and how many more or less are in one category than in another.

CONNECTION TO ENGLISH LANGUAGE ARTS

W.1.7 Participate in shared research and writing projects (e.g., explore a number of "how-to" books on a given topic and use them to write a sequence of instructions).

R.1.1 Ask and answer questions about key details in a text.

Supporting All Students, All Standards

Integrating the Three Dimensions of Learning

This lesson focuses on how the external parts of plants allow plants to survive and grow (**DCI Structure and Function**). The lesson begins with children exploring the different parts of plants and continues with children exploring how the structure of each part helps the plant to live (**CCC Structure and Function**). Children will explore how people design solutions to problems by mimicking how plant parts function (**CCC Influence of Engineering, Technology, and Science on Society and the Natural World**). Finally, children will use what they have learned about plant structure and function to design, build, and share a solution to a human problem. (**DCI Defining and Delimiting Engineering Problems**) (**SEPs Asking Questions and Defining Problems / Constructing Explanations and Designing Solutions**).

Professional Development

Go online to view **Professional Development videos** with strategies to integrate CCCs and SEPs, including the ones used in this lesson.

Build on Prior Knowledge

Children should already know and be prepared to build on the following concepts:

- A living thing has parts that help it survive.
- The natural world gives scientists and engineers ideas to help solve problems.

Differentiate Instruction

Lesson Vocabulary

- mimic

Reinforcing Vocabulary To help children remember the vocabulary word, have them take turns mimicking a partner's behavior. Then have them use the word in a sentence. Remind children to look for the highlighted word as they proceed through the lesson.

RTI/Extra Support Supply children with plants for hands-on discovery. Provide examples of different plant parts. Allow children to explore each part. Encourage children to use descriptive words for each part.

Extension Children who want to find out more can do research on plants in different environments. Children should use their data to make a poster that illustrates the parts of a plant in each environment, and how those parts help the plant survive in its environment.

ELL Be sure to point out all labels, pictures, captions, and headings throughout the lesson to assist children with strategies to summarize chunks of content. Discuss with children real-life connections to content, and provide hands-on examples of materials when possible to best support the needs of these learners.

Lesson Problem

Lesson Objective

Design a solution to a human problem by mimicking how plants use their parts to survive and grow.

About This Image

Ask: Have you ever seen a tree like this one? What parts does it have? What do you notice about the trunk? What about the roots? Lead children in a discussion about what parts of the tree help it live and grow.

 Structure and Function

Alternative Engage Strategy

Take a Hike	👥 small groups ⏱ 20–30 minutes

Begin with a discussion about plants. List types of plants that children can find outside in your region. Allow 5 minutes for children to brainstorm and discuss.

Then take children on a walk to a nearby park or other grassy area. Encourage them to look for one of the plants they named. Invite them to draw a picture of the plant and label any parts they know. Remind children not to touch any plants outside unless they know they are safe.

Lesson 1

Engineer It • What Parts Help Plants Live?

This tree has parts that help it live.

By the End of This Lesson
I will know the parts of a plant. I will be able to explain how plants give people ideas to solve problems.

140

© Houghton Mifflin Harcourt • Image Credits

Can You Solve It?

From Seed to Design The natural world can give people
ideas to solve problems. Watch the video to learn more. If the
video is not available, children can use the images on the page.

Ask children to record their initial thoughts about how plants
give people ideas to solve problems. Accept all reasonable
answers. At the end of this lesson, children will revisit this video
as part of the Lesson Check.

Collaboration

Build on Prior Knowledge You may want children to
view and discuss the video as a whole class activity.

*Think about what you saw in the video and plants you see
every day. Have you ever thought about looking at a plant
to get an idea for a design? What human-made objects
are like parts of plants? Use details from the video and
evidence, or facts, to support your answer.*

From Seed to Design

Explore online. ▶

Plants give people ideas to solve problems.

Can You Solve It?

✏️ How did the maple seed give people
ideas to make the helicopter blades?

Accept all reasonable answers.

_____

_____

_____

_____

_____

© Houghton Mifflin Harcourt • Image Credits:

Lesson 1 • Engineer It • What Parts Help Plants Live?   141

Plant Parts

3D Learning Objective

Children will identify parts of flowering plants and construct explanations of how the parts help plants survive, grow, and meet their needs.

DCI Structure and Function . . . .

CCC Structure and Function . . . .

Ask: How do you think thorns protect plants? Thorns are sharp, so it is harder for animals to eat the plant. How do flowers and fruit help plants grow? Seeds form in flowers and fruit holds seeds. The seeds grow into new plants.

SEP Constructing Explanations and Designing Solutions . . . .
Explain to children that the way each plant part works depends on its structure, or how it is shaped. **Ask:** How do roots keep a plant in place? Roots are able to grow under the ground. They spread out and make it harder for the plant to be pulled from the ground.

Differentiate Instruction

ELL Use multiple pictures to illustrate each plant part. Show several pictures of roots and say *roots*. Show several pictures of stems and say *stem*. Show several pictures of thorns and say *thorns*. Show several pictures of flowers and say *flower*. Show several pictures of fruit and say *fruit*. Have children repeat each term aloud with you as you say it.

Plant Parts

Explore online.

● A fruit holds seeds.

● Food for the plant is made in leaves.

● Water moves through the stem to other parts of the plant.

● Seeds form in flowers. Seeds grow into new plants.

● Thorns protect the plant from animals.

● Roots take up water and hold the plant in the ground.

Circle the part where seeds are made.

Put an X on the part that holds the plant.

Each part of a plant helps the plant live.

142

© Houghton Mifflin Harcourt • Image Credits:

Do the Math! • Ask 4 or 5 people which plant part is their favorite. Show the data in the graph.

Represent Data
Go to the online handbook for tips.

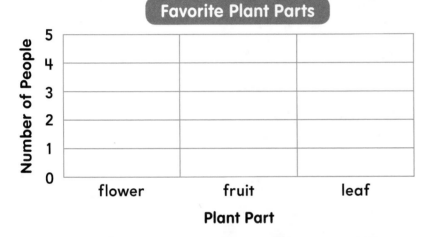

Favorite Plant Parts

(Graph: y-axis "Number of People" labeled 0–5; x-axis "Plant Part" with categories: flower, fruit, leaf)

 Apply What You Know

Evidence Notebook • Observe a real plant. Draw and label it in your Evidence Notebook. Use evidence to describe what each plant part does.

Do the Math! • Represent Data

Children should fill in one rectangle for each person's choice. **Ask: How does the graph tell you which part was chosen the most and which part was chosen the least?** The tallest bar shows the part that was chosen the most. The shortest bar shows the part that was chosen the least.

 Represent Data Children can sort data into groups and show the data in a graph. Use bars to show the amount in each group.

Differentiate Instruction

RTI/Extra Support Provide children with a table to collect data. Show them how to use tally marks to record data as it is collected. Show children how each tally mark corresponds to a rectangle on the graph.

Extension Have groups share their graphs. Discuss the different graphs. Did each group have similar results? Why do you think this might be?

✋ **FORMATIVE ASSESSMENT**

Evidence Notebook

Children will need to observe and sketch a real plant. Plan to have several types of plants available in the classroom, or take children outside to observe plants in nature. Encourage children to list details underneath their sketches about how each part helps the plant live.

Scoring Guidelines

- accurately identifies the location of the roots, stem, thorns (if applicable), leaves, flowers (if applicable), and fruit (if applicable)
- describes how each part helps the plant live

Shape Up

3D Learning Objective

Children will **construct explanations** of how the shape and stability of structure of plant parts are **related to their function(s)**.

DCI Structure and Function . . . .

CCC Structure and Function . . . .

To help children understand the concept of tubes inside of stems and roots, it may be helpful to do a demonstration with a straw to show how liquid moves through tubes. **Ask: How is the shape of roots and stems connected to how they work?** Roots and stems have long tubes inside. Water moves through the tubes to different parts of a plant. **Ask: How does the shape of the thorn help keep animals from eating the plant?** The thorn is pointed and sharp. If an animal tries to eat the plant, it will be poked by the thorn.

 Structure and Function Tell children to think of things in nature or things that people make. Point out that the shape of a thing is connected to how it works.

SEP **Constructing Explanations and Designing Solutions** . . . .

Ask: How is the shape of a leaf connected to how it works? Do you think leaves would work the same way if they were a different shape? Leaves are flat, which allows them to catch sunlight. If leaves were a different shape, they may not be able to catch sunlight as well.

Shape Up

How does the shape of each plant part help the plant work?

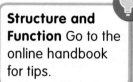 **Structure and Function** Go to the online handbook for tips.

Explore online. ▶

Roots have tubes inside. Water moves from soil into the tubes.

Stems have tubes inside. Water moves through the tubes to flowers and leaves.

Thorns are sharp. Thorns keep animals from eating a plant.

Leaves have flat, green surfaces that catch sunlight. They also have openings that take in air.

144

© Houghton Mifflin Harcourt • Image Credits:

Fruits are shaped to hold seeds inside. They protect seeds.

Look at the shape of this plant part. How does it work?

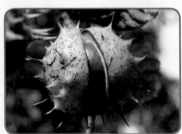

Ⓐ It moves water to the plant's parts.

Ⓑ It holds seeds inside.

Ⓒ It catches light.

Apply What You Know

Evidence Notebook • Work with a group. Cover the leaf of a plant with dark paper. What do you think will happen to the leaf after two weeks? Use evidence to explain. Record your explanation in your Evidence Notebook.

 CCC Structure and Function . . . .

Children should choose B. Children should look at the shape of the part to help determine how it works. If children are confused by the thorns or spines on the plant part, direct their attention to what the plant part is holding. **Ask: What is this plant part?** a fruit **How can you tell?** It is holding a seed.

Connection to Earth and Space Sciences

Earth and the Solar System Plants need sunlight to live and grow. The amount of sunlight a place receives changes from season to season. This can affect how plants grow. Have children think about how the amount of sunlight from season to season affects how plants grow in their area.

FORMATIVE ASSESSMENT

Evidence Notebook

Children predict and record what will happen to a leaf when it is covered with aluminum foil. Have children record not only their prediction, but also their reasoning behind it. Remind children to use evidence to support their reasoning.

Address the possible misconception that the paper holds some kind of "special" property for blocking light or changing the color of leaves. If time allows, the experiment can be carried out to check children's predictions.

Scoring Guidelines

- gives a reasonable prediction
- relates the shape and function of a leaf to the prediction

Looking to Nature

3D Learning Objective

Children will explore how the **shape and function** of **plant parts give people ideas for designs**.

Collaboration

Think, Pair, Share Divide children into pairs. Have each pair brainstorm words that describe both the leaves and the solar panels.

CCC Structure and Function . . . .

DCI Structure and Function . . . .

Ask: How are the shapes of leaves and solar panels similar? How does this help both the leaves and the solar panels work? Both the leaves and the solar panels have large, flat surfaces. This allows for a large surface area to come into contact with sunlight. **How are solar panels like leaves?** They both collect sunlight.

Looking to Nature

Explore online. ▶

Look at the pictures to see how plants give people ideas.

▼

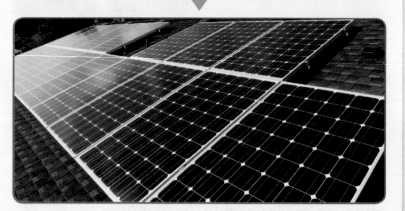

Leaves take in sunlight to make food. The solar panels take in sunlight and change it into energy.

146

© Houghton Mifflin Harcourt • Image Credits:

Explore online. ▶

Thorns gave people the idea to make barbed wire fences.

People get ideas from plants. People **mimic**, or copy, what they see in nature to make designs. The designs solve problems.

Lesson 1 • Engineer It • What Parts Help Plants Live?   147

© Houghton Mifflin Harcourt • Image Credits:

CCC **Influence of Engineering, Technology, and Science on Society and the Natural World. . . .**

Ask: Which do you think came first: thorns or barbed wire? Why? Thorns came first because they are found in nature. **How are the shapes of the thorns and barbed wire similar? How does this help both do their jobs?** They both have sharp points. The sharp points of the thorns keep animals away from plants. The sharp points of the wire keep people away from animals. **Why were thorns a good model for a barbed wire fence?** Thorns work in a way that people wanted fences to work. They looked at thorns and got an idea for the fence.

Collaboration

Small Groups Take a tour of the classroom or the school. Point out different human-made objects that have features similar in structure and function to plant parts. Ask small groups to find an object that has parts inspired by a plant. Have each group present to the class by introducing the object and explaining its connection to plant structure and function.

 CCC **Influence of Engineering, Technology, and Science on Society and the Natural World. . . .**

Children should choose A. Children should be able to see that the trees are similar in shape to the columns of the building.

Ask: What plant part is the trunk of a tree? a stem What are some words you could use to describe a trunk of a tree? tall, sturdy, strong Why do you think these trees are a good model to use when designing a building? Tree trunks are very sturdy and strong. Columns that are designed like them will support the building. They hold up the ceiling like the trunks hold up the tree branches.

🖐 **FORMATIVE ASSESSMENT**

Read, Write, Share! • Evidence Notebook

In pairs, children will research both plants and human designs that are similar in structure and function. Provide children with a variety of sources such as fiction and nonfiction books and online photo galleries. Allow children to record their answers in paragraphs or in chart form. Children should provide evidence from the lesson or from personal experience to support their ideas.

Scoring Guidelines

- provides examples of designs that are similar to plants
- uses evidence to show the connection between structure and function

💡 **Participate in a Research Project** Remind children that when they research, they are finding facts about a topic. Explain how to use the index and the table of contents to find sources of information. Children should ask questions like, Which pages have facts for my topic?

Which plant gave the idea for the building?

Ⓐ   Ⓑ   Ⓒ

🖐 **Apply What You Know**

Read, Write, Share! • Evidence Notebook • Work with a partner. Research pictures of plants. Name designs that look like those plants. Use evidence to tell how you know.

Plants Give Ideas

Plants Give Ideas

Explore online. ▶

This cactus has folds on its stem. The folds make shade for the plant. The shade keeps the cactus cool in the hot sun.

This tree can tilt its leaves. Then the sun does not hit the leaves directly. That keeps the tree cool.

This cactus shrinks down into the cool desert soil when the weather is hot.

Some plants have ways to keep cool in the heat.

© Houghton Mifflin Harcourt • Image Credits:

3D Learning Objective

Children will **construct explanations** of how the shape and stability of the structure of plant parts are **related to their function(s)**. Children will **design a solution to a human problem** by **applying knowledge of plant parts**.

DCI Structure and Function . . . .

CCC Structure and Function . . . .

Direct children to look at the leaves of the second plant and have them compare these leaves to the leaves of the plant in the Looking to Nature section. **Ask: How are these leaves different from the leaves that gave the idea for solar panels?** These leaves are different because they tilt to take in less sun.

CCC Influence of Engineering, Technology, and Science on Society and the Natural World . . . .

Ask: Can you think of any technology that works like tilting leaves? How is the technology similar? Sample answer: Window blinds rotate to adjust how much sun comes through. This helps regulate the amount of light and the temperature in a room.

Differentiate Instruction

RTI/Extra Support Make a class chart to organize what has been covered in the lesson so far. The columns should be: Plant Part, Shape (or Structure), Job (or Function), and Technology. Invite children to use words or pictures to fill in the chart.

Extension Invite children to find pictures in books and magazines to add to the chart.

Differentiate Instruction

RTI/Extra Support Provide images of plant parts. Have children describe the parts and how their shape helps them do their job. Then help children connect those jobs to problems that people might want to solve.

Extension Have children write a paragraph explaining the connection between the plant and their design.

 FORMATIVE ASSESSMENT

In small groups, children will observe plant parts and make connections between their structure and function. Have children brainstorm ways the function of a plant part could be used as an idea to solve a human problem. Children should provide a labeled sketch of their design and explain how the design solves a problem. Make sure children use evidence to support their answers.

Scoring Guidelines

• provides examples of plant structures that could be used as models to solve problems
• uses evidence to show the connection between structure and function

Constructing Explanations and Designing Solutions Explain to children that scientists and engineers use materials to design a device that solves a specific problem. Tell them to observe something that happens in nature and use the facts to describe what happened.

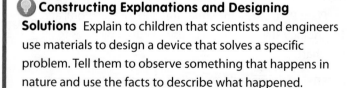

 Apply What You Know

Work with a small group. Observe a plant. Talk about its shape and what its parts do. Use ideas from the plant to think of a new design.

Constructing Explanations and Designing Solutions Go to the online handbook for tips.

✏️ Draw and label your design. Write about how it solves a problem.

> Children should draw and label a picture that shows their design.

Children should write sentences to tell how the design solves a problem.

150

Name_____

Hands-On Activity
Engineer It • Use Ideas from Plants to Design a Solution

Materials • craft materials

Ask a Question
How can I use an idea from a plant to design something that would keep me cool?

Test and Record Data   Explore online.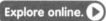

Step 1

Explain the problem. Gather information about it.

Check children's work.

Step 2

Think about the parts of plants. Plan your solution.

Lesson 1 • Engineer It • What Parts Help Plants Live?   151

Hands-On Activity 👥 pairs ⏱ 1 class period

Engineer It • Use Ideas from Plants to Design a Solution

3D Learning Objective

SEP **Constructing Explanations and Designing Solutions** . . . .

Children will use an idea from a plant to design and build something that would help keep them cool on hot days. They will use the design process to solve their problem. Children will work with partners to identify plants to use for ideas and draw a picture of how they could make something that would keep them cool. Then partners will use a variety of craft materials to make what they planned.

Suggested Materials craft materials

Preparation

This activity can be an extension from the Apply What You Know exercise in the Plants Give Ideas section of the lesson. Children can look at the plant pictures in the Plants Give Ideas section or at pictures of plants for ideas.

Activity

As a class, view the video. Then discuss the question that will need to be answered. Have children record the question.

DCI **Defining and Delimiting Engineering Problems** . . . .

SEP **Asking Questions and Defining Problems** . . . .

STEP 1 To help children gather information, use probing questions. **Ask: What is the problem? Why is it a problem? Where can you go to get some ideas of how to solve the problem? What are some ideas for possible solutions?**

STEP 2 Have children identify parts of their solution that are like plant parts. Have them describe how to build these parts so they function like the plant parts that inspired them.

Hands-On Activity, continued

CCC **Structure and Function** . . . .

STEP 3 Direct children to use a variety of materials to build their solution. Encourage them to think beyond what the material is traditionally used for. **Ask: How is this material like a plant part? How will it make your solution work?**

SEP **Constructing Explanations and Designing Solutions** . . . .

STEP 4 Ask: What ideas did you get from plant parts? Sample answer: The cactus has folds that make shade for the plant. I made folds in the material of the hat to make shade for my head.

Claims, Evidence, and Reasoning

In this section, children will have peer and teacher feedback as per EQuIP rubric. **Ask: How does your evidence support your claim?** Sample answer: My claim is that making a hat with folds will make shade and keep me cool. My evidence supports this because I am cooler when wearing the hat.

	Scoring Rubric for Hands-On Activity
3	States a claim supported with evidence that their solution solves the problem.
2	States a claim somewhat supported with evidence that their solution solves the problem.
1	States a claim that is not supported with evidence.
0	Does not state a claim and does not provide evidence.

Step 3

Build your solution.

Step 4

Share your solution. Explain how you used ideas from plant parts in your design.

> Check children's work.

Make a claim that answers your question.

Sample answer: I used the idea of folds on a cactus to design a

folded hat that would keep me cool.

What is your evidence?

Sample answer: My evidence is that I observed that the folds of

the hat helped keep me cool.

152

Explore online. ▶   Guide children to the Interactive Online Student Edition where they can choose from and explore both paths.

Take It Further

People in Science & Engineering • Janine Benyus

Introduce children to Janine Benyus, a biologist and a writer who helps inventors find and copy ideas from plants and animals that will help them solve their problems.

CCC **Influence of Engineering, Technology, and Science on Society and the Natural World.** . . . .
A biologist studies living things and their relationship to the environment. **Ask: What does a biologist know that would be useful in designing solutions based on ideas from nature?** Biologists know about the parts of living things and how those parts are used in nature. They can think of designs that mimic these parts. **Ask: How does copying ideas from plants and animals help solve human problems?** People see how things work in the natural world and use those ideas to make designs.

Take It Further

People in Science & Engineering •
Janine Benyus

Explore more online.

Plants We Eat

Explore online. ▶

Janine Benyus helps inventors copy ideas from plants and animals to solve problems.

Benyus says she is a nature nerd!

She was named a "Hero of the Environment" for her work.

She has written six books about nature.

Take It Further, continued

Read, Write, Share! • Ask Questions

Remind children to ask about important details or things that are unclear. Children should start questions with words such as *who, what, when, where, why,* and *how.*

Differentiate Instruction

ELL Have children ask the questions first and pay close attention to their partners' answers. Children can use partners' answers to model their own responses to the same questions.

Explore more online. ▶

Plants We Eat

Children investigate different plants we eat and determine which plant parts are eaten.

Ask Janine Benyus

Read, Write, Share!

> **Ask Questions** Go to online handbook for tips.

Work with a partner. Write questions for Janine Benyus. Then do an interview. One partner acts as Janine Benyus. The other partner asks questions. Then switch roles.

Check children's work. Children's questions should be based on

the information provided about Janine Benyus.

154

© Houghton Mifflin Harcourt • Image Credits:

Explore online. ▶   Have children explore online to find out more about how plants give people ideas for designs.

Lesson Check

Name_____

Explore online. ▶

Can You Solve It?

✏️➤ How did the maple seed give people ideas to make the helicopter blades?

Be sure to

• Tell how nature helps people solve problems.

Sample response: People copy what they see in nature to make

designs. The designs solve problems. People copied the shape of

the maple seed to make the helicopter blades.

_____

_____

_____

Lesson Check

Can You Solve It?

Have children reread their answers to the Can You Solve It? prompt at the beginning of the lesson.

CCC **Influence of Engineering, Technology, and Science on Society and the Natural World** . . . .

Children should connect the structure and function of plant parts to human designs that have similar functions.

SEP **Constructing Explanations and Designing Solutions** . . . .

If children have difficulty responding to the Can You Solve It? question, have children look through the lesson and identify human designs that mimic plant structures in nature.

DCI **Structure and Function** . . . .

Have children discuss some of the plant parts and human designs they saw in the lesson. **Ask: Can you name a plant part that gave an idea for a human design?** Sample answer: Leaves gave an idea for solar panels. **Ask: How do you think the shape and function of leaves gave the idea for solar panels?** Leaves are flat so they can take in sunlight. People probably looked at the leaves and designed a flat panel that could also take in sunlight.

Scoring Guidelines

• Children should explain how nature helps people solve problems.

• Children should offer a reasonable explanation about how the maple seed gave people the idea for the helicopter blades.

Lesson Check, continued

SUMMATIVE ASSESSMENT
Self Check

1. Children should choose B—They move water to other plant parts. If children choose A or C, direct them to the Shape Up section of the lesson. Have them read the information for roots and stems and identify their similarities in function.

2. Children should choose C—They help the plant make new plants. If children choose A or B, direct them to the Plant Parts section of the lesson. Have children identify the role of thorns and the role of roots. Discuss how these roles are different from the roles of flowers, fruits, and seeds.

3. Children should choose A—They stick to things. If children choose B or C, ask them to look at the shape and material of the burrs and the hook-and-loop fastener. Ask children to think if they have a shape that would be good for taking in sunlight. Ask them if they think both things are found in nature.

Self Check

1. How are roots and stems alike?

   Ⓐ They make food for the plant.

   Ⓑ They move water to other plant parts.

   Ⓒ They help the plant make new plants.

---

2. How do flowers, fruits, and seeds help a plant?

   Ⓐ They stop animals from eating the plant.

   Ⓑ They keep the plant in the ground.

   Ⓒ They help the plant make new plants.

---

3. Look at the seeds on the dog and the hook-and-loop fastener. How are they alike?

   Ⓐ They stick to things.

   Ⓑ They take in sunlight.

   Ⓒ They are both found in nature.

156

© Houghton Mifflin Harcourt • Image Credits:

4. Which plant part gave people the idea for each invention? Draw lines to match the pictures.

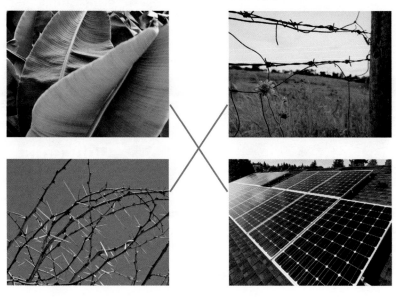

5. Tari wants to invent a way to take the salt out of seawater. Which plant would be best for her to study for ideas?

Ⓐ a tree that lives in salt water

Ⓑ a flower that lives in a garden

Ⓒ a cactus that lives in a desert

4. Children should match the banana palm leaf with the solar panels and the bush with thorns with the barbed wire fence. If children make incorrect matches, direct them to the Looking to Nature section of the lesson. Have them describe the structure and function of each plant part and then identify the technology that has similar characteristics.

5. Children should choose A—a tree that lives in salt water. If children choose B or C, have them reread the item and underline words that give details about the problem Tari wants to solve, such as *salt* and *sea water*. Then, direct children to the Plant Parts and Shape Up sections of the lesson. Have children identify which plant parts are useful to help solve the problem.

© Houghton Mifflin Harcourt • Image Credits:

Lesson 1 • Engineer It • What Parts Help Plants Live?   157

Engineer It • What Body Parts Help Animals Stay Safe?

Building to the Performance Expectation

The learning experiences in this lesson prepare children for mastery of:

1-LS1-1 Use materials to design a solution to a human problem by mimicking how plants and/or animals use their external parts to help them survive, grow, and meet their needs.

 Trace Tool to the NGSS
Go online to view the complete coverage of these standards across this lesson, unit, and time.

 **Science & Engineering Practices** (SEP)

 **Disciplinary Core Ideas** (DCI)

 **Crosscutting Concepts** (CCC)

Constructing Explanations and Designing Solutions
Use materials to design a device . . .
▶ **VIDEO** SEPs: Constructing Explanations and Designing Solutions/Engaging in Argument from Evidence

Developing and Using Models
Develop a simple model based on . . .
▶ **VIDEO** SEP: Developing and Using Models

Analyzing and Interpreting Data
Analyze data from tests . . .
▶ **VIDEO** SEPs: Analyzing and Interpreting Data / Using Mathematical and Computational Thinking

LS1.A: Structure and Function
All organisms have external parts. Different animals use their body parts in different ways to see, hear, grasp objects, protect themselves, move from place to place, and seek, find, and take in food, water and air. Plants also have different parts (roots, stems, leaves, flowers, fruits) that help them survive and grow.

ETS1.A: Defining and Delimiting Engineering Problems
Before beginning to design a solution, it is important to clearly understand the problem.

ETS1.C: Optimizing the Design Solution
Because there is always more than one possible solution to a problem, it is useful to compare and test designs.

Structure and Function
The shape and stability of structures of natural and designed objects are related to their function(s).
▶ **VIDEO** CCC: Structure and Function

Influence of Engineering, Technology, and Science on Society and the Natural World
Every human-made product is designed by applying some knowledge of the natural world and is built using materials derived from the natural world.

CONNECTIONS TO MATH

1.MD.A.2 Express the length of an object as a whole number of length units, by layering multiple copies of a shorter object (length and unit) end to end; understand that the length measurement of an object is the number of same-size length units that span it with no gaps or overlaps.

CONNECTIONS TO ENGLISH LANGUAGE ARTS

W.1.7 Participate in shared research and writing projects (e.g., explore a number of "how-to" books on a given topic and use them to write a sequence of instructions).

Supporting All Students, All Standards

Integrating the Three Dimensions of Learning

In this lesson, children use materials with characteristics similar to those of animal parts (**CCC Influence of Engineering, Technology, and Science on Society and the Natural World**) to construct a solution to a human problem—a shoe that protects feet from cold (**SEPs Constructing Explanations and Designing Solutions / Developing and Using Models / Analyzing and interpreting Data**) (**DCIs Defining and Delimiting Engineering Problems / Optimizing the Design Solution**). Children begin by exploring how the structure of animal parts is related to their function (**CCC Structure and Function**) and exploring how those parts keep animals safe (**DCI Structure and Function**).

 Professional Development Go online to view **Professional Development videos** with strategies to integrate CCCs and SEPs, including the ones used in this lesson.

Build on Prior Knowledge

Children should already know and be prepared to build on the following concepts:

- Animals have body parts with particular functions.
- People invent technology with particular functions.
- It is a normal part of solving a problem to compare and test solutions.

Differentiate Instruction

RTI/Extra Support Supply children with additional images of animals and ask them to sort the animals in various ways. **Ask: Which animals would run away from danger? Why? Which animals might be good at hiding? Why do you think so?**

Extension Children could investigate various pieces of sports equipment that are designed to keep us safe, for example, shin guards in soccer, a helmet in baseball, or shoulder pads in football. Invite children to share a piece of sports equipment with the class and identify an animal's body part that functions in a similar way.

ELL As children view the photographs of animals in this lesson, encourage them to find the name of the animal on the page with the photograph and say it aloud together. Children could build a class poster or picture book of animals they know.

Lesson Problem

Lesson Objective

Design a solution to a human problem by mimicking how animals use parts of their body for protection.

About This Image

Ask: What do you think this fish uses to stay safe? As you explore, you'll learn how animals' body parts help them stay safe.

 **Structure and Function**

Alternative Engage Strategy

What Animal Am I?	👥 whole class
	⏱ 10–15 minutes

Invite children to choose an animal to mimic for their classmates. Encourage them to emphasize a certain way of moving that is characteristic of that animal. After a short time, allow other children to guess the animal that is being portrayed. Have children who guess correctly explain how they knew what animal their classmate was mimicking.

Guide children to recognize that different animals have body parts that allow them to move in different ways. Engage children in a discussion about how these body parts and movements might be helpful to the animals.

Lesson 2 Engineer It • What Body Parts Help Animals Stay Safe?

Animals have body parts that keep them safe.

By the End of This Lesson

I will tell how body parts keep animals safe. I will be able to explain how animals give people ideas to solve problems.

158

Staying Safe

A hedgehog rolls into a ball when it is in danger. It has spines all over. Animals do not want to eat a spiny hedgehog!

Explore online. ▶

Can You Solve It?

✏️ What ideas can you get from a hedgehog to keep something safe?

Accept all reasonable answers.

_____

_____

Lesson 2 • Engineer It • What Body Parts Help Animals Stay Safe?

159

Can You Solve It?

Staying Safe Show the video of the hedgehog rolling into a ball. If the video is not available, children may view the photos on the page.

Ask children to record their ideas about what we can learn from the way a hedgehog protects itself. Accept all reasonable answers. At the end of this lesson, children will revisit this this question and their answers as part of the Lesson Check.

Collaboration

Build on Prior Knowledge Have children list three things they know that have spines. For example, children might list a cactus, a fish, or another animal. Discuss how the spines protect each thing.

Moving Away from Danger

3D Learning Objective

Children observe **animal parts** and how those **parts have specific functions** that allow the animals to move away from danger.

(DCI) Structure and Function . . . .

Ask: **What does the animal in each photograph do to move away? What body part helps it do that?** The kangaroo hops using its strong legs. The squirrel climbs using its claws. The dolphin swims using its tail and flippers. The butterfly flies using its wings.

(CCC) Structure and Function . . . .

Ask: **Do you think a kangaroo would be good at swimming quickly? Why or why not?** Probably not. It doesn't have smooth skin or flippers. **Ask:** **Do you think a butterfly would be good at running away?** No, it has very short legs.

💡 **Structure and Function** Think of things in nature. Tell how the shape of a thing is connected to how it works.

Differentiate Instruction

ELL Help children identify the action words that describe how each animal moves. To reinforce these action words, invite children to act out each word as they say it aloud.

Moving Away from Danger

Explore online. ▶

A kangaroo hops on its back legs to stay safe. It uses its tail for balance.

A squirrel climbs to stay safe. It has sharp claws that help it climb.

A dolphin swims fast to stay safe. It uses its tail and flippers to swim.

A butterfly has wings to fly. This makes it hard to catch.

Some animals use body parts to move away from danger to stay safe.

160

💡 **Structure and Function** Go to the online handbook for tips.

© Houghton Mifflin Harcourt • Image Credits:

✏️➡ Draw a line to match the animal to the way it moves in order to stay safe.

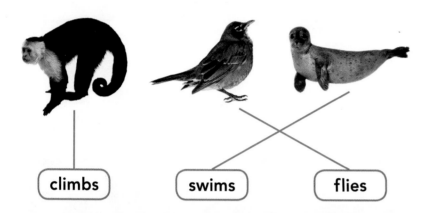

climbs   swims   flies

DCI Structure and Function. . . . .

Before children draw lines to match each animal with the way it moves, ask them to name the body parts that each animal might use to help it move. Highlight the relationship between the body part and the primary means of movement, and help children generalize this relationship to other animals. **Ask: What other animals might fly to stay safe? Do they have wings?** A bat flies and has wings. A mosquito flies and has wings.

Help children make connections between the way something works in the natural world and how it could inspire solutions to problems in society. **Ask: What can you learn about hopping from watching a kangaroo?** It takes strong legs to make long hops. **Ask: What can you learn about flying from watching a butterfly?** Wings that are big, but very thin, can help something fly.

✋ Apply What You Know

Read, Write, Share! • Evidence Notebook • Work with a partner. Research how animals move to stay safe. Draw pictures of the animals. Write **runs**, **climbs**, **swims**, or **flies** to tell how they move. Use evidence to tell how you know.

💡 **Participate in a Research Project** Go to the online handbook for tips.

Lesson 2 • Engineer It • What Body Parts Help Animals Stay Safe?

161

✋ FORMATIVE ASSESSMENT

Read, Write, Share! • Evidence Notebook
Children will work with a partner to draw and label pictures of animals moving to stay safe. Encourage children to show the body parts in their drawings that help the animals move.

Scoring Guidelines
• illustrates how different animals move away from danger
• provides evidence of why the animals are able to move in these ways

 Participate in a Research Project Remind children to share the tasks of researching, drawing, and writing fairly.

Hiding from Danger

3D Learning Objective

Children observe how **animal body characteristics (camouflage)** help **animals hide from danger**.

CCC Structure and Function . . . .

Help children see that the body characteristics that help an animal blend in depend on the animal's environment. For example, an arctic hare's white fur will blend in with snow in the arctic, but it will not blend into a leafy forest. **Ask: What might help an animal hide on a beach?** a light brown color **What might help an animal hide on a tree trunk?** very rough skin that looks like tree bark

DCI Structure and Function . . . .

To emphasize the diversity of animal structures and functions, invite children to share other examples they know of animals hiding from danger. **Ask: What other animals do you know that use their shape or color to hide? Explain how they do it.** A green frog can hide among water plants because it's green. A mouse looks like the leaves on the forest floor so it can hide there.

CCC Influence of Engineering, Technology, and Science on Society and the Natural World . . . .

Ask children to describe aquariums they have seen, or view a video of an aquarium. **Ask: Is it easy to see the animals that live in the aquarium? Why or why not?** If there are plants, rocks, or other features that occur in the animals' natural environment in the aquarium, it probably isn't easy to see the animals. Encourage children to see that while an aquarium is made by humans, taking care to make it as close as possible to the animals' natural environment can give the animals places to hide.

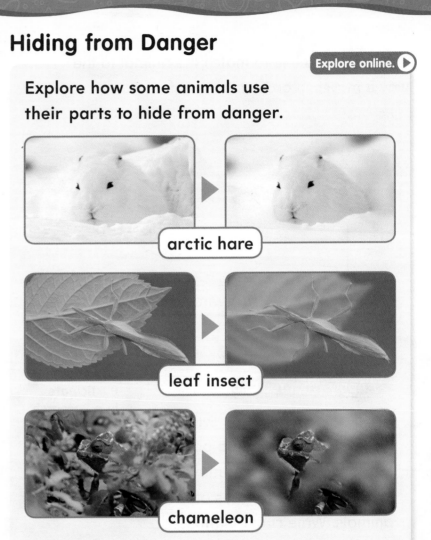

Hiding from Danger

Explore online. ▶

Explore how some animals use their parts to hide from danger.

arctic hare

leaf insect

chameleon

These animals are hard to see in their environments. This helps them stay safe.

162

🖍️▷ Circle each animal whose color could help it hide in this forest.

toad

squirrel

toucan

Apply What You Know

Use an idea you got from an animal. What could you wear during a game of hide-and-seek to help you hide? Draw a design. Share your design with others.

DCI Structure and Function . . . .

Children should circle the toad and the squirrel. They should look at the color of the toad and squirrel to determine if they can hide in the forest. If children choose the toucan, ask them to look again at the color of the toucan's beak and think about if it would blend into the forest.

SEP Developing and Using Models . . . .

Ask: Suppose you wanted to build a tree fort in a forest like this one, and you wanted it to blend into the forest. How could you use color or shape to help you? I could paint it different shades of green to blend in with the leaves. I could put branches on the outside of it.

✋ FORMATIVE ASSESSMENT

Children will use what they know about animals blending into their environments to suggest what they could wear to help them hide in a game of hide-and-seek. Guide children to understand that the shape and color of the clothing or other items they design should depend on the environment where they are playing the game.

Scoring Guidelines
- designs clothing using colors or shapes that would help them blend into their environment in a game of hide-and-seek

© Houghton Mifflin Harcourt • Image Credits:

Facing Danger

3D Learning Objective

Children observe how **animal body characteristics** help animals face danger.

 ccc Structure and Function . . . .

Draw children's attention to the words that describe the animal body parts they see on this page. **Ask: What word describes a porcupine's quills?** sharp **Ask: Why is that important for keeping the porcupine safe?** Other animals will stay away so it doesn't get hurt.

 FORMATIVE ASSESSMENT

Evidence Notebook

Children will use what they have learned about animals' body coverings to design a box to keep things safe. Introduce the topic by discussing the dangers from which a box can protect something.

Scoring Guidelines
- designs a box with safety features
- tells how they used ideas from animals to design the box

💡 **Structure and Function** Remind children to think about what harm might come to the box (the problem) and then think about what they know about animals' body coverings that could provide a solution to the problem.

Facing Danger

Explore online. ▶

 A turtle has a <u>hard shell</u> that keeps its body safe.

 A porcupine has <u>sharp quills</u> that keep its body safe.

 An eagle has <u>sharp talons</u> it uses to protect itself.

✏️ Draw a line under the name of the body part that keeps each animal safe.

Some animals have body parts that help them face danger.

 Apply What You Know

Evidence Notebook • Design a box to keep things safe. Use ideas from animals. Add parts to your box. Use evidence to explain how the parts keep it safe.

💡 **Structure and Function** Go to the online handbook for tips.

164

Staying Safe in Weather

Staying Safe in Weather

Explore online.

A red fox has a thick coat of fur in winter. It keeps the fox warm.

A walrus has a thick layer of blubber, or fat. It keeps the walrus warm.

A jackrabbit has big ears. They give off heat to keep the jackrabbit cool.

A blue jay fluffs up its feathers to stay warm.

Animals have body parts that help them stay safe from the weather.

© Houghton Mifflin Harcourt • Image Credits:

Lesson 2 • Engineer It • What Body Parts Help Animals Stay Safe?

165

3D Learning Objective

Children observe how **animal characteristics (body coverings)** help animals stay safe from severe weather.

DCI Structure and Function . . . .

Point out that while the fox and the walrus both need to stay warm, they have different body parts and body coverings that help them stay warm. **Ask: How does each animal stay warm?** The fox has thick fur, and the walrus has a layer of blubber. **Why do you think they use different ways of keeping warm?** The fox needs to run, and that would be difficult with a thick layer of blubber. The walrus needs to swim, and a thick layer of fur might slow it down.

Have children use what they have learned to consider how other animal body parts or body coverings might protect the animal from extreme weather. **Ask: A duck's feathers are lightly covered in oil. How might that help protect the duck in winter?** It helps the duck stay dry in the water, which helps it stay warm. **Ask: A dog has a long tongue that it can pant with. How might that help the dog in summer?** It can help the dog cool down in hot weather.

CCC Structure and Function . . . .

It might not be obvious to children why the jackrabbit's large ears help give off heat. **Ask: How do you think the jackrabbit's big ears give off heat?** Listen to all answers and then explain that in large ears the animal's warm blood flows close to the skin, where it is cooled a bit by the air around it.

Influence of Engineering, Technology, and Science on Society and the Natural World. . . .
Many heating and cooling tools made by humans are based on the same principal as that used by the desert fox's ears. Show children a photo of the coils on a refrigerator or a car radiator. Explain that a liquid flows through the thin coils and releases heat to the air. **Ask: Which animal has a body part that works a little like this?** The jackrabbit or the desert fox. **How is it similar?** A thin part helps the animal or the refrigerator give heat off to the air around it.

Children should circle the ears of the fox. If children have trouble identifying the correct part, refer them to the information about how the jackrabbit stays cool in the section Staying Safe in Weather.

Connection to Engineering Design

Defining and Delimiting Engineering Problems
Encourage children to think about how engineers might look to nature to help solve human problems. Remind them that engineers must first define a problem. Then, they might look to animals to get ideas for a solution.

 FORMATIVE ASSESSMENT

Evidence Notebook
Children will experience the insulating effect of blubber by protecting one hand with shortening and putting both hands into cold water. Provide soap, water, and towels to clean up afterward.

Scoring Guidelines
• tells that the hand with shortening felt warmer
• explains, with evidence, how blubber helps animals keep warm

 Circle the body part that keeps the fox cool.

 Apply What You Know

Evidence Notebook • Put one hand in an empty bag. Put the other hand in a bag with shortening. Put your hands into cold water. Tell which hand stays warmer. How does blubber keep animals warm? Use evidence to tell how you know.

166

Animals as Models

Explore online. ▶

Engineers got ideas from shark scales to make swimsuits.

The feet of a gecko stick to things. Engineers got ideas from geckos to make a tape that does not slip.

People get ideas from animals to solve problems.

Lesson 2 • Engineer It • What Body Parts Help Animals Stay Safe?

167

© Houghton Mifflin Harcourt • Image Credits:

Animals as Models

3D Learning Objective

Children relate the **structure and function of human products** to **animal body parts that solve similar problems** related to motion and adhesion in different environments.

DCI Structure and Function . . . .

Have children look at the photograph of the gecko. **Ask: What does the gecko's feet help it do?** climb

SEP Constructing Explanations and Designing Solutions . . . .

Draw children's attention to each human solution that is based on an animal model. **Ask: What problem might the new swimsuits help swimmers solve?** Sample answer: They wanted to swim faster, but couldn't. **Ask: What problem might the strong tape that does not slip solve?** It will stay where you place it.

Structure and Function . . . .

Guide children to notice the characteristics of each body part that humans might want to copy. **Ask: What is it about the frog's feet that helps the frog swim so quickly?** They are webbed between the toes so they push more water with every kick. **Ask: What is it about an orca that helps it dive underwater?** Its shape moves easily through the water.

Differentiate Instruction

RTI/Extra Support Have children move small and large pieces of cardboard through the air while a classmate stands nearby to feel the wind. Guide children to see that a frog's feet work like the large piece of cardboard, moving more water than small, unwebbed feet.

Extension Provide modeling clay and a container of water. Challenge children to design an experiment to demonstrate how the orca's shape allows it to dive in water more easily than an animal with a less streamlined shape.

 FORMATIVE ASSESSMENT

Do the Math! • Use Nonstandard Units to Measure Length

Children will design and test two paper airplane models, comparing how far each model flies.

Scoring Guidelines
• creates two different paper airplanes
• describes how much farther one model flies than the other, using nonstandard units

 Use Nonstandard Units to Measure Length
Encourage children to choose a reasonable unit to measure how far their paper airplanes flew.

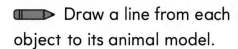 Draw a line from each object to its animal model.

Influence of Engineering, Technology and Science Go to the online handbook for tips.

 Apply What You Know

Do the Math! • Design a paper airplane. Look at pictures of birds for ideas. Build and test your airplane. Measure how far it flies. Build a new model. Measure how far it flies. Compare your results.

Use Nonstandard Units to Measure Length Go to the online handbook for tips.

© Houghton Mifflin Harcourt • Image Credits

168

Hands-On Activity

Engineer It • Design a Shoe

Name_____

Materials • ice • scissors • craft materials

Ask a Question

How can you protect your feet from ice?

Test and Record Data Explore online. ▶

Step 1

Find a problem. How could you use ideas from animals to solve the problem?

Step 2

Plan two solutions.

Children should draw or write plans for their solutions.

Lesson 2 • Engineer It • What Body Parts Help Animals Stay Safe?

169

Hands-On Activity 👥 small groups ⏱ 1 class period

Engineer It • Design a Shoe

3D Learning Objective

SEP **Constructing Explanations and Designing Solutions . . . .**

Children identify a problem related to keeping feet safe and use ideas about animals body parts to develop a solution to the problem.

Suggested Materials construction paper, markers, scissors, other craft materials, and ice packs for testing

Preparation

Gather a variety of craft materials and clean recyclable items that children may want to use in their shoe design.

Activity

STEP 1 Show children pictures or videos of arctic animals and identify characteristics that help those animals keep their feet safe. If children have trouble identifying a problem, have them imagine what it would be like to spend all day walking on a very cold surface.

STEP 2 If children have trouble planning two solutions to their problem, encourage them to plan one solution, then choose one part of that solution to change to create a second solution.

DCI **Defining and Delimiting Engineering Problems . . . .**

Some children may begin working on a solution before they understand the problem. Remind them to be clear about the problem they are trying to solve before they begin the planning step of the activity.

Hands-On Activity, continued

STEP 3 Allow time for children to build their solutions. If some children finish before others, you could suggest that children who are still building could ask one of the children who have finished for help constructing their solution. Remind helpers that they should follow the plan created by the builder.

STEP 4 Children could test their designs by placing one hand in each of their designs, holding both designs over an ice pack, and observing which design keeps their hand warmer.

DCI **Optimizing the Design Solution** . . . .

Point out that comparing and testing two designs is useful. Even if one design is clearly better, you can learn things from the other design that can help you improve your product.

Claims, Evidence, and Reasoning

Children should make a claim about how their preferred solution helps protect feet from cold. They should cite evidence that their hand stayed warm when tested. **Ask: How do you know one of your solutions will protect feet better than your other solution?** When I tested them both, my hand stayed warm in one shoe longer than it did in the other shoe.

Scoring Rubric for Hands-On Activity	
3	States a claim supported with evidence that the shoe design protects feet from cold.
2	States a claim somewhat supported with evidence that the shoe design protects feet from cold.
1	States a claim that is not supported by evidence.
0	Does not state a claim and does not provide evidence.

Step 3

Build your solutions. Follow your plan.

Step 4

Test your solutions. How can you improve them? Share your solutions with others.

Children should explain how they would improve their

solutions.

_____

Make a claim that answers your question.

Sample answer: I used an idea from a polar bear's foot to design

my shoe. I added materials like cotton balls and pipe cleaners to

the bottom of the shoe.

What is your evidence?

Sample answer: The pipe cleaners kept the shoe from slipping on

the ice. The cotton balls kept the shoe warm.

_____

170

Explore online. ▶   Guide children to the Interactive Online Student Edition where they can choose from and explore both paths.

Take It Further

Careers in Science & Engineering •
Bioengineer

Explore more online.

New Body Parts for Animals

A bioengineer is a kind of engineer. Bioengineers design things to help people. They also look for ways to help the environment.

Explore online. ▶

Bioengineers can work in labs. They make new medicines to help people who are sick.

© Houghton Mifflin Harcourt • Image Credits:

Take It Further

Careers in Science & Engineering •
Bioengineer

Children explore the career of a bioengineer. Bioengineers use math and science to design new products that help people and the environment.

DCI **Defining and Delimiting Engineering Problems...**

Remind children of some key tasks in designing something new. Write the following steps on strips of paper and read them aloud to children:

Test a solution.

Design a solution.

Improve the solution.

Understand the problem.

Find materials.

Have children place the tasks in the order a bioengineer would perform them. Understand the problem. Design a solution. Find materials. Test the solution. Improve the solution. Encourage children to justify the order they choose.

Take It Further, continued

Children should choose A and C. If children choose B, have them review the information about bioengineers. **Ask: Is studying rocks one of the main things that bioengineers do?**

DCI **Defining and Delimiting Engineering Problems** . . . .

Ask: What kinds of information might a bioengineer need before designing a solution? Sample answer: They would need to know what is polluting the water or air, or what problem a farmer is having with a crop.

Collaboration

Think, Pair, Share Ask children to think about what problem they might try to solve if they were a bioengineer. Have them share ideas with a classmate, then invite children to share some ideas as a class.

Explore more online. ▶

New Body Parts for Animals

Children observe how people design parts for animals that are injured.

Bioengineers find new ways to clean air and water. They also help farmers grow food in ways that are safer.

© Houghton Mifflin Harcourt • Image Credits:

What does a bioengineer do? Choose all correct answers.

Ⓐ helps clean air and water

Ⓑ studies rocks

Ⓒ makes new medicine

172

Explore online. ▶   Have children explore online to find out more about how a hedgehog stays safe.

Lesson Check

Name_____

Explore online. ▶

Can You Solve It?

✏️▷ What ideas can you get from a hedgehog to keep something safe?

Be sure to
- Tell how a hedgehog's body parts keep it safe.
- Describe how you got your idea from the hedgehog.

Sample answer: A hedgehog has spines to keep its body safe. I

can use this idea to design a fence with spines to keep animals

out of a garden.

_____

_____

Lesson 2 • Engineer It • What Body Parts Help Animals Stay Safe?   173

Lesson Check

Can You Solve It?

Have children reread their answers to the Can You Solve It? prompts at the beginning of the lesson.

DCI **Structure and Function** . . . .

Reinforce the important role body part characteristics play in keeping animals safe. **Ask: What words could you use to describe the body parts that keep a hedgehog safe?** spines, rolls into a ball

DCI **Defining and Delimiting Engineering Problems...**

Remind children to think about a problem people might have that could be solved by something that acts like the spines of the hedgehog.

CCC **Structure and Function** . . . .

Help children see how the shape and structure of an effective solution are related to the solution's function. **Ask: How does the shape of the hedgehog's parts help protect the hedgehog?** The hedgehog is covered by sharp spines. The spines cover the whole hedgehog when it rolls up. **Ask: How does your idea to keep people safe work in a similar way?** Sample answer: The fence has spines all over it.

Scoring Guidelines

- Children should explain that a hedgehog's spines keep it safe.
- Children should identify an idea to keep something safe that has a structure and function similar to a hedgehog's spines.
- Children should describe the problem their idea could help solve.

Lesson Check, continued

SUMMATIVE ASSESSMENT
Self Check

1. Children should choose A—feathers, and B—blubber. If children choose C, remind them that animals have body parts that keep them warm and have them read the question again to decide if talons are a body part that keep an animal warm.

2. Children should choose B—shell. If children choose A, acknowledge that turtles may use their legs to move away from danger, and ask children which body part turtles are most likely to use to escape quickly. If children choose C, have them read the question again and identify what animal it is asking about.

3. Children should circle the seal and the frog. If children circle the raccoon, have them look closely at the photograph of the raccoon and ask whether it has any body parts that look like they would help it swim quickly.

Self Check

1. Which body parts keep animals warm? Choose all correct answers.

   Ⓐ feathers

   Ⓑ blubber

   Ⓒ talons

2. What body part keeps a turtle safe from other animals?

   Ⓐ legs

   Ⓑ shell

   Ⓒ fur

3. Circle the animals you could use as models for making something that helps you swim faster.

© Houghton Mifflin Harcourt • Image Credits:

174

4. Draw a line to match each animal model to the object an engineer designed.

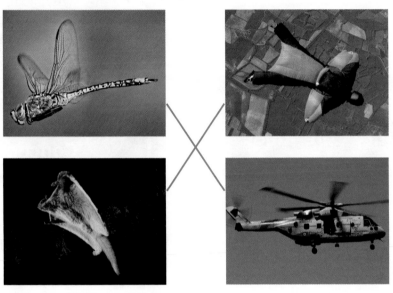

5. Which material would you use to act like blubber? Choose the best answer.

(A) rubber

(B) wood

(C) plastic

© Houghton Mifflin Harcourt • Image Credits:

Lesson 2 • Engineer It • What Body Parts Help Animals Stay Safe?   175

4. Children should draw a line from the dragonfly to the helicopter and a line from the flying squirrel to the wingsuit. If children make other connections, point out that flying squirrels glide through the air and ask which human technology helps people glide. Point out that the dragonfly has wings that move quickly and ask which human technology has quick-moving wings.

5. Children should choose A—rubber. If children choose B or C, ask them to describe how blubber feels and moves. Then ask them which of the materials would feel and move most like blubber.

Engineer It • What Body Parts Help Animals Meet Their Needs?

Building to the Performance Expectation

The learning experiences in this lesson prepare children for mastery of:

1-LS1-1 Use materials to design a solution to a human problem by mimicking how plants and/or animals use their external parts to help them survive, grow, and meet their needs.

Trace Tool to the NGSS
Go online to view the complete coverage of these standards across this lesson, unit, and time.

(SEP) Science & Engineering Practices

Constructing Explanations and Designing Solutions
Use materials to design a device that solves a specific problem or a solution to a specific problem.

▶ **VIDEO** SEPs: Constructing Explanations and Designing Solutions / Engaging in Argument from Evidence

Analyzing and Interpreting Data
Analyze data from tests ...

▶ **VIDEO** SEPs: Analyzing and Interpreting Data / Using Mathematics and Computational Thinking

(DCI) Disciplinary Core Ideas

LS1.A: Structure and Function
All organisms have external parts. Different animals use their body parts in different ways to see, hear, grasp objects, protect themselves, move from place to place, and seek, find, and take in food, water, and air. Plants also have different parts (roots, stems, leaves, flowers, fruits) that help them survive and grow.

ETS1.A: Defining and Delimiting Engineering Problems
Before beginning to design a solution, it is important to clearly understand the problem.

(CCC) Crosscutting Concepts

Structure and Function
The shape and stability of structures of natural and designed objects are related to their function(s).

▶ **VIDEO** CCC Structure and Function

Influence of Engineering, Technology, and Science on Society and the Natural World
Every human-made product is designed by applying some knowledge of the natural world and is built using materials derived from the natural world.

CONNECTIONS TO MATH

1.MD.C.4 Organize, represent, and interpret data with up to three categories; ask and answer questions about the total number of data points, how many in each category, and how many more or less are in one category than in another.

CONNECTIONS TO ENGLISH LANGUAGE ARTS

W.1.7 Participate in shared research and writing projects (e.g., explore a number of "how-to" books on a given topic and use them to write a sequence of instructions).

Supporting All Students, All Standards

Integrating the Three Dimensions of Learning

This lesson focuses on how the body parts of animals allow animals to meet their needs (DCI Structure and Function). The lesson begins with children exploring how the body parts of animals help animals meet their needs (CCC Structure and Function). Children will explore how people design solutions to problems by mimicking animal parts (CCC Influence of Engineering, Technology, and Science on Society and the Natural World). Finally, children will use what they have learned about animal body parts and function to design, build, and share a solution to a problem (DCI Defining and Delimiting Engineering Problems) (SEPs Constructing Explanations and Designing Solutions / Analyzing and Interpreting Data).

 Professional Development Go online to view **Professional Development videos** with strategies to integrate CCCs and SEPs, including the ones used in this lesson.

Build on Prior Knowledge

Children should already know and be prepared to build on the following concepts:
- A living thing has parts that help it survive.
- The natural world gives scientists and engineers ideas to help solve problems.

Differentiate Instruction

Lesson Vocabulary
- gills
- lungs

Reinforcing Vocabulary To help children remember each vocabulary word, have them draw an illustration of each word. Then have them write the word beneath the illustration, define it, and use it in a sentence. Remind children to look for these highlighted words as they proceed through the lesson.

RTI/Extra Support Supply children with additional images of animals. Provide examples of different animal parts. Allow children to talk about each part. Encourage children to use descriptive words for each part.

Extension Children who want to find out more can do research on animals in different habitats. Children should use their data to make a poster that illustrates the animals in each habitat and how those animals use their body parts to help them survive in their habitat.

ELL Be sure to point out all labels, pictures, captions, and headings throughout the lesson to assist children with strategies to summarize chunks of content. Discuss with children real-life connections to content, and provide hands-on examples of materials when possible to best support the needs of these learners.

Lesson Problem

Lesson Objective

Design a solution to a human problem by mimicking how animals use their body parts to meet their needs.

About This Image

Ask: Have you ever seen a bird like this one? What kind of bird is it? a hummingbird What is the bird doing? eating or drinking from the flower What do you notice about its beak? It is long. Lead children in a discussion about what parts of the bird help it live and grow.

 Structure and Function . . . .

Alternative Engage Strategy

Animals Around Us	👥 small groups ⏱ 20–30 minutes

Begin with a discussion about animals. List types of animals that live in the surrounding area that children are familiar with and can identify. Allow 5 minutes for children to brainstorm and discuss.

In small groups, invite chidren to draw a picture of the animals they discussed and label any body parts they know. Have the children share their drawings and discuss how different animals have different types of bodies and different body parts.

Lesson 3

Engineer It • What Body Parts Help Animals Meet Their Needs?

Animals have body parts that help them get food.

By the End of This Lesson

I will be able to tell how body parts help animals meet their needs. I will be able to explain how animals give people ideas to solve problems.

© Houghton Mifflin Harcourt • Image Credit:

176

Can You Solve It?

Meeting Their Needs People get ideas from animals for inventions. Watch the video to learn more. If the video is not available, have children use the image on the page.

Ask children to record their initial thoughts about how people use the ideas they get from animals to solve problems. Children will revisit this question and their answers as part of the Lesson Check.

Meeting Their Needs

A giraffe has a long neck and a long sticky tongue. It uses both to help it reach leaves.

Explore online. ▶

Collaboration

Build on Prior Knowledge You may want children to view and discuss the video as a whole class activity. In this way, you can assess their prior knowledge on animals parts and functions.

Think about what you saw in the video. What do living things need in order to survive? What parts of an animal help it with these needs? Use details from the video and evidence, or facts, to support your answer.

Can You Solve It?

✏️▷ How can you get an idea from the giraffe to make a tool that reaches high places?

Accept all reasonable answers.

_____

_____

Lesson 3 • Engineer It • What Body Parts Help Animals Meet Their Needs? 177

© Houghton Mifflin Harcourt • Image Credits:

Parts to Find Food

3D Learning Objective

Children will **identify parts of an animal** and **construct explanations** of **how the parts help animals survive, grow, and meet their needs**.

(DCI) Structure and Function . . . .

Ask: How do eyes help animals meet their needs? Animals use their eyes to find food and to watch for predators.

(CCC) Structure and Function . . . .

Ask: What do these pictures have in common? They both show animal eyes. **Ask:** How are they different? They show different types of animal eyes. **Ask:** Why do you think different types of animals have different types of eyes? The animal eyes are different because different animals need different things. Some need to see well in the dark, and some need to see in all directions.

(SEP) Constructing Explanations and Designing Solutions . . . .

Explain to children that the structure of a pair of eyes depends on its use. **Ask: How does the shape or size of an animal's eyes help it meet its needs?** Because animals need different things they have different types of eyes. The shape or size can help the animal survive.

Differentiate Instruction

ELL Use multiple pictures to show different types of animals and their eyes. Show several pictures of eyes and say *eyes*. Give an explanation of the unique features of an animal's eyes such as *helps to see in dark*, or *helps to see all around*. Have children repeat each term aloud with you as you say it.

Parts to Find Food

How do animals use eyes and ears to find food and stay safe?

Explore online. ▶

A tiger hunts mostly at night. It has eyes that can <u>see in the dark</u>!

A dragonfly has eyes that can <u>see in all directions</u>! This helps it find insects and stay safe from birds.

✏️ ➡ Draw a line under two ways animals use their eyes to find food.

178

© Houghton Mifflin Harcourt • Image Credits:

Explore online. ▶

A fox hunts for food. It has ears that face forward to hear animals.

A rabbit uses its nose to find plants. It has ears that turn. It listens for animals that might want to eat it.

A bat uses its ears to find food. The bat makes sounds. It listens for the sounds to come back to it.

Lesson 3 • Engineer It • What Body Parts Help Animals Meet Their Needs?   179

CCC Structure and Function . . . .

Ask: How do you use your ears and nose? To hear things and to smell things. **Ask:** How do you think animals use their ears and nose? Do they use them the same way you do? Animals use their ears to hear and nose to smell, but they use them in different ways, like to find food and protect themselves.

DCI Structure and Function . . . .

Ask: Do you think the shape of the bat's ears is connected to the way the ear works? Sample answer: The bat's ear is probably shaped so that it can hear sounds come back to it.

Differentiate Instruction

RTI/Extra Support Provide children with a more detailed description of why the fox needs to follow animal sounds so that they understand the concept. Explain why the rabbit's ears need to turn and how this helps the animal meet its needs.

Extension Challenge children to write a short paragraph about how animals use their eyes, ears, and noses to help meet their needs. Children can share their paragraphs in small groups or with the class.

Collaboration

Build on Prior Knowledge Review with children the meanings of the terms *sound* and *smell*. Have children brainstorm examples from their own experiences of using their sense of sound or smell to understand what is happening around them. Guide children to recognize that animals use the senses the same way we do to meet their needs.

Structure and Function . . . .

Children should circle the wolf and the polar bear. They should draw a square around the deer. Children should look at the shape of the animals' ears and what they have explored to determine which animals eat other animals and which animals eat plants. The animals with ears that face forward eat other animals. The animal with ears that turn and face to the side eat plants.

SEP **Constructing Explanations and Designing Solutions** . . . .

Ask: What do you think the child is doing in the pictures? **Why?** She is cupping her ears so that they face forward like the ears of an animal that eats other animals. She is using the cones to shape ears like the ears of animals that eat plants. **Ask: How could doing these things help you make something that allows you to hear like an animal?** They could give me an idea for making something with the same shape as the ears of an animal.

✋ FORMATIVE ASSESSMENT

Evidence Notebook

Children should identify the similarities and differences between their ears and animal ears. They should explain how they could use an idea from what they have explored about animal ears to make something that would help them to hear better. Make sure that children use evidence to support their answer.

Scoring Guidelines

• identifies the similarities and differences between their ears and animal ears
• provides an idea from animal ears to help make something that helps them hear better
• uses evidence to support their answer

💡 **Structure and Function** Tell children to think of things in nature or things that people make. Point out that the shape of a thing is connected to how it works.

✏️▷ Circle animals that eat other animals. Draw a square around animals that eat plants.

✋ Apply What You Know 💡

Evidence Notebook • Compare your ears to animal ears. How could you use an idea from animal ears to make something that helps you hear better? Use evidence to explain. Write your answer.

Structure and Function Go to the online handbook for tips.

180

Parts to Eat Food

3D Learning Objective

Children will explore how animals use **their body parts** to grab and eat food.

DCI Structure and Function . . . .

Ask: Why is it important that frogs have a long sticky tongue and not flat teeth like a deer? The frog's long sticky tongue helps it catch insects. Teeth wouldn't help it to do that.

Differentiate Instruction

RTI/Extra Support Some children have difficulty with the concept that animals use body parts other than their mouths to grab and eat food. Remind children that some animals use other body parts to bring the food to their mouths to eat (in the same way that we use our hands).

Extension Have children research animals that have not yet been discussed. Children should discover how these animals grab and eat food.

Parts to Eat Food

Explore online. ▶

A bear has sharp claws to grab fish. It has sharp teeth for tearing food.

A deer has front teeth for pulling up plants. It has flat teeth for chewing plants.

A frog has a sticky tongue to grab insects. It pulls the insect into its mouth to eat.

Animals use body parts to grab and eat food.

© Houghton Mifflin Harcourt • Image Credits:

Lesson 3 • Engineer It • What Body Parts Help Animals Meet Their Needs?   181

DCI Structure and Function . . . .

Children should choose A, B, and C. Animals can use claws, teeth, and tongues to grab food. If a child does not choose all three answer choices, direct them back to the photographs and text on the previous page.

Collaboration

Think, Pair, Share Divide children into pairs. Have each pair brainstorm words that describe the different body parts animals use to grab and eat food.

Which body parts can animals use to grab food? Choose all the correct answers.

Ⓐ claws

Ⓑ teeth

Ⓒ tongue

FORMATIVE ASSESSMENT

Do the Math! • Organize, Represent, and Interpret Data

Children will work with the class to collect data. Have children come up with questions to ask and answer using the data from the chart. Remind children to use evidence in support of their reasoning.

💡 **Organize, Represent, and Interpret Data** Remind children to organize data into groups and sort the data into a chart or graph. Remind children that each mark can stand for one thing.

  Apply What You Know

Do the Math! • Work with your class. Learn about human teeth. Find out how many flat teeth people have. Find out how many sharp teeth people have. Make a tally chart. Ask and answer questions about the information in the chart.

Organize, Represent, and Interpret Data
Go to the online handbook for tips.

© Houghton Mifflin Harcourt • Image Credits:

182

Parts to Breathe

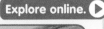

A fish has gills. **Gills** are body parts that take in oxygen from water.

Dolphins have lungs. They swim to the surface to breathe. **Lungs** are body parts that take in air.

Animals need to take in oxygen. They have different body parts to help them take in oxygen.

© Houghton Mifflin Harcourt • Image Credits:

Lesson 3 • Engineer It • What Body Parts Help Animals Meet Their Needs?   183

Parts to Breathe

3D Learning Objective

Children will explore how animals use **their body parts to take in oxygen**.

Structure and Function . . . .

Ask: What might happen if fish had lungs? Fish would have to come to the surface to breathe air.

Explain to children that most land animals use lungs to take in oxygen. Children may think that all animals that live in the water have gills. Explain that animals such as dolphins, whales, seals, sea otters, and turtles live in water but rise to the surface of water to take in air.

SEP Constructing Explanations and Designing Solutions . . . .

Children may not know what oxygen is. Explain that oxygen is a gas that all animals need to take in. **Ask: How can animals that live under the water take in oxygen?** Animals that live under the water have gills that take in oxygen from water. **Ask: How is this different from animals who live on the land or animals that come to the surface of water to breathe?** Animals that live on the land and that come to the surface of water have lungs to breathe.

Parts to Take in Water

3D Learning Objective

Children will explore how animals use **their body parts to take in water**.

DCI **Structure and Function** . . . .

Discuss with children that all animals must have water to survive. **Ask:** Why do you think animals have different body parts to take in water? Animals have different body shapes and sizes. They also live in different places, so they need different ways to take in water.

Collaboration

Small Groups Have children work in small groups to write a paragraph about an animal. Children should include the body parts of that animal and how those parts help the animal find food, grab and eat food, and breathe. Each group can share its paragraph with the class.

Differentiate Instruction

RTI/Extra Support Make a class chart to organize what has been covered in the lesson so far. The columns should be: Parts to Find Food, Parts to Breathe, Parts to Take in Water. Invite children to use words or pictures to fill in the chart.

Extension Invite children to find pictures in books and magazines to add to the chart.

Parts to Take In Water

Explore online. ▶

An elephant uses its trunk to take in water. Then it moves the water into its mouth.

A fish lives in water. Its body needs water, too. A fish takes in water through its skin and gills.

A horse uses its mouth to drink water. It drinks like you do when you drink from a water fountain.

Animals need water to live. They have different body parts to take in water.

184

© Houghton Mifflin Harcourt • Image Credits:

Structure and Function Go to the online handbook for tips.

✏️ Write **lungs** or **gills** to tell what each animal uses to take in oxygen.

| lungs | gills | lungs |

Apply What You Know

Read, Write, Share! • Look in books with a partner. Find one animal that uses lungs and one animal that uses gills. Use evidence to tell how you know.

Participate in a Research Project Go to the online handbook for tips.

© Houghton Mifflin Harcourt • Image Credits:

---

ccc Structure and Function . . . .

Children should write *lungs* for the sea otter, *gills* for the shark, and *lungs* for the zebra. If children incorrectly identify what each animal uses to breathe, refer back to the descriptions of gills and lungs. **Ask: How are gills and lungs different?** Gills take in oxygen from water, and lungs take in oxygen from air.

 Structure and Function Remind children to think of things in nature or things people make. Tell how the shape of a thing is connected to how it works. Tell how the fact that something doesn't change is connected to how it works.

🤚 **FORMATIVE ASSESSMENT**

Read, Write, Share! • Participate in a Research Project

In pairs, children will research both animals that use lungs to take in oxygen and animals that use gills to take in oxygen. Provide children with a variety of sources such as nonfiction books and online photo galleries. Allow children to record their answers in paragraphs or in chart form. Children should provide evidence to support their ideas.

Scoring Guidelines
• provides examples of an animal that uses lungs to take in oxygen and an animal that uses gills to take in oxygen
• provides sufficient evidence to support claims

Participate in a Research Project Remind children that when they research, they are finding facts about a topic. Instruct them on how to use the index and the table of contents to find sources of information. Children should ask questions like, Which pages have facts for my topic?

Animals as Models

3D Learning Objective

Children will explore how engineers **design solutions to human problems** by **mimicking the structure and function of animals in the natural world**.

CCC **Influence of Engineering, Technology, and Science on Society and the Natural World** . . . .

Discuss with children that engineers often study how animals use their body parts to help solve human problems. **Ask:** **How is the bird's beak like the new design for the bullet train?** Both are long and pointy.

SEP **Constructing Explanations and Designing Solutions** . . . .

Ask: **What was the problem with the train?** It was too loud. **Ask:** **What did the engineer do to fix the problem?** He gave the train a pointy front like a beak. **Ask:** **What do you think made the engineer think he should try that?** He saw that the bird didn't make a sound when it went into the water. He saw that the bird had a pointy beak. He thought maybe the beak being pointy kept it from making noise.

Differentiate Instruction

ELL Provide images of animals and body parts. Have children describe the animals and body parts and list the features that allow the body parts to work. Then help children connect how they work to problems that people might want to solve.

Animals as Models

Explore online. ▶

Look at the pictures. How did engineers get ideas from animals to solve problems?

Japan had a fast train with a problem. It made a loud sound going through tunnels. An engineer saw a bird that could dive without making a sound. He gave the train a pointy front like the bird's beak. Now the train goes through tunnels without making noise.

© Houghton Mifflin Harcourt • Image Credits:

186

Engineers made a machine that sends sounds into water. They got ideas from bats. The sounds bounce off fish to help fishing boats find them.

Engineers got ideas from spider webs to build large nets. The nets collect drops of water from the air. The drops go into pipes.

© Houghton Mifflin Harcourt • Image Credits:

Explore online. ▶

Lesson 3 • Engineer It • What Body Parts Help Animals Meet Their Needs?   187

CCC Influence of Engineering, Technology, and Science on Society and the Natural World . . . .

Discuss with children that engineers often study how animals use their body parts to help solve human problems. **Ask: How is the machine that fishing boats use like the sounds a bat makes?** Both send sounds out and wait for them to come back. The bat sends out sounds to help it find food and the boat sends out sounds to find fish.

Connection to Physical Science

Wave Properties Start a discussion with children about the sonar machine and sound. **Ask: What do you think engineers needed to know about sound to make the machine?** Sample answer: They needed to know how sound travels to make the machine. They needed to know that sound would bounce off the fish.

SEP Constructing Explanations and Designing Solutions . . . .

Ask: What is the idea that engineers got from the spider web? collecting drops of water **Ask: What did the engineer use this idea to make? Why?** The engineer made a big net that collects water drops from fog in the air. This is so the water can go into pipes and be used in dry places that need more water.

CCC **Influence of Engineering, Technology, and Science on Society and the Natural World** . . . .

Children should match the woodpecker to the ice pick, the cat eyes to the road reflectors, and the elephant trunk to the robotic arm. If children do not match the correct tool to the animal, discuss how each tool works and provide the similarity between the tool and the animal. For example, the cat eyes "glow" in the dark like the road reflectors.

Differentiate Instruction

ELL Review the terms *evidence, model,* and *tool.* Provide additional images of tools that have been modeled after animals. Have children describe their own experiences using any of the tools.

 FORMATIVE ASSESSMENT

Evidence Notebook

Children will look at classroom tools to think of what animal each tool could have been modeled after.

Remind children to think of things that people make and to think about how the shape of a thing is connected to how it works. Encourage children to discuss ideas in groups and then write answers in their Evidence Notebook. Remind them to use evidence to tell how the animal could have been a model for the tool.

Scoring Guidelines
- accurately describes the classroom tool and the animal it could be modeled after
- identifies similarities between the two animals and the tool
- provides sufficient evidence to support claims

 Draw a line from the animal to the object that was made with an idea from the animal.

 Apply What You Know

Evidence Notebook • Look at classroom tools. What animal could have been a model for each tool? Discuss your ideas with classmates. Write your answers. Use evidence to tell how the animal could have been a model for the tool.

188

Hands-On Activity   👥 small groups   🕐 1 class period

Engineer It • Use Ideas from Animals

3D Learning Objective

SEP   **Constructing Explanations and Designing Solutions** . . . .

Children will use an idea from an animal to design and build a tool that would help them pick up food. They will use the design process to solve their problem. Children will look for an animal to mimic and draw a picture of their design. Then children will use a variety of craft materials to build what they planned. Children will share their tool with a partner and talk about how it solves the problem.

Suggested Materials   animal books, craft materials (craft sticks, coffee stirrers, toothpicks, plastic utensils, scissors, glue or tape), craft paper, chenille sticks, rubber bands, food to test

Preparation

Preassemble material bundles for groups. Children will need a variety of sources that show and describe different animals. Alternatively, children may do this activity as a whole class if materials are limited.

Activity

As a class, view the video. Then discuss the question that will need to be answered. Have children record the question.

DCI   **Defining and Delimiting Engineering Problems** . . . .

STEP 1 To help children gather information, use probing questions. **Ask: What is the problem? Why is it a problem? Where can you go to get some ideas of how to solve the problem? What are some ideas for possible solutions?**

STEP 2 Have children identify parts of their design that are like animal parts. Have them describe how to build these parts so they function like the animal parts that inspired them.

Name_____

🔍 Hands-On Activity

Engineer It • Use Ideas from Animals

| Materials | • animal books | • craft materials |

Ask a Question

How can you use ideas from animals to design a new tool for picking up food?

Test and Record Data   Explore online. ▶

Step 1

Use ideas from animals. Look in animal books. Observe how animals use their body parts to pick up food.

Step 2

Plan and build two solutions.

Check children's work.

Lesson 3 • Engineer It • What Body Parts Help Animals Meet Their Needs?   189

Hands-On Activity, continued

CCC **Influence of Engineering, Technology, and Science on Society and the Natural World** . . . .

STEP 3 Encourage children to think about materials beyond what they are traditionally used for. **Ask: How is this material like an animal part? How does it make your tool work?**

SEP **Analyzing and Interpreting Data** . . . .

Children should analyze data from their tests to see if their solution solved the problem. Give children the opportunity to redesign their solutions.

Claims, Evidence, and Reasoning

Children should make a claim that identifies how their tool is like an animal part. **Ask: What characteristics of your tool are like the characteristics of the animal part?** Sample answer: The tool is long and skinny like a bird's beak.

Scoring Rubric for Hands-On Activity	
3	States a claim supported with evidence about the tool.
2	States a claim somewhat supported with evidence about the tool.
1	States a claim that is not supported by evidence.
0	Does not state a claim and does not provide evidence.

Step 3

Test your tool. Compare it with other classmates. How did you use an idea from an animal to solve the problem?

Make a claim that answers your question.

Sample answer: I can look at how an animal part is shaped and how it picks up food. I can design something with the same shape to pick up food.

What is your evidence?

Sample answer: I designed something that had the same shape as a bird's beak. I tested the tool and it worked.

190

Explore online. ▶ Guide children to the Interactive Online Student Edition where they can choose from and explore both paths.

Take It Further

Animals Can Use Tools!

Explore more online.

Hear Like a Bat ▶

Explore online. ▶

People use tools to help solve problems. What tools can animals use?

Dolphins use an ocean sponge to brush away sand to look for food. The sponge protects the dolphin's nose from rocks.

A sea otter floats with a rock on its chest. It hits a clam shell with the rock to crack it open. Then it eats the clam inside.

An elephant uses a tree branch to scratch its itchy back.

© Houghton Mifflin Harcourt • Image Credits:

Lesson 3 • Engineer It • What Body Parts Help Animals Meet Their Needs?   191

Take It Further

Animals Can Use Tools!

Introduce children to the concept of animals using tools to help solve problems. Animals use tools for different reasons. Some use tools for finding and reaching food.

CCC **Influence of Engineering, Technology, and Science on Society and the Natural World** . . . .

Ask: How do you use a sponge? to wipe things off or clean things How is the dolphin using the sponge in a similar way? The dolphin is wiping the sand away. **Ask:** Look at the picture of the elephant. How did the tree branch help the elephant solve its problem? The tree branch scratched a part of its body that the elephant could not reach. **Ask:** How is this similar to how a person uses a backscratcher? A person uses a backscratcher like an elephant uses a tree branch: to scratch a part of the body that cannot be reached.

SEP **Constructing Explanations and Designing Solutions** . . . .

Ask: How do animals use tools to help solve problems? Animals find things in nature to use as tools to help them solve problems.

Collaboration

Small Groups Have children discuss other ways that animals may use tools. Groups can make a list of ways animals use tools they find in nature to help solve problems they may have.

Take It Further, *continued*

Children should choose C. If children choose A, remind them that chimpanzees are not good swimmers and ask them to think about what the chimps want to do and why the stick is being used. If children select B, remind them that sticks can be used to paddle a boat and to think about what the chimps are trying to do.

Differentiate Instruction

RTI/Extra Support Have children act out the different ways in which animals use tools.

Extension Have children research online more ways that animals use items from nature as tools to help meet their needs. Children can make a poster to share with the class.

Explore more online. ▶

Hear Like a Bat

Children explore how a bat uses its ears to fly in the dark and find food.

Chimpanzees will sometimes go in the water. But chimps are not good swimmers.

How do you think this chimp is using a stick to help it cross the river? Choose the best answer.

Ⓐ to help it swim

Ⓑ to help it paddle

Ⓒ to see how deep the water is

192

© Houghton Mifflin Harcourt • Image Credits:

Explore online. ▶   Have children explore online to find out more about how a giraffe reaches leaves.

Lesson Check

Name_____

Explore online. ▶

Can You Solve It?

✏️➤ How can you get an idea from the giraffe to make a tool that reaches high places?

Be sure to

• Tell how the giraffe uses its body parts to reach food in high places.

• Tell about an idea this gives you for making a tool that can grab something in a high place.

Sample answer: A giraffe has a long neck and tongue to reach

food in high places. I could make a tool with a long arm and a

grabbing part on the end to reach something in a high place.

Lesson 3 • Engineer It • What Body Parts Help Animals Meet Their Needs?   193

Lesson Check

Can You Solve It?

Have children reread their answers to the Can You Solve It? prompt at the beginning of the lesson.

CCC **Influence of Engineering, Technology, and Science on Society and the Natural World** . . . .

Children should connect the structure and function of parts of animals to structures that people use that have similar functions.

SEP **Constructing Explanations and Designing Solutions** . . . .

If children have difficulty responding to the Can You Solve It? prompt, have children look back through the lesson and identify human-made structures that are modeled on animal structures.

DCI **Structure and Function** . . . .

Have children discuss some of the animal parts they observed in this lesson. **Ask: Why do different parts of animals have different shapes?** Different parts have different functions. **How do the different shapes help keep the animal alive?** Some parts are long and pointy like bird beaks to reach food. Other parts are shaped a certain way to hear sounds better, like a fox's ears.

Scoring Guidelines

• Children should effectively communicate how people use the ideas they get from animals to solve problems.

• Children should explain how people use animal's structures as models for human-made structures with similar functions.

Lesson Check, continued

SUMMATIVE ASSESSMENT
Self Check

1. Children should choose A—eyes; and B—ears. If children choose C, direct them to the Parts to Find Food section of the lesson. Have them read the statements for the body parts animals use to help them find food.

2. Children should choose C—a frog's tongue. If children choose A or B, direct them to the Parts to Eat Food section of the lesson. Have children identify how the frog catches its food.

3. Children should circle the middle picture of the mole. If they circle the dragonfly or the tree frog, remind them that the dragonfly and tree frog do not have parts that help them dig. Revisit the Animals as Models section of the lesson.

Self Check

1. Which body parts can animals use to find food? Choose all the correct answers.

   Ⓐ eyes

   Ⓑ ears

   Ⓒ gills

2. You want to design a sticky tool to grab objects. Which animal part would you use as a model?

   Ⓐ a groundhog's claws

   Ⓑ a bear's teeth

   Ⓒ a frog's tongue

3. Which of these animals would you use as a model for making a digging tool? Circle the correct answer.

© Houghton Mifflin Harcourt • Image Credits:

194

4. Which body part does a land animal use to take in oxygen?

(A) gills

(B) lungs

(C) ears

5. An engineer came up with an idea for a new kind of thumbtack. The pointy part of the thumbtack only comes out when it is being used. Which part of a cat do you think an engineer used for an idea?

(A) cat claws that come out when a cat stretches

(B) cat eyes that can see in low light

(C) a cat tongue that can take dirt off fur

4. Children should choose B—lungs. If children choose A or C, have them reread the Parts to Breathe section of the lesson.

5. Children should choose A—cat claws that come out when a cat stretches. If children choose B or C, have them reread the item stem and underline the word *pointy*. Then have them revisit the Animals as Models section of the lesson.

How Do Plants and Animals Respond to Their Environment?

Building to the Performance Expectation

The learning experiences in this lesson prepare children for mastery of:

1-LS1-1 Use materials to design a solution to a human problem by mimicking how plants and/or animals use their external parts to help them survive, grow, and meet their needs.

 Trace Tool to the NGSS
Go online to view the complete coverage of these standards across the lesson, unit, and time.

 SEP **Science & Engineering Practices**

Constructing Explanations and Designing Solutions
Make observations (firsthand or from media) to construct an evidence-based account for natural phenomena.

 VIDEO SEPs: Constructing Explanations and Designing Solutions / Engaging in Argument from Evidence

DCI **Disciplinary Core Ideas**

LS1.D: Information Processing
Animals have body parts that capture and convey different kinds of information needed for growth and survival. Animals respond to these inputs with behaviors that help them survive. Plants also respond to some external inputs.

CCC **Crosscutting Concepts**

Cause and Effect
Simple tests can be designed to gather evidence to support or refute student ideas about causes.

 VIDEO CCC: Cause and Effect

CONNECTIONS TO MATH

MP.4 Model with mathematics.

1.MD.A.2 Express the length of an object as a whole number of length units, by laying multiple copies of a shorter object (the length unit) end to end; understand that the length measurement of an object is the number of same-size length units that span it with no gaps or overlaps.

CONNECTION TO ENGLISH LANGUAGE ARTS

W.1.7 Participate in shared research and writing projects (e.g., explore a number of "how-to" books on a given topic and use them to write a sequence of instructions).

Supporting All Students, All Standards

Integrating the Three Dimensions of Learning

This lesson focuses on how plants and animals respond to their environments (**CCC Cause and Effect**). Children make observations from pictures about plant growth patterns in different light and water conditions. They then carry out an investigation to construct an explanation of the effects of light on plant growth (**SEP Constructing Explanations and Designing Solutions**). Children also explore how the senses of sight, hearing, and smell help animals process information and react to their environment (**DCI Information Processing**) and construct explanations for changes in animals' physical characteristics and behaviors in different seasons.

Professional Development

Go online to view **Professional Development videos** with strategies to integrate CCCs and SEPs, including the ones used in this lesson.

Build on Prior Knowledge

Children should already know and be prepared to build on the following concepts:

- Different plants and animals have different characteristics.
- Plants need water, air, and light to grow.
- Plants and animals have different parts to help them live, stay safe, and meet their needs.
- Our senses help us gather information about our environment.
- Winter and summer can have different weather patterns.

Differentiate Instruction

Lesson Vocabulary

- adaptation
- environment

Reinforcing Vocabulary To help children remember the vocabulary words, work as a class to make a mural for each word. To help children remember the vocabulary word *adaptation*, draw their attention to the root word *adapt*. Remind children that adapt means change. Have children draw pictures of things changing. To help children remember the word *environment*, draw a big circle and label it *Environment*. Encourage children to draw living and nonliving things that are in their environment inside the circle. Remind children to look for these highlighted words as they proceed through the lesson.

RTI/Extra Support Help children connect plant and animal adaptations and migrations to their own experiences and stories they might be familiar with. For example, children may have seen flocks of birds flying south for the winter, or they may have read stories or seen movies in which animals hibernate. Encourage children to share these experiences. If possible, find and read stories related to animal adaptation or migration.

Extension Children who want to find out more can work in pairs to conduct research about a particular plant or animal they are interested in to learn more about how it reacts to changes in its environment. Children can make a poster or a slide show to share what they learn.

ELL Work with children to label a diagram of key plant parts involved in adaptations (e.g., roots, leaves, stem) and a diagram of animal parts involved in gathering information (e.g., nose, eyes, whiskers). Display these for children to refer to as needed.

Lesson Phenomenon

Lesson Objective

Make observations to describe how behaviors of living things help them grow and survive.

About This Image

Ask: Where might these birds be going? Why? As you explore, you'll find out how animals move and how animals and plants change to get what they need.

 Information Processing

Alternative Engage Strategy

Dressing for the Weather	small groups 15–20 minutes

Begin by asking children how they decide what to wear when they go outside. Guide the discussion to focus on how we adapt our clothing choices to changes in the weather, for example, by wearing raincoats, warm coats, or short sleeves. Allow 5 minutes for children to brainstorm and discuss.

Then have children work in small groups to contrast their behavior in different environmental conditions (for example, cold days versus warm days, or wet days versus dry days). Invite groups to share some of their ideas. Ask children whether they know of any plants or animals that change in different seasons. Allow 5 minutes for children to share and discuss.

Lesson **4**

How Do Plants and Animals Respond to Their Environment?

Some animals move to get what they need.

By the End of This Lesson

I will be able to tell how plants and animals respond to the places where they live.

196

Plants Change to Grow

Have you ever seen trees like this? These trees are growing in unusual ways!

Explore online. ▶

© Houghton Mifflin Harcourt • Image Credits: (l) ©MaksymGolovinov/iStock/Getty Images; (r) ©Aries Yu/EyeEm/Getty Images; (c) ©Makarov668/iStock/Getty Images

Can You Explain It?

✏️▶ Why are the trees growing in unusual ways?

Accept all reasonable answers.

_____

_____

Lesson 4 • How Do Plants and Animals Respond to Their Environment?   197

Can You Explain It?

Plants Change to Grow Plants grow in some interesting ways. Look at the images to see some examples. If the images are not available, children can look at the plants on the page.

Have children record their ideas about why the trees in these pictures are growing the way they are. At the end of this lesson, children will revisit this question and their answers as part of the Lesson Check.

Collaboration

Build on Prior Knowledge You may want children to view and discuss the pictures one at a time as a whole-class activity. In this way, you can assess their understanding of plant needs and how those needs can affect plants' growth.

Ask: What does a tree need to survive? sunlight and water What part uses sunlight? the leaves What part helps the tree get water? the roots

Have children look at each tree. **Ask: What do you notice about its trunk (or leaves, or roots)? Why might it grow that way?** Sample asnwers: Some trees grow tall to reach more sunlight. Others grow long roots to reach water that is far away.

Plant Places

3D Learning Objective

Children **make observations** to describe how plants **use information about their environment** to **change their behaviors and characteristics** to help them grow and survive.

 SEP **Constructing Explanations and Designing Solutions** . . . .

Discuss with children that characteristics or parts of a plant help the plant get what it needs to live and grow. **Ask: Why do some plants have long roots while others don't? Why do some plants have tall trunks like trees while others don't? Use evidence to support your answer.** Sample answers: Plants that grow where there is a lot of water don't need long roots because trees with long roots can grow to take in water from far away. Trees that grow in open areas don't need tall trunks to reach the sunlight because there is nothing blocking the sunlight from the leaves.

 FORMATIVE ASSESSMENT ───────────

Do the Math! • Measure Length
Ask: How many cubes tall is each plant? Sample answer: One is 4 cubes tall and the other is 19 cubes tall. **Which plant is taller? How do you know?** Sample answer: The plant that is 19 cubes tall is taller because 19 is greater than 4.

Scoring Guidelines
• measures the plants accurately with the connecting cubes
• lists evidence that supports their claim that the plants can grow where they live

💡 **Use Nonstandard Units to Measure Length** Remind children to connect the cubes for a more accurate measurement.

Plant Places

Explore online. ▶

 A rain forest has tall trees. Some plants grow on trees to reach the sunlight.

 A desert gets very little rain. Many desert plants have thick stems and leaves to hold water.

Plants have adaptations to live in different places. An **adaptation** is something that helps a living thing survive in its environment. An **environment** is all the living and nonliving things in a place.

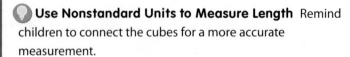 **Apply What You Know**

Do the Math! • Find two plants and draw them. Use connecting cubes to measure the plants. Use evidence to tell how the plants can grow where they live.

 Use Nonstandard Units to Measure Length Go to the online handbook for tips.

198

© Houghton Mifflin Harcourt • Image credits: (t) ©comidor9/iStock/Getty Images; (b) ©Woltek/iStock/Getty Images

Hands-On Activity
Change How a Plant Grows

Name_____

 Hands-On Activity

Materials
- a shoebox
- a bean plant
- scissors
- cup of water

Ask a Question

How do plants grow to get sunlight?

Test and Record Data   Explore online.

Step 1

Put the shoebox near a window. Place the plant in the box. Then close the box.

Step 2

Observe the plant for two weeks. Water the soil when it is dry.

© Houghton Mifflin Harcourt

Lesson 4 • How Do Plants and Animals Respond to Their Environment?

199

Hands-On Activity 👥 pairs 🕐 1 class period plus 10 minutes each day for 2 weeks

Change How a Plant Grows

3D Learning Objective

SEP **Constructing Explanations and Designing Solutions** . . . .

Children make observations from an investigation to construct an evidence-based account for a plant's growth pattern.

Suggested Materials a shoe box, a bean plant, scissors, a cup of water

Preparation

Provide bean plants, or other fast-growing seedlings, or plant seeds 10 days or more in advance to provide seedlings of an appropriate size. Have the shoeboxes cut in advance. Make sure the hole is about three inches in circumference. Allow children time to observe and water the plant each day for 2 weeks.

Activity

CCC **Cause and Effect** . . . .

Discuss with children the cause and effect relationship between plants and sunlight. **Ask: Why do plants need sunlight?** to live and grow **Ask: Why might a plant grow in an unusual direction?** to reach the sunlight **Ask: Why is there a hole in the box?** to see if the plants will adapt

STEP 1 If a window is not available, the boxes can be set near a bright light that is on for several hours each day. Children should turn their boxes so the holes are facing the light source.

STEP 2 Children may require assistance in measuring and pouring an appropriate amount of water. Pouring too little or too much water can affect how the plant grows.

Hands-On Activity, continued

STEP 3 Consider establishing a short time every day for making observations and caring for the plants. Encourage children to record the date and anything they notice about the plant's growth. Have children share their observations in small groups.

DCI **Information Processing** . . . .

Guide children to connect their plant's growth pattern to the benefits the plant obtained by growing that way. **Ask: In what direction did your plant grow? What was your plant able to get by growing in that direction?** My plant grew sideways and down towards the hole in my box to get more more sunlight.

Claims, Evidence, and Reasoning

Children should make a claim that plants grow toward a source of light. They should cite evidence that the plants grew toward the hole in their box. **Ask: How do you know your plant didn't grow toward the hole so that it could get more water or more air?** I put water in the plant's pot and air was everywhere in the box. Sunlight was the only thing that the plant could get more of by growing toward the hole.

Scoring Rubric for Hands-On Activity	
3	States a claim supported with evidence about why the plant grew the way it did.
2	States a claim somewhat supported with evidence about why the plant grew the way it did.
1	States a claim that is not supported by evidence.
0	Does not state a claim and does not provide evidence.

Step 3

Record your observations. Why did your plant grow the way it did? Compare the way your plant grew with the way another group's plant grew.

Children should record their observations.

_____

_____

Make a claim that answers your question.

Sample answer: Plants grow toward sunlight. Plants may

grow sideways or around other things to reach sunlight.

What is your evidence?

Sample answer: The plant grew toward the sunlight.

It grew sideways in the box toward the light coming

through the hole.

200

Plants and Seasons

How do plants survive in different seasons?

winter   spring   summer   fall

Some trees lose their leaves in winter. <u>There is less sunlight and water to make food.</u> In spring and summer, sunlight and water help new leaves grow. In fall, leaves change color and begin to drop off.

 Underline what causes some trees to lose leaves in winter.

 Explore online.

 Apply What You Know

Evidence Notebook • What might happen if a plant did not get sunlight? Use evidence to explain your ideas. Draw and write about a way to test your ideas.

Cause and Effect
Go to the online handbook for tips.

Plants and Seasons

3D Learning Objective

Children **make observations to explain** how plants respond to the changing seasons. Children use their observations to identify the cause and effect relationships related to plant adaptation.

DCI Information Processing . . . .

Ask: How does the weather change throughout the year? Sample answer: Days are longer and temperatures are warmer in summer than in winter. **Ask:** How does the tree change as the weather changes? Sample answer: When the days get longer in the spring, trees grow leaves to take in the sunlight.

FORMATIVE ASSESSMENT

Evidence Notebook
Children will describe some possible effects of a plant not getting sunlight, and an investigation they might conduct to test their hypothesis. Remind children to use evidence to support their ideas about what would happen.

Scoring Guidelines
- provides a claim about the effects of a plant not getting enough light
- lists evidence that supports their claim

Cause and Effect Remind children a cause is what makes something happen, and an effect is the result. In this case, the cause is not enough sunlight.

Animals Use Senses

3D Learning Objective

Children **use an animal's physical characteristics as evidence** to help them identify **how the animal captures information about its surroundings**. Children observe the **effects of those characteristics** on the animal's sensory abilities.

DCI Information Processing . . . .

Discuss the five senses with children. As children name each sense, write it as a heading on the board. Point out that animals use their senses to gather information about their environment. Ask for examples from childrens' own experiences. **For example, birds listen to one another's calls, and dogs can smell food through a bag.** Write children's responses on the board under the appropriate sense heading.

SEP Constructing Explanations and Designing Solutions . . . .

Have children look carefully at each of the photographs and draw upon their own knowledge and experiences to find evidence that might help explain why each animal uses its particular sense to get information about its environment. **Ask: Why would it be helpful for a prairie dog to be good at seeing long distances?** It lives on the prairie where the ground is flat and there is nothing in the way. It can see danger from far away.

Differentiate Instruction

ELL Have children make posters showing the five senses. The posters should include labels for the body parts used by each sense and examples of what children might see, feel, taste, hear, and smell. Children can use the posters as a resource as they work through the lesson.

Animals Use Senses

Explore online. ▶

A prairie dog uses its eyes and nose to notice the things around it. It will warn others if it sees or smells danger.

A great white shark has eyes that see well. It uses its ears to feel movements in the water.

A mouse does not see well at night. It uses its nose to smell for food. It uses its whiskers to feel in the dark.

© Houghton Mifflin Harcourt • Image Credits: (t) ©DLILLC/Cardinal/Corbis; (c) ©Alastair Pollock Photography/Moment/Getty Images; (b) ©Martin Fowler/Alamy

202

Moles do not see well. What body parts do you think it uses to notice things and find food? Choose all the correct answers.

Ⓐ nose

Ⓑ eyes

Ⓒ whiskers

 Apply What You Know

Evidence Notebook • Work in a group. Talk about how you use your eyes, ears, nose, and hands to notice the things around you. Write your ideas. Then share your ideas.

Lesson 4 • How Do Plants and Animals Respond to Their Environment?   203

ᴅᴄɪ Information Processing . . . .

Children should choose A and C. If children choose B, remind them that a mole does not see well and guide children to look for body parts a mole can use to find food. You may want to have children close their eyes and think about which of their senses they could use to find food with their eyes shut. Discuss which sense a mole would experience with each body part.

Connection to Physical Science

Information Technologies and Instrumentation
Ask children how they learn about their environment. As children suggest ideas, encourage them to see that as well as relying on information they gather directly, humans have developed tools including books, telephones, radios, televisions, and computers to help them gather information from farther away.

 FORMATIVE ASSESSMENT

Evidence Notebook
Children will work in small groups to list ways they use their eyes, ears, nose, and hands to gather information about their environment. Remind children to include specific examples of how they use each body part.

Scoring Guidelines
• provides at least two examples of how he or she uses each of the body parts listed: eyes, ears, nose, and hands

Animals on the Move

3D Learning Objective

Children **observe animals migrating** in response to changes in the weather. Children use their observations to identify **what causes animals in their own area to migrate**.

 Information Processing . . . .

Discuss with children how animals can gather information about their environment. **Ask: What information might each animal gather that causes it to move from one place to another**? Sample answers: The wildebeest might find all the grass in one area is dry or eaten. The whales and the penguins might feel the water getting colder.

SEP Constructing Explanations and Designing Solutions . . . .

Ask: What evidence tells you that the different types of animals move because of a change in the weather? How do you know there isn't another reason they move? The animals in the group move at the same time, and they move at the same time every year when the weather changes.

Collaboration

Small Groups Have children work in small groups to research another animal that moves because of changes in the weather. Start by brainstorming animals to research. Provide children with appropriate research materials or Internet sites. Groups can share their research with the class.

Animals on the Move

Explore online. ▶

Why do some animals move to other places when the weather changes?

Every year, wildebeests travel a long way to find food. They move to where it rains and plants grow.

Gray whales live in cold waters. Every winter, they swim to warmer waters to have young.

© Houghton Mifflin Harcourt

204

In winter, emperor penguins move away from the ocean to have young. By summer, their young are big enough to swim and hunt.

Why do some animals move to another place when there are changes in the weather? Choose all the correct answers.

Ⓐ to find food

Ⓑ to hide from danger

Ⓒ to have young

Apply What You Know

Read, Write, Share! • Work with a partner. Learn about an animal in your area that moves when the weather changes. Draw a picture of the animal. Tell about why the animal moves. Use evidence to tell how you know.

Participate in a Research Project
Go to the online handbook for tips.

SEP Constructing Explanations and Designing Solutions . . . .

Children should choose A and C. If children choose B, have children brainstorm possible causes of danger for different animals. Discuss whether animals can find danger in only one location or in different locations. Children should recognize that danger is present wherever animals live.

Differentiate Instruction

RTI/Extra Support Have children work in small groups to role play a group of a particular kind of animal sensing a change in the environment and moving to another location to find food or stay warm. Tell children to show clearly the animals reacting to the change and to show how the animals benefit from moving. Allow children to narrate their role play.

Extension Have children write and illustrate a short story about an animal that responds to a change in the environment and decides to migrate.

 FORMATIVE ASSESSMENT

Read, Write, Share! • **Participate in a Research Project**
Children perform research to learn about a migratory animal that lives in their area. Provide children with a variety of resources, including books and appropriate Internet sites.

Scoring Guidelines
• uses words and pictures to describe an animal and how it moves with changing seasons
• provides evidence to support the claim that the animal moves with changing seasons

Participate in a Research Project Remind children to provide evidence for the animal's migration, as well as describing it.

© Houghton Mifflin Harcourt

Animals and Seasons

3D Learning Objective

Children **gather evidence** to explain **adaptations animals have developed in response to environmental conditions**. Children use their observations to identify **adaptations and how those adaptations enable animals to survive**.

DCI Information Processing . . . .

Discuss with children that not all animals respond to environmental change in the same way. **Ask: What animals do you know of that move to another place when winter comes?** Sample answer: Many birds and butterflies move to a warmer place. **Ask: What animals change with the seasons?** Sample answer: Foxes grow thick fur, squirrels gather nuts, and bears rest or sleep in dens.

SEP Constructing Explanations and Designing Solutions . . . .

Ask: How does eating food help the groundhog prepare? How does growing thick fur help the fox prepare? Use evidence to support your answer. Sample answers: The groundhog eats a lot of food so it can sleep all winter without having to eat again. The fox's thick fur helps keep it warm like a coat.

 FORMATIVE ASSESSMENT

Evidence Notebook

Children will conduct research to learn about an animal in their area. They will describe how the animal changes with the seasons and provide evidence to support their claims. Provide access to print resources or online resources.

Scoring Guidelines
• describes how an animal adapts to changing seasons
• provides evidence to support a claim that the animal adapts to changing seasons

Animals and Seasons

Explore online. ▶

What adaptations help animals live in the same place all year?

To get ready for winter, a groundhog <u>eats a lot of food</u>. Then it <u>digs a home under the ground</u> and sleeps all winter long.

A red fox grows thick fur and eats more to get ready for winter.

 Draw a line under the words that tell how a groundhog gets ready for winter.

 Apply What You Know

Evidence Notebook • Learn about an animal in your area. How does it change with the seasons? Use evidence to tell how you know.

206

Explore online. ▶ Guide children to the Interactive Online Student Edition where they can choose from and explore both paths.

Take It Further

Careers in Science & Engineering •
Forest Ranger

Children explore the career of a forest ranger. Forest rangers watch for forest fires to protect plants and animals. A forest ranger also educates the public about plants and animals and how to protect them.

DCI Information Processing . . . .

Discuss with children the importance of protecting places where plants and animals live. **Ask: How do animals know when the place where they live has been harmed?** Sample answer: Animals use their body parts to learn about their surroundings. They might notice that the forest smells different. **Ask: What happens to the animals if a forest is damaged by a fire?** Sample answer: The animals might decide to move somewhere else.

CCC Cause and Effect . . . .

Discuss with the children the effect a forest fire, or other damage to the forest, will have on the plants and animals that live there. **Ask: How does a forest fire affect the plants and animals that live there?** Sample answer: Animals will lose their homes and food they eat. Plants may burn.

Take It Further

Careers in Science & Engineering •
Forest Ranger

Explore more online.
Insects in Winter

A forest ranger works to protect places where plants and animals live.

Explore online. ▶

A forest ranger watches for forest fires. A fire can quickly destroy plants and animals. It can also harm people visiting the forest.

A forest ranger tells people about the plants and animals that live in the forest. The ranger talks about how to protect the plants and animals that live in a forest.

Lesson 4 • How Do Plants and Animals Respond to Their Environment?   207

Take It Further, continued

Children should choose C. If children choose A or B, discuss with children what they would observe in a picture of the forest ranger watching for fires or protecting an animal.

DCI Information Processing . . . .

Discuss with children the importance of of a forest ranger's job. **Ask: Why is it important for a forest ranger to teach people about the forest and how to protect it?** Sample answer: It is important to teach people about the forest so they can find out how to keep it safe from fire and other damage. Since plants and animals get what they need in the forest, this will protect the plants and animals that live there.

Collaboration

Partners Have children work with a partner to role play the job of a forest ranger. Children can take turns playing the roles of forest ranger and forest visitor. The visitor will ask questions about animals discussed in this lesson. The forest ranger will draw upon his or her knowledge to answer the questions. This activity can be used as a lesson review.

Explore more online. ▶

Insects in Winter

Children explore what happens to insects in winter.

Look at the photo of the forest ranger.

© Houghton Mifflin Harcourt • Image Credits: ©Johann Schumacher/Photolibrary/ Getty Images

What is this forest ranger doing? Choose the best answer.

Ⓐ watching for fires

Ⓑ helping an animal

Ⓒ teaching people

208

Lesson Check

Name_____

Explore online. ▶

Can You Explain It?

✏▷ Why are the trees growing in unusual ways?

Be sure to

• Tell what plants need to grow and live.

• Tell how these trees are growing to get the things they need in their environment.

Sample answer: A tree needs sunlight, air, and water to grow.

These trees are growing in unusual ways to get the things they

need in their environment.

Lesson Check

Can You Explain It?

Have children reread their answers to the Can You Explain It? prompts at the beginning of the lesson.

SEP **Constructing Explanations and Designing Solutions** . . . .

Guide children to consider evidence from the Hands-On Activity, Change How a Plant Grows, as they suggest why the trees might be growing in strange ways. **Ask: How is this tree like the plants we grew in boxes?** The plants and the tree all grew in unusual directions to reach the light.

DCI **Information Processing** . . . .

Encourage children to think about or draw a picture of an atypical tree. Then have them compare their picture with a typical tree. **Ask: How is your tree different from other trees you have seen?** Sample answer: It is growing at an angle. **Ask: What is different about its surroundings?** Sample answer: The ground is not flat. **Ask: How might the tree's surroundings have affected how it grew?** Sample answer: It is growing towards the sun, instead of straight up, so it can get more light.

Scoring Guidelines

• Children should identify a plant's needs for sunlight and water.
• Children should describe how trees respond to their environment.
• Children should explain the cause and effect relationship that results in trees having unusual growth patterns.

Lesson Check, continued

SUMMATIVE ASSESSMENT
Self Check

1. Children should choose C—to get sunlight. If children choose A, reinforce that there is water in the soil. Ask children what plants need that might be up high. Some children may benefit from reviewing the investigation Change How a Plant Grows. If children choose B, remind them that air is everywhere.

2. Children should choose B—water and sunlight. If children choose A or C, review what plants need to grow, and ask children what changes when spring arrives.

3. Children should choose A—to sense danger; and B—to find food. If children choose C, direct them to reread the Animals Use Senses section of this lesson. Ask guiding questions as children read to highlight how each animal uses its senses. Remind children that they use senses to observe. Ask children what senses they use when they are eating, and guide children to understand that eating is itself not a sense.

Self Check

1. Why do some plants grow on trees?

   (A) to get water

   (B) to take in air

   (C) to get sunlight

2. What do trees get in the spring that causes them to grow new leaves?

   (A) water and wind

   (B) water and sunlight

   (C) water and snow

3. How do animals use their eyes, ears, and nose to notice the things in their environment? Choose all correct answers.

   (A) to sense danger

   (B) to find food

   (C) to eat food

210

4. Hector thinks that a plant will grow toward light. Which test should he do to prove that a plant grows toward light?

Ⓐ He should grow a plant in a box with no light.

Ⓑ He should grow a plant in a box that lets some light in.

Ⓒ He should grow a plant in a box with no water.

5. Draw a line to match each animal to how it gets ready for winter.

| grows thick fur | digs a home under the ground |

4. Children should choose B—He should grow a plant in a box that lets some light in. If children choose A or C, ask them what they expect to observe, and whether those observations will help them decide whether a plant grows toward light.

5. Children should draw a line from the picture of the groundhog to "digs a home under the ground" and from the picture of the fox to "grows thick fur." If children indicate that the fox digs a home under the ground, direct them to reread the Animals and Seasons section of the lesson.

Unit 4 Performance Task

Engineer It • Design a House

👥 small groups ⏱ 2 class periods

Objective
Children will **define a problem** and **design a solution** by applying the **structure and function** of the **parts of water plants**.

Suggested Materials
books about water plants, craft materials, container of water

Preparation
Collect cardboard, foam, string, sticks, dowels, and other craft materials in advance of this activity. Bring in a plastic tub or other large container and arrange for sink access.

 SEP Asking Questions and Defining Problems . . . .

Ask: Why do you think it's important to define the problem before you begin to plan a solution? Sample answer: If I don't understand the problem, then I can't begin to plan solutions.

STEPS

Step 1 • Define a Problem
Ask: What does your house need to be able to do? Sample answer: It needs to be built on or near water.

SEP Constructing Explanations and Designing Solutions . . . .

Step 2 • Plan and Build
Ask: How could learning about water plants help you to design a house that will be built near water? Sample answer: I could look at the shape and function of parts of plants that live near water, and design something that has similar parts.

Step 3 • Test and Improve
Guide children as they test their solutions.

 ## Unit 4 Performance Task
Engineer It • Design a House

> **Materials**
> - books about water plants
> - craft materials
> - container of water

STEPS

Step 1

Find a Problem You want to design a house that could be built near or on the water.

Step 2

Plan and Build Look at plants that grow in or near the water. Use ideas from the plants to plan at least two solutions. Build your solutions.

© Houghton Mifflin Harcourt

Step 3

Test and Improve Test your solutions. How can you improve your solutions?

212

Step 4

Redesign

Make changes to the materials or how you put the materials together. Test your new solutions.

Step 5

Communicate Share your solutions. Compare solutions with others. Use evidence to tell how your solution solves the problem.

✔ Check

_____ I used ideas from plants to plan and build my house.

_____ I tested my house by putting it in water.

_____ I redesigned my house to make it work better.

_____ I shared my house with others.

© Houghton Mifflin Harcourt

Step 4 • Redesign

 Structure and Function . . . .

Prompt children to make changes as a result of their tests. Children may need to change the structure of their houses, or they may need to change their materials. Children should retest their houses to evaluate their changes. **Ask: Did your changes make the design better? How do you know?** Sample answer: The changes made the design better. Before, the stilts of the house got too wet and broke apart. I changed the material of the stilts from paper to wood. Now the house stands in the water.

Step 5 • Communicate

Children should communicate their results, and include an explanation for each step of a design process that they followed. Children should explain, based on their test results, how parts of a water plant can be mimicked to improve the design of a house built on or near water.

Scoring Rubric for Performance Task	
3	Builds, tests, and redesigns a model house that can withstand water and remain in place. Shares solution with others using evidence to tell how the solution solves the problem.
2	Builds and tests a model house, but does not redesign it. Shares solution with others, but does not provide evidence that it solves the problem.
1	Builds a model house, but does not test or redesign it. Does not share solution with others or provide evidence.
0	Does not build, test, or redesign a model house.

Unit 4 Review

SUMMATIVE ASSESSMENT

1. Children should connect the roots to take in water from soil; the leaves to make food for the plant; and the thorns to protect the plant from animals. If children do not complete this correctly, review the parts of a plant and how they function. By completing Plant Parts and Shape Up in Lesson 1, children explored parts of plants, and how the they help plants survive, grow, and meet their needs.

2. Children should choose B—a plant with seeds that are carried by water. If children choose A or C, reinforce that designs often mimic things in nature. By completing Looking to Nature in Lesson 1, children explored how people design solutions to problems by mimicking how plants use their parts.

3. Children should choose C—talons. If children choose A or B, reinforce that animals use their body parts to protect themselves in different ways. Explain that some animals do use horns and shells to protect themselves, but an eagle does not. An eagle has talons. By completing Facing Danger in Lesson 2, children explored how body parts help animals face danger by providing physical protection or a threat.

Unit 4 Review   Name _____

1. Draw a line to match the plant parts to the words that tell how they help the plant.

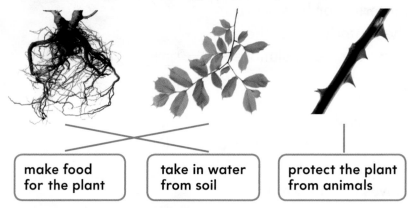

| make food for the plant | take in water from soil | protect the plant from animals |

2. Alonso wants to design a waterproof box that can float. Which plant would be best to study for ideas?
   (A) a plant with seeds that are carried by wind
   (B) a plant with seeds that are carried by water
   (C) a plant with seeds that stick to the fur of animals

3. Which body part helps an eagle stay safe from other animals?
   (A) horns
   (B) shell
   (C) talons

214

4. Look at the picture. Which body parts help keep this musk ox safe? Choose all correct answers.

Ⓐ thick fur
Ⓑ hard shell
Ⓒ big horns

5. Look at the picture. Which tool mimics this bird's bill?

Ⓐ   Ⓑ   Ⓒ

6. Which body parts do animals use to take in oxygen? Choose all correct answers.

Ⓐ lungs
Ⓑ gills
Ⓒ fins

---

4. Children should choose A—thick fur; and C—big horns. If children choose B, reinforce that different animals have body parts that work in different ways to help them. A hard shell helps some animals stay safe, but a musk ox does not have this kind of body part. By completing Facing Danger and Staying Safe in Weather in Lesson 2, children explored how body parts help animals protect themselves from danger and severe weather.

5. Children should choose A—the photograph of the tongs. If children choose B or C, reinforce that the shape of a human tool and the way it moves can mimic an animal's body part. Discuss all answer choices to verify children understand the way each tool works. Ask them to compare the shape and function to the bird's bill. By completing Animals as Models in Lesson 3, children explored how engineers design solutions to human problems based on animals' body parts.

6. Children should choose A—lungs; and B—gills. If children choose C, or did not select both A and B, reinforce that animals have different body parts to help them take in oxygen. If children did not choose "lungs", they may have limited their selection to external body parts. Reinforce that lungs help take oxygen into the body. By completing Parts to Breathe in Lesson 3, children explored body parts that animals use to take in oxygen.

7. Children should choose C—a machine that helps find fish. If children choose A or B, have them think about if those tools use sound. By completing Animals as Models in Lesson 3, children explored how engineers design solutions to problems.

8. Children should choose B—There is little sunlight and water for the tree to make food. If children choose A, discuss how winter affects plants. If children choose C, discuss if animals help a tree live and grow. By completing Plants and Seasons in Lesson 4, children explored how plants respond to seasonal changes.

9. Children should choose C—eyes. If children choose A or B, discuss how hawks use their eyes. They don't have whiskers, and their beak helps them eat. By completing Animals Use Senses in Lesson 4, children explored how animals get information.

10. Children should choose B—to have their young. If children choose A or C, explain that newborn whales do not have enough blubber to protect against cold water. By completing Animals on the Move in Lesson 4, children explored how some animals migrate in response to changes in the weather.

3D Item Analysis	1	2	3	4	5	6	7	8	9	10
SEP Constructing Explanations and Designing Solutions		•					•			
DCI Structure and Function	•	•	•	•	•	•	•		•	
DCI Information Processing							•	•	•	•
CCC Structure and Function	•	•	•	•	•	•			•	
CCC Influence of Engineering, Technology, and Science on Society and the Natural World		•			•		•			
CCC Cause and Effect										•

7. Engineers observed how bats use sound to find food. What tool did this help engineers invent?
   Ⓐ a fast train that is very quiet
   Ⓑ road markers that glow in the dark
   Ⓒ a machine that helps find fish

8. Look at the tree. Why did it lose its leaves in winter?

   Ⓐ There is too much sunlight and water for the tree to make food.
   Ⓑ There is little sunlight and water for the tree to make food.
   Ⓒ The animals that live in the tree moved to a warmer place.

9. What body part helps this hawk find food?
   Ⓐ whiskers
   Ⓑ beak
   Ⓒ eyes

10. Why do gray whales swim to warmer waters in winter?
    Ⓐ to find fish to eat
    Ⓑ to have their young
    Ⓒ to escape danger

216

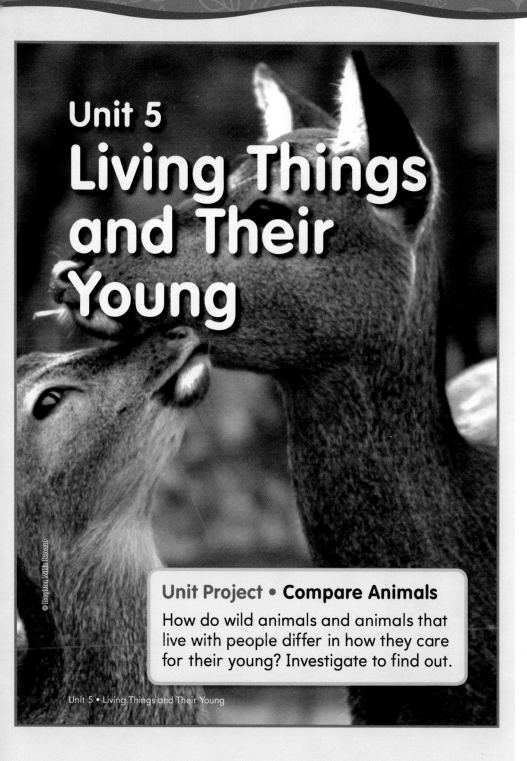

Unit 5
Living Things and Their Young

Unit Project • Compare Animals

How do wild animals and animals that live with people differ in how they care for their young? Investigate to find out.

Unit 5 • Living Things and Their Young

© Houghton Mifflin Harcourt

Unit 5 • Living Things and Their Young

Unit Overview

In this unit, children will…
- compare young plants with parent plants.
- observe patterns to explain how plants of the same kind are alike and different.
- compare young animals with parent animals.
- observe patterns to explain how animals of the same kind are alike and different.
- describe how plants and animals respond to their environments to meet their needs.
- describe how behavior patterns of parents and offspring help offspring survive.

About This Image

Guide children in a discussion about the animals on this page. **Ask: Are these the same kind of animal? How do you know?** Yes, they have the same parts and both have fur. They are both deer. They look alike. **Ask: Which one of these animals could be the parent of the other animal? How do you know?** The bigger deer is the parent. Parents are bigger than young animals.

Unit Project • **Compare Animals**

Have children plan and conduct an investigation to compare how wild animals and animals that live with people care for their young. Discuss what kind of animals they will include in the investigation. Have children brainstorm questions that could be answered, such as: "How are the needs of an animal that lives in the wild and an animal that lives with people alike and different?", "How do wild animals get what they need?", and "How would a parent take care of its young in the wild?"

More support for the Unit Project can be found on pp. 219I–219L.

Unit 5 At a Glance

The learning experiences in this unit prepare children for mastery of:

Performance Expectations

LS1-2 Read texts and use media to determine patterns in behavior of parents and offspring that help offspring survive.

LS3-1 Make observations to construct an evidence-based account that young plants and animals are like, but not exactly like, their parents.

Explore online. ▶

In addition to the print resources, the following resources are available online to support this unit:

Unit Pretest

Lesson 1 How Do Plants Look Like Their Parents?
- Interactive Online Student Edition
- Lesson Quiz

Lesson 2 How Do Animals Look Like Their Parents?
- Interactive Online Student Edition
- Lesson Quiz

You Solve It Watch Us Grow

Lesson 3 How Do Animals Take Care of Their Young?
- Interactive Online Student Edition
- Lesson Quiz

Unit Performance Task

Unit Test

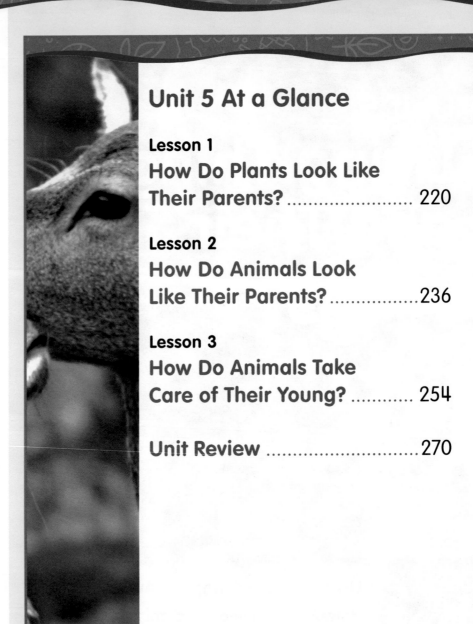

Unit 5 At a Glance

218

© Houghton Mifflin Harcourt

Unit Vocabulary

parent a plant or animal that makes young like itself (p. 222)

offspring the young of a plant or animal (p. 222)

trait something that living things get from their parents (p. 231)

behavior a way an animal acts (p. 256)

Vocabulary Game • Guess the Word

Materials
- 1 set of word cards

How to Play
1. Work with a partner to make word cards.
2. Place the cards face down in a pile.
3. One player picks the top card but does not show it.
4. The second player asks questions until he or she guesses the word correctly.
5. Then the second player takes a card.

Unit Vocabulary

The Next Generation Science Standards emphasize explanation and demonstration of understanding versus rote memorization of science vocabulary words. Keep in mind that these vocabulary words are tools for clear communication. Use these words as a starting point, not an end goal, for children to build deeper understanding of science concepts.

Children can explore all vocabulary words in the **Online Glossary**.

Vocabulary Strategies

- Have children review the vocabulary words. Then have children work in pairs to share an example of each word and explain why they think it's an example. Have pairs record their examples to refer back to during the unit.
- Have children think about how each word relates to living things. Have children share their ideas with a partner.

Differentiate Instruction

RTI/Extra Support Pronounce each word and have children repeat it after you. Have children find each highlighted word within the unit content. Have children work in pairs and explain to a partner what they think each word means based on the surrounding context of imagery and text.

Extension Have children select two vocabulary words and work in small groups to illustrate and explain the words to a kindergarten child.

Vocabulary Game • Guess the Word

Preparation Guide children in making the vocabulary game cards. Assign children to teams. Appoint one scorekeeper and rotate children through the position during gameplay. Establish a winning score or set number of terms per round.

Integrating the NGSS* Three Dimensions of Learning

Building to the Performance Expectations

The learning experiences in this unit prepare children for mastery of the following Performance Expectations:

From Molecules to Organisms: Structures and Processes

1-LS1-2 Read texts and use media to determine patterns in behavior of parents and offspring that help offspring survive.

Heredity: Inheritance and Variation of Traits

1-LS3-1 Make observations to construct an evidence-based account that young plants and animals are like, but not exactly like, their parents.

Assessing Student Progress

After completing the lessons, the **Unit Project** **Compare Animals** provides children with opportunities to practice aspects of and to demonstrate their understanding of the Performance Expectations as they plan and conduct an investigation to compare how wild animals and animals that live with people care for their young.

Additionally, children can further practice or be assessed on aspects of the Performance Expectations by completing the **Unit Performance Task** **Match Animals and Their Young,** in which children obtain information from books to make a card game about animals and their young. They will describe patterns that explain how parents and their offspring are alike and different.

Lesson 1
How Do Plants Look Like Their Parents?

In Lesson 1, children focus on the similarities and differences between adult plants and their young. Children investigate these phenomena by classifying plants based on shared traits **(CCC Patterns).** They discuss how the transfer of traits from parent plants to their young results in plants that look alike **(DCI Inheritance of Traits).** Children observe, illustrate, and discuss variation among plants of the same kind **(DCI Variation of Traits).** During a hands-on activity, children make observations about how plants of the same kind grow to construct evidence **(SEP Constructing Explanations and Designing Solutions).**

Lesson 2
How Do Animals Look Like Their Parents?

In Lesson 2, children focus on the similarities and differences between animals and their offspring. Children explore how animals change as they grow and observe patterns in these changes **(DCI Inheritance of Traits) (CCC Patterns).** Children compare parts of young animals and their parents **(CCC Patterns)** through a hands-on activity **(SEP Constructing Explanations and Designing Solutions).** Children compare and contrast coverings of young and adult animals. They explore variations among animals of the same kind **(DCI Variation of Traits).**

Lesson 3
How Do Animals Take Care of Their Young?

In Lesson 3, children focus on patterns in behavior of parents and offspring that help them survive. Children explore how animals take care of their young **(CCC Patterns) (SEP Scientific Knowledge is Based on Empirical Evidence) (DCI Growth and Development of Organisms).** They describe behavioral patterns of parents and offspring that help offspring get food **(CCC Patterns) (SEP Scientific Knowledge is Based on Empirical Evidence) (DCI Growth and Development of Organisms).** They discover how animals teach their offspring to get food and stay safe **(CCC Patterns) (SEP Obtaining, Evaluating, and Communicating Information) (DCI Growth and Development of Organisms).**

Standards Supported by This Unit

 Explore Online. Online only.

Next Generation Science Standards	Unit Project	Lesson 1	Lesson 2	Lesson 3	Unit Performance Task	You Solve It
SEP Constructing Explanations and Designing Solutions	•	•	•			
SEP Obtaining, Evaluating, and Communicating Information	•			•	•	
SEP Scientific Knowledge is Based on Empirical Evidence				•		•
DCI **LS3.A** Inheritance of Traits		•	•		•	
DCI **LS3.B** Variation of Traits		•	•			•
DCI **LS1.B** Growth and Development of Organisms	•			•		•
CCC Patterns	•	•	•	•	•	•

NGSS* Across the Grades

Before
From Molecules to Organisms: Structures and Processes

K-LS1-1 Use observations to describe patterns of what plants and animals (including humans) need to survive.

Grade 1
From Molecules to Organisms: Structures and Processes

1-LS1-2

Heredity: Inheritance and Variation of Traits

1-LS3-1

After
From Molecules to Organisms: Structures and Processes

3-LS1-1 Develop models to describe that organisms have unique and diverse life cycles but all have in common birth, growth, reproduction, and death.

Heredity: Inheritance and Variation of Traits

3-LS3-1 Analyze and interpret data to provide evidence that plants and animals have traits inherited from parents and that variation of these traits exists in a group of similar organisms.

3-LS3-2 Use evidence to support the explanation that traits can be influenced by the environment.

 **Trace Tool to the NGSS™** Go online to view the complete coverage of these standards across this grade level and time.

3D Unit Planning

Lesson 1 How Do Plants Look Like Their Parents? pp. 220–235

Overview

Objective Make observations to explain the differences and similarities between plant parents and their offspring.

SEP Constructing Explanations and Designing Solutions
DCI **LS3.A** Inheritance of Traits
DCI **LS3.B** Variation of Traits
CCC Patterns

Math and **English Language Arts** standards and features are detailed on lesson planning pages.

Print and Online Student Editions	Explore online.
ENGAGE	Lesson Phenomenon pp. 220–221 Can You Explain It? Plants of the Same Kind	▶ Can You Explain It? Pictures and audio
EXPLORE/ EXPLAIN	Young and Old Compare Parts Compare Adult Plants Hands-On Activity Grow Carrot Tops pp. 229–230	Hands-On Worksheet You Solve It Watch Us Grow
ELABORATE	Take It Further pp. 231–232 People in Science & Engineering • Gregor Mendel	Take It Further Watch a Pumpkin Grow
EVALUATE	Lesson Check p. 233 Self Check pp. 234–235	Lesson Quiz

Hands-On Activity Planning

Grow Carrot Tops

Objective Children grow two carrot plants from carrot tops, record their observations, compare the plants, and look for patterns. They make a claim and support the claim by using evidence gathered from their observations.

👥 small groups
🕐 10 minutes/day for 10 days

Suggested Materials
- two carrot tops
- small bowl of water

Preparation/Tip

Organize and bundle materials for groups. Prepare enough carrot tops for each group to grow two. Provide access to water.

Lesson 2 How Do Animals Look Like Their Parents? pp. 236–253

Overview

Objective Make observations to explain the differences and similarities between animal parents and their offspring.

SEP Constructing Explanations and Designing Solutions
DCI **LS3.A** Inheritance of Traits
DCI **LS3.B** Variation of Traits
CCC Patterns

Math and **English Language Arts** standards and features are detailed on lesson planning pages.

Print and Online **Student Editions**	Explore online. ▶
ENGAGE	**Lesson Problem** pp. 236–237 **Can You Solve It?** Related Animals	▶ **Can You Solve It?** Video
EXPLORE/ EXPLAIN	**Animals Grow** **Compare Parts** **Compare Body Coverings** **Animals of the Same Kind** **Hands-On Activity** Observe Brine Shrimp pp. 241–242	**Hands-On** Worksheet
ELABORATE	**Take It Further** pp. 249–250 The Butterfly Life Cycle	**Take It Further** Pet Investigation
EVALUATE	**Lesson Check** p. 251 **Self Check** pp. 252–253	Lesson Quiz

🔍 Hands-On Activity Planning

Observe Brine Shrimp

Objective Children explore how brine shrimp hatch and change as they grow into adults. Children observe the shrimp over time and record information about their body features. They compare and contrast the adult shrimp and use this information to construct evidence.

👥 whole class
🕐 10-15 minutes every other day for 2 weeks

Suggested Materials
- container with water
- brine shrimp eggs
- iodine-free salt
- baking soda
- hand lens

Preparation/Tip

The teacher should prepare the water in advance. Add 2 tablespoons of salt and $\frac{1}{4}$ teaspoon of baking soda for every liter of water. Set aside 10-15 minutes every other day for two weeks to make observations.

3D Unit Planning, continued

Lesson 3 How Do Animals Take Care of Their Young? pp. 254–269

Overview

Objective Determine patterns in how animal parents and offspring behave in ways that help the offspring survive.

SEP Obtaining, Evaluating, and Communicating Information

SEP Scientific Knowledge is Based on Empirical Evidence

DCI **LS1.B** Growth and Development of Organisms

CCC Patterns

Math and **English Language Arts** standards and features are detailed on lesson planning pages.

	Print and Online Student Editions	Explore online. ▶
ENGAGE	Lesson Phenomenon pp. 254–255 Can You Explain It? Animals Help Their Young	▶ Can You Explain It? Video
EXPLORE/ EXPLAIN	Staying Safe Finding Food Young Animals Learn Hands-On Activity Compare How Animals Learn pp. 263–264	Hands-On Worksheet
ELABORATE	Take It Further pp. 265–266 Careers in Science & Engineering • Zookeeper	Take It Further On Their Own
EVALUATE	Lesson Check p. 267 Self Check pp. 268–269	Lesson Quiz

🔍 Hands-On Activity Planning

Compare How Animals Learn

Objective Children gather information on how polar bears and lions teach their young to find food and stay safe. They use this information to construct evidence about how the animals are alike and different. 👥 small groups ⏱ 1 class period	**Suggested Materials** • a computer • animal books

Preparation/Tip

Locate books on polar bears and lions from the school's library or a local library. Schedule time at the computer center if you do not have a computer in the classroom. View websites and books in advance for appropriateness.

3D Unit Planning

You Solve It

Go online for an additional interactive opportunity.

Watch Us Grow

This interactive activity offers practice in support of **1-LS3-1.**

SEP Scientific Knowledge is Based on Empirical Evidence

DCI LS3.B Variation of Traits

DCI LS1.B Growth and Development of Organisms

CCC Patterns

3D Learning Objectives

- Children understand that most young plants and animals have the same or similar body features as their parents.
- Children demonstrate an understanding that plants and animals look similar to their parents but not exactly alike.

Activity Problem

- Children are given images of a bean plant and a gosling growing and compare these images to images of the adult bean plant or goose.
- At each developmental stage of either the bean plant or the gosling, children compare and contrast the young plant or animal to the adult.

Interaction Summary

The activity presents scenarios for children to observe, explore, compare, and contrast the body features of young plants and animals and their parents.

- Children select either the bean plant or the gosling to watch them as they develop. In either case there is an image of an adult on the screen for children to compare and contrast the young organism to.
- At each stage children drop labels (e.g. "have flowers" "don't have flowers") into "buckets" next to the young and the parent images or both.
- Children will demonstrate success by dropping the correct labels next to the young and/or adult at each stage.

Assessment

Pre-Assessment

Assessment Guide, Unit Pretest

The Unit Pretest focuses on prerequisite knowledge and is composed of items that evaluate children's preparedness for the content covered within this unit.

Formative Assessment

Interactive Worktext, Apply What You Know, Lesson Check, and Self Check

Summative Assessment

Assessment Guide, Lesson Quiz

The Lesson Quiz provides a quick assessment of each lesson objective and of the portion of the Performance Expectation aligned to the lesson.

Interactive Worktext, Performance Task pp. 270–271

The Performance Task presents the opportunity for children to collaborate with classmates in in order to complete the steps of each Performance Task. Each Performance Task provides a formal Scoring Rubric for evaluating children's work.

Interactive Worktext, Unit 5 Review, pp. 272–274

Assessment Guide, Unit Test

The Unit Test provides an in-depth assessment of the Performance Expectations aligned to the unit. This test evaluates children's ability to apply knowledge in order to explain phenomena and to solve problems. Within this test Constructed Response items apply a three-dimensional rubric for evaluating children's mastery on all three dimensions of the Next Generation Science Standards.

Assessment Online

Go online to view the complete assessment items for this unit.

Differentiate Instruction

Leveled Readers

The Science & Engineering Leveled Readers provide additional nonfiction reading practice in this unit's subject area.

On Level
What Can We Learn About Animals?
What Is a Plant?
These readers reinforce unit concepts and include response activities for your children.

Extra Support
What Can We Learn About Animals?
What Is a Plant?
These readers share title, illustrations, vocabulary, and concepts with the On-Level Reader; however, the text is linguistically accommodated to provide simplified sentence structures and comprehension aids. They also include response activities.

Enrichment
Amazing Animals
Weird and Wacky Plants
These high-interest, nonfiction readers will extend and enrich unit concepts and vocabulary and include response activities.

Teacher Guide
The accompanying Teacher Guide provides teaching strategies and support for using all the readers.

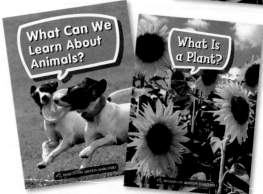

ELL

English Language Learner support resources include a glossary and Leveled Readers in Spanish and English. ELL teaching strategies appear throughout this unit:

pp. 220B, 227, 236B, 238, 254B, 262

RTI/Extra Support

Strategies for children who need extra support appear throughout this unit:

pp. 219, 220B, 226, 236B, 244, 254B, 259, 265

Extension

Strategies for children who have mastered core content and are ready for additional challenges appear throughout this unit:

pp. 219, 220B, 226, 236B, 244, 254B, 259, 265

Leveled Readers All readers are available online as well as in an innovative, engaging format for use with touchscreen mobile devices. Contact your HMH Sales Representative for more information.

Connecting with NGSS

Connections to Community

Use these opportunities for informal science learning to provide local context and to extend and enhance unit concepts.

At Home

Tree Leaves Have children work with a family member to collect a variety of leaves from trees. Children should categorize their tree leaves according to shape and size. Help children identify the type of tree the leaf came from. Have children share their findings with the class and explain how they know which leaf came from which tree.
Use with Lesson 1.

Animal Families Have children work with a family member to cut out pictures of animals and their offspring. Then have children make a poster or collage of the different animal families. Children can present their poster or collage to the class and explain how the animals and their offspring are alike and different.
Use with Lesson 2.

In the Community

Visiting Plants Plan a class field trip to a local orchard or nursery. Have children develop a list of questions they want to ask about how young plants are similar to and different from their parents. Have children record the answers to their questions.
Use with Lesson 1.

Guest Speaker Invite a veterinarian to speak to the class about how animals and their offspring are alike and different. Have them also talk about how parents and their young display behaviors that help them survive. Have children prepare questions for him or her to answer. Encourage children to ask a mix of appropriate science questions.
Use with Lesson 2 or 3.

Home Letters Go online to view the Home Letters for this unit.

Collaboration

Collaboration opportunities in this unit:

Build on Prior Knowledge
pp. 221, 237, 255

Think, Make, Pair, Share
p. 224

Small Groups
pp. 232, 250, 257, 266

Think, Write, Pair, Share
p. 247

Jigsaw
p. 240

Connections to Science

Connections to Science opportunities in this unit:

Connection to Engineering Design
Lesson 1, p. 222

Connection to Earth and Space Sciences
Lesson 2, p. 240

Connection to Earth and Space Sciences
Lesson 3, p. 257

Unit Project

Unit Project   👥 small groups   🕐 2 class periods
Compare Animals

Have children plan and conduct an investigation to compare how animals in the wild with animals that live with people. Discuss what kind of animals they will include in the investigation. Have children brainstorm questions that should be answered, such as: How are the needs of an animal that lives in the wild and an animal that lives with people alike and different? How would a parent take care of its young in both environments? Are there any differences in the animal depending on where it lives?

3D Learning Objective

SEP Obtaining, Evaluating, and Communicating Information
Explore differences between wild animals and animals that live with people by planning and conducting an investigation.
Collect data to use as evidence to answer a question.
Construct an argument using evidence to support a claim.

Skills and Standards Focus

This project supports building children's mastery of **Performance Expectation 1-LS1-2.**

SEP Constructing Explanations and Designing Solutions
SEP Obtaining, Evaluating, and Communicating Information
DCI Growth and Development of Organisms
CCC Patterns

Suggested Materials

- pictures of different environments
- several books on animals

Preparation

Show pictures of different environments, such as a forest or a farm. Share details about how each environment has several types of animals living in the environment. Have children share what kind of animals they might find in each picture. Guide children to begin brainstorming questions they can answer in their investigation and where they can look to find the answers to their questions.

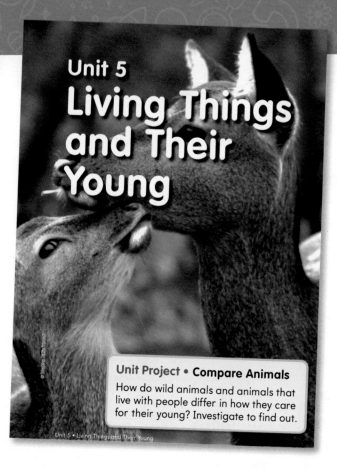

Unit 5
Living Things and Their Young

Unit Project • Compare Animals
How do wild animals and animals that live with people differ in how they care for their young? Investigate to find out.

Unit 5 • Living Things and Their Young

Differentiate Instruction

RTI/Extra Support Children can be provided with two or three animals that live in different environments along with specific questions to answer. They can then choose their method to investigate.

Extension Have children compare differences in an animal depending on its environment. For example, does an elephant that lives in the wild display similar behaviors as an elephant that lives in a zoo?

Name _____

Unit 5 Project
Compare Animals

Where do animals live? Can you think of two animals that can live in the wild and live with people? Write your ideas of the lines below. Then choose one animal that can live in both a wild or natural environment and live with people. Plan and conduct an investigation to find out how the animal cares for their young in both environments, and if there are any differences in the animal living in the wild and living with people.

Children should write their idea they have for an animal that lives in

both places and how they care for their young.

_____

_____

Materials
Draw and label the materials you will need.

Children should draw and label materials. The following are possible materials children can use for this investigation: books, pictures, computer.

Unit 5 Project • Page 1 of 3

Unit 5 Project
Compare Animals

SEP Obtaining, Evaluating, and Communicating Information . . . .

Pose the unit project question to children. Encourage them to think of how wild animals and animals that live with people differ in how they care for their young. Discuss all of the ideas as a class. Have children choose one animal that lives in both environments to investigate similarities and differences.

Children investigate how one animal that lives in the wild is similar and different than when the same animal lives with people. Children select one animal that can live in both environments to discover patterns. They will compare the animal for differences in behavior, interaction with the environment, and social behaviors in how they care for their young. **Ask: How do you think the animal is the same in both environments? What do you think may be different about the animal when both environments are compared?** I think the animal will still care for their young in the same way within both environments. I think one difference will be that the animal in the environment living with people will be more friendly.

ESSENTIAL QUESTIONS Prepare children for their project by asking the following questions.

- Where do animals live in the wild?
- Where do we find animals living with people?
- What evidence can be collected to show how animals take care of their young?
- Do you think there is a difference in how animals take care of their young depending on their environment?

Ask: Can you think of an animal that lives in the wild that also lives with people? What differences do you think you will see? A fish can live in the river and also in a fishbowl in a person's home. A fish living in the river finds its own food while a fish living in a fishbowl is fed by a person.

Steps

Children investigate similarities and differences between one animal that lives in the wild and with people.

SEP **Obtaining, Evaluating, and Communicating Information** . . . .

Before beginning the investigation, have children discuss different environments where animals live, such as a forest, a zoo, and a home.

Ask: Where do animals live? **Animals live in trees, in the water, underground, and in our homes.** Challenge children to identify one animal that lives in the wild and with people. **Ask: Can you think of one animal that lives in the wild and with people?** **The penguin can live in the wild and in a zoo with people.** **Ask: Do you think where the animal lives will make them change how they raise their young?** **The animals that live with people might not have to worry about their safety or finding food as much as the animal living in the wild.** Refer children to Lesson 3 How Do Animals Take Care of Their Young? to begin their observations.

Have children plan the steps of their investigation on one animal living in the wild compared to the same animal living with people. At the end of the investigation, children need to be able to tell what similarities and differences they found in their selected animal. They should record their observations using words and pictures.

Data

Children evaluate the information found during the investigation to note similarities and differences.

CCC **Patterns** . . . .

Remind children that patterns in the natural world can be observed, used to describe phenomena, and used as evidence. **Ask: What are some patterns in nature?** **Sample answer: animals meeting their needs, animals taking care of their young, animals hiding from danger**

Steps Write the steps you will do.

Answers may vary but should reflect a logical order of steps in the investigation. Sample steps listed:

1. Select one animal that can live in the wild and with people.

2. List how the animal living in the wild cares for their young.

3. List how the animal living with people cares for their young.

4. Compare the animal for ways it is the same in both environments.

5. Compare the animal for ways it is different in both environments.

Data
Record your data.

Answers and drawings may vary but should reflect that the animal cares for their young in both environments.

animal living in the wild   animal living with people

Analyze Your Result

Look for patterns in your data.

Restate Your Question

Write the question you investigated.

Answers should identify the question children initially chose at the

beginning of the investigation.

Claims, Evidence, and Reasoning

Make a claim that answers your question.

Answers should compare how their animal cares for their young in

both environments.

Review the data. What evidence from the investigation supports your claim?

Answer should cite evidence from the investigation to support the

comparison made between the animal that lives in the wild and the

animal that lives with people.

Discuss your reasoning with a partner.

Unit 5 Project • Page 3 of 3

Analyze Your Result

Have children analyze their data. Elicit from them any patterns they noticed. Encourage them to share their data with the other groups in order to compare research results. **Ask: What patterns did you observe?** I observed that the animal takes care of its young whether it lives in the wild or with people. However, how the animal cares for its young in each environment can be different.

Claims, Evidence, and Reasoning

Children should state a claim about the similarities and differences in how an animal that lives in the wild cares for its young compared to one living with people. Review with children what it means to make a claim. Guide them to understand that the data they collected will be used as evidence to support their claim. They should site evidence to support their claim by using their drawings and written notations.

Ask: What claim can you make? Some animals might take care of their young differently depending on their environment. **Ask: How does your evidence support your claim?** Evidence of how the animal they have researched taking care of their young should be provided. Encourage children to discuss their reasoning.

Ask: What can you use as evidence from your investigation? the data and research collected, such as the drawings or writings

Scoring Rubric for Unit Project	
3	States a claim supported with evidence about how animals are alike and different in their care of their young in different environments
2	States a claim somewhat supported with evidence about how animals are alike and different in their care of their young in different environments
1	States a claim that is not supported by evidence
0	Does not state a claim and does not provide evidence

How Do Plants Look Like Their Parents?

Building to the Performance Expectation

The learning experiences in this lesson prepare children for mastery of:

1-LS3-1 Make observations to construct an evidence-based account that young plants and animals are like, but not exactly like, their parents.

Trace Tool to the NGSS
Go online to view the complete coverage of these standards across this lesson, unit, and time.

 SEP Science & Engineering Practices

Constructing Explanations and Designing Solutions
Make observations (firsthand or from media) to construct an evidence-based account for natural phenomena.

▶ **VIDEO** SEPs: Constructing Explanations and Designing Solutions / Engaging in Argument from Evidence

 DCI Disciplinary Core Ideas

LS3.A: Inheritance of Traits
Young animals are very much, but not exactly like, their parents. Plants also are very much, but not exactly, like their parents.

LS3.B: Variation of Traits
Individuals of the same kind of plant or animal are recognizable as similar but can also vary in many ways.

 CCC Crosscutting Concepts

Patterns
Patterns in the natural world can be observed, used to describe phenomena, and used as evidence.

CONNECTIONS TO MATH

1.MD.A.1 Order three objects by length; compare the lengths of two objects indirectly by using a third object.

1.MD.A.2 Express the length of an object as a whole number of length units, by laying multiple copies of a shorter object (the length unit) end to end; understand that the length measurement of an object is the number of same-size length units that span it with no gaps or overlaps. Limit to contexts where the object being measured is spanned by a whole number of length units with no gaps or overlaps.

CONNECTION TO ENGLISH LANGUAGE ARTS

W.1.7 Participate in shared research and writing projects (e.g., explore a number of "how-to" books on a given topic and use them to write a sequence of instructions).

Supporting all Students, All Standards

Integrating the Three Dimensions of Learning

This lesson focuses on the similarities and differences between adult plants and their young. Initially, children investigate these phenomena by classifying plants based on shared traits (**CCC Patterns**). They will discuss how the transfer of traits from parent plants to their young results in plants that look alike (**DCI Inheritance of Traits**). As the lesson progresses, they observe, illustrate, and discuss variation among plants of the same kind (**DCI Variation of Traits**). During a Hands-On Activity, children make observations about how plants of the same kind grow to construct evidence (**SEP Constructing Explanations and Designing Solutions**).

Professional Development Go online to view **Professional Development videos** with strategies to integrate CCCs and SEPs, including the ones used in this lesson.

Build on Prior Knowledge

Children should already know and be prepared to build on the following concepts:

- A plant is a growing, living thing.
- Living things make new living things.
- Many plants have common parts, including stems, leaves, flowers, seeds, and fruit.
- Plants make seeds and new plants grow from seeds.

Differentiate Instruction

Lesson Vocabulary

- trait
- parent
- offspring

Reinforcing Vocabulary To help children remember these vocabulary words, ask them to make a poster of animal parents and offspring. They can cut out pictures and label them with the vocabulary word *parent* or *offspring*. Ask children to tell about one *trait* that the parent animal shares with their offspring. Remind children to look for the highlighted words as they proceed through the lesson.

RTI/Extra Support Provide additional opportunity for hands-on discovery. Ask children to save a few seeds from fruit eaten at home or school. Begin by providing examples of commercial seed packets for children to investigate. Explain that the picture on the front of the packet shows how the parent plant looks. Help children find information on the packets about some traits to expect in the young plants. Finally, guide children to design their own seed envelopes for the seeds they collected.

Extension Children who want to find out more can do research on how some traits are more helpful for a plant to live, grow, or make new plants.

ELL Be sure to point out all labels, pictures, captions, and headings throughout the lesson to assist children with strategies to summarize chunks of content. Discuss with children real-life connections to content and provide hands-on examples of materials when possible to best support the needs of these learners.

Lesson Phenomenon

Lesson Objective

Make observations to explain the differences and similarities between plant parents and their offspring.

About This Image

Guide children to look at the field of flowers in the photograph. **Ask: What do you see in the picture?** water, sun, flowers, trees **Which of those things are living?** flowers, trees **Look at the flowers. How many kinds of flowers do you see?** one **How do you know?** Accept all reasonable answers.

 **Constructing Explanations and Designing Solutions**

Alternative Engage Strategy

Plant Portraits	 small groups 20–30 minutes

Ahead of time, gather several photographs or cards of plants with prominent features. Place each photograph into a folder to allow viewing by one person at a time.

Have children form groups. Explain to children that the members of each group will all draw the same kind of plant. Give one volunteer from each group a plant photograph, advising them not to show it to others in the group. Then have the volunteer describe the plant to the rest of the children while they draw. (e.g. "It has a very long stem".) Encourage the children to ask clarifying questions as they draw (e.g. "Are the leaves pointy or round?"). Allow 15 minutes for this activity.

Have each group share their drawings and photograph with the whole class. Encourage them to think about how their drawings look alike and different. Allow 10 minutes to share their results.

Lesson 1 How Do Plants Look Like Their Parents?

This field has flowers that are the same kind.

By the End of This Lesson
I will be able to explain how plants of the same kind can be alike and different.

220

© Houghton Mifflin Harcourt · Image Credits: ©Radius Images/Alamy Stock Photo/ Getty Images

Can You Explain It?

Plants of the Same Kind We can make observations to determine whether plants are the same kind. Go online to look at the pictures and listen to the audio. If you are unable to go online, use the photographs on the page.

Ask children to record their thoughts about how the two plants are alike and different. Children will see this question again in the Lesson Check, and a have a chance to modify their answers at that time.

Collaboration

Build on Prior Knowledge You may want children to view the photographs as a whole class activity. In this way, you can assess their prior knowledge of plant traits. Think about the plants in the pictures. How are the plants the same? How are they different? Do you think these plants are the same kind of plant? How do you know?

Plants of the Same Kind

How are the young plants like the parent plant?
How are they different from the parent plant?

young plants

Explore online. ▶

parent plant

Can You Explain It?

✏ How can you tell if two plants are the same kind of plant?

Accept all reasonable answers.

_____

_____

_____

Young and Old

3D Learning Objective

Children **observe a pattern of differences** between **young trees and parent trees to gather evidence** of how **offspring** may start life **with different features than their parent plant**.

Patterns . . . .

Ask: How would you describe the trees in each of the pictures? Sample answer: Young trees have a small trunk and a few straight branches with some green leaves. Parent trees have a thicker trunk and large, bent branches covered with flowers. If children interpret flowers as white or pink leaves, point out areas with green leaves and explain that the tree is covered with flowers. **Ask: Do the young trees have flowers?** No

DCI Inheritance of Traits . . . .

Read and discuss the labels below each picture. **Ask: Why are the trees on the right labeled** *parent cherrry trees*? They made new trees similar to themselves. **What do you think these young cherry trees will look like when they get older?** They'll grow to look like their parents.

Connection to Engineering Design

Developing Possible Solutions Lead a discussion about the different kinds of fruit people pick from plants. For each fruit, guide children to identify a plant trait that could cause a problem in picking the fruit (e.g., tall trees, thorny bushes, fruit too heavy to carry). In groups, have children discuss and draw a possible solution to one of the problems discussed. Ask each group to share their solution with the class.

Young and Old

Explore online. ▶

| young cherry trees | parent cherry trees |

The young cherry trees do not have flowers yet. They will grow flowers.

A **parent** is a plant or animal that makes young like itself. Parent plants make young plants. The young plants may look different from the parent plants. But they will grow to look like the parent plants. **Offspring** are the young of a plant or an animal.

222

© Houghton Mifflin Harcourt • Image Credits: (l) ©DWalker44/Getty Images; (r) ©Stephen Saks/Getty Images

Have children explore to find out more about how young plants may be different than their parent plants.

Circle the parts on the parent tree that are different from the parts on the young tree.

young tree

parent tree

Apply What You Know

Evidence Notebook • Do research. Draw pictures to show how a young plant may look different from its parent plant. Use evidence to tell how you know. Then look for patterns in your pictures.

Patterns
Go to the online handbook for tips.

Lesson 1 • How Do Plants Look Like Their Parents?

223

SEP **Constructing Explanations and Designing Solutions** . . . .

Discuss with children the trees in the picture. **Ask: Which tree is the parent tree?** taller tree with flowers **What evidence supports your answer?** It has many of the same traits as the smaller tree, but its trunk is bigger and it's old enough to grow flowers. Explain that when trees grow flowers, they are old enough to be parents and make new trees.

CCC **Patterns** . . . .

Ask: How are the trees different? The parent tree is taller, has a thicker trunk, and has flowers. **Ask: How are the trees alike?** The trees are the same kind and have the same shaped leaves.

 FORMATIVE ASSESSMENT

Evidence Notebook

Have children think about what happens when a young plant becomes an adult, and draw pictures to represent differences between adult and young plants. Encourage them to identify and discuss patterns in their pictures. Ask children to justify features of their drawings with evidence from the lesson or from personal observations.

Scoring Guidelines
• includes parts that are exclusive to either a young plant or an adult plant
• uses evidence and describes patterns

Patterns Remind children that when they observe nature, they can look for a pattern, or things that repeat. Have them use the pattern to describe what happens and as proof of an idea.

Compare Parts

3D Learning Objective

Children **compare patterns** between a **young plant and a parent plant** to **explain how they are alike and different**.

SEP **Constructing Explanations and Designing Solutions** . . . .

Guide children's attention to the labels on each photograph. Provide help as needed to read and pronounce the word *coleus*. Explain that it is a kind of plant. **Ask: If there were no labels on these pictures, would we know they are the same kind of plant?** yes **What evidence supports your observation?** They have the same parts. The leaves are the same shape and colors.

CCC **Patterns** . . . .

Ask: Do the plants share a trait for a color pattern? If so, describe it. Yes, every leaf is red in the middle and green at the edges. **Suppose these plants are right next to each other. You see a leaf on the floor. How could you tell which plant dropped the leaf?** Sample answer: If it came from the young coleus plant, it would be smaller and have more green around the edge.

DCI **Inheritance of Traits** . . . .

Ask: Do you think the young plant will look exactly the same as the parent plant as it grows? Sample answer: The young plant might be a different size or have a different number of leaves than its parent.

Collaboration

Think, Make, Pair, Share Have children draw plants with different traits. Have children switch drawings with their partner and describe the traits of the plants.

Compare Parts

How are young plants and parent plants alike and different? Look closely at the pictures.

Explore online. ▶

young coleus plant

parent coleus plant

© Houghton Mifflin Harcourt • Image Credits: (l) ©VStock/Getty Images; (r) ©Mim Friday/Alamy; (r) ©Mim Friday/Alamy

Most young plants have parts that look like the parts of their parents. The leaves may have the same shape. But the young plants may have smaller or fewer leaves.

224

✏️ This leaf is from an adult beech tree. Circle the picture that shows a young beech tree.

© Houghton Mifflin Harcourt • Image Credits: (t) ©Tom Chance/Getty Images; (bc) ©Stuart Scott/Alamy; (bl) ©blickwinkel/Alamy; (br) ©Kathy Collins/Getty Images

✋ **Apply What You Know**

Read, Write, Share! • Work in a small group. Choose an adult plant. Research what the plant looks like when it is young. Draw a picture to compare the young plant to the adult plant.

💡 **Participate in a Research Project**
Go to the online handbook for tips.

SEP Constructing Explanations and Designing Solutions . . . .

Ask: If you can only see the leaves of the adult beech tree, how will you know which young tree is also a beech tree? I will compare the beech tree leaves with the leaves on each young tree.

CCC Patterns . . . .

Ask: What will you observe about the leaves on each young tree? I will look at the shape of each leaf to compare it with the adult leaf. Discuss the shape of each sapling's leaves.

DCI Inheritance of Traits . . . .

Ask: Which one is the young beech tree? the picture in the center How do you know? The shape of the leaves is the same. The other young trees have leaves that are not like the adult beech tree leaves.

✋ **FORMATIVE ASSESSMENT**

Read, Write, Share! • Participate in a Research Project
Children work in small groups to research how an adult plant looks when it is young. Provide access to resources such as books, magazines, or digital sources. Children should use descriptions and photographs to help them illustrate how their plant looks as an adult and as a young plant.

Scoring Guidelines
• accurately represents parts of an adult and young plant
• identifies differences between adult and young plants

💡 **Participate in a Research Project** Remind children that when they research, they are finding facts about a topic. Describe how to use the index and the table of contents to find sources of information.

Compare Adult Plants

3D Learning Objective

Children **observe and gather evidence of** how plants of the same kind **can have similarities and differences**.

 Patterns . . . .

Explain that all of the plants in the pictures are tulips. **Ask: How would you describe this kind of plant to someone who has never seen it before?** Tulips have flowers that are round at the bottom and pointy at the top, they have long stems, and thin, pointy, green leaves.

 Variation of Traits . . . .

Remind children that plants get traits from a parent. Those traits make the plant look the way it does. Think about traits for shape, color, and size. **Ask: Which of these traits is the same for these tulips?** shape of the flowers, stems, and leaves **Which of these traits can be different?** color of the flowers and size of the stems, leaves, and flowers

---

Differentiate Instruction

RTI/Extra Support Some children may have difficulty understanding how plants of the same kind can have obvious differences. Ask them to write about or draw their favorite ice cream. When a number of children have shared descriptions or drawings, discuss the differences in each. Have children explain what makes them all ice cream.

Extension Have children make a chart showing examples of plant traits observed by each sense. Ask them to report to the class which senses they use most often, and which sense is least likely to help them observe plant traits.

Compare Adult Plants

How are adult plants of the same kind alike and different?

Explore online.

These tulips are different heights.

The flowers of these tulips are different colors.

The leaves on these tulips have the same shape. But the leaves are not the same size.

226

 This flower is a lily. Circle the picture that also shows a lily.

Apply What You Know

Evidence Notebook • Work in a group. Sort pictures of plants. Which are the same kind? Use patterns you observe to help you. Use evidence to explain how you sorted. Record in your Evidence Notebook.

Patterns Go to the online handbook for tips.

SEP Constructing Explanations and Designing Solutions . . . .

Ask: Do any of these other flowers look exactly the same as this lily? no How can you use your observations about the first lily to look for another lily? Observe the other flowers to see if there are any similarities between the first lily and the other three.

DCI Variation of Traits . . . .

Ask: Do any of the bottom flowers have pointed petals? Yes, the first and third flowers do. Point to the third flower. Do you think this flower with pointed petals is a lily? no Why not? It has too many petals. The lily has six. Do you think this first flower is a lily? Why? Yes, its petals are similar in number and shape.

Differentiate Instruction

ELL Have children draw two different plants. Provide sentence frames for children to practice describing and comparing traits of the two plants.

 FORMATIVE ASSESSMENT

Evidence Notebook

Children work in groups to sort pictures of plants by kind. Provide photographs of several varieties of the same kind of plants. Encourage children to discuss their observations about each plant as they decide which ones should be sorted together and to justify their decisions with evidence.

Scoring Guidelines

- identifies patterns to justify decisions
- provides sufficient evidence to support explanation

Patterns Remind children to observe the plants and look for a pattern, something that repeats. The patterns you see will help you decide which plants are the same kind.

Do the Math! • Compare and Order Length

Discuss with children that height is one way plants of the same kind can be different. Provide enough plants of different heights for each group of children to choose four. Ideally, the containers should be the same height. Guide children as they use paper clips to measure the plants. Encourage children to write down the height of each plant in paper clips. Children may choose to use this data, or they may visually compare the height of the four plants. Allow children to order the plants from shortest to tallest before they draw and write about what they did.

Compare and Order Length Compare four plants. Place the four plants next to one another. Be sure the bottom of all the plants line up. Which plant is tallest? Which is shortest?

Use Nonstandard Units to Measure Length Choose a plant to measure first. Line up paper clips along the plant. Count the paper clips to measure the plant's length.

Do the Math! • Work with a group. Find four plants. Use paper clips to find the height of each plant. Then compare the heights of your plants. Order them from shortest to tallest.

Compare and Order Length Go to the online handbook for tips.

Draw to show how you ordered. Write about what you did.

Children should draw four plants in order from shortest to tallest.

Sample answer: I measured each plant. Then I put them in order with the shortest first and the tallest last.

228

Hands-On Activity

Grow Carrot Tops

Name _____

Materials • two carrot tops • small bowl of water

Ask a Question

How do plants of the same kind look alike and different?

Test and Record Data **Explore online.** ▶

Step 1

Place the bowl of carrots in a sunny place.

Step 2

Observe the carrots each day for ten days. Record your observations.

© Houghton Mifflin Harcourt

Lesson 1 • How Do Plants Look Like Their Parents?   229

Hands-On Activity 👥 small groups ⏱ 10 minutes/day for 10 days

Grow Carrot Tops

3D Learning Objective

SEP **Constructing Explanations and Designing Solutions** . . . .

Children grow two carrot plants from carrot tops and record observations over a ten-day span, compare the plants, and look for patterns. Children will then make a claim and support that claim using evidence from their observations during the investigation.

Suggested Materials carrot tops, small bowls of water

Preparation

Organize and bundle materials for groups. Prepare enough carrot tops for each group to grow two. Provide access to water.

Activity

Guide children to write a question by asking about the materials and the video, if used as support. Remind children about the content of the lesson as they write their own question. **Ask: Think about the lesson. What could we explore with these materials?** Have children record a question.

STEP 1 Discuss the first step. **Ask: Why does the bowl need to be in a sunny place?** Carrots are plants, and plants need sunlight to grow.

STEP 2 To help children gather information, use probing questions. **Ask: What will you observe?** Sample answers: How much the carrots grow, changes in the way the carrots look, and changes in the way they feel to the touch. Remind children to record their observations.

Hands-On Activity, continued

(CCC) Patterns . . . .

STEP 3   Ask: How did the carrot tops look when you started? They were small carrot tops. **What parts changed?** The carrot and the top changed. **How did they change?** They got taller and changed shape.

(SEP) Constructing Explanations and Designing Solutions . . . .

STEP 4 Discuss the question again with children to determine whether they have enough information to make a claim. **Ask: What kind of evidence will support your claim?** Accept all reasonable answers.

Claims, Evidence, and Reasoning

Children should make a claim that identifies a pattern of growth that results in very similar, but not identical, plants. **Ask: Did you identify any patterns? How does it compare to patterns you observed about other plants?** Sample answer: All of the leaves on both plants were the same color and shape. My carrot plants look alike, but when I look closer, I can see differences. This is like other plants I saw in this lesson.

Scoring Rubric for Hands-On Activity	
3	States a claim supported with evidence about how two plants of the same kind can be alike and different
2	States a claim somewhat supported with evidence about how two plants of the same kind can be alike and different
1	States a claim that is not supported by evidence
0	Does not state a claim and does not provide evidence

Step 3

Compare the carrots. Look for patterns in their parts and size.

Step 4

Tell how plants of the same kind are the same and how they are different. Use the patterns you found as evidence.

Sample answer: The plants have leaves that look the same,

but the size and number of the leaves are different.

_____

Make a claim that answers your question.

Sample answer: When I grow two plants of the same kind, the

leaves and other parts look the same, but the number and size

of the leaves are different.

What is your evidence?

Sample answer: I grew two carrot plants and observed them.

The kind of leaves and parts were the same, but the number and

size were different.

230

Explore online. ▶ Guide children to the Interactive Online Student Edition where they can choose from and explore both paths.

Take It Further

People in Science & Engineering •
Gregor Mendel

Children investigate Gregor Mendel's work to apply and extend knowledge about how young plants look similar to and different from their parent plants.

Gregor Mendel is known as the "father of modern genetics." He was a botanist who discovered the basic principles of heredity by doing experiments in his garden. His findings showed how traits are passed through generations of living things.

CCC Patterns . . . .

As a class, read the information about Gregor Mendel. Discuss his experiments with pea plants and traits. Remind children that an experiment is one way to look for a pattern. **Ask: What kind of patterns did Mendel want to find?** patterns that explain how traits are passed from parents to offspring

DCI Inheritance of Traits . . . .

Explain to children that Mendel used two plants to make new plants. Sometimes he used two plants that looked different from each other. When he did this, he observed that the new plant sometimes had many traits from just one parent, and sometimes it had traits from both parents.

SEP Constructing Explanations and Designing Solutions . . . .
Ask: How does this explain why three plants from the same two parents might not look very much alike? The first plant has more traits from one parent. The second plant has more traits from the other parent. The third plant has some traits from both parents.

Take It Further

People in Science & Engineering •
Gregor Mendel

Explore more online.
Watch a
Pumpkin Grow

Explore online. ▶

© Houghton Mifflin Harcourt

Gregor Mendel was a scientist. He used many pea plants to do experiments. He grew young plants from parent plants with different traits. A **trait** is something living things get from their parents.

Lesson 1 • How Do Plants Look Like Their Parents?

231

Take It Further, continued

Children should choose C—young. If children choose A or B, they may have the misconception that traits travel through soil or roots to reach a new plant. **Ask: How do plants make new plants?** They make seeds. Remind children that young plants grow from seeds. Explain that seeds contain the traits that parent plants pass to a new plant.

DCI **Variation of Traits**. . . . .

Discuss with children the chart showing some of the traits Gregor Mendel observed. **Ask: What happened when Mendel grew plants from parents with different traits?** The new plants had traits from both parents. **What kinds of traits did he compare?** seed shape, seed color, and flower color **When young pea plants have different color flowers or seeds than the parent, is it still a pea plant? Explain.** Yes, they have all of the same parts and grow peas. They can look a little different from the parent plants.

Collaboration

Small Groups Have children work in small groups to discuss the chart of Mendel's findings. Encourage children to ask each other questions, to use evidence to support their arguments, and to agree with or refute a claim.

Explore more online. ▶

Watch a Pumpkin Grow

Children investigate how pumpkins grow.

Seed		Flower
Shape	Color	Color
Round	Yellow	White
Wrinkled	Green	Pink

Mendel looked at traits like seed shape, seed color, and flower color. He found that young plants had traits from both parents.

Mendel looked at how adult pea plants pass traits to their _____.

Ⓐ soil

Ⓑ roots

Ⓒ young

232

© Houghton Mifflin Harcourt

Explore online. ▶ Have children explore online to find out more about young plants and parent plants.

Lesson Check

Name _____

young plants

Explore online. ▶

parent plant

Can You Explain It?

✏▷ How can you tell if two plants are the same kind of plant? Be sure to

• Tell how plants of the same kind can be alike and different.

• Explain how you can observe patterns to tell if two plants are the same kind of plant.

Sample answer: Plants of the same kind can have different

heights and colors, but they usually have the same parts. I can

observe patterns in the shape and size of parts to tell if plants

are of the same kind.

Lesson Check

Can You Explain It?

Have children reread their answers to the Can You Explain It? prompts at the beginning of the lesson.

SEP **Constructing Explanations and Designing Solutions** . . . .

If children have difficulty responding to the Can You Explain It? prompt, have them look through the lesson and identify patterns to use as evidence that the two plants pictured are the same kind.

CCC **Patterns** . . . .

Have children review some of the plant parts they observed in this lesson. **Ask: Did the young cherry trees look exactly like the parent cherry trees?** No; the young cherry trees were smaller and did not have flowers. **When those young cherry trees grow, will they have the same parts as the parent cherry trees?** yes **Think about the tulip pictures we observed. Did the tulips all have the same parts?** yes **Did they look exactly alike?** No; the flowers were different colors. Some tulips were taller or had bigger leaves. **How can thinking about these patterns help you to tell if two plants are the same kind?** You can compare these patterns with patterns you observe in other plants.

Scoring Guidelines

• Children should describe how plants of the same kind are alike and different.

• Children should effectively explain how patterns can be used as evidence to answer the question.

Lesson Check, continued

SUMMATIVE ASSESSMENT
Self Check

1. Children should choose B—similar. If children choose A or C, guide them to the pictures showing a young plant and a parent plant in the Young and Old and Compare Parts sections of the lesson. Have them compare the way the plants look.

2. Children should choose A—Their leaves are the same shape. If children choose B or C, guide them to the pictures showing a young plant and a parent plant in the Compare Parts section of the lesson. Have them compare the way the plants look.

3. Children should choose C—a plant with leaves that are like the young plant's leaves. If children choose A or B, guide them to the results of the Compare Parts section of the lesson.

Self Check

1. How do most young plants and their parent plants look?

Ⓐ exactly alike

Ⓑ similar

Ⓒ very different

2. Observe this young plant and its parent plant. What pattern do you see?

young plant

parent plant

Ⓐ Their leaves are the same shape.

Ⓑ Their leaves are different colors.

Ⓒ The young plant has more leaves than the parent plant.

3. Cate sees a young plant in a park. She wants to find an adult plant that is the same kind of plant. What should Cate look for?

Ⓐ a plant that is the same size

Ⓑ a plant with the same number of leaves

Ⓒ a plant with leaves that are like the young plant's leaves

234

4. Draw a line to match each young plant to its parent plant.

5. Which statements are true?
Choose all correct answers.

Ⓐ All tulips are red.

Ⓑ Tulip flowers can be different colors.

Ⓒ Some tulips are taller than others.

4. Children draw a line from the top left picture to the bottom right picture, and from the bottom left picture to the top right picture. If children connect the wrong pictures, guide them to the Compare Parts sections of the lesson.

5. Children should choose B—Tulip flowers can be different colors; and C—Some tulips are taller than others. If children choose A, or did not choose B or C, guide them to the Compare Adult Plants section of the lesson. Guide children to look for clues in the text and pictures.

Lesson 2 — How Do Animals Look Like Their Parents?

Building to the Performance Expectation

The learning experiences in this lesson prepare children for mastery of:

1-LS3-1 Make observations to construct an evidence-based account that young plants and animals are like, but not exactly like, their parents.

Trace Tool to the NGSS
Go online to view the complete coverage of these standards across this lesson, unit, and time.

SEP — Science & Engineering Practices

Constructing Explanations and Designing Solutions
Make observations (firsthand or from media) to construct an evidence-based account for natural phenomena.

 VIDEO SEPs: Constructing Explanations and Designing Solutions / Engaging in Argument from Evidence

DCI — Disciplinary Core Ideas

LS3.A: Inheritance of Traits
Young animals are very much, but not exactly like, their parents. Plants also are very much, but not exactly, like their parents.

LS3.B: Variation of Traits
Individuals of the same kind of plant or animal are recognizable as similar but can also vary in many ways.

CCC — Crosscutting Concepts

Patterns
Patterns in the natural world can be observed, used to describe phenomena, and used as evidence.

CONNECTIONS TO MATH

MP.5 Use appropriate tools strategically.

1.MD.A.1 Order three objects by length; compare the lengths of two objects indirectly by using a third object.

CONNECTION TO ENGLISH LANGUAGE ARTS

RI.1.1 Ask and answer questions about key details in a text.

W.1.7 Participate in shared research and writing projects (e.g., explore a number of "how-to" books on a given topic and use them to write a sequence of instructions).

Supporting All Students, All Standards

Integrating the Three Dimensions of Learning

This lesson focuses on the similarities and differences between animals and their offspring. The lesson begins with children exploring how animals change as they grow and observing patterns in these changes **(DCI Inheritance of Traits) (CCC Patterns)**. Next, children compare parts of young animals and their parents **(CCC Patterns)**, and extend this exploration with a hands-on activity **(SEP Constructing Explanations and Designing Solutions)**. As they observe coverings of animals, children will compare and contrast coverings of young and adult animals. Lastly, children will explore variations among animals of the same kind **(DCI Variation of Traits)**.

 Professional Development Go online to view **Professional Development videos** with strategies to integrate CCCs and SEPs, including the ones used in this lesson.

Build on Prior Knowledge

Children should already know and be prepared to build on the following concepts:
- There are many different kinds of animals.
- Different kinds of animals can share some features.
- Animals change and grow as they get older.

Differentiate Instruction

RTI/Extra Support Provide additional examples of young animals and their parents. Show children pictures or videos of young animals and their parents, and discuss how they are alike and how they are different.

Extension Children who want to find out more can do research on other kinds of young animals and their parents. Children can share their findings with the class by making a poster or other display that shows how the young animals and their parents are similar and how they are different.

ELL Be sure to point out all labels, pictures, captions, and headings throughout the lesson to assist children with strategies to summarize chunks of content. Discuss with children real-life connections to content and provide hands-on examples of materials when possible to best support the needs of these learners.

Lesson Problem

Lesson Objective

Make observations to explain the differences and similarities between animal parents and their offspring.

About This Image

Guide children to look at the photograph of the young koala and its parent. **Ask: Which koala is the parent?** the bigger one **How do you know?** Adults are bigger than young animals. **How else are the young koala and its parent different?** Sample answer: The young koala has smaller eyes and its fur looks fluffier. **How are they alike?** Sample answer: They have the same parts and both are furry.

 **Inheritance of Traits**

Alternative Engage Strategy

We Are Family	👥 whole class 🕐 10–15 minutes

Provide children with pictures of adult and young animals. Discuss how the young animals are similar to their parents, and how they are different. Make a chart listing similarities and differences. Encourage children to think about details and also about general characteristics.

Lesson 2

How Do Animals Look Like Their Parents?

A young koala looks like its parent.

By the End of This Lesson
I will be able to tell how animals of the same kind can be alike and different.

© Houghton Mifflin Harcourt • Image Credits: ©GuyLePage/Getty Images

236

Related Animals

Look at the adult swan and her young. What can you tell about the birds?

Explore online. ▶

Can You Solve It?

✏️➤ You see a young animal. You want to find an adult animal that is of the same kind. What should you look for?

Accept all reasonable answers.

_____

_____

_____

Can You Solve It?

Related Animals Watch the video of the swans. If the video is not available, guide children to look at the photograph on the page. **Ask:** You see a young animal. You want to find an adult animal that is the same kind. What should you look for? Discuss children's ideas and accept all answers. At the end of this lesson, children will revisit their response as part of the Lesson Check.

Remind children not to be concerned if they are unsure of their answers. They will see this question again at the end of the lesson, and use what they've found out in the lesson to revise their responses as needed.

Collaboration

Build on Prior Knowledge Have children work in pairs to draw a picture of a young animal and its parents. Children can share their drawings and explain how the young animals are like their parents, and how they are different.

Animals Grow

3D Learning Objective

Children **observe patterns in how young animals grow and change in order to construct evidence**. They describe how young animals and their parents are alike and different.

DCI Inheritance of Traits . . . .

Ask: How are the newborn panda and the adult panda alike? Sample answer: They both have four legs. **Ask:** How are the 3-week-old panda and the adult panda alike? Sample answer: They have the same markings. How are the 3-month-old panda and the adult panda alike? Sample answer: They have the same markings and their ears look the same.

CCC Patterns . . . .

Ask: What do you notice about the panda as it gets older? It gets bigger and starts to look more like an adult panda. Tell children that this is also true of other kinds of animals, and it is a pattern. Remind children that a pattern is something that happens again and again. Have children look at the photographs of the pandas and think about the photographs of the koalas and swans. **Ask:** What pattern do you notice about the sizes of parent animals and young animals? Parent animals are bigger than young animals.

Differentiate Instruction

ELL Review the different words used to describe the growth stages among animals. Have children make flash cards for *newborn, young animal*, *parent*, and *adult*. Children can write each word on one side of a flash card, and draw a picture or write words or phrases in their native language on the other side.

Animals Grow

newborn

Explore online. ▶

3 weeks old

3 months old

1 year old

Parent animals make young animals like themselves. Young animals are smaller than their parents. They will grow to look like their parents. Look at how a panda changes as it grows into an adult.

238

adult

What is the same about a panda that is three months old and a panda that is an adult? Choose all correct answers.

Ⓐ They are the same size.

Ⓑ They have the same color fur.

Ⓒ They are the same shape.

Apply What You Know

Evidence Notebook • Draw pictures to show an animal when it is young and when it is an adult. Talk with a partner about your animals. How do they grow and change? Use evidence to tell how you know. Look for patterns in your pictures.

💡 **Patterns** Go to the online handbook for tips.

Lesson 2 • How Do Animals Look Like Their Parents?

239

© Houghton Mifflin Harcourt • Image Credits: ©Geostock/Getty Images

DCI **Inheritance of Traits** . . . .

Children should choose B—They have the same color fur; and C—They are the same shape. If children answer incorrectly, have them look back at the four photographs on the previous page.

CCC **Patterns** . . . .

Some children may struggle with the different perspectives of the photographs that make the 3-week-old, 3-month-old, and adult pandas appear to be the same size. If children choose A, **Ask: What pattern did we observe in the size of young animals and their parents?** Young animals are smaller than their parents.

 FORMATIVE ASSESSMENT ────

Evidence Notebook

Children draw pictures to show an animal when it is young and when it is an adult. Make sure that children use evidence to support the changes they identify. You may want to provide children with pictures of young animals and their parents as resources to ensure variation among children's drawings.

Scoring Guidelines

• draws pictures to show an animal when it is young and when it is an adult

• explains how the animal grows and changes

• provides evidence to show how animals grow and change

💡 **Patterns** Tell children that they can observe patterns in nature. Look for a pattern, or things that repeat. Use the pattern to describe what happens, or as proof of an idea.

Compare Parts

3D Learning Objective

Children **observe patterns** in how the body features of young animals and their parents are alike and different **in order to construct evidence**.

 Inheritance of Traits . . . .

Ask: Do young animals have the same body parts and features as their parents? How do you know? No. Some body parts and features don't grow until the young get older.

 Patterns . . . .

Brainstorm a list of young animals that have body parts and features like their parents, and a list of young animals that do not. **Ask:** What pattern did we observe in the body parts and features of young animals and their parents? Most young animals have parts and features like their parents.

Collaboration

Jigsaw Assign each small group an animal to research in order to find out how its body parts and features are alike and different from its parents. After researching, form new groups so that each group has each animal represented. Children share their findings with members of the group.

Connection to Earth and Space Science

Patterns Discuss other patterns in nature. **Ask:** What pattern do you see as the sun appears to move across the sky? Every day, the sun appears to rise in one part of the sky and appears to set in another part of the sky.

Compare Parts

Explore online. ▶

An elephant parent has big ears and a long trunk. A young elephant has big ears and a long trunk, too.

A young rhino looks much like its parent, but it does not have a horn. It will grow a horn like its parent.

Think about young animals. How can you tell what kind of animal they are? One way is to look at their body parts. Most young animals have parts like their parents.

240

Hands-On Activity

Observe Brine Shrimp

Name _____

Materials
- container with water
- brine shrimp eggs
- hand lens

Ask a Question
Do young animals of the same kind look different from each other as they grow?

Test and Record Data Explore online. ▶

Step 1

Add the brine shrimp eggs to the water.

Step 2

Children should record their observations.

Observe the brine shrimp every other day for two weeks. Record your observations.

Lesson 2 • How Do Animals Look Like Their Parents?   241

© Houghton Mifflin Harcourt

Hands-On Activity whole class ⏱ 10–15 minutes every other day for 2 weeks

Observe Brine Shrimp

3D Learning Objective

SEP Constructing Explanations and Designing Solutions . . . .

Children explore how brine shrimp hatch and change as they grow into adults. Children will observe the shrimp over time and record information about their body features. They will compare and contrast the adult shrimp and use this information to construct evidence.

Suggested Materials container with water, brine shrimp eggs, iodine-free salt, baking soda, hand lens

Preparation
The teacher should prepare the water in advance. Add two tablespoons of salt and $\frac{1}{4}$ teaspoon of baking soda for every liter of water. Set aside 10–15 minutes every other day for two weeks to make observations.

Activity
Read the title and ask children to develop a question.

STEP 1 Observe children as they add the brine shrimp eggs to the water. Alternatively, have children observe you as you add the brine shrimp to a single, large container.

STEP 2 Designate a time every other day for children to make observations. Children may use words and drawings to record their observations. Encourage children to include as much detail as possible. You may want to take a digital photograph every other day to record the status of the brine shrimp for children who are absent during observation time, or for extra support.

SEP Constructing Explanations and Designing Solutions . . . .

Ask: What do you observe about the brine shrimp? What has changed since your last observation? Do all of the shrimp look the same? If not, how are they different? Answers will vary throughout the investigation.

Lesson 2 • How Do Animals Look Like Their Parents?   **241**

Hands-On Activity, continued

💡 **Use Appropriate Tools** Review with children how to use a hand lens. Ask them how the lens helps them compare the shrimp.

STEP 3 Have children refer to their data as they compare the size, shape, and parts of the brine shrimp. Children can share their observations with the rest of their group for additional data.

CCC Patterns ....

Ask: What parts or features does an adult brine shrimp have? How are these like the parts or features of a young brine shrimp? How are these different from the parts and features of a young brine shrimp? Answers will vary.

Claims, Evidence, and Reasoning

Children should write a claim that explains whether animals of the same kind look different from each other as they grow. They should cite evidence to support their claim, including any patterns they observed in the brine shrimp. **Ask:** Did all of the brine shrimp look the same during each observation? What was different? Sample answer: The brine shrimp did not all look the same during each observation. They were the same shape, but some were different sizes.

Scoring Rubric for Hands-On Activity	
3	Writes a claim about the features of young animals as they grow and uses evidence to support their claim
2	Writes a claim about the features of young animals as they grow that is supported with weak evidence
1	Writes a claim about the features of young animals as they grow but is not supported with evidence
0	Does not state a claim and does not provide evidence

Step ③

Compare the size, shape, and parts of the brine shrimp. How are the brine shrimp the same? How are they different? Use the patterns you found as evidence.

Sample answer: The shape of the shrimp are the same, but some

of the shrimp are different sizes.

Make a claim that answers your question.

Sample answer: Young animals of the same kind can look different

from each other as they grow.

What is your evidence?

Sample answer: My evidence is what I observed when the brine

shrimp grew. The shape of the shrimp were the same, but some of

the shrimp were different sizes.

242

 This is a young anteater. Circle the picture below that shows an adult anteater.

 Apply What You Know

Evidence Notebook • Observe animals. What body parts does each animal have? How can you tell if the animal is young or an adult? Use evidence to tell how you know. Record your answers.

Constructing Explanations and Designing Solutions
Go to the online handbook for tips.

Lesson 2 • How Do Animals Look Like Their Parents?

243

CCC Patterns ....

Children should circle the third photograph. **Ask:** What pattern did we observe in the body parts of young animals and their parents? Most young animals have body parts like their parents.

DCI Inheritance of Traits ....

Ask: What body parts does this young anteater have? It has a long snout, floppy ears, and small eyes. Will the adult anteater have the same body parts or different body parts? It will have the same body parts.

 FORMATIVE ASSESSMENT

Evidence Notebook
Children observe animals and describe their body parts. Allow children to use words or pictures. Then have children tell whether the animal is young or an adult. Make sure that children use evidence to support their claims. This activity can also be completed as *Think, Pair, Share!*

Scoring Guidelines
- describes an animal's body parts
- writes a claim about whether the animal is young or an adult
- uses evidence to support their claim

 Constructing Explanations and Designing Solutions Children can use their observations to make explanations. Observe something that happens in nature. Use the facts observed to describe what happened.

Compare Body Coverings

3D Learning Objective

Children **compare and contrast the body features of young animals and their parents**. They **observe patterns** of how young animals are alike and different from their parents **in order to construct evidence**.

(CCC) Patterns ....

Discuss with children that many young animals and their parents have the same type of body covering. Tell children that this is a pattern. **Ask: How are the young raccoon and the adult raccoon alike?** They both have the same color fur. **How are the young chicken and the adult chicken alike?** They both have feathers.

(DCI) Inheritance of Traits ....

Ask: How are the young chicken and the adult chicken different? They are different colors. Their feathers have different textures. The adult has different feathers on its face. **How do you know the adult chicken is the young chicken's parent, even though their coverings are not the same?** They have other parts that are the same. They have the same kind of feet. They both have wings and beaks.

Differentiate Instruction

RTI/Extra Support Guide children as they work in pairs or small groups to make a T-chart of coverings in adult animals and their young. Children may use words and/or drawings.

Extension Have children choose an animal from the lesson, and make a poster that compares the young and adult animal. Children should include body coverings, body parts, and sizes of the young and adult animal.

Compare Body Coverings

Some body coverings are scales, fur, or feathers. How are the body coverings of young animals and their parents alike and different?

Explore online.

young raccoon   **adult raccoon**

Raccoons have dark fur around their eyes. The young and the adult have the same color fur.

young chicken   **adult chicken**

A young chick has yellow, fluffy feathers. It will grow new feathers and look more like its parent.

244

 Observe each animal. Then draw a line to match each parent animal to its young.

Apply What You Know

Read, Write, Share! • Research an animal. Find out how it grows. Tell what it is like when it is young and when it is an adult. Draw pictures to show what you found.

Participate in a Research Project Go to the online handbook for tips.

 Patterns . . . .

Children should draw a line from the top left animal to the middle right animal; from the middle left animal to the bottom right animal; and from the bottom left animal to the top right animal. **Ask: How can you use an animal's body coverings to match it to its young?** Animals and their young have the same type of body covering. This is a pattern.

 Inheritance of Traits . . . .

Ask: What body parts or features do each pair of animals have? The lizards have the same shape, body covering, legs, and eyes. The turtles have the same shell. The skunks have the same stripes and tail.

Constructing Explanations and Designing Solutions . . . .

Ask: What evidence can you construct to support the claim that young animals and their parents have body coverings that are alike, but not exactly the same? Sample answer: A young skunk has black fur like its parent, but it has different white markings.

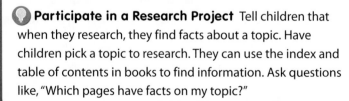 **FORMATIVE ASSESSMENT**

Read, Write, Share! • Participate in a Research Project

Children will research an animal. Allow children to complete this activity in pairs and share their findings with others.

Scoring Guidelines
- researches an animal and finds out how it grows
- describes the young animal and the adult animal
- draws pictures to share findings

Participate in a Research Project Tell children that when they research, they find facts about a topic. Have children pick a topic to research. They can use the index and table of contents in books to find information. Ask questions like, "Which pages have facts on my topic?"

Animals of the Same Kind

3D Learning Objective

Children **observe patterns** in how **the body features of animals of the same kind are alike and different** in order to construct evidence.

DCI Variation of Traits . . . .

Discuss the photographs of the fish and the dogs. Explain that the fish are the same kind of fish and the dogs are the same kind of dog. **Ask: How are the fish alike?** They have the same body parts: fins, tails, gills, and scales. **How are they different?** They are different colors and sizes. **How are the dogs alike?** They are the same shape and size, and have the same body parts. **How are they different?** They are different colors.

Discuss with children that young animals often share the same body parts and body coverings with their parents and with other adult animals. Explain that sometimes animals can have different body coverings, or be different sizes from other animals that are the same kind. Encourage children to draw on personal experiences and share examples of variation. **Ask: Have you or someone you know ever had a pet dog or cat? Did the pet look the same as its brothers and sisters?** Accept all reasonable answers.

CCC Patterns . . . .

Explain to children that even though not all of the animals look the same, the young animals will still look like their parents in some ways. **Ask: What do you think the young dogs would look like?** Sample answer: I think they would have four legs and a tail with the same shape face. I think they would be covered with fur, but it might be a different color.

Animals of the Same Kind

How can animals of the same kind be alike and different?

Explore online. ▶

These fish are all the same kind. They have the same body parts. But they are not the same size. They also have different colors and markings.

These dogs are all the same kind. They all have four legs and a tail. They all have fur. But their fur is different colors.

246

Look at the animals. Circle the two that are the same kind of animal. Look for patterns.

Patterns Go to the online handbook for tips.

CCC Patterns . . . .

Children should circle the two dogs on the sofa. **Ask: How can you decide if two animals are the same kind?** Sample answer: They have the same body parts and the same type of body covering.

Patterns Remind children that there are patterns in nature. Observe nature. Look for a pattern, or things that repeat. Use the pattern to describe what happens. Use the pattern as proof of an idea.

DCI Variation of Traits . . . .

Ask: How are the two dogs alike? They are the same shape and their body parts look the same. **How are they different?** They are different colors and different sizes.

Collaboration

Think, Write, Pair, Share Have children work with a partner. Each child thinks of a kind of animal and writes about how some of those animals are alike and some are different. For example, if the type of animal chosen is birds, the child could compare blue birds and cardinals. Children share their ideas with their partner.

© Houghton Mifflin Harcourt

Lesson 2 • How Do Animals Look Like Their Parents? 247

Do the Math! • Compare and Order Length

Children should label the brown dog 3, the black dog 1, and the white dog 2. If children order the dogs from tallest to shortest, remind them to read the directions carefully. **Ask: How can you find which dog is tallest and which dog is shortest?** I can compare the brown dog to the white dog. Then I can compare the brown dog to the black dog. Since the brown dog is taller than both dogs, I know that the brown dog is the tallest. Then I compare the black dog and the white dog, and I see the black dog is the shortest.

 Compare and Order Length Remind children that when you compare, you look for how things are alike and different. When you put things in order by length or height, you compare them and look for the ones that are the longest or tallest and the shortest.

DCI **Variation of Traits.** . . . .

Look at the three dogs. **Ask: What is alike and different about the dogs?** Sample answer: They all seem to be the same kind of dog; they all have four legs and a tail. The dogs are all different sizes and colors.

✋ FORMATIVE ASSESSMENT

Evidence Notebook
Children should work in pairs to complete their research and make their claims. Make sure that children use evidence to support their statements about how the animals are alike and different.

Scoring Guidelines
- identifies animals of the same kind
- explains how the animals are alike and different
- uses evidence to support their claims

Do the Math! • Compare the dogs. Put them in order from shortest to tallest. Write 1, 2, or 3.

 **Compare and Order Length** Go to the online handbook for tips.

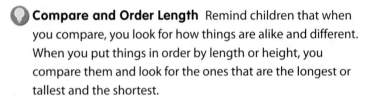

| 3 | 1 | 2 |

 Apply What You Know

Evidence Notebook • Work with a partner. Look through books for animals of the same kind. Tell how they are alike and different. Use evidence to tell how you know. Draw the animals in your Evidence Notebook.

Explore online. ▶   Guide children to the Interactive Online Student Edition where they can choose from and explore both paths.

Take It Further

The Butterfly Life Cycle

Explore more online.

Pet Investigation ➤

Explore online. ▶

Some young animals look very different from their parents. One example is a butterfly. A butterfly makes big changes as it grows. It begins its life inside an egg.

A caterpillar hatches from the egg.

The caterpillar becomes a pupa. It makes a hard covering.

An adult butterfly comes out of the covering. One day it may lay eggs.

© Houghton Mifflin Harcourt

Lesson 2 • How Do Animals Look Like Their Parents?   249

Take It Further

The Butterfly Life Cycle

Children will explore the butterfly life cycle. Explain to children that a life cycle shows how an animal grows and changes from a young animal into an adult animal. The butterfly is an example of an adult animal that looks very different from its young. Its life cycle has four main stages—egg, larva (or caterpillar), pupa, and adult. This cycle repeats once an adult butterfly lays eggs.

CCC Patterns . . . .

Ask: **What does it mean for something to happen in a cycle?** it happens again and again **How is a life cycle a pattern?** Sample answer: The steps happen again and again, with adults laying eggs, caterpillars hatching from the eggs, caterpillars becoming a pupa, and coming out as an adult butterfly. The cycle starts again and repeats when an adult butterfly lays eggs.

DCI Inheritance of Traits. . . . .

Explain that although caterpillars do not look like adult butterflies, they grow and change to look like their parents. **Ask: What happens when a caterpillar becomes a pupa?** It becomes a butterfly. **How is the adult butterfly like its parents?** Sample answer: They have the same body parts and they might have the same color body covering.

Take It Further, continued

Read, Write, Share! • Ask and Answer Questions

Remind children when asking questions to ask about important details or things that are unclear. Children should start questions with words such as *who, what, when, where, why,* and *how.*

Collaboration

Small Groups After children have written their questions, have them form small groups with children who asked a similar question. Children can research and formulate answers together, and then share their results with the class.

Ask and Answer Questions Remind children to stop and ask themselves questions as they read. Ask about important ideas and details. Look for the answers in the text and the pictures.

ccc Patterns . . . .

Children should number the caterpillar 2, the pupa 3, and the butterfly 4. If children have difficulty with the activity, have them draw the four pictures on index cards and place them in order.
Ask: What hatches out of the egg? a caterpillar What does the caterpillar become? a pupa What comes out of the hard covering? a butterfly

Explore more online. ▶

Pet Investigation

Children will interview others to find out more about the pets they own.

Read, Write, Share!

✏️➤ What other questions do you have about the butterfly life cycle? Write your questions. Do research to answer them.

> **Ask and Answer Questions**
> Go to the online handbook for tips.

Children should ask and answer questions about the butterfly

life cycle.

✏️➤ Order the pictures to show the butterfly's life cycle. The first one is done for you.

1

4

3

2

250

© Houghton Mifflin Harcourt

LESSON 2   Engage • Explore/Explain • Elaborate • **Evaluate**

Explore online. ▶   Have children review the video of the swans from the Engage page.

Lesson Check

Name _____

Explore online. ▶

Can You Solve It?

✏️ You see a young animal. You want to find an adult animal that is the same kind. What should you look for? Be sure to

- Tell how animals of the same kind can be alike and different.
- Explain how you can observe patterns to tell if two animals are the same kind of animal.

Sample answer: Animals of the same kind can have different

sizes and colors, but they usually have the same parts. I can

observe patterns in the shape and size of parts to tell if animals

are of the same kind.

Lesson 2 • How Do Animals Look Like Their Parents?   251

© Houghton Mifflin Harcourt • Image Credits: ©CJ Park/Shutterstock

Lesson Check

Can You Solve It?

Have children reread their answers to the Can You Solve It? prompts at the beginning of the lesson.

🔵DCI Inheritance of Traits . . . .

Ask: **How are most young animals like their parents? How are they different?** Sample answer: Most young animals have the same body parts and features and the same type of body covering as their parents. Most young animals are smaller than their parents, and might have body coverings that are different colors or different textures.

🔵DCI Variation of Traits . . . .

Ask: **Can two animals be different colors and different sizes but still be the same kind of animal?** yes **What else can you look for to help you know if the animals are the same kind or different kinds?** Sample answer: I can look at the body parts and body coverings. If the animals are the same kind, they will have the same body parts even if they are different sizes, and the same type of body covering even if they are different colors.

🔵CCC Patterns . . . .

Ask: **What patterns can you look for to help you know if two animals are the same kind?** Sample answer: I can look for the same body parts and the same body covering. **What patterns can you look for to help you find an adult animal that is the same kind as a young animal?** Sample answer: I can look for an animal that has the same body parts but is bigger.

Scoring Guidelines

- Children should tell how animals of the same kind can be alike and different.
- Children should effectively explain how they can observe patterns to tell if two animals are the same kind.

Lesson 2 • How Do Animals Look Like Their Parents? 251

Lesson Check, continued

SUMMATIVE ASSESSMENT
Self Check

1. Children should choose A—Young animals have parts like their parents; and B—Young animals grow to look like their parents. If children choose C, ask them to read the statement carefully. Make sure children understand that young animals are smaller than their parents.

2. Children should choose B—scales. If children choose A or C, guide them to review the Compare Body Coverings part of the lesson. Remind children that most young animals have the same type of body covering as their parents, even if the body coverings do not look exactly the same. Discuss with children the various pairs of young animals and their parents shown in this part of the lesson, and reinforce the pattern.

3. Children should choose B—They have the same pattern on their fur. If children choose A or C, discuss the animals shown in each picture. Guide children to recognize that the animals in each picture are different sizes, and they have the same body parts. Review with children the key patterns discussed in this lesson— young animals are smaller than their parents; young animals and their parents have the same or similar body coverings; and young animals and their parents have the same body parts.

Self Check

1. Which is true about most young animals and their parents? Choose all correct answers.

   Ⓐ Young animals have parts like their parents.

   Ⓑ Young animals grow to look like their parents.

   Ⓒ Young animals are bigger than their parents.

2. Marco sees a young animal that has scales on its body. The young animal's parent will likely have _____.

   Ⓐ fur

   Ⓑ scales

   Ⓒ a shell

3. Observe each young animal and its parent. What pattern do you see?

   Ⓐ They are the same size.

   Ⓑ They have the same pattern on their fur.

   Ⓒ They have different body parts.

252

4. Draw a line to match each parent to its young.

---

5. Amy observes two dogs that are the same kind.
   Which sentences could be true about the dogs?

   Ⓐ The dogs are different colors.

   Ⓑ One dog has fur and one dog has feathers.

   Ⓒ One dog is smaller than the other dog.

4. Children should match the top left picture with the top right picture and the bottom left picture with the bottom right picture. If children do not match the pictures correctly, instruct them to review the Compare Parts section of the lesson. Then have children look carefully at the body parts of each animal to help them match each parent to its young.

5. Children should choose A—The dogs are different colors; and C—One dog is smaller than the other dog. If children do not choose any answer choices, have them read the question again and underline the phrase *could be true*. Explain that this phrase means the statement is possible, but doesn't always have to be true. If children require additional support, instruct them to review the Animals of the Same Kind part of the lesson.

 **Lesson 3**

How Do Animals Take Care of Their Young?

Building to the Performance Expectation

The learning experiences in this lesson prepare children for mastery of:

1-LS1-2 Read texts and use media to determine patterns in behavior of parents and offspring that help offspring survive.

 Trace Tool to the NGSS
Go online to view the complete coverage of these standards across this lesson, unit, and time.

 SEP **Science & Engineering Practices**

Obtaining, Evaluating, and Communicating Information
Read grade-appropriate texts and use media to obtain scientific information to determine patterns . . .

 VIDEO SEP: Obtaining, Evaluating, and Communicating Information

Scientific Knowledge is Based on Empirical Evidence
Scientists look for patterns and order when making observations about the world.

DCI **Disciplinary Core Ideas**

LS1.B Growth and Development of Organisms
Adult plants and animals can have young. In many kinds of animals, parents and the offspring themselves engage in behaviors that help the offspring to survive.

CCC **Crosscutting Concepts**

Patterns
Patterns in the natural world can be observed, used to describe phenomena, and used as evidence.

CONNECTIONS TO MATH

1.NBT.B.3 Compare two two-digit numbers based on the meanings of the tens and one digits, recording the results of comparisons with the symbols >, =, and <.

1.NBT.C.5 Given a two-digit number, mentally find 10 more or 10 less than the number, without having to count; explain the reasoning used.

CONNECTIONS TO ENGLISH LANGUAGE ARTS

RI.1.1 Ask and answer questions about key details in a text.

W.1.8 With guidance and support from adults, recall information from experiences or gather information from provided sources to answer a question.

Supporting All Students, All Standards

Integrating the Three Dimensions of Learning

This lesson focuses on patterns in behavior of parents and offspring that help them survive. The lesson begins as children explore how animals take care of their young (CCC Patterns) (SEP Scientific Knowledge is Based on Empirical Evidence), (DCI Growth and Development of Organisms). Children describe behavioral patterns of parents and offspring that help offspring get food (CCC Patterns) (SEP Scientific Knowledge is Based on Empirical Evidence), (DCI Growth and Development of Organisms). Then, children discover how animals teach their offspring to get food and stay safe (CCC Patterns), (SEP Obtaining, Evaluating, and Communicating Information), (DCI Growth and Development of Organisms).

Professional Development Go online to view **Professional Development videos** with strategies to integrate CCCs and SEPs, including the ones used in this lesson.

Build on Prior Knowledge

Children should already know and be prepared to build on the following concepts:

- Animals are living things.
- Animals look like their parents.
- Problems can be solved through asking questions, analyzing information, and using models.

Differentiate Instruction

Lesson Vocabulary
- behavior

Reinforcing Vocabulary Remind children to look for this highlighted word as they proceed through the lesson. To help children remember the word *behavior*, have them note that the root word is *behave*. Then, have children use the root word and the new word in a sentence.

RTI/Extra Support Locate pictures of adult animals taking care of their young. Cut each picture into two, one that includes the adult and one that includes the young. Allow children to match the parent with the young, and explain why they think it is a match.

Extension Challenge children to keep a log as they find animals taking care of their young over a given time. Have children make a chart of their findings to display or present to the class.

ELL Be sure to point out all labels, pictures, captions, and headings throughout the lesson to assist children with strategies to summarize chunks of content. Discuss with children real-life connections to content and provide hands-on examples of materials when possible to best support the needs of these learners.

Lesson Phenomenon

Lesson Objective

Determine patterns in how animal parents and offspring behave in ways that help the offspring survive.

About This Image

Ask: **What do you think is happening in this picture?** Sample answers: The mother is comforting her young. The mother is taking care of her young. **Ask:** **Why do you think the mother is doing this?** Accept all reasonable answers. As you explore, you will find out how adult animals take care of their young.

 Growth and Development of Organisms

Alternative Engage Strategy

Helping Young Survive	pairs ⏱ 15–25 minutes

Ask: **What kinds of things do parents do for their children? Why do you think they do these things?**

Allow children time to discuss and describe what parents do for children and explain why they think these adults do these things. Record these for the class to see.

Then have children work in pairs to identify how animals do similar things for their young. Children may write or draw to record their thinking. Allow each pair to present their ideas to the class.

Lesson
3
How Do Animals Take Care of Their Young?

Animals care for their young in different ways.

By the End of This Lesson

I will be able to describe patterns in how animals help their young survive.

254

Animals Help Their Young

Explore online. ▶

Many animals help their young survive. This frog carries her tadpole up a tree. She puts it in water inside a flower. The tadpole gets what it needs to live and grow in the water.

© Houghton Mifflin Harcourt • Image Credits: © Michael Doolittle / Alamy Stock Photo

Can You Explain It?

✏️ How do animals help their young survive?

Accept all reasonable answers.

_____

_____

_____

Lesson 3 • How Do Animals Take Care of Their Young?

255

Can You Explain It?

Animals Help Their Young Some adult animals help take care of their young. Play the video to see how this kind of frog helps its young. If the video is unavailable to view, guide children to look at the picture. Guide children to identify the animals in the picture and describe the behavior taking place.

Ask children to record their initial thoughts about how animals help their young survive. Accept all reasonable answers. At the end of this lesson, children will revisit this question and their answers as part of the Lesson Check.

Collaboration

Build on Prior Knowledge You may want children to view and discuss the video as a whole-class activity. In this way, you can assess their prior knowledge on how animals take care of their young. **Ask: How is this frog helping her young?** The adult frog is placing her young in water because it needs water to survive.

Staying Safe

3D Learning Objective

Children **observe and describe** behavioral **patterns** animal parents and offspring exhibit that help **offspring stay safe**.

DCI Growth and Development of Organisms . . . . .

Discuss with children that some parent animals take care of their young by keeping them safe. They have certain behaviors that keep the young safe. **Ask: What does the word behavior mean when we talk about animals?** A *behavior* is the way an animal acts.

SEP Obtaining, Evaluating, and Communicating Information . . . .

Review the text and pictures of the animals with children. **Ask: What behaviors keep young rabbits safe?** Young rabbits hide in the grass while the mother is gone. They call back and forth with one another. **Ask: What behaviors keep young prairie dogs safe?** Adults bark to warn their group when there is danger nearby.

SEP Scientific Knowledge is Based on Empirical Evidence . . . .

Discuss with children how the prairie dog and rabbits have behaviors that are alike and different. **Ask: What patterns do you observe in how both animals behave?** Both animals have behaviors that keep the young animals safe.

Staying Safe

A **behavior** is a way an animal acts. What are some behaviors that help keep young animals safe?

Explore online.

Young rabbits hide in the grass to stay safe. They wait for their mother to come back. They listen for her call and then call back to her.

Prairie dogs live in groups. They bark to warn the group when danger is near.

256

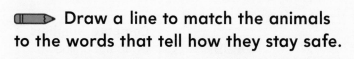 Draw a line to match the animals to the words that tell how they stay safe.

hide to stay safe   bark when in danger

Lesson 3 • How Do Animals Take Care of Their Young?   257

© Houghton Mifflin Harcourt • Image Credits: (b) © Jeff Mauritzen/ National Geographic/ Getty Images; (t) © stephen jones / Alamy Stock Photo

ccc Patterns . . . .

Remind children that a pattern is an event or occurrence that repeats, or happens over and over again. Discuss with children that animals display patterns of behavior that help them stay safe. **Ask: What pattern of behavior does a young rabbit display?** The young rabbits hide to stay safe. **Ask: What pattern of behavior does a prairie dog display?** Prairie dogs bark when they see danger. They also hide to stay safe.

Collaboration

Small Groups Place children in small groups. Provide each group with a picture of an animal that helps keep its young safe. (Some examples could include a penguin with an egg, a cat licking her young, an eagle building a nest, or an alligator carrying her young.) Have each group research behaviors of the animal and how it helps keep its young safe. Children can discuss their findings with the class.

Connection to Earth and Space Sciences

Patterns Patterns can be found in many places in the natural world. Discuss with children that the sun appears to move across the sky in a predictable pattern. Each day, the sun appears to rise in one part of the sky, move across the sky, and set in another part of the sky. Challenge children to describe other patterns they have observed in nature.

DCI **Growth and Development of Organisms** . . . . .

Discuss with children that a mother wolf spider keeps her eggs safe by carrying them in an egg sac on her abdomen. Once the young spiders hatch, they crawl onto their mother's abdomen for protection.

Do the Math! • Compare Numbers

Ask: Which symbol should we use to complete this number sentence? Children will use the symbol > to finish the number sentence, 64 > 48.

 Compare Numbers You can compare numbers to find out which number is greater. Remember to look at the tens place when you compare numbers. The number with more tens is greater. If the tens are the same, look at the ones. The number with more ones is greater.

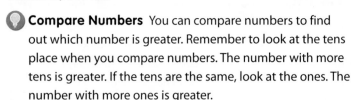 **FORMATIVE ASSESSMENT**

Evidence Notebook

Children find pictures of animals and their young staying safe. Monitor children as they discuss animal behaviors that keep the animals safe. Guide children to make a chart to show any patterns they find.

Scoring Guidelines

• accurately describes patterns to show how animals help their offspring stay safe
• identifies and describes patterns observed

 Patterns • Obtaining, Evaluating, and Communicating Information Remind children that a pattern is an event or occurrence that happens again and again. Discuss how information from texts and other sources can be used to help determine patterns in nature. Guide children to observe patterns to describe animals' behavior.

Do the Math! • One wolf spider carries 64 eggs in an egg sac. Another wolf spider carries 48 eggs. Compare the numbers. Write <, >, or =.

Compare Numbers
Go to the online handbook for tips.

64   (>)   48

 Apply What You Know

Evidence Notebook • Work with classmates. Find pictures of animals and their young staying safe. Talk about what the animals do to stay safe. Make a chart to show the patterns you found.

Patterns •
Obtaining,
Evaluating, and
Communicating
Information
Go to the online handbook for tips.

© Houghton Mifflin Harcourt

258

Finding Food

3D Learning Objective

Children **observe and describe** behavioral **patterns** animal parents and offspring exhibit that help offspring get food.

🔵DCI Growth and Development of Organisms . . . . .

Ask: What do you do when you are hungry? get something to eat, ask for something to eat **Ask:** What do you think you would do if you could not get your own food and you were hungry? I'd ask for something to eat. **Ask:** What do you think is happening in this picture? The young birds are chirping for their parents to let them know they are hungry.

🔵CCC Patterns . . . .

Discuss with children the behaviors the robins and the sea lions are displaying. **Ask: What is the same about the behavior of these two animals?** Young robins and young sea lions call out to their parent when it is time to eat, and this is a form of communication. **Ask: Is this a pattern in behavior that all animals display when they need to eat?** No, some may do this, but other young animals may not need to communicate this way to get food. For example, lions and other predators return from hunting with food for their young without the young calling out.

Differentiate Instruction

RTI/Extra Support To help children understand the meaning of the word *communication*, display pictures of people communicating. For example, people giving an order to a server in a restaurant, a doctor giving information to a patient, a teacher giving information to students, and a police officer directing traffic with a whistle.

Extension Children can research to find other predatory animals that hunt and bring food back to their young.

Finding Food

Explore online. ▶

Young robins make noise when they are hungry.

A mother sea lion calls to her pup to feed it. The pup calls back.

Animals need food to live. Many animals feed their young. Young animals show behaviors that help them get food from their parents.

Lesson 3 • How Do Animals Take Care of Their Young?

259

Scientific Knowledge is Based on Empirical Evidence . . . .

Remind children how scientists look for patterns when observing the natural world. These patterns and observations can be used as evidence. Have children observe the pictures of the two animals and their young. Have them look for patterns. **Ask: What evidence do you have that the young animals were making a noise to get food?** Parents brought food to the young animals.

 ### FORMATIVE ASSESSMENT

Evidence Notebook

Discuss what animals children have seen around their neighborhood or the school. **Ask: Have you seen any of these animals trying to find food?** Monitor children as they continue to discuss what animals they have seen do to find food and survive. Allow children to make a chart showing any patterns they observe during their discussion. Guide children to use evidence to support their answers.

Scoring Guidelines

- describes behaviors of animals finding food to survive
- identifies and describes patterns observed
- uses evidence to support the answer

💡 **Patterns • Scientific Knowledge is Based on Empirical Evidence** Guide children to observe patterns, or things that repeat, to describe what happens. Remind children that patterns can be found by observing the natural world.

 Circle the animal parent that feeds its young when the young make noise.

✋ **Apply What You Know**

Evidence Notebook • Observe animals around your school. What are the animals doing to find food and survive? Use evidence to tell how you know. Talk with a partner. Make a chart to show the patterns you observe.

💡 **Patterns • Scientific Knowledge is Based on Empirical Evidence** Go to the online handbook for tips.

260

© Houghton Mifflin Harcourt • Image Credits: (l) © Westend61 GmbH / Alamy Stock; Photo; (r) © Andy Sacks/Oxford Scientific/Getty Images

Young Animals Learn

3D Learning Objective

Children will **observe and describe** behavioral **patterns** animal parents teach their young that help the young find food and stay safe.

DCI Growth and Development of Organisms . . . . .

Discuss with children how young animals stay with their parents to learn how to find food and stay safe. **Ask: What do bear cubs need to learn?** Bear cubs need to learn how to catch fish so they can eat. **Ask: What do leopard cubs need to learn?** Leopard cubs learn to move around in their environment so they can stay safe. **Ask: Why do you think moving around can help animals stay safe?** They can find places to hide from other animals, and they look for places that have the things they need to live.

CCC Patterns . . . .

Remind children that a pattern is an event or occurrence that happens over and over. **Ask: What patterns might you see in the behavior of animals when they are learning to find food or stay safe?** Bears will show a pattern of going to water to find fish, and leopards will show a pattern of moving to find new places to rest and stay safe.

Young Animals Learn

Explore online. ▶

Bear cubs learn to catch fish for food.

Leopard cubs learn to move around to stay safe.

Some young animals learn from their parents. They stay with their parents for a few years. They watch what their parents do to find food and stay safe.

© Houghton Mifflin Harcourt • Image Credits: (t) © Ignacio Yufera / FLPA / Science Source; (b) © Uwe Skrzypczak / Alamy Stock Photo

Obtaining, Evaluating, and Communicating Information . . . .

Discuss with children what is happening in the picture. **Ask: What are the orangutans doing?** The orangutans are eating bananas. **Ask: What do you think the mother is teaching her young?** She is teaching the young orangutan to find food.

Differentiate Instruction

ELL Have books with animal names available for children to practice learning animal names that might not be familiar. Display photos in the classroom of animals with labels for ELL students to practice.

 FORMATIVE ASSESSMENT ━━━━

Read, Write, Share! • Recall Details • Ask and Answer Questions

With a partner, children reflect on what they have read about how parents take care of their young. Partners then make a list of ways that the parents act the same as and differently from their young.

Scoring Guidelines
- compares the behavior of bears, leopards, and orangutans as they teach their young how to find food and stay safe
- provides evidence to support similarities and differences noted in their comparison

Recall Details • Ask and Answer Questions Remind children to think about important ideas and details as they read. Asking and answering questions about the text helps identify and understand the key details in the text.

What is this orangutan teaching its young to do?

Ⓐ find fruit

Ⓑ hide in a den

Ⓒ catch small animals

 Apply What You Know

Read, Write, Share! • Think about how different animal parents take care of their young. Work with a partner to answer these questions—How do the animal parents act the same? How do they act differently?

Recall Details • Ask and Answer Questions Go to the online handbook for tips.

262

Hands-On Activity

Compare How Animals Learn

Name_____

Materials • a computer • animal books

Ask a Question

How do polar bears and lions learn from their parents?

Test and Record Data Explore online.

Step 1

Work with a partner. Research polar bears and lions. Use a computer and animal books to collect information.

Step 2

Find out how polar bears and lions teach their young to find food. Find out how they teach their young to stay safe.

© Houghton Mifflin Harcourt

Hands-On Activity 👥 small groups 🕐 1 class period

Compare How Animals Learn

3D Learning Objective

SEP **Obtaining, Evaluating, and Communicating Information** . . . .

Children gather information on how polar bears and lions teach their young to find food and stay safe. They use this information to construct evidence about how the animals are alike and different.

Suggested Materials a computer and animal books.

Preparation

Locate books on polar bears and lions from the school's library or a local library. Schedule time at the computer center if you do not have a computer in the classroom. View websites and books in advance for appropriateness.

Activity

Read the title and ask children to develop a question.

STEP 1 Observe children as they collect information. If children struggle with doing research, guide them to online websites they can use or to sections of the books.

STEP 2 In order to keep children on topic in their research, remind them of the question they are trying to answer.

DCI **Growth and Development of Organisms** . . . . .

Ask: What are some things animal parents do to teach their young that are the same as other animal parents? What are some of the different things animal parents do as they teach their offspring to survive? Accept all reasonable answers.

Hands-On Activity, continued

STEP 3 Guide children to look for patterns in how polar bears and lions learn from their parents.

 **Patterns** . . . .

Ask: What patterns do you see in how polar bears and lions teach their young? Sample answer: Polar bear and lion parents both teach their young to find food.

Guide children to make a claim that answers the question about how polar bears and lions train their young to find food and stay safe.

Claims, Evidence, and Reasoning

Children should write a claim that describes how polar bears and lions are similar in teaching their offspring to survive, and how they are different in teaching their offspring to survive. They should cite evidence to support their claims. **Ask: How are these two animals the same?** Sample answer: Both animals need to train their young how to find food. **How are these two animals different?** Polar bears have to teach their young how to fish, and lions have to teach their young how to hunt.

Scoring Rubric for Hands-On Activity

3	States a claim supported with evidence about similarities and differences in the ways animal parents teach their young
2	States a claim somewhat supported with evidence about similarities and differences in the ways parents teach their young
1	States a claim that is not supported by evidence
0	Does not state a claim and does not provide evidence

Step 3

Write or draw pictures to show what you found. Look for patterns in how the young animals learn from their parents.

Check children's drawings.

Sample answer: Polar bear young and lion young watch their parents hunt. They watch their parents to learn how to stay safe.

Make a claim that answers your question.

Sample answer: Polar bear young and lion young watch their parents to learn how to survive. This helps them learn to live on their own.

What is your evidence?

Sample answer: My evidence is the facts I researched in books and online.

264

LESSON 3   Engage • Explore/Explain • **Elaborate** • Evaluate

Explore online. ▶   **Guide children to the Interactive Online Student Edition where they can choose from and explore both paths.**

Take It Further

Careers in Science & Engineering •
Zookeeper

Explore more online.

On Their Own

Explore online. ▶

What does a zookeeper do? Zookeepers care for the animals in a zoo. They observe how animals act. They look for patterns to learn the best way to care for the animals.

Zookeepers give animals the food and water they need to live. They keep the animals and their environments clean.

© Houghton Mifflin Harcourt • Image Credits: (b) © Günter Peters/ullstein bild via Getty Images; (t) © Oli Scarff/Getty Images

Lesson 3 • How do Animals Take Care of Their Young?   265

Take It Further

Careers in Science & Engineering • Zookeeper

Children investigate what a zookeeper does to learn more about how animals survive.

A zookeeper typically has a science degree in biology, zoology, animal science, or wildlife management. Their responsibilities include feeding, health care, and taking care of the animals' environments. They are often involved in scientific research and public education. Zookeepers study animal behaviors in order to learn more about many kinds of animals.

SEP **Obtaining, Evaluating, and Communicating Information** . . . .
Guide children to look at the pictures of zookeepers taking care of animals and read the text that tells what a zookeeper does. **Ask: Have you ever been to a zoo? What kind of things have you seen zookeepers do when they are with an animal?** Children may have seen zookeepers feeding or grooming animals.

Differentiate Instruction

RTI/Extra Support To help children remember the word *zookeeper* and what it means, guide children to recognize this is a compound word. Discuss the two words, *zoo* and *keeper,* and how their meaning changes when they become one word, *zookeeper*.

Extension Children who want to find out more about zookeepers can research online or collect information from nonfiction books.

Take It Further, continued

Children match each photograph to a phrase that describes what each zookeeper is doing.

SEP **Scientific Knowledge is Based on Empirical Evidence** . . . .

Discuss what the zookeepers in the pictures are doing to help the animals survive. **Ask: Which picture shows what the words below the pictures tell?** Children should match each picture with the correct phrase: feeds animals, cleans environment, or observes animals. **Ask: What pattern do you see in what zookeepers do?** Sample answer: All of the zookeepers are taking care of the animals so they stay healthy and survive.

Do the Math! • Use Mental Math

You can find 10 more without counting 10 ones. To find 10 more, add one to the number of tens. The number of ones stays the same. **Ask: How many animals does Zoo B have?** Children will use mental math to find the solution to 10 more than 80.

💡 **Use Mental Math** Remind children that mental math can be used as a strategy instead of counting by ones.

Collaboration

Small Groups Place children in small groups. Have each group write a mental math word problem about a zookeeper. Then have children swap word problems with another group and solve them.

Explore more online. ▶

On Their Own

Children explore how some parent animals do not have to take care of their young. The young care for themselves.

✏️ Draw a line to match each picture to the words that tell about it.

| feeds animals | cleans environment | observes animals |

Do the Math! • Zoo A has 80 animals. Zoo B has 10 more animals than Zoo A. How many animals does Zoo B have?

💡 **Use Mental Math** Go to the online handbook for tips.

Ⓐ 70

Ⓑ 81

Ⓒ 90

266

Explore online.   Have children review how animals take care of their young.

Lesson Check

Name _____

Explore online. ▶

Can You Explain It?

✏️➤ How do animals help their young survive? Be sure to

• Describe patterns in how some animals act to take care of their young.

• Explain how this helps the young survive.

Sample answer: Parent animals hide their young or warn them

of danger. Parent animals bring food when a young animal calls.

Parent animals teach their young to find food. These things help

young animals grow, stay safe, and learn to live on their own.

Lesson 3 • How do Animals Take Care of Their Young?   267

Lesson Check

Can You Explain It?

Have children reread their answers to the Can You Explain It? prompt at the beginning of the lesson.

 Patterns . . . .

Review the picture from the Engage page and discuss the ways some animals take care of their young. **Ask: What are some of the patterns of behavior we have seen that show how animals take care of their young?** Children should be able to describe patterns of behavior exhibited by parent animals and their young that help the young find food and stay safe.

 Obtaining, Evaluating, and Communicating Information . . . .

Review the Can You Explain It? question. **Ask: What was your favorite of the animals we discussed, and what did it do to help its offspring?** Accept all answers that describe a behavior discussed during the lesson.

DCI **Growth and Development of Organisms** . . . . .

Guide children to describe and explain animal behaviors that help their young find food or stay safe. **Ask: Can you write about some of the patterns we have seen that show what animals do to take care of their young?** Accept all answers that describe patterns of what animals do to take care of their young.

Scoring Guidelines

• Children should describe patterns of how animal parents take care of their young.

• Children should explain how this helps young animals survive.

• Children should use evidence to explain their answers.

Lesson Check, continued

SUMMATIVE ASSESSMENT
Self Check

1. Children should choose both B—by calling to its young, and C—by hiding its young. If children choose A, remind children that feeding its young is important for helping the young animal grow, but feeding will not keep the young animal safe.

2. Children should make the following three matches:

   1. top left picture with bottom right picture

   2. middle left picture with top right picture

   3. bottom left picture with middle right picture

   If children make incorrect matches, discuss how the pictures show the following three behaviors: 1) staying safe using a shelter, 2) riding on a parent's back, and 3) keeping close to a family group.

Self Check

1. How might an animal keep its young safe? Choose all correct answers.

   Ⓐ by feeding its young

   Ⓑ by calling to its young

   Ⓒ by hiding its young

2. Draw a line to match animals that stay safe in the same way.

268

3. Observe each bird and its young. What pattern do you see?

Ⓐ The parent bird is teaching its young to fly.

Ⓑ The parent bird is feeding its young.

Ⓒ The parent bird and its young are staying safe.

4. Which sentence is **true**?

Ⓐ Young animals make noise only when they are in danger.

Ⓑ All young animals make the same noises.

Ⓒ Some animals and their young make noises to find each other.

5. How long do bear cubs and leopard cubs stay with their mothers?

Ⓐ a few days

Ⓑ a few weeks

Ⓒ a few years

3. Children should choose B—The parent bird is feeding its young. If children choose A, remind children that these birds are not teaching their young in this picture. If children choose C, remind children that while the eagle may be safe in the nest, the penguins may not be safe where they are.

4. Children should choose C—Some animals and their young make noises to find each other. If children choose A, remind children that some birds, such as cardinals, make noise even when they are not in danger. If children choose B, remind children that the birds in question 3, an eagle and a penguin, do not make the same noise.

5. Children should choose C—a few years. If children choose A or B, guide children to review the Animals Learn from Their Parents section of the lesson. Bear cubs and leopard cubs stay with their parents for a few years.

Unit 5 Performance Task

Match Animals and Their Young

👥 small groups 🕐 2 class periods

Objective
Children **obtain information from books** to make picture cards about animals and their young. They will **describe patterns** that explain **how parents and their offspring are alike and different**.

Suggested Materials
books about animals, crayons, construction paper, scissors

Preparation
Collect an assortment of grade-appropriate books.

SEP **Obtaining, Evaluating, and Communicating Information** . . . .

Ask: How will reading books about animals and their young help you to draw the animals? I can look for patterns to compare parent animals and young animals.

STEPS

Step 1
DCI **Inheritance of Traits** . . . .

Ask: If you choose an adult animal but do not find information about its young, can you just draw a smaller animal that looks like the adult? Why or why not? No, the young animal is probably smaller, but there may be other things about the young animal that are different from the adult animal.

Step 2
Advise children to make all ten cards as close in size as possible.

Step 3
Have children decide which animal each group member will draw.

 Unit 5 Performance Task
Match Animals and Their Young

Materials
- books about animals
- construction paper
- crayons
- scissors

STEPS

Step 1
Look in books to find out about animals and their young. Choose five kinds of animals.

Step 2
Cut ten cards from the paper. Make sure they are the same size.

Step 3
Draw adult animals on five of the cards. Draw their young on the other five cards.

270

Step 4

Put the cards face down on a table. Ask a friend to turn over two cards. If the cards match, tell how the adult and young are alike and different.

Step 5

Take turns flipping over the cards until all the adults and young are matched. What patterns do you see?

✔ Check

_____ I researched animals and their young.
_____ I made ten animal cards.
_____ I played a matching game.
_____ I compared animals and their young.

Step 4

DCI Inheritance of Traits . . . .

Encourage children to make observations about size, coloring, body coverings, and body parts as they compare and contrast each pair of animals. Ask children to explain how they decided which cards matched. **Ask: How did you know each pair was a match?** I looked at the parts, size, and covering of each animal. The young animals had similar parts and coverings, but they were smaller.

Step 5

CCC Patterns . . . .

Say: Describe the patterns in how the adults are alike and different from their young. The young all have the same kind of body covering as their parent. They also have the same parts. Sometimes the young were a different color from the parent. The parents are bigger than the young.

	Scoring Rubric for Performance Task
3	Makes picture cards, matches animals correctly, compares animals, and describes patterns.
2	Makes picture cards and matches animals correctly, but does not compare animals or describes patterns.
1	Makes picture cards, but does not match animals correctly, does not compare animals, and does not describe patterns.
0	Does not make picture cards, match animals correctly, compare animals, or describe patterns.

Unit 5 Review

1. Children should choose A—the first plant. If children choose B or C, reinforce that young plants usually have leaves that are the same shape as a parent. The young plant may have smaller or fewer leaves than its parent. By completing Compare Parts in Lesson 1, children observed how most young plants have parts that look like the parts of their parents.

2. Children should choose A—Their flowers can be different colors; and B—They can have different numbers of leaves. If children choose C, reinforce that the size, number, and color of parts of plants of the same kind can be different. Plants of the same kind always grow the same kinds of fruits. By completing Compare Adult Plants in Lesson 1, children explored how plants of the same kind can have similarities and differences. Plants of the same kind may look alike, but may also have differences.

3. Children should choose B—a smaller plant with leaves that are the same shape. If children choose A or C, reinforce that a young plant of the same kind would be smaller and have the same shape leaves. The leaves would not be bigger than an adult plant. By completing Young and Old and Compare Parts in Lesson 1, children compared a young plant with a parent plant to explain how they are different.

Unit 5 Review · Name _____

1. Observe this young plant. Which plant is its parent? Look for patterns.

(A)   (B)   (C)

---

2. How can plants of the same kind be different? Choose all correct answers.
   - (A) Their flowers can be different colors.
   - (B) They can have different numbers of leaves.
   - (C) They can grow different kinds of fruits.

---

3. Zak found a plant in his yard. He wants to find a young plant of the same kind. What should he look for?
   - (A) a smaller plant with bigger leaves
   - (B) a smaller plant with leaves that are the same shape
   - (C) a plant that is the same size

272

4. Draw lines to match each young animal with its parent.

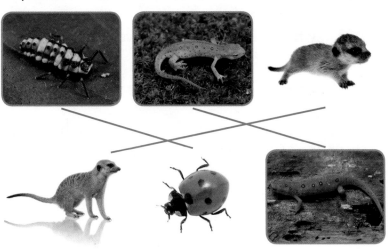

5. Kim sees an animal with fur on its body. What will a young animal of the same kind have on its body?
  Ⓐ feathers
  Ⓑ a shell
  Ⓒ fur

6. Which is true about young animals and their parents? Choose all correct answers.
  Ⓐ Young animals are smaller than their parents.
  Ⓑ Young animals are always different colors from their parents.
  Ⓒ Young animals are the same kind of animal as their parents.

4. Children should draw a line from the top left animal to the bottom middle animal; from the top middle animal to the bottom right animal; and from the top right animal to the bottom left animal. Children may choose not to connect the insects because they observe differences in their color and length. Reinforce that although they have these differences, the shape and structure of the parent ladybug and young ladybug are similar. By completing the Take It Further in Lesson 2—The Butterfly Life Cycle, children explored the life cycle of butterflies to observe how an adult animal can look different from its young. By completing Compare Parts and Compare Body Coverings in Lesson 2, children compared the body features of young animals and their parents.

5. Children should choose C—fur. If children choose A or B, reinforce that most young animals and their parents have the same type of body covering. By completing Compare Body Coverings in Lesson 2, children explored how young animals look similar to and different from their parents.

6. Children should choose A—Young animals are smaller than their parents; and C—Young animals are the same kind of animal as their parents. If children choose B, ask them to think about whether they have ever seen a young animal that is the same color as its parents. By completing Animals Grow and Animals of the Same Kind in Lesson 2, children explored how young animals grow and change.

7. Children should choose B—They are different sizes. If children choose A or C, have them think about how animals of the same kind can be different. Remind them that most animals of the same kind have the same body coverings and kinds of parts.

8. Children should choose A—how to stay safe; and B—how to find food. If children choose C, they may be confused because parents often respond by meeting the needs of a young animal when it makes noise. However, young animals can make noise from the time they are born. Reinforce that a young animal watches an adult to learn how to find food and stay safe.

9. Children should choose C—to help them get food from their parents. If children choose A or B, reinforce that young animals make noise to let their parents know they are hungry.

10. Children should choose B—the birds on a branch; and C—the duck feeding the ducklings. If children choose A, they may have thought the swan was teaching its young how to get food. The other pictures show the parent animals in the act of feeding its young. Reinforce that parents often provide food for offspring.

3D Item Analysis	1	2	3	4	5	6	7	8	9	10
SEP Constructing Explanations and Designing Solutions	•			•						•
SEP Obtaining, Evaluating, and Communicating Information				•	•					
DCI Inheritance of Traits	•	•	•	•	•					
DCI Variation of Traits	•	•	•				•	•		
DCI Growth and Development of Organisms								•	•	•
CCC Patterns	•	•		•		•	•			•

7. Bella sees two horses that are the same kind, but they do not look exactly alike. How might they be different?
Ⓐ They have different body coverings.
Ⓑ They are different sizes.
Ⓒ They have different numbers of legs.

8. Which are things an animal parent might teach its young? Choose all correct answers.
Ⓐ how to stay safe
Ⓑ how to find food
Ⓒ how to make noise

9. Why do many young birds make noise?
Ⓐ to find their way back home
Ⓑ to hide from danger
Ⓒ to help them get food from their parents

10. Which animals are feeding their young? Look for patterns. Choose all correct answers.

274

Unit 6
Objects and Patterns in the Sky

Unit Project • Explore the Moon's Phases

How can you model the moon's phases? Investigate to find out.

© Houghton Mifflin Harcourt

Unit 6 • Objects and Patterns in the Sky

Unit Overview

In this unit, children will…

- identify and describe objects in the sky.
- use evidence to describe predictable patterns of the sun, moon and stars.
- observe and model patterns of the moon's phases.
- use observations to describe characteristics of each season.
- predict patterns of change that take place from season to season.
- use observations to compare the amount of daylight from season to season.
- explore how seasons affect people and animals.

About This Image

Guide children in a discussion about the moon's phases.
Ask: What do we call the large ball of rock in the nighttime sky? the moon **Ask: Why does the moon look different throughout the month?** As the moon moves, different amounts of light are reflected from the sun. Encourage children to provide reasonable answers, and steer them away from any misconceptions they might have about objects and their patterns in the sky.

Unit Project • Explore the Moon's Phases

Have children plan and conduct an investigation about how they can model the moon's phases. Discuss what the investigation should include. Have children brainstorm questions that could be answered, such as: "What are the moon's phases?" and "What causes these phases?"

To begin, review the phases of the moon with children, and cover any information that will help them model the moon's phases. More support for the Unit Project can be found on pp. 277I–277L.

Unit 6 At a Glance

The learning experiences in this unit prepare children for mastery of:

Performance Expectations

ESS1-1 Use observations of the sun, moon, and stars to describe patterns that can be predicted.

ESS1-2 Make observations at different times of year to relate the amount of daylight to the time of year.

Explore online.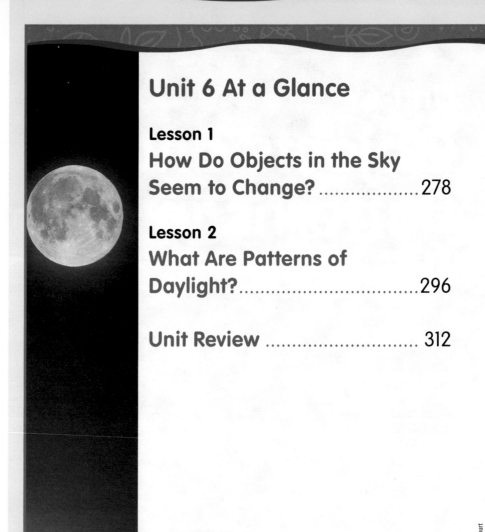

In addition to the print resources, the following resources are available online to support this unit:

Unit Pretest

Lesson 1 How Do Objects in the Sky Seem to Change?
- Interactive Online Student Edition
- Lesson Quiz

You Solve It Eyes on the Sky!

Lesson 2 What Are Patterns of Daylight?
- Interactive Online Student Edition
- Lesson Quiz

Unit Performance Task

Unit Test

276

© Houghton Mifflin Harcourt

Unit Vocabulary

star an object in the sky that gives off its own light (p. 280)

sun the star closest to Earth (p. 280)

moon a large ball of rock that circles Earth (p. 286)

phases the moon's pattern of light and shadow as the moon moves (p. 288)

season a time of year with a certain kind of weather (p. 298)

Vocabulary Game • Show the Word

Materials
• 1 set of word cards

1. Work with a partner to make word cards.
2. Place the cards face down in a pile.
3. Pick a card, but do not show the word.
4. Draw or act out the word for your partner to guess.
5. When the word is guessed correctly, your partner picks a card to draw or act out.

Unit Vocabulary

The Next Generation Science Standards emphasize explanation and demonstration of understanding versus rote memorization of science vocabulary words. Keep in mind that these vocabulary words are tools for clear communication. Use these words as a starting point, not an end goal, for children to build deeper understanding of science concepts.

Children can explore all vocabulary words in the **Online Glossary**.

Vocabulary Strategies

• Have children review the vocabulary words. Then have children work in pairs to share an example of each word and explain why they think it's an example. Have pairs record their examples.
• Have children think about how each word relates to patterns seen in the sky. Have children share their ideas with a partner.

Differentiate Instruction

RTI/Extra Support Pronounce each word, and have children repeat it after you. Have children find each highlighted word within the unit content. Have children work in pairs and explain to a partner what they think each word means based on the surrounding context of imagery and text.

Extension Have children select two vocabulary words and work in small groups to illustrate and explain the words to a kindergarten child.

Vocabulary Game • Show the Word

Preparation Assign children to partners. Distribute blank cards. Have children write vocabulary words on cards. Remind children that only the partner guessing should speak during a turn. If time permits, encourage children to play a second round, this time drawing words previously acted out and vice versa.

Integrating the NGSS* Three Dimensions of Learning

Building to the Performance Expectations

The learning experiences in this unit prepare children for mastery of the following Performance Expectations:

Earth's Place in the Universe

1-ESS1-1 Use observations of the sun, moon, and stars to describe patterns that can be predicted.

1- ESS1-2 Make observations at different times of year to relate the amount of daylight to the time of year.

Assessing Student Progress

After completing the lessons, the **Unit Project • Explore the Moon's Phases** provides children with opportunities to practice aspects of and to demonstrate their understanding of the Performance Expectations as they plan and conduct an investigation about the moon.

Additionally, children can further practice or be assessed on aspects of the Performance Expectations by completing the **Unit Performance Task • Explore Short and Long Days,** in which children observe the growth of plants exposed to different amounts of sunlight and collect and analyze data that explains how seasonal patterns of daylight affect plant growth.

Lesson 1
How Do Objects in the Sky Seem to Change?

In Lesson 1, children focus on observing, describing, and predicting patterns in the way the sun, moon, and stars appear to move across the sky **(DCI The Universe and its Stars)**. Children make observations of objects in the daytime sky and the nighttime sky and use those observations to answer questions about the motion of the objects they see in the sky **(SEP Analyzing and Interpreting Data)**. In the process, children explore the apparent motion of these objects as examples of natural events that are repeated through time **(CCC Scientific Knowledge Assumes an Order and Consistency in Natural Systems)**, and learn to make assumptions about phenomena using observed repetitions as evidence **(CCC Patterns)**.

Lesson 2
What Are Patterns of Daylight?

In Lesson 2, children focus on how the amount of daylight in a day is related to the time of year **(DCI Earth and the Solar System)**. After an introduction to the seasons, children observe, describe, and predict seasonal patterns of sunrise and sunset **(DCI Earth and the Solar System)**. They observe how seasonal changes affect plants and animals **(CCC Patterns)**. Children explore these patterns through a variety of interactions and one hands-on activity **(SEP Planning and Carrying Out Investigations)**.

Standards Supported by This Unit

 Explore online. Online only.

Next Generation Science Standards	Unit Project	Lesson 1	Lesson 2		Unit Performance Task	You Solve It
SEP Analyzing and Interpreting Data	•	•			•	
SEP Planning and Carrying Out Investigations	•		•			•
DCI **ESS1.A** The Universe and its Stars	•	•				•
DCI **ESS1.B** Earth and the Solar System	•		•		•	
CCC Patterns	•	•	•		•	•
CCC Scientific Knowledge Assumes an Order and Consistency in Natural Systems		•				

NGSS* Across the Grades

Before	**Grade 1**	**After**
Coverage of the **Performance Expectations** within this unit originates in Grade 1.	**Earth's Place in the Universe** **1-ESS1-1** **1-ESS1-2**	**Earth's Place in the Universe** **5-ESS1-1** Support an argument that differences in the apparent brightness of the sun compared to other stars is due to their relative distances from Earth. **5-ESS1-2** Represent data in graphical displays to reveal patterns of daily changes in length and direction of shadows, day and night, and the seasonal appearance of some stars in the night sky.

Trace Tool to the NGSS™ Go online to view the complete coverage of these standards across this grade level and time.

3D Unit Planning

Lesson 1 How Do Objects in the Sky Seem to Change? pp. 278–295

Overview

Objective Identify and describe objects in the sky and observe and describe predictable patterns of the sun, moon, and stars.

SEP Analyzing and Interpreting Data
DCI **ESS1.A** The Universe and its Stars
CCC Patterns
CCC Scientific Knowledge Assumes an Order and Consistency in Natural Systems
Math and **English Language Arts** standards and features are detailed on lesson planning pages.

	Print and Online Student Editions	Explore online. ▶
ENGAGE	Lesson Phenomenon pp. 278–279 Can You Explain It? Objects	▶ Can You Explain It? Video
EXPLORE/ EXPLAIN	The Daytime Sky Patterns in the Daytime Sky The Nighttime Sky Patterns in the Nighttime Sky 🔍 Hands-On Activity Observe the Pattern of the Sun pp. 283–284	Hands-On Worksheet You Solve It Eyes on the Sky!
ELABORATE	Take It Further pp. 291–292 **People in Science & Engineering •** Dr. Sarah Ballard	Take It Further Space Technology
EVALUATE	Lesson Check p. 293 Self Check pp. 294–295	Lesson Quiz

Hands-On Activity Planning

Observe the Pattern of the Sun

Objective Children explore the sun's apparent movement across the daytime sky. They use their observations to make a claim that answers their question. 👥 individuals 🕙 10 minutes for each observation over 2 days	**Suggested Materials** • drawing paper • clock

Preparation/Tip
Try to arrange times for children to observe the sun's position in the morning, at noon, and in the afternoon on two different days.

Lesson 2 What Are Patterns of Daylight? pp. 296–311

Overview

Objective Make observations at different times of year to relate the amount of daylight to the time of year.

SEP Planning and Carrying Out Investigations
DCI **ESS1.B** Earth and the Solar System
CCC Patterns
Math and **English Language Arts** standards and features are detailed on lesson planning pages.

	Print and Online Student Editions	Explore online. ▶
ENGAGE	Lesson Problem pp. 296–297 Can You Solve It? Patterns of Daylight	▶ Can You Solve It? Video
EXPLORE/ EXPLAIN	The Four Seasons Spring and Summer Fall and Winter Patterns of Daylight	Hands-On Worksheet
	Hands-On Activity Observe Patterns of Sunset pp. 305–306	
ELABORATE	Take It Further pp. 307–308 **Careers in Science & Engineering •** **Circadian Biologist**	Take It Further The Midnight Sun
EVALUATE	Lesson Check p. 309 Self Check pp. 310–311	Lesson Quiz

🔍 Hands-On Activity Planning

Observe Patterns of Sunset

Objective Children compare what time the sun sets in three different seasons. Children make a claim about how the time of sunset changes from season to season.

👥 small groups
🕐 1 class period

Suggested Materials
- a calendar
- a computer
- crayons
- drawing paper

Preparation/Tip

Gather materials for groups. Arrange access to a variety of resources that include daily sunset data. Alternatively, children may use the Internet to complete this activity.

3D Unit Planning, continued

 You Solve It   Go online for an additional interactive activity.

Eyes on the Sky!

This interactive activity offers practice in support of **1 -ESS1-2**.

SEP Planning and Carrying Out Investigations
DCI **ESS1.A** The Universe and its Stars
CCC Patterns

3D Learning Objectives
- Children model the moon phases by moving a ball-on a stick around their head, with a light bulb used to model the sun.
- Children predict the order of the moon's phases during the month and check to see if they are correct by using a simulation of the different moon phases throughout a month.

Activity Problem
- Children use a model to see how the moon orbits Earth. Children photograph their models at each stage and match them up to actual phases of the moon.
- They use their data from the model to predict the order of moon phases for a 30-day cycle, starting with a specific moon phase.
- After making their predictions, they will use a 30-day night-sky simulator to determine if their predictions were correct, and they can revise their predictions if needed.

Interaction Summary
- Use a moon and Earth ball-stick model. They take pictures of their model at different positions, comparing them to pictures of actual moon phases.
- Make a prediction for moon phases for 30 days starting with the new moon.
- Use a simulator to determine if their predictions are correct.

Assessment Planning

Pre-Assessment
Assessment Guide, Unit Pretest
The Unit Pretest focuses on prerequisite knowledge and is composed of items that evaluate children's preparedness for the content covered within this unit.

Formative Assessment
Interactive Worktext, Apply What You Know, Lesson Check, and Self Check

Summative Assessment
Assessment Guide, Lesson Quiz
The Lesson Quiz provides a quick assessment of each lesson objective and of the portion of the Performance Expectation aligned to the lesson.

Interactive Worktext, Performance Task pp. 312–313
The Performance Task presents the opportunity for children to collaborate with classmates in in order to complete the steps of each Performance Task. Each Performance Task provides a formal Scoring Rubric for evaluating children's work.

Interactive Worktext , Unit 6 Review, pp. 314–316
Assessment Guide, Unit Test
The Unit Test provides an in-depth assessment of the Performance Expectations aligned to the unit. This test evaluates children's ability to apply knowledge in order to explain phenomena and to solve problems. Within this test, Constructed Response items apply a three-dimensional rubric for evaluating children's mastery on all three dimensions of the Next Generation Science Standards.

 **Assessment Online**   Go online to view the complete assessment items for this unit.

Teacher Notes

Differentiate Instruction

Leveled Readers

The Science & Engineering Leveled Readers provide additional nonfiction reading practice in this unit's subject area.

On Level
How Can We Observe and Record Weather?
How Does the Sky Seem to Change?
These readers reinforce unit concepts, and include response activities for your children.

Extra Support
How Can We Observe and Record Weather?
How Does the Sky Seem to Change?
These readers share title, illustrations, vocabulary, and concepts with the On-Level Reader; however, the text is linguistically accommodated to provide simplified sentence structures and comprehension aids. They also include response activities.

Enrichment
Move It!
A Closer Look at Telescopes
These high-interest, nonfiction readers will extend and enrich unit concepts and vocabulary, and include response activities.

Teacher Guide
The accompanying Teacher Guide provides teaching strategies and support for using all the readers.

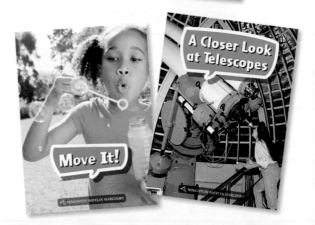

ELL

English Language Learner support resources include a glossary and Leveled Readers in Spanish and English. ELL teaching strategies appear throughout this unit:

pp. 278B, 287, 296B, 302

RTI/Extra Support

Strategies for children who need extra support appear throughout this unit:

pp. 277, 278B, 281, 296B, 299, 308

Extension

Strategies for children who have mastered core content and are ready for additional challenges appear throughout this unit:

pp. 277, 278B, 281, 296B, 299, 308

Leveled Readers

All readers are available online as well as in an innovative, engaging format for use with touchscreen mobile devices. Contact your HMH Sales Representative for more information.

Connecting with NGSS

Connections to Community

Use these opportunities for informal science learning to provide local context, and to extend and enhance unit concepts.

At Home

Star Gazing Have children view the sky at night, with or without a telescope. If children live in the city, allow them to use pictures of the nighttime sky. Children should draw an illustration of what the moon looks like, and identify the phase of the moon. Children can add the stars they also see in the nighttime sky and identify any constellations they (or their parents) may know. Have children share their findings with the class, and explain which phase the moon is in and any constellation they knew. *Use with Lesson 1.*

My Seasons Have children work with family members to draw a picture of their favorite hobbies according to the seasons. What are the things they enjoy doing depending on the season? How do seasonal changes affect what you do? *Use with Lesson 2.*

In the Community

Farm Visits Plan a class field trip to a local farm. Have children develop a list of questions they want to ask about how the seasons affect the farm. Guide children to think about possible problems the farmer may have during the different seasons. Have children record the answers to their questions. *Use with Lesson 2.*

Guest Speaker Invite an astronomer to speak to the class about interesting things in the sky at night. Have children prepare questions for him or her to answer. Encourage children to ask a mix of appropriate science and engineering questions. *Use with Lesson 1.*

Collaboration

Collaboration opportunities in this unit:

Build on Prior Knowledge
pp. 279, 297

Whole Class
p. 290

Small Groups
p. 301

Think , Pair, Share
p. 282

Connections to Science

Connections to Science opportunities in this unit:

Connection to Physical Science
Lesson 1, p. 289

Connection to Life Science
Lesson 2, p. 304

Home Letters Go online to view the Home Letters for this unit.

Unit Project

Unit Project 👥 small groups ⏱ 2 class periods

Explore the Moon's Phases

Have children plan and build a model to demonstrate the moon's phases. Discuss what kind of objects they will include in the investigation. Have children brainstorm questions that should be answered, such as: "What are the phases of the moon?", "What causes these phases?", "How does the moon change?", "How does the sun change?", "What patterns do we see in light?", or "How is the Earth involved in the moon's phases?"

3D Learning Objective

SEP Analyzing and Interpreting Data
Observe the interaction of the sun, Earth, and our moon to investigate and describe pattern of the moon's phases. Collect data to use as evidence to answer a question. Construct an argument using evidence to support a claim.

Skills and Standards Focus

This project supports building children's mastery of **Performance Expectation 1-ESS1-1.**

SEP Analyzing and Interpreting Data
SEP Planning and Carrying Out Investigations
DCI The Universe and its Stars
DCI Earth and the Solar System
CCC Patterns

Suggested Materials

- pictures of the moon's phases
- different sized balls, such as ping pong balls, tennis balls, or Styrofoam balls
- different sized rods, drinking straws, or twine
- construction paper
- crayons, paints, or markers
- modeling clay

Preparation

Have pictures that show the different phases of the moon. Share details about how the moon can look different at night. Have children share what they know about the moon's phases. Guide children to begin brainstorming questions they can answer during their investigation to discover what causes the moon's phases and where they can look to find the answers to their questions. Finally, guide children to share ideas on what they need to build a model that can show the moon's phases and how this phenomenon occurs.

Unit 6
Objects and Patterns in the Sky

Unit Project • Explore the Moon's Phases
How can you model the moon's phases? Investigate to find out.

Differentiate Instruction

RTI/Extra Support Show children pictures of the moon's phases that includes the positioning of the sun and Earth to make the connection more defined.

Extension Have children compare other planets in the solar system that have moons. Ask children to consider if these planet's moons would also have phases similar to our moon.

Name _____

Unit 6 Project

Explore the Moon's Phases

What are the moon's phases? What causes these phases? How can you model the moon's phases? Write your two ideas on the lines below. Then choose one. Plan and conduct an investigation to find out what causes the moon's phases, then build a model to display your findings.

Children should write two ideas they have to discover and explain the

phases of the moon.

_____

Materials
Draw and label the materials you will need.

Children should draw and label materials. The following are possible materials children can use to investigate the causes of the moon's phases: books, internet

The following are possible materials children can use for their model: ping pong balls, modeling clay, tennis balls, string, short dowel rods, Styrofoam balls, light source, construction paper, crayons, or paints.

Unit 6 Project • Page 1 of 3

© Houghton Mifflin Harcourt Publishing Company

Unit 6 Project
Explore the Moon's Phases

SEP Analyzing and Interpreting Data . . . .

Pose the unit project question to children. Encourage them to think of how they could build a model to demonstrate the phases of the moon. Discuss all of the ideas as a class. Have children choose which method they would like to complete from the list.

Children investigate what causes the moon's phases and build a model to demonstrate what changes. Children select one method from the class discussion to build a model that represents the moon's phases. They investigate why we see the different phases. **Ask: Why do we see the moon in the sky at night? Why do you think the moon seems to change?** We can see the moon at night because the light from the sun hits the moon's surface and reflects the light from the sun. It changes because sometimes the light from the sun doesn't hit all of the moon.

ESSENTIAL QUESTIONS Prepare children for their project by asking the following questions.

- Why do we see the moon in the sky at night?
- Does the moon actually change?
- Why does it seem like the moon changes?
- How could you build a model that can show the cause for the moon's phases?

Ask: How can we investigate why the moon seems to change? What materials would you need to show how the moon looks during the different phases? We can look in our science book and other books. We will need some round objects and a light source.

Steps

Children plan and carry out an investigation of the moon's phases to construct a model that explains how this happens.

SEP **Planning and Carrying Out Investigations . . . .**

Before beginning the investigation, have children observe the properties of the moon and how we view the moon from Earth.

Ask: Why do we see the moon as different shapes at night? The moon reflects sunlight and sometimes, Earth gets in the way and causes a shadow on the moon. Challenge children to identify the order of the phases and the relationship between the sun, Earth, and the moon. **In which phase does the entire surface of the moon reflect the sun's light?** The full moon happens when the entire moon's surface reflects the sun's light. Refer children to Lesson 1 Patterns in the Nighttime Sky. Have them record their observations using words and pictures.

Data

Children will design and test their model that demonstrates the moon's phases.

DCI **The Universe and its Stars . . . .**

Ask: How does the sun cause the moon's phases? The sun gives off the light that hits the moon to cause the changes in how we see the moon. **How does the Earth cause the moon's phases?** The Earth sometimes gets in the path of the light that goes to the moon and causes a shadow on the moon.

CCC **Patterns . . . .**

Remind children that patterns in the natural world can be observed, used to describe phenomena, and used as evidence. **Ask: What patterns can we find as we study the causes of the moon's phases?** The sun gives off light that bounces or reflects off of the moon. Sometimes, the entire moon does not reflect the sun's light because the Earth gets in the way. This is what causes the different phases of the moon. Refer children to Lesson 1 How Do Objects in the Sky Seem to Change?

Steps Write the steps you will do.

Answers may vary but should reflect a logical order of steps in the project. Sample steps listed:

1. Identify the question guiding the investigation.

2. Discover what causes the moon's phases.

3. Plan how to build the model.

4. Gather materials needed for the model.

5. Build the model to show how the moon's phases happen.

6. Test the model to make sure it explains the moon's phases.

7. Finish the model so it explains the moon's phases.

Data

Record your data.

Answers and drawings may vary but should reflect a relationship between the sun, earth, and moon that causes the moon's phases. Answers and drawings should also reflect the model.

Unit 6 Project • Page 2 of 3

Analyze Your Result

Does the model explain the moon's phases?

Restate Your Question

Write the question you investigated.

Answers should identify the question children initially

Chose at the beginning of the investigation (Step 1).

Claims, Evidence, and Reasoning

Make a claim that answers your question.

Answers should explain what causes the moon's phases and should

include how the model shows the phases.

Review the data. What evidence from the investigation supports your claim?

Answers should describe how the model supports their

Explanation of what causes the moon's phases.

Discuss your reasoning with a partner.

Unit 6 Project • Page 3 of 3

Analyze Your Result

 Analyzing and Interpreting Data . . . .

Have children analyze their model. Elicit from them any patterns they noticed. Encourage them to share their model with the other groups in order to compare test results.

Claims, Evidence, and Reasoning

Children should understand that the moon's phases are a reflection of the light from the sun and depend on the placement of the Earth's and moon's rotation. They should site evidence to support their claim by using their drawings, written notations, and recorded times.

Ask: What claim can you make? The cause of the moon's phases depends on how much light from the sun hits the moon instead of the Earth. How does your evidence support your claim? My model demonstrates how the sun's light is reflected differently off of the moon depending on where the Earth is placed. Encourage children to discuss their reasoning.

DCI **Earth and the Solar System** . . . .

Ask: How does the Earth move in our solar system? The Earth orbits the sun. How does our moon move in the solar system? The moon orbits the Earth. How does this cause the phases of the moon? Sometimes, the Earth gets the light from the sun instead of letting it travel all the way to our moon.

Scoring Rubric for Unit Project	
3	States a claim supported with evidence to explain the phases of the moon
2	States a claim and somewhat supported with evidence to explain the phases of the moon
1	States a claim that is not supported by evidence
0	Does not state a claim and does not provide evidence

How Do Objects in the Sky Seem to Change?

Building to the Performance Expectation

The learning experiences in this lesson prepare children for mastery of:

1–ESS1–1 Use observations of the sun, moon, and stars to describe patterns that can be predicted.

 Trace Tool to the NGSS
Go online to view the complete coverage of these standards across this lesson, unit, and time.

 SEP ## Science & Engineering Practices

Analyzing and Interpreting Data
Use observations (firsthand or from media) to describe patterns in the natural world in order to answer scientific questions.

▶ **VIDEO** SEPs: Analyzing and Interpreting Data / Using Mathematics and Computational Thinking

DCI ## Disciplinary Core Ideas

ESS1.A: The Universe and its Stars
Patterns of the motion of the sun, moon, and stars in the sky can be observed, described, and predicted.

 CCC ## Crosscutting Concepts

Patterns
Patterns in the natural world can be observed, used to describe phenomena, and used as evidence.

Scientific Knowledge Assumes an Order and Consistency in Natural Systems
- Science assumes natural events happen today as they happened in the past.
- Many events are repeated.

CONNECTION TO MATH

1.G.A.3 Partition circles and rectangles into two and four equal shares, describe the shares using the words *halves, fourths,* and *quarters,* and use the phrases *half of, fourth of,* and *quarter of.* Describe the whole as two of, or four of the shares. Understand for these examples that decomposing into more equal shares creates smaller shares.

CONNECTION TO ENGLISH LANGUAGE ARTS

W.1.8 With guidance and support from adults, recall information from experiences or gather information from provided sources to answer a question.

Supporting All Students, All Standards

Integrating the Three Dimensions of Learning

This lesson focuses on observing, describing, and predicting patterns in the motion of the sun, moon, and stars (**DCI The Universe and its Stars**). Children make observations of objects in the daytime sky and the nighttime sky, and use those observations to answer questions about the motion of the objects they see in the sky (**SEP Analyzing and Interpreting Data**). In the process, children explore the motion of these objects as examples of natural events that are repeated through time (**CCC Scientific Knowledge Assumes an Order and Consistency in Natural Systems**) and learn to make assumptions about phenomena using observed repetitions as evidence (**CCC Patterns**).

 Professional Development

Go online to view **Professional Development videos** with strategies to integrate CCCs and SEPs, including the ones used in this lesson.

Build on Prior Knowledge

Children should already know and be prepared to build on the following concepts:

- The sun appears in the daytime sky.
- The moon and stars appear in the nighttime sky.
- A pattern is something that repeats.
- Time can be measured using hours and minutes.

Differentiate Instruction

Lesson Vocabulary

- star
- sun
- moon
- phases

Reinforcing Vocabulary To help children remember the vocabulary words *star*, *sun*, and *moon*, choose two of the objects and have children tell what the difference is between them. For example, a star gives off its own light and the moon doesn't. Invite children to make up riddles for others to solve. For example, "You can see me in the daytime sky. What am I?"

RTI/Extra Support Use a light bulb to represent a star. Show children that when the light bulb is far away it looks like a small spot of light, like the way most stars look to us. When the light bulb is closer, like the way the sun appears to us, it seems brighter. Use a ball wrapped in aluminum foil to represent the moon. Show how light from the light bulb reflects off the ball, as the sun's light reflects off the moon.

Extension Children who want to find out more can research the names of some of the bright stars or constellations in the nighttime sky and share them with the class.

ELL Point out and reinforce words associated with times of day including *daytime*, *nighttime*, *early morning*, *noon*, and *late afternoon*. To help children put these words into context, talk with children about what they might be doing at each time of day.

Lesson Phenomenon

Lesson Objective

Identify and describe objects in the sky and observe and describe predictable patterns of the sun, moon, and stars.

About This Image

Ask: What do you see in this photograph?   Sample answer: I see too many stars to count in the sky.   Use the discussion as an opportunity for children to share their knowledge about the sky and the objects we see in it.   **Ask:** What do you know about stars?   Stars are bright. Most of them are very far away.   Do we always see stars like this in the sky?   No, we only see them at night.

 The Universe and its Stars

Alternative Engage Strategy

Sky Sorting	small groups ⏱ 15–20 minutes

Have children list objects they see in the sky. For example, they might list the sun, clouds, stars, and the moon. Write each object on the board as children say it. Allow 5 minutes for this activity. Have children work in small groups to sort the objects into those they see during the day and those they see at night. Then provide cards to each group with the objects' names on them. Allow 10 minutes for this activity. Invite children to share and discuss how they sorted each object. Some objects, such as the moon, can be seen both at night and during the day.

Lesson 1

How Do Objects in the Sky Seem to Change?

Objects in the nighttime sky seem to change.

By the End of This Lesson
I will be able to describe objects in the sky and predict their patterns.

278

Can You Explain It?

Objects in the Sky The objects we see in the sky seem to move. Play the video to see how objects appear to move in the sky.

If the videos are unavailable to view, guide children to look at the pictures of the daytime and nighttime sky. Ask children to record their initial thoughts about how the objects in the sky seem to change. Accept all reasonable answers. At the end of this lesson, children will revisit this question and their answers as part of the Lesson Check.

Collaboration

Build on Prior Knowledge Guide children to look at the two photographs. **Ask: What do you see that is the same in both photographs?** the buildings, the trees, and the roads **What do you see that is different?** One sky is light and one is dark; I see the moon in the nighttime photograph. Use Think, Pair, Share to have children recall other changes they have observed in the sky at different times of night or day. Encourage children to begin to think about what might be the cause of each change they mention.

Objects in the Sky

daytime

Explore online. ▶

nighttime

You can see objects in the daytime sky.

You can see objects in the nighttime sky.

Can You Explain It?

✏️ How do objects in the sky seem to change?

Accept all reasonable answers.

_____

_____

_____

_____

© Houghton Mifflin Harcourt • Image Credits: ©Stockelements/Shutterstock

Lesson 1 • How Do Objects in the Sky Seem to Change?

279

The Daytime Sky

3D Learning Objective

Children **observe the daytime sky** and describe **the pattern of the appearance of the sun.** Children **use their observations as evidence to support a claim.**

 DCI The Universe and its Stars . . . .

Have children relate the photograph on the left to what they see every day in the daytime sky. **Ask: When do you see the sun in the sky?** I see the sun in the sky during the day. **Ask: Have you ever seen the moon in the sky during the day?** Sample answer: Yes, I have seen the moon during the day a few times. If time permits, go outside and observe the daytime sky with children.

 CCC Patterns . . . .

Encourage children to start thinking about the pattern of how the sun appears in the daytime sky. **Ask: Is the sun in the daytime sky?** Sample answer: Yes, I see the sun in the daytime sky unless it is cloudy. Remind children that even on days when it is cloudy, the sun is still in the daytime sky.

 FORMATIVE ASSESSMENT

Evidence Notebook

Children work with a partner to describe what they know about the sun in the daytime sky. They will include evidence based on their reading and firsthand observations. Children will record facts about the sun in sentence form. Encourage children to help their partners provide evidence for each description of the sun.

Scoring Guidelines

• writes factual sentences about the sun
• provides evidence for each fact

The Daytime Sky

sun from Earth

Explore online. ▶
sun close up

You can see objects in the daytime sky. You may see the sun and sometimes the moon. The sun is a star. A **star** is an object in the sky. It gives off its own light. The **sun** is the star closest to Earth. It is made of hot gases. It gives off light and heat.

 Underline two sentences that tell facts about the sun. Possible answers shown.

 Apply What You Know

Evidence Notebook • Work with a partner. Talk about what you know about the sun in the daytime sky. Use evidence to tell how you know. Then write sentences about it in your Evidence Notebook.

280

© Houghton Mifflin Harcourt

Patterns in the Daytime Sky

Explore online. ▶

early morning

08:00

noon

12:00

late afternoon

04:00

Each day, Earth turns all the way around. This makes the sun seem to move across the sky.

In early morning the sun seems low in the sky. At noon the sun seems to be directly above us. By late afternoon it seems to be low again, but on the other side of the sky. This pattern repeats each day.

© Houghton Mifflin Harcourt

Lesson 1 • How Do Objects in the Sky Seem to Change?

281

Patterns in the Daytime Sky

3D Learning Objective

Children observe the movement of the sun in the daytime sky and use their observations as evidence to support a claim about the pattern of the sun's movement from day to day.

DCI The Universe and its Stars . . . .

Have a child describe the position of the sun and of shadows in each picture. Discuss that just as the sun appears to move across the sky, shadows change as Earth moves. The sun's light shines on objects from different directions throughout the day. The shadows change in size and position. **Ask: What words did you hear that help describe the sun's position in the sky?** Sample answers: low, high, rise, move across, go down List the words and phrases for children to refer to.

Differentiate Instruction

RTI/Extra Support Some children may have difficulty with the idea that Earth moves and the sun stays still. Place a large picture of the sun on the wall. Have children stand facing the opposite wall to represent Earth. Have children slowly turn in a counterclockwise direction toward the picture of the sun. **Ask: What moved?** Earth **What seemed to move?** the sun

Extension Children may be aware that while it is day in the United States, it is night in other parts of the world. Challenge children to talk with a classmate and use what they know about Earth's movement to explain how it can be a different time in two different places.

DCI The Universe and its Stars . . . .

Children should draw a line from the first picture to late afternoon, the second picture to noon, and the last picture to early morning. If children have trouble matching the pictures, refer them back to what they explored about the pattern of the sun in the daytime sky. **Ask: Where does the sun appear to be in the sky in the early morning? Where does it appear to be at noon? Where does it appear to be in the late afternoon?**

SEP Analyzing and Interpreting Data . . . .

Have children use their observations of how the sun appears to move across the sky to describe this pattern. **Ask: How is the sun appearing to move across the sky a pattern?** Sample answer: It repeats each day. The sun appears to rise in the morning, and move across the sky throughout the day.

Collaboration

Think, Pair, Share Have children complete their matches and share what they did with a classmate. Encourage children to talk about and compare their answers. If children have different answers, ask them to share why they chose the answers they did.

✏️ Match each picture to the word or words that describe it.

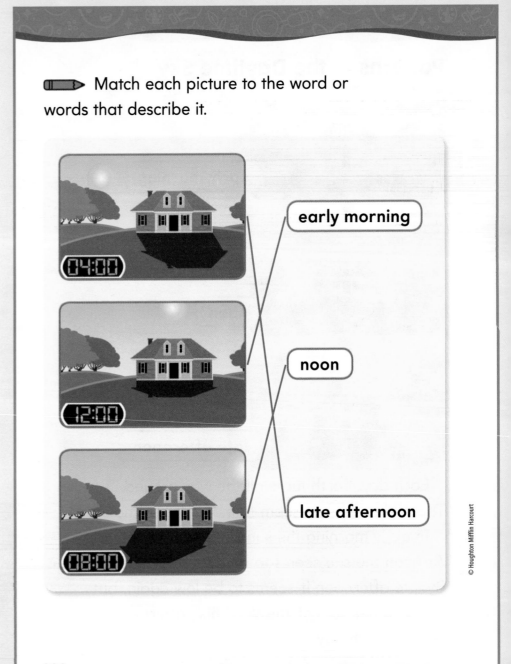

early morning

noon

late afternoon

© Houghton Mifflin Harcourt

282

Hands-On Activity
Observe the Pattern of the Sun

Name_____

| Materials | • drawing paper |

Ask a Question

How does the sun appear to move across the daytime sky?

Test and Record Data   Explore online. ▶

Step 1

Choose a time in the morning. Record the time.

Check children's work.

Step 2

Go outside. Draw a picture to record the position of the sun. Be sure not to look directly at the sun.

Drawings may vary but children should draw a picture that shows the morning sun, an object, and the shadow made by the object.

Step 3

Look for an object that makes a shadow. Draw a picture of the object and its shadow.

Lesson 1 • How Do Objects in the Sky Seem to Change?

283

Hands-On Activity 👥 individuals ⏱ 10 minutes for each observation over 2 days

Observe the Pattern of the Sun

3D Learning Objective

SEP **Analyzing and Interpreting Data** . . . .

Children explore the sun's apparent movement across the daytime sky. They will use their observations to make a claim that answers their question.

Suggested Materials drawing paper, clock

Preparation

Try to arrange times for children to observe the sun's position in the morning, at noon, and in the afternoon on two different days.

Activity

As a class, view the video. Then discuss the question that will need to be answered. Have children record the question.

STEP 1 If necessary, review how to read a clock and record times to the nearest hour.

STEP 2 Be sure to tell children not to look directly at the sun.

DCI **The Universe and its Stars** . . . .

Guide children to focus on important features in their drawings, such as the sun, an object, and the object's shadow. **Ask: What is the purpose of the pictures you will draw?** The pictures need to show the position of the sun and the position of a shadow.

STEP 3 Guide children to show the location and approximate size of the shadow. Suggest children look for an object that is permanent so it will be in the same place when they go outside later in the day.

Hands-On Activity, continued

DCI The Universe and its Stars . . . .

STEP 4 Have children make all three observations in the same location and facing the same direction to ensure they can see patterns in their series of pictures. **Ask: Why is it important to make all of your observations in the same location?** It will help compare differences in the location of the sun and the size and shape of the shadow. Assist children in recording the times of day they go outside and observe.

CCC Patterns . . . .

SEP Analyzing and Interpreting Data . . . .

STEP 5 Guide children to use their observations and data to identify patterns. **Ask: How can observing again on another day help you make a claim about a pattern?** Observing again will help see if there is a pattern in how the sun appears to move across the sky.

Claims, Evidence, and Reasoning

Children should make a claim that the sun appears on the same side of the sky every morning, passes overhead at noon, and appears on the other side of the sky every afternoon. They should cite evidence that they observed the same pattern on two different days.

Scoring Rubric for Hands-On Activity	
3	States a claim supported with evidence about the pattern of how the sun moves in the sky
2	States a claim somewhat supported with evidence about the pattern of how the sun moves in the sky
1	States a claim that is not supported by evidence
0	Does not state a claim and does not provide evidence

Step 4

Repeat steps 2 and 3 at noon and again in the afternoon. Compare the position of the sun and the shadows at the different times of day.

Children should draw a picture that shows the noontime sun overhead, an object, and the shadow made by the object.	Children should draw a picture that shows the late afternoon sun, an object, and the long shadow made by the object.

Step 5

Do the activity again another day. What patterns do you see?

Make a claim that answers your question.

Sample answer: The pattern of the sun is that it appears on one side of the sky in the morning, overhead at noon, and on the other side of the sky in the afternoon. This pattern repeats day after day.

What is your evidence?

Sample answer: My evidence is that I observed the sun at different times of the day on different days and found the same pattern.

284

Read, Write, Share! • Think about what you saw in the activity. Has the sun always seemed to move this way? Look in books or on the Internet to find out more.

Recall Information • Order and Consistency Go to the online handbook for tips.

 Record what you think.

Accept all reasonable answers.

_____

_____

_____

 Apply What You Know

Work with a partner. Make a model of the sun in the daytime sky. Use your model to explain the pattern of how the sun seems to move.

© Houghton Mifflin Harcourt

Read, Write, Share! • Recall Information

Children should recall information from the lesson and the hands-on activity to gather evidence to answer the question, "Has the sun always seemed to move this way?" Have books available that describe the sun's movement in the sky or bookmark websites that present information about the sun's movement in an age-appropriate way.

 Scientific Knowledge Assumes an Order and Consistency in Natural Systems . . . .

Ask: Do you think the sun moved this way a few years ago? What about many, many years ago? Sample answer: The sun seems to move like this every day. I think the sun moved like this a few years ago, and many, many years ago.

 Recall Information Remind children that when they recall information, they think about what they have explored and investigated to use as evidence.

Order and Consistency Encourage children to think about the repetition of how the sun moves in the sky. Remind them that many natural events repeat. They looked at how the sun moves over two days, but the sun moves like this every day of the year.

 FORMATIVE ASSESSMENT

Children will work with a partner to build a simple model of the sun. Children record their observations and use them as evidence to explain the pattern of the sun's apparent movement.

Scoring Guidelines
- makes a simple, accurate model of the sun's position in the sky in the morning, at noon, and in the afternoon
- explains the pattern of the sun's apparent movement, using observations from the model as evidence

The Nighttime Sky

3D Learning Objective

Children observe the nighttime sky and describe the pattern of appearance of objects in the nighttime sky. Children use their observations as evidence to support a claim.

SEP Analyzing and Interpreting Data . . . .

Begin by asking children what questions they have about the moon. Record four or five of their questions on the board. Have children observe the photographs of the moon and read the text together. Help children see that observations—their own and other people's—can help them answer scientific questions about the moon. **Ask: What have you explored that can help you answer some of your questions?** Sample answer: It says that the moon is a large ball of rock. I wondered what the moon was made of, so that helps me answer my question. **How could you find answers to your other questions?** Sample answer: I could look in other books, search on the Internet, or observe the moon at night.

CCC Patterns . . . .

Reinforce the idea that observations of patterns can be used as evidence of natural events. **Ask: How do you think people decided that the moon circles Earth?** Sample answer: Maybe they observed the moon for a long time and saw that it moved slowly across the sky every night.

The Nighttime Sky

Explore online. ▶

moon from Earth

moon close up

Night always follows day. On many nights you can see the moon in the sky. The **moon** is a large ball of rock that circles Earth. The moon seems to shine, but the moon does not give off its own light. The moon reflects light from the sun.

 Write a fact about the moon.

Sample answer: The moon is a large ball of rock that circles Earth.

_____

_____

286

Explore online.

On a clear night, you can see many stars. Stars are balls of hot gases. <u>These gases give off light. This light is what you see from Earth.</u> Stars look tiny because they are far away. A telescope can help you see them better. It makes objects look bigger.

 Underline the sentence that tells why you can see stars.

Apply What You Know

Work with a group. Make a picture dictionary about the nighttime sky. List the objects in the nighttime sky. Draw a picture for each object. Write sentences to tell about it.

Lesson 1 • How Do Objects in the Sky Seem to Change?   287

---

ccc Patterns . . . .

Have children think about when they can see stars in the sky. **Ask: When can you see the sun in the sky?** during the day **When can you see other stars in the sky?** at night **Does this pattern repeat? Explain.** Yes, this pattern repeats every day. I see the sun in the daytime sky and and I see other stars in the nighttime sky.

Ask: Why do you think you can't see stars in the daytime sky? The sun makes the sky so bright that you cannot see the light from the stars.

Differentiate Instruction

ELL Encourage children to read their picture dictionaries they made in the Apply What You Know aloud with a partner. Keep these dictionaries available for children to refer to throughout the lesson.

FORMATIVE ASSESSMENT

Children work in small groups to make a picture dictionary that includes pictures and descriptions of objects in the nighttime sky. Encourage children in each group to work together to make sure that the facts they include are correct, and to check that words are spelled correctly so the dictionaries can be used for reference.

Scoring Guidelines
- includes clear titled drawings of objects in the nighttime sky, including stars and the moon
- includes one or more facts about each object in the nighttime sky

Patterns in the Nighttime Sky

3D Learning Objective

Children **observe the pattern of the moon in the nighttime sky and the pattern of stars in the sky** and **use their observations to describe the patterns.** They use evidence **to describe how natural events repeat.**

DCI The Universe and its Stars . . . .

Explain that the moon moves around Earth. As it moves, it looks different to us. It takes about 29 days for the moon to move around Earth one time. **Ask: What is the effect of the moon moving around Earth?** The moon looks different to us on different days. **Ask:** What do we call the different shapes that we see? phases

SEP Analyzing and Interpreting Data . . . .

Ask: How long does it take for the moon to go through all of its phases? about 29 days **Describe in your own words the pattern of moon phases.** Accept all reasonable answers that describe the pattern from one phase to the next.

💡 **Patterns** Remind children to observe nature and look for a pattern, or things that repeat. They can use the pattern to describe what happens, or as proof of an idea.

Do the Math! • Describe Shares

Children identify that the full moon looks like a whole circle and the first-quarter moon and the third-quarter moon look like half circles. **Ask: What do you know about the two halves of a circle?** They are exactly the same size.

💡 **Describe Shares** Remind children that a whole can be partitioned into two equal shares, and each share is one half. One whole is two of these shares.

Patterns in the Nighttime Sky

new moon

first-quarter moon

full moon

third-quarter moon

Explore online. ▶

The shape of the moon seems to change. These changes are called phases. **Phases** are the moon's pattern of light and shadow that you see as the moon moves. The phases repeat each month.

💡 **Patterns** Go to the online handbook for tips.

Do the Math! • ✏️▷ Draw an X on the phase of the moon that looks like a whole circle. Draw a box around the phases that look like half of a circle.

💡 **Describe Shares** Go to the online handbook for tips.

288

These are stars you can see during the summer.

These are stars you can see during the winter.

The sun is the only star you can see during the day. But the stars you see each night are not always the same. They change with the seasons.

© Houghton Mifflin Harcourt

SEP Analyzing and Interpreting Data . . . .

Ask: What patterns in the sky can you see in these pictures? The sun is visible during the day, but not at night. Stars are visible at night, but not during the day. The sun is in the sky every day in summer and winter. Some stars are visible in winter, and other stars are visible in summer.

CCC Scientific Knowledge Assumes an Order and Consistency in Natural Systems . . . .

Reinforce the idea that science assumes natural events happen today as they happened in the past. **Ask: Suppose you were standing in the place in the picture many, many years ago. Do you think you would see the same stars in the sky?** Sample answer: Yes, I think I would see the same stars in the sky. I think the stars probably looked the same way many years ago.

Connection to Physical Science

Electromagnetic Radiation Explain to children that the moon does not actually give off its own light. The moon appears to give off light because it reflects light from the sun. The light the moon reflects from the sun is sometimes so bright that we can see the moon during the day.

The Universe and its Stars . . . .

Children should choose A— The sun is the only star you can see during the day; and C— Many stars are different at different times of the year. If children choose B, have them review the pictures of the summer and winter nighttime skies on the previous page. **Ask: Are the stars in the same places in both skies?** no

SEP Analyzing and Interpreting Data . . . .

Remind children of the role observations play in answering scientific questions. **Ask: What observations helped you decide whether answer choice A was correct?** When I look at the photographs of the winter daytime sky and the summer daytime sky, I only see the sun. I don't see any other stars.

Collaboration

Whole Class Have children work in pairs to write a sentence about an object in the sky. The sentence can be true or false. Then have each pair read their sentence to the class. Invite other children to make a claim about whether the sentence is true or false, and to present evidence to support their claim. Allow children who wrote the sentence to confirm if the sentence is indeed true or false.

 FORMATIVE ASSESSMENT

Evidence Notebook

Children work in small groups to make a model of the phases of the moon, and use their models to tell about the pattern of the phases of the moon. They will explain, using evidence, how the moon seems to change.

Scoring Guidelines

- makes an accurate model of the phases of the moon
- shows phases in the correct order
- explains how the moon seems to change, using evidence from the lesson

Which sentences are facts about the patterns of the stars? Choose all correct answers.

(A) The sun is the only star you can see during the day.

(B) The stars at night in the winter are the same as the stars at night in the summer.

(C) Many stars are different at different times of the year.

 Apply What You Know

Evidence Notebook • Work with a group. Make a model of the phases of the moon. Use your model to tell about the pattern of phases of the moon. How does the moon seem to change? Use evidence to tell how you know. Record your answers in your Evidence Notebook.

290

LESSON 1   Engage • Explore/Explain • **Elaborate** • Evaluate

Explore online. ▶   Guide children to the Interactive Online Student Edition where they can choose from and explore both paths.

Take It Further

People in Science & Engineering •
Dr. Sarah Ballard

Explore more online. → Space Technology

Explore online. ▶

Dr. Sarah Ballard is an astronomer. An astronomer studies objects in the sky. Dr. Ballard searches for new planets. A planet is a large object in space that moves around a sun or a star. Earth is a planet.

© Houghton Mifflin Harcourt

Lesson 1 • How Do Objects in the Sky Seem to Change?   291

Take It Further

People in Science & Engineering • Dr. Sarah Ballard

Children investigate what an astronomer does. They are introduced to Dr. Sarah Ballard and her work searching for new planets. Dr. Ballard is an exoplanetary astronomer at the Massachusetts Institute of Technology. She has helped discover four new exoplanets! She thinks it's exciting that there could be a planet in space that is very similar to Earth.

DCI **The Universe and its Stars** . . . .

Discuss with children how Dr. Ballard uses observations in her work. **Ask: What kinds of things do you think Dr. Ballard observes?** Sample answers: stars, planets, patterns, movements **Ask: How do you think her observations help her?** She might see something no one else has seen before. She might see a pattern that tells her what an object in the sky is doing.

CCC **Scientific Knowledge Assumes an Order and Consistency in Natural Systems** . . . .

Tell children that some astronomers study the sky to learn about what happened in the past. **Ask: How can observing patterns today help an astronomer learn about the past?** Sample answer: If something happens today that is part of a pattern, it probably happened a long time ago.

Take It Further, continued

SEP Analyzing and Interpreting Data . . . .

Discuss the model that Dr. Ballard is standing next to. **Ask: Why do you think it is helpful to make models of tools?** Sample answer: A model helps you plan the tool. The model can help you see if the tool will work. **How do you think Dr. Ballard will use the satellite when it is built?** Sample answer: I think she will use it to explore planets and other things in the sky.

Children should choose A—They study objects in the sky; and B—They find new planets. If children choose C, review what an astronomer does. **Ask: What do astronomers mainly do?** Explain that while an astronomer could study an animal, this is not what astronomers mainly do.

Explore more online. ▶

Space Technology

Children are introduced to some of the technology that scientists use to learn about space.

Explore online. ▶

This is a model of a satellite that Dr. Ballard will use.

© Houghton Mifflin Harcourt

What do astronomers do? Choose all correct answers.

Ⓐ They study objects in the sky.

Ⓑ They find new planets.

Ⓒ They study animals.

292

Explore online. ▶ Have children review the video of the daytime and nighttime skies from the Engage page.

Lesson Check

Name _____

daytime

Explore online. ▶

nighttime

Can You Explain It?

✏️▸ How do objects in the sky seem to change?

Be sure to

• Tell how objects seem to change in the sky.

• Describe the pattern of changes.

Sample answer: Objects seem to move across the sky. Each day

the sun rises and sets. The moon seems to change shape over

one month. These are patterns.

_____

_____

Lesson 1 • How Do Objects in the Sky Seem to Change?   293

Lesson Check

Can You Explain It?

Have children reread their answers to the Can You Explain It? prompts at the beginning of the lesson.

DCI The Universe and its Stars . . . .

Ask: **What pattern do you see in how the sun appears to change?** The sun appears to rise in one part of the sky, move across the sky, and set each day. **What pattern do you see in how the moon appears to change?** The moon appears to change shape throughout the month.

SEP Analyzing and Interpreting Data . . . .

Remind children of the importance of using observations to provide evidence for their explanations. **Ask: What have you observed that you can use as evidence for your explanation?** Sample answer: I observed the position of the sun and of shadows at different times of day. I observed that the moon goes through all of its phases about every 29 days.

Scoring Guidelines

• Children should describe how some objects change in the sky.
• Children should provide examples of the changes they describe.
• Children should identify why the changes are patterns.

Lesson Check, continued

SUMMATIVE ASSESSMENT
Self Check

1. Children should choose A—Earth turns all the way around. If children choose B or C, refer them to the Patterns in the Daytime Sky section of the lesson. Have them read the text to determine which object turns around.

2. Children should label the first picture "noon," the second picture "late afternoon," and the third picture "night." If children label the pictures differently, refer them to their observations in the Hands-On Activity. **Ask: Where in the sky did you observe the sun at noon?** very high in the sky **Where did you observe it in the late afternoon?** low in the sky

3. Children should choose B—7. If children choose A or C, guide them to see that the sun rises once each day in a week. **Ask: How many days are in a week?** seven **How many times does the sun rise each day?** one time Children could use tallies while they say the days of the week aloud to help them count the sunrises for one week.

Self Check

1. What causes the sun to seem to move in patterns?

   Ⓐ Earth turns all the way around.

   Ⓑ The sun turns all the way around.

   Ⓒ The moon turns all the way around.

2. Write words from the box to label each picture.

   | night | late afternoon | noon |

   noon   late afternoon   night

3. How many times does the sun seem to rise in one week?

   Ⓐ 1

   Ⓑ 7

   Ⓒ 14

294

4. What is the moon?

Ⓐ a large star that circles Earth

Ⓑ a large ball of rock that circles Earth

Ⓒ a large ball of rock that blocks light from the sun

5. What are the phases of the moon? Write the numbers to show the correct order. The first one has been done for you.

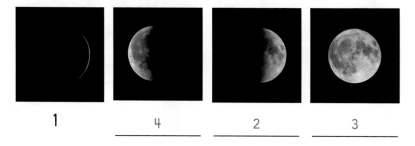

1   4   2   3

6. What are the patterns of objects in the sky? Choose all correct answers.

Ⓐ The sun seems to move in the daytime sky.

Ⓑ All stars appear in the daytime sky.

Ⓒ The moon seems to change shape during the month.

4. Children should choose B—a large ball of rock that circles Earth. If children circle A or C, refer them to the description of the moon in The Nighttime Sky section of the lesson. **Ask: Does the moon give off its own light like a star?** **no** **Why does the moon appear to give off light?** **It reflects the sun's light.**

5. Children should number the pictures 4, 2, 3 from left to right. If children indicate an order different from this, have them look at the models they built of the phases of the moon. Ask them to choose the model that matches the picture labeled 1. **Ask: Which model shows the next phase?** If necessary, refer children to the images of phases of the moon in the Patterns in the Nighttime Sky section of the lesson.

6. Children should choose A—The sun seems to move in the daytime sky; and C—The moon seems to change shape during the month. If children choose B, **Ask: When do we see most stars?** **at night** If children do not choose A, refer them to their observations in the Hands-On Activity. **Ask: Where did the sun appear in the morning? In the afternoon?** **It appeared lower in the sky in the morning, and higher in the sky in the afternoon.** If children do not choose C, have them look at the photographs of the phases of the moon in the Patterns in the Nighttime Sky section of the lesson.

What Are Patterns of Daylight?

Building to the Performance Expectation

The learning experiences in this lesson prepare children for mastery of:

1-ESS1-2 Make observations at different times of year to relate the amount of daylight to the time of year.

Trace Tool to the NGSS
Go online to view the complete coverage of these standards across this lesson, unit, and time.

 **SEP** **Science & Engineering Practices**

DCI **Disciplinary Core Ideas**

 CCC **Crosscutting Concepts**

Planning and Carrying Out Investigations
Make observations (firsthand or from media) to collect data that can be used to make comparisons.

▶ **VIDEO** SEP: Planning and Carrying Out Investigations

ESS1.B: Earth and the Solar System
Seasonal patterns of sunrise and sunset can be observed, described, and predicted.

Patterns
Patterns in the natural world can be observed, used to describe phenomena, and used as evidence.

CONNECTIONS TO MATH

MP.2 Reason abstractly and quantitatively.

1.OA.A.1 Use addition and subtraction within 20 to solve word problems involving situations of adding to, taking from, putting together, taking apart, and comparing, with unknowns in all positions, e.g., by using objects, drawings, and equations to represent the problem.

CONNECTIONS TO ENGLISH LANGUAGE ARTS

W.1.7 Participate in shared research and writing projects (e.g., explore a number of "how-to" books on a given topic and use them to write a sequence of instructions).

W.1.8 With guidance and support from adults, recall information from experiences or gather information from provided sources to answer a question.

Supporting All Students, All Standards

Integrating the Three Dimensions of Learning

This lesson focuses on how the amount of daylight in a day is related to the time of year **(DCI Earth and the Solar System)**. After an introduction to the seasons, children observe, describe, and predict seasonal patterns of sunrise and sunset **(DCI Earth and the Solar System)**. They will observe how seasonal changes affect plants and animals **(CCC Patterns)**. Within the Explore/Explain sections, children will explore these patterns through a variety of interactions and one hands-on activity **(SEP Planning and Carrying Out Investigations)**.

 Professional Development

Go online to view **Professional Development videos** with strategies to integrate CCCs and SEPs, including the ones used in this lesson.

Build on Prior Knowledge

Children should already know and be prepared to build on the following concepts:

- The sun and other objects in the sky seem to change.
- The sun seems to move across the sky throughout the day. It leaves our sight, or sets, each night. It reappears, or rises, in the sky each morning.
- The sun gives Earth light and warmth.
- Living things need sunlight to live.

Differentiate Instruction

Lesson Vocabulary
- season

Reinforcing Vocabulary To help children remember this vocabulary word, help them form a real-life connection. Discuss with children how to determine in which season they were born. Ask children to describe the kind of weather they might expect during their "birth season." Remind children to look for the highlighted word as they proceed through the lesson.

RTI/Extra Support Provide an additional opportunity for hands-on discovery. Label four boxes or suitcases with the name of each season. Provide an assortment of clothing and accessories such as a heavy jacket, light sweater, sleeveless shirt, gloves, sandals, rain boots, sunglasses, knit hat, rain hat, and sun hat. Allow children to choose items to pack for each season. Encourage them to justify their selections. If articles of clothing and accessories are not available, provide photos from magazines or ask children to draw items.

Extension Children who want to find out more can explore uses of the word *season* that connect annual activities to certain times of the year. Provide them with a phrase such as *strawberry season, baseball season, or leaf-peeping season*. Ask them to research what the phrase means and determine how it connects to a season (e.g. strawberries are done growing and ready to be picked in spring, most professional baseball games are played in summer because the weather is warm, leave-peeping happens when leaves change color in the fall). Children can share what they found out with the class by making a poster or concept map.

ELL Be sure to point out all labels, pictures, captions, and headings throughout the lesson to assist children with strategies to summarize chunks of content. Discuss with children real-life connections to content and provide hands-on examples of materials when possible to best support the needs of these learners.

Lesson Problem

Lesson Objective

Make observations at different times of year to relate the amount of daylight to the time of year.

About This Image

Guide children's attention to the scenery in the landscape photograph. **Ask: What do you see in the picture?** mountains, snow, sky, sun **Is it daytime or nighttime?** daytime **When will it be nighttime?** when the sun sets **What season is it?** winter **How do you know?** the snow Lead children in a discussion about how this place would look at other times of the year.

 Earth and the Solar System

Alternative Engage Strategy

Plan a Picnic	small groups 20–30 minutes

Have children work in small groups to plan a picnic dinner. Children may write or draw to make a poster to tell about the picnic. Encourage them to choose a season for the picnic.

Allow 10 minutes for this part of the activity. Discuss children's lists and the seasons depicted in their work.

Then discuss how the sun sets at different times as the seasons change. Have children work in their small groups to discuss how their choice of season might affect their plans for a picnic dinner. Encourage them to think about how their plans may need to change. Ask them to work together to find a solution to any problems. Allow 10 minutes for this part of the activity.

Lesson 2 **What Are Patterns of Daylight?**

Patterns of daylight change throughout the year.

By the End of This Lesson
I will be able to describe patterns of daylight.

296

Patterns of Daylight

spring

summer   Explore online. ▶

winter

fall

The amount of daylight and the seasons change throughout the year. What patterns do they follow?

Can You Solve It?

✏️ You want to plant flowers in seasons with the most daylight. Which seasons would you choose?

Accept all reasonable answers.

Can You Solve It?

Patterns of Daylight We can observe changes throughout the year. Play the video to see how one place changes. If the video is not available, children can use the photographs on the page.

Children record their thoughts about the observed changes. At the end of the lesson, children will revisit this question as part of the Lesson Check. At this point, children should be able to describe patterns of change that occur with each season.

Collaboration

Build on Prior Knowledge You may want children to view and discuss the video as a whole-class activity. In this way, you can assess their prior knowledge of seasonal patterns.

Think about what you saw in the video. What changes did you observe? What part of the video showed the warmest weather? Explain. Which part was lightest? Why? Living things need the sun for light and heat. Describe any living things you saw in the video. How did they change?

Where you live, different times of year may have more or less sunlight. Are some times of year better for some activities than other times of year? How would you predict which time of year might be best for outdoor activities? Use evidence from the video, or from your own experiences, to support your answers.

LESSON 2   Engage · **Explore/Explain** · Elaborate · Evaluate

Explore online. ▶   Have children explore to find out more about each season and seasonal patterns.

The Four Seasons

3D Learning Objective

Children **observe and compare** seasonal changes. They use their observations to **identify a pattern** of seasons in a year.

SEP Planning and Carrying Out Investigations....

Ask: What do you see in these pictures? Sample answers: trees, land, sky, seasons Do you think these photographs were taken on the same day? no Explain. Sample answers: trees looks different, one has snow, flowers are blooming in some

CCC Patterns.............................

Lead a discussion about the pattern of seasons. Explain that the arrows in the center of the pictures show a cycle or a pattern. **Ask: What do you think the arrows show?** the order of seasons and the pattern that they repeat over in the same order each year

Ask: Do any of these photographs remind you of the weather outside today? What season do you think it is now? How do you know? Accept all reasonable answers. Point to the photograph of the current season. **Ask: Which season will come next? What happens once we finish the last season?** The pattern will begin again with the current season because the pattern repeats.

 FORMATIVE ASSESSMENT

Children will make a collage to exhibit a collection of objects related to one of the seasons. Provide a variety of pictures and craft materials. Encourage children to write sentences to describe the collage. Ask children to share evidence from the lesson, or from personal experience, to support their choices.

Scoring Guidelines
- provides examples of objects or sentences related to the season of choice
- uses evidence to show the connection between selected objects and the season of choice

The Four Seasons

spring   summer

winter   fall

A **season** is a time of year with a certain kind of weather. The four seasons are spring, summer, fall, and winter. The pattern of seasons repeats year after year.

✋ **Apply What You Know**

Make a collage that shows a season. Label your collage with the season. Write sentences to tell about it. Share your collage with the class.

298

Spring and Summer

3D Learning Objective

Children **observe to collect data about** spring and summer and **use their observations as evidence to describe** spring and summer. Children **predict the pattern** of changes that take place from winter to spring and spring to summer.

SEP Planning and Carrying Out Investigations . . . .

Ask: **What are the children in the picture doing?** holding an umbrella in the rain **What season do you think this picture shows?** spring **Why?** rain, clothing is for rainy, mild weather

CCC Patterns . . . .

Remind children that seasons happen in a repeating pattern. Point out that although they are exploring spring first, there was a season before spring. **Ask: What season comes before spring?** winter **What changes happen as winter turns to spring?** The air gets warmer; it may rain often; there are more hours of daylight; plants begin to grow.

Ask: What is happening to the tree in the picture? It is growing flowers. **Do trees grow flowers in winter?** No. Many trees are bare during the winter. Flowers might not survive in the cold weather.

Differentiate Instruction

RTI/Extra Support Some children may have difficulty with the concept that it can rain in any season, but it may rain more in spring. Discuss why water in the air falls as rain from clouds in spring, but might fall as snow during the winter.

Extension Have children research the amount of rainfall during each season for your area, and create a picture graph to show the number of inches of rain in each season. Ask them to explain their picture graph to the class.

Spring

Explore online. ▶

Spring comes after winter. The air gets warmer. There are more hours of daylight than in winter. Spring days may be rainy, so people may wear light jackets. Warmer air and more daylight help plants begin to grow.

 Write a sentence that describes spring.

Sample answer: Spring is the season after winter

when the air gets warmer.

Lesson 2 • What Are Patterns of Daylight?

299

Spring and Summer, continued

SEP **Planning and Carrying Out Investigations . . . .**

Ask: What are the children doing in the picture?   riding bikes
What season do you think this picture shows?   summer   Why?
People are playing outside. It is warm enough to wear light
clothing.

CCC **Patterns . . . .**

Remind children that seasons happen in a repeating pattern. **Ask:**
What season comes before summer? spring **Ask: What changes**
happen as spring turns to summer? It is sunny and the air gets
very warm; there is a lot of daylight; you can wear lighter clothes;
plants begin to grow flowers and fruit.

FORMATIVE ASSESSMENT ━━━━

**Read, Write, Share! • Participate in a Research
Project**
Children work in small groups to research spring and summer.
Provide access to resources such as books, magazines, and
digital sources. Children will write and illustrate two facts to
share with their group. Children should look for things that
repeat to identify patterns for each season. Children will use
patterns as evidence to support their facts.

Scoring Guidelines
• accurately describes the facts about each season
• identifies patterns in seasonal changes
• presents patterns as evidence to support claims

💡 **Participate in a Research Project • Patterns**
Remind children that when they research, they are finding
facts about a topic. Provide instruction on how to use the
index and the table of contents to find sources of information.
Remind children to observe nature and look for things that
repeat to identify patterns. They can use patterns to help
describe what happens, and as evidence to prove an idea.

Summer

(Explore online.)

   Summer follows spring. The first day of
summer has the most hours of daylight. <u>Summer
days are often hot and sunny.</u> People dress to
stay cool. Flowers and fruit grow on plants.

✏️ Underline the sentence that describes
summer weather.

Apply What You Know

Read, Write, Share! • Research
spring and summer. Write two
new facts about each season.
Draw a picture for each fact.
Then share your work. Compare
facts. Did you find any patterns?

💡 **Patterns •
Participate
in a Research
Project** Go to
the online
handbook
for tips.

300

Fall and Winter

Fall

Fall comes after summer. There are fewer hours of daylight than in summer. Some animals store food for winter. The leaves of many trees change color and drop off. This is because there is less daylight.

✏️ Write a sentence that describes fall.

Sample answer: Fall comes after summer. There are fewer hours

of daylight in fall than in summer.

_____

Lesson 2 • What Are Patterns of Daylight?   301

3D Learning Objective

Children **observe to collect data about** fall and winter and **use their observations as evidence to describe** fall and winter. Children **predict the pattern** of changes that take place from summer to fall and fall to winter.

SEP Planning and Carrying Out Investigations . . . .

Ask: What season do you think these pictures show? fall **Why?** colorful leaves; leaves on the ground **What is this squirrel holding?** a nut, food **The squirrel may not eat the nut right away. Instead, it might store the nut. What does that mean?** The squirrel may save it for later. **Why would the squirrel do that?** The trees and plants stop growing food. If the squirrel saves it, he will have food for the winter.

CCC Patterns . . . .

Remind children that seasons happen in a pattern. We started reading about spring. Then we learned about summer. **Ask: Why do you think we are going to talk about fall now?** fall is the next season in the pattern **What changes happen as summer turns to fall?** The air gets cooler, leaves fall from trees, there is less daylight, and plants stop growing food.

Collaboration

Small Groups Have each group select an animal and act out how it prepares for winter. You may want to assign an animal to each group. Guide children to think about how different animals would use their senses to determine that the season is changing. In turn, groups can present their animals to the class for further discussion.

Fall and Winter, continued

SEP **Planning and Carrying Out Investigations . . . .**

Ask: What are the people doing in the picture? Sample answer: ice skating What season do you think this picture shows? winter Why? I see ice, snow, and people wearing warm clothing. **Why are they wearing this kind of clothing?** This heavier clothing helps people stay warm in the cold weather.

CCC **Patterns . . . .**

Remind children that seasons happen in a repeating pattern. **Ask: What season comes before winter?** fall **What changes happen as fall turns to winter?** The air gets colder. There are fewer hours of daylight than in any other season. People wear heavier clothes. Some animals grow thick fur. **Ask: How has the animal in the picture prepared for winter?** Sample answer: It grew thicker fur to help keep it warm.

Differentiate Instruction

ELL Review the words *season, spring, summer, fall,* and *winter*. Fold a sheet of paper into fourths. Have children write the word *seasons* in large letters across the top of the page. Children should write the name of a season in each section of the paper. Ask children to draw pictures to show each word.

Winter

Explore online.

Winter follows fall. The first day of winter has the fewest hours of daylight. Winter is the coldest time of year. Some places get snow. People wear coats to keep warm. Some animals grow thick fur.

 Write a sentence that describes winter.

Sample answer: Winter is the coldest time of year and some

places get snow.

_____

302

Do the Math! • This chart shows the seasons that some children like best.

How many more children chose summer than spring?

Ⓐ 5   Ⓑ 3   Ⓒ 4

Solve Word Problems Go to the online handbook for tips.

✋ Apply What You Know

Read, Write, Share • Evidence Notebook • Why do you think the weather changes throughout the year? Use what you know about the seasons as evidence.

Recall Information Go to the online handbook for tips.

Lesson 2 • What Are Patterns of Daylight?

303

Do the Math! • Solve Word Problems

Children should choose C—4. If children choose A, they may have miscounted or subtracted the data for fall instead of spring. If they choose B, they may have subtracted the winter total from the spring total. Point out that the season names *summer* and *spring* tell them what data to use. The word *more* and the phrase *summer than spring* tell that they need to find the difference between the quantities for each season.

 Solve Word Problems Remind children to read word problems carefully to help them choose the correct operation to solve the problem. Allow children to use counters to show each part of the problem.

✋ FORMATIVE ASSESSMENT

Read, Write, Share! • Evidence Notebook
Children work in groups to describe the pattern of the seasons in a year. Then children use what they know about the seasons as evidence to explain why the weather changes throughout the year.

Scoring Guidelines
- describes a relationship between daily amounts of sunlight and seasonal patterns
- provides sufficient evidence to support their explanation

 Recall Information Remind children to listen carefully to the question. They should ask themselves *What information is this question asking about?* and *Do I remember the information?* Children should review the reading to find answers. They can also look in books and on the Internet.

Patterns of Daylight

3D Learning Objective

Children **observe the time of sunset** throughout the year. They will **describe a pattern** of daylight, and **use it to compare** it with **seasonal patterns**.

 DCI **Earth and the Solar System** . . . .

Ask: In which season does the sun set earliest?   In winter the sun sets before 5 o'clock.   **In which season does the sun set latest?**   In summer the sun sets after 8 o'clock.   **Which season has the most hours of daylight?**   summer   **Why do some days have more daylight than others?**   the amount of daylight changes from season to season

---

Connection to Life Science

Information Processing Discuss with children that plants need sunlight to live and grow. **Ask: Why do plants grow toward sunlight?** Plants depend on sunlight to make food. The leaves lean towards the light for photosynthesis. Without sunlight green plants cannot survive.

 FORMATIVE ASSESSMENT

Evidence Notebook
Children work with a partner as they identify patterns of daylight hours for each season. Children should describe how the patterns of daylight relate to the time of year.

Scoring Guidelines
• accurately compares the amount of daylight in a season relative to other seasons
• provides sufficient evidence to support the seasonal pattern of daylight

---

Patterns of Daylight

Explore online. ▶

winter–4:43 at night

spring–7:13 at night

summer–8:29 at night

fall–6:57 at night

The amount of daylight changes from season to season. The sun rises and sets at different times during the year. This pattern repeats each year. Take a look at what time the sun sets in one place at the start of each season.

 Apply What You Know

Evidence Notebook • Work with a partner. Use evidence to explain the patterns of daylight during the year. Write your explanations in your Evidence Notebook.

304

© Houghton Mifflin Harcourt

Hands-On Activity 👥 small groups 🕐 1 class period
Observe Patterns of Sunset

3D Learning Objective

SEP Planning and Carrying Out Investigations . . . .

Children compare what time the sun sets in three different seasons. Children make a claim about how the time of sunset changes from season to season.

Materials calendar, computer, crayons, drawing paper

Preparation

Gather materials for groups. Arrange access to a variety of resources that includes daily sunset data. Alternatively, children may use the Internet to complete this activity.

Activity

As a class, view the video. Then discuss the question that will need to be answered. Have children record the question.

STEP 1 Guide children as they gather and record information. Remind them how to use a calendar to find the date, and lead a discussion to identify the current season. Observe and support children as they look up and record the time the sun will set.

CCC Patterns . . . .

STEP 2 Guide children to recall the pattern of seasons through the year and to use the pattern to identify the next two seasons. **Ask: What is the pattern of seasons throughout the year?** spring, summer, fall, winter **Which season always comes after this one? Which season comes after that?** Have them select a day for each season. Provide support as needed as the children research what time the sun will set on each of these days.

Name_____

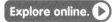
Hands-On Activity
Observe Patterns of Sunset

Materials	• a calendar	• a computer
	• crayons	• drawing paper

Ask a Question

How does sunset change from season to season?

Test and Record Data **Explore online.**

Step 1

Identify the season and the date. Together, look up what time the sun will set that day.

Step 2

Look up what time the sun will set on a day in the next two seasons.

Hands-On Activity, continued

SEP Planning and Carrying Out Investigations . . . .

STEP 3 Ask: How can you use the information about the times you saw in the section Patterns of Daylight to help you identify a pattern in your data? I can compare my data to times from the Patterns in Daylight section.

Reason Abstractly and Quantitatively Children should look for patterns in their data, and apply what they found to the context of the question.

Claims, Evidence, and Reasoning

Children should make a claim that identifies the pattern of sunset as it relates to the selection of seasons. They should cite evidence to support the claim, including citing patterns observed earlier in this lesson. **Ask:** Did you identify a pattern? How does it compare to other patterns? Sample answer: I looked up the times of sunset in different seasons. I compared my results with the results I studied earlier in this lesson. The patterns are the same.

Scoring Rubric for Hands-On Activity	
3	States a claim supported with evidence about how the time the sun sets changes from season to season
2	States a claim somewhat supported with evidence about how the time the sun sets changes from season to season
1	States a claim that is not supported by evidence
0	Does not state a claim and does not provide evidence

Step 3

Compare all the times you found. Record any patterns.

Make a claim that answers your question.

Sample answer: In winter, the sun sets earliest. In summer, the sun sets latest. In spring and fall, it sets at a time between winter and summer. This pattern repeats year after year.

_____

_____

What is your evidence?

Sample answer: I looked up the times of sunset in different seasons. I found a pattern in the data.

_____

_____

_____

306

Explore online. ▶   Guide children to the Interactive Online Student Edition where they can choose from and explore both paths.

Take It Further

Careers in Science & Engineering • Circadian Biologist

Children investigate what a circadian biologist studies to develop a deeper understanding of how seasons affect people and animals.

ccc Patterns . . . .

A biologist studies living things and their relationship to the environment. **Ask: Why does a circadian biologist observe and identify human or animal patterns?** The circadian biologist compares these patterns with patterns of seasons and daylight. **How will comparing these patterns help a biologist learn?** If the patterns are related, it may provide evidence to explain how living things are affected by their environment.

DCI Earth and the Solar System . . . .

Some people like to use an alarm clock that slowly turns on a light similar to sunlight. **Ask: How would a circadian biologist explain the reason why that type of alarm clock wakes people from sleep?** Patterns of light and darkness send signals to your brain to make you feel sleepy. When the clock lights up the environment before the sun rises, it tricks your brain into following a new pattern. **Ask: In which season would this type of light be most useful? Explain.** It would be helpful in winter. The sun rises later and sets earlier. People may have trouble waking up in the dark.

Take It Further

Careers in Science & Engineering • Circadian Biologist

Explore more online. ▶

The Midnight Sun

Explore online. ▶

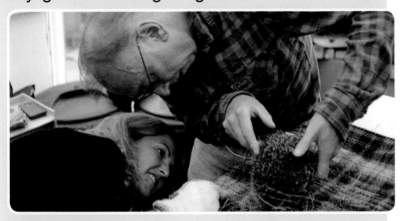

Circadian biologists study how seasons and daylight affect living things.

You may feel sleepier in fall and winter. Circadian biologists found out why. There is less daylight in fall and winter. This makes you feel sleepier.

Less daylight affects animals, too. They sense that it is time to get ready for winter.

© Houghton Mifflin Harcourt • Image Credits: (t) ©Simon Dack/Alamy; (b) ©Ed Reschke/Getty Images

Take It Further, continued

Children make observations about people and animals in their home or community. They should use evidence from their observations to support their claim as to how they are affected and how they change.

CCC Patterns . . . .

Discuss the types of animals children might observe in their homes or community. **Ask: What kinds of animals live near you?** Answers may include common or exotic house pets or animals that live outside. **Do the seasons affect these animals? How? Do you notice changes in the way they look? Do they act in a different way?** Accept all reasonable answers.

Differentiate Instruction

RTI/Extra Support Some children might have limited experience with animals. Ask them to interview a classmate who has a pet.

Extension Challenge children to find out more about how seasonal changes affect plants. Children may decide to research a certain type of plant, such as garden plants, houseplants, or trees.

Explore more online. ▶

The Midnight Sun

Children investigate how animals and plants are affected in places with periods of nearly 24 hours of daylight.

Think about the people and animals in your home or community. How do the seasons affect them? How do they change?

 Draw a picture to show what happens. Then write about it.

Accept all reasonable answers.

308

© Houghton Mifflin Harcourt

Lesson Check

Name _____

spring

summer

Explore online. ▶

winter

fall

Can You Solve It?

✏️ You want to plant flowers in seasons with the most daylight. Which seasons would you choose?

Be sure to

• Tell how knowing patterns of daylight helped you solve the problem.

Sample answers: I would plant flowers in spring and in summer.

Spring and summer have the most hours of daylight.

Fall and winter have fewer hours of daylight.

Lesson Check

Can You Solve It?

Have children reread their answers to the Can You Solve It? prompts at the beginning of the lesson.

SEP Planning and Carrying Out Investigations . . . .

Lead a discussion about how knowing the pattern of daylight through the year can help solve the problem. **Ask: What is the longest day of the year?** the first day of summer **What is the shortest day of the year?** the first day of winter

DCI Earth and the Solar System . . . .

Guide children to think about the patterns they observed in the video. **Ask: Now that you know about the seasons and patterns of daylight, think about how much daylight is in each season. Which seasons have the most daylight?** spring and summer

CCC Patterns . . . .

Ask: How do you think the amount of daylight affects plants and animals? Why do plants grow better in the spring and summer? The amount of sunlight directly relates to the rate of plant growth. The more sunshine there is, the more growth there is.

Scoring Guidelines

• Children should describe the pattern of sunlight.
• Children should compare the amount of sunlight during the different seasons.
• Children should effectively explain how the change of sunlight relates to the seasons.

Lesson Check, continued

SUMMATIVE ASSESSMENT
Self Check

1. Children should number the pictures 4, 3, 2, from left to right. If children complete the blanks incorrectly, ask them guiding questions. Point to the first photograph. **Ask: Which season is already labeled with the number 1?** spring **How do you know this photo shows spring?** Flowers are blooming. **Which season comes after spring?** summer **Which photograph shows summer?** the last photo on right **How do you know?** The children have warm weather clothes and cool treats. **Which season comes after summer?** fall **Which photo looks like fall?** the third photo **How do you know?** the colorful leaves Point to the remaining photograph. **Ask: How do you know what season is in this photograph?** It is winter because there is snow. **Winter comes after which season?** fall

2. Children should choose B—The sun sets earlier in winter. If children choose A or C, direct them to the Patterns of Daylight section of the lesson. Remind them that the photographs show the same time of day in different seasons. Have them compare the pictures of winter to the pictures of summer.

Self Check

1. Write the numbers 2, 3, and 4 to show the order of the seasons. The first one has been done for you.

spring	winter	fall	summer
1	4	3	2

2. This family is eating dinner at the same time in winter and summer. Which is true about when the sun sets?

winter   summer

Ⓐ The sun sets earlier in summer.

Ⓑ The sun sets earlier in winter.

Ⓒ The sun sets at the same time in winter and summer.

310

3. Spring and fall have about the same number of hours of _____.

Ⓐ rain

Ⓑ sunset

Ⓒ **daylight**

4. If the sun sets at 7 o'clock on the first day of spring, when will it set on the first day of summer?

Ⓐ earlier than 7 o'clock

Ⓑ **later than 7 o'clock**

Ⓒ at the same time

5. Which is a pattern of daylight?

Ⓐ **The amount of daylight changes from day to day with the seasons.**

Ⓑ The amount of daylight changes from year to year.

Ⓒ The amount of daylight never changes.

3. Children should choose C—daylight. If children choose A or B, direct them to the results of the Patterns of Daylight section of the lesson. Guide children to observe the times the sun sets in spring and fall. Both times are close to 7 o'clock.

4. Children should choose B—later than 7 o'clock. If children choose A or C, direct them to the Spring and Summer sections of the lesson. Guide children to look for clues in the reading.

5. Children should choose A—The amount of daylight changes from day to day with the seasons. If children choose B or C, direct them to the Spring and Summer sections of the lesson. Guide children to look for clues in the reading.

Unit 6 Performance Task

Explore Short and Long Days

 small groups ⏱ 1 class period and then 10 minutes a day for 2 weeks

Objective

Children **observe the growth patterns** of plants exposed to different amounts of sunlight, and **collect and analyze data** that explains how seasonal patterns of daylight affect plant growth.

Suggested Materials

two seedlings of the same kind, water, paper clips

Preparation

Have enough seedlings for each group to choose two. Identify sunny and dark places where children can place the seedlings.

SEP **Planning and Carrying Out Investigations** . . . .

Ask: Why should you record your observations at the beginning of the investigations? So I can compare how much the two seedlings have changed over time.

STEPS

Step 1

CCC **Patterns** . . . .

Ask: Why should you record your measurements at the beginning of the investigation? I can use the measurements later to identify patterns in how each seedling grew.

Step 2

DCI **Earth and the Solar System** . . . .

Ask: Which seedling do you think should get less sun, the one labeled *winter* or *spring*? Why? Winter, because plants get less sunlight during the winter.

 Unit 6 Performance Task
Explore Short and Long Days

Materials
- two seedlings of the same kind
- water
- paper clips

STEPS

Step **1**

Label one seedling **winter** and the other seedling **spring**. Measure the height of each seedling with paper clips. Record your observations.

Step **2**

Place the seedlings in a sunny window. After one hour, put the **winter** seedling in a dark place. Leave the **spring** seedling in the sunny window.

Step **3**

Put the **winter** seedling in the window for only one hour each day.

312

© Houghton Mifflin Harcourt

Step 4

Observe the seedlings for two weeks. Water the soil when it is dry. Measure and record the results every day.

Step 5

Use evidence to tell why a plant in spring might grow more than a plant in winter. Compare your results with the results of other classmates.

✅ Check

_____ I gave the **spring** seedling long days of sunlight.

_____ I gave the **winter** seedling short days of sunlight.

_____ I observed the seedlings for two weeks and recorded my observations every day.

_____ I explained why a plant in spring might grow more than a plant in winter.

_____ I compared my results to the results of my classmates.

© Houghton Mifflin Harcourt

Step 3

As a class, discuss the best time of day to place the winter seedling in the sunlight.

Step 4

 Patterns . . . .

Ask: Why should you measure and record your results every day?
So I can look for a pattern in how the two seedlings grow.

Step 5

 Analyzing and Interpreting Data . . . .

Children should use their observations as evidence to describe how much each seedling grew, and to explain how this simulates the way seasonal patterns of daylight might affect plants. Encourage children to look for patterns as they compare their results with those of their classmates.

Scoring Rubric for Performance Task	
3	Performs the investigation as directed, obtains and records data, uses evidence to describe how seasonal patterns of daylight affect plants, and compares results with others.
2	Performs the investigation as directed, obtains and records data, uses evidence to describe how seasonal patterns of daylight affect plants, but does not compare results with others.
1	Attempts to perform the investigation as directed, but does not obtain and record data, does not use evidence to describe how seasonal patterns of daylight affect plants or compare results with others.
0	Does not perform the investigation, does not obtain and record data, does not use evidence to describe how seasonal patterns of daylight affect plants, and does not compare results with others.

Unit 6 Review

1. Children should choose B—sun; and C—star. If children choose A, reinforce that the sun is a star. Stars, including the sun, give off light and heat. By completing The Daytime Sky in Lesson 1, children observed pictures of the sun, and explored how it is a star that is close to Earth.

2. Children should choose A—in the morning. If children choose B or C, reinforce that the sun first appears in the sky, or rises, at the beginning of each day. By completing Patterns in the Daytime Sky in Lesson 1, children observed how the sun appears to move in the daytime sky.

3. Children should choose B—high in the noon sky. If children choose A or C, review how shadows appear at different times of the day. By completing the Hands-On activity in Lesson 1, children explored the position of the sun and shadows at different times of the day.

4. Children should choose A—The sun seems to move across the sky. If children choose B or C, encourage them to think about how often the pattern of the moon's phases and the seasons change. By completing Lessons 1 and 2, children observed the movement of the sun in the sky, explored the pattern of the phases of the moon, and explored the pattern of the seasons.

Unit 6 Review   Name _____

1. Which objects give off their own light? Choose all correct answers.
   Ⓐ moon
   🅑 sun
   🅒 star

---

2. When does the sun seem to rise?
   🅐 in the morning
   Ⓑ at noon
   Ⓒ at night

---

3. Look at the shadow in the picture. Where does the sun seem to be?
   Ⓐ low in the morning sky
   🅑 high in the noon sky
   Ⓒ low in the afternoon sky

---

4. Which pattern repeats every day?
   🅐 The sun seems to move across the sky.
   Ⓑ The shape of the moon seems to change.
   Ⓒ The seasons change.

314

5. What phase of the moon does the picture show?
   Ⓐ new moon
   Ⓑ half moon
   Ⓒ **full moon**

6. Look at the pictures. Write a word from the word box to label the season each picture shows.

   | fall | spring | summer | winter |

   winter   spring   summer   fall

7. Which season follows summer?
   Ⓐ spring
   Ⓑ **fall**
   Ⓒ winter

© Houghton Mifflin Harcourt • Image Credits: (bcl) ©Ulrich Krellner/iStock/Getty Images; (tr) ©Peter Gridley/Getty Images; (bl) ©SaintCanada/iStock/Getty Images; (bcl) ©gallimaufry/Shutterstock; (br) ©Marcin Pawinski/Hemera/Getty Images

5. Children should choose C—full moon. If children choose A or B, review the phases of the moon. By completing Patterns in the Nighttime Sky in Lesson 1, children explored the patterns of the moon's phases.

6. Children should label the pictures from left to right as: winter, spring, summer, fall. If children do not label the pictures in that order, reinforce that the pattern of the seasons is the same each year. Observations about the tree's branches can help identify the season in each picture. By completing The Four Seasons in Lesson 2, children explored pictures of seasonal changes to identify the pattern of seasons in a year.

7. Children should choose B—fall. If children choose A or C, review the order of the seasons. By completing Fall in Lesson 2, children explored patterns associated with fall.

8. Children should choose A—There are fewer hours of daylight than summer; and B—Some animals move to warmer places. If children choose C, reinforce that the days get shorter and the air gets cooler in fall. Encourage children to think about how people dress when the air gets cooler. By completing Fall in Lesson 2, children explored characteristics of fall.

9. Children should choose C—the first day of summer. If children choose A or B, reinforce that there are more hours of sunlight in summer, and the first day of summer is the longest day of the year. By completing Summer in Lesson 2, children explored patterns associated with summer.

10. Children should choose A—Winter has fewer hours of daylight than summer. If children choose B or C, reinforce that winter has the fewest hours of daylight than any other season. By completing Winter in Lesson 2, children explored patterns associated with winter.

3D Item Analysis	1	2	3	4	5	6	7	8	9	10
SEP Analyzing and Interpreting Data			•		•	•				
SEP Planning and Carrying Out Investigations						•				
DCI The Universe and its Stars	•	•	•	•	•					
DCI Earth and the Solar System						•		•	•	•
CCC Patterns		•	•	•	•	•	•	•	•	•

8. Which statements are true about fall? Choose all correct answers.
   Ⓐ There are fewer hours of daylight than summer.
   Ⓑ Some animals move to warmer places.
   Ⓒ People dress to stay cool.

9. Which day of the year has the most hours of daylight?
   Ⓐ the first day of winter
   Ⓑ the first day of spring
   Ⓒ the first day of summer

10. How is winter different from summer?
   Ⓐ Winter has fewer hours of daylight than summer.
   Ⓑ Winter has more hours of daylight than summer.
   Ⓒ Winter has the same number of hours of daylight as summer.

316

Resources

Integrating Reading and Science Instruction

This listing compiles readers and trade books that align with the topical organization of the Performance Expectations and Disciplinary Core Ideas for Grade 1 of the NGSS, and the units contained within the *HMH Science Dimensions™* program. Titles are arranged according to their approximate Guided Reading Levels.

As with all materials you share with your class, we suggest you review the books first to ensure their appropriateness. While titles are available at time of publication, they may go out of print without notice.

Waves: Light and Sound—Units 1–3

Level E
Day and Night by Storad, Conrad (Rourke Publishing)

Level H
Light Makes a Rainbow by Sharon Coan (Shell Educational Publishing/TCM)
What Are Sound Waves? by Johnson, Robin (Crabtree Publishing Company)

Level I
Music Around the World by Char Benjamin (Shell Educational Publishing/TCM)
Sources of Light by Nunn, Daniel (Capstone Press)

Level K
Shadow Puppets by Rigby Staff (Rigby/Steck-Vaughn)

Level L
Sounds by Rigby Staff (Rigby/Steck-Vaughn)

Read Aloud
The Shape of Me and Other Stuff by Dr. Seuss (Penguin Random House)

Structure, Function, and Information Processing—Units 4–5

Level C
Who Do I Look Like? by Lundgren, Julie K. (Rourke Publishing)

Level D
Animal Mothers by Kalman, Bobbie (Crabtree Publishing Company)
Mammal Moms and Their Young by Freeman, Marcia S. (Rourke Publishing)

Level E
A New Skin by Rigby Staff (Rigby/Steck-Vaughn)
Animal Helpers by Rigby Staff (Rigby/Steck-Vaughn)
Animal Mothers and Babies by Rice, Dona (Shell Educational Publishing/TCM)
Colorful Animals by Rigby Staff (Rigby/Steck-Vaughn)
Funny Insects by Rigby Staff (Rigby/Steck-Vaughn)
How Do Baby Animals Grow? by Hutchinson, Caroline (Newmark Learning)
How Plants Grow by Herweck, Dona (Shell Educational Publishing/TCM)
Inside Nests by Rigby Staff (Rigby/Steck-Vaughn)
Leaves by Mitchell, Melanie S. (Lerner Publishing Group)
Out of the Egg by Rigby Staff (Rigby/Steck-Vaughn)
Plant Parts: Roots, Stems, and by Griffin, Maeve (Rosen Publishing)
What Is A Mammal? by Carson, Janet (Rosen Publishing)
What Is Hatching? by Kalman, Bobbie (Crabtree Publishing Company)
Where do Plants Live? by Hutchinson, Caroline (Newmark Learning)

Level F

A Safe Place to Sleep by Rigby Staff (Rigby/Steck-Vaughn)

Animal Shapes by Rigby Staff (Rigby/Steck-Vaughn)

Ears by Rigby Staff (Rigby/Steck-Vaughn)

Going Buggy! by Rice, Dona (Shell Educational Publishing/TCM)

Growth and Change by Rice, Dona (Shell Educational Publishing/TCM)

Hearing by Rigby Staff (Rigby/Steck-Vaughn)

How do Plants Help us? by Kalman, Bobbie (Crabtree Publishing Company)

Legs, No Legs by Rigby Staff (Rigby/Steck-Vaughn)

Shell Homes by Rigby Staff (Rigby/Steck-Vaughn)

Shells by Rigby Staff (Rigby/Steck-Vaughn)

Smelling! by Rigby Staff (Rigby/Steck-Vaughn)

Smells All Around Us by Rigby Staff (Rigby/Steck-Vaughn)

Level G

Animals Homes by Rigby Staff (Rigby/Steck-Vaughn)

Changing Shape by Pyers, Greg (Rigby/Steck-Vaughn)

Fangs by Rigby Staff (Rigby/Steck-Vaughn)

Frogs and Toads and Tadpoles, Too! by Fowler, Allan (Grolier/Scholastic Library Publishing)

Hairy Caterpillars by Rigby Staff (Rigby/Steck-Vaughn)

It's A Fruit, It's A Vegetable, It's A Pumpkin by Fowler, Allan (Grolier/Scholastic Library Publishing)

Jellyfish by Rigby Staff (Rigby/Steck-Vaughn)

Jumping Spiders by Rigby Staff (Rigby/Steck-Vaughn)

Knowing About Noses by Fowler, Allan (Grolier/Scholastic Library Publishing)

Plant Adaptations by Lundgren, Julie (Rourke Publishing)

Poisonous Animals by Gibson, Brylee (Rigby/Steck-Vaughn)

Rock Pools by Rigby Staff (Rigby/Steck-Vaughn)

Spiders Are Not Insects by Fowler, Allan (Grolier/Scholastic Library Publishing)

The Five Senses: Hearing by Rissman, Rebecca Leigh (Capstone Press)

The Five Senses: Smelling by Rissman, Rebecca Leigh (Capstone Press)

The Five Senses: Tasting by Rissman, Rebecca Leigh (Capstone Press)

The Five Senses: Touching by Rissman, Rebecca Leigh (Capstone Press)

What Are Bulbs and Roots? by Aloian, Molly (Crabtree Publishing Company)

What Are Stems? by Aloian, Molly (Crabtree Publishing Company)

Level H

Amazing Animal Senses! by Hutchinson, Caroline (Newmark Learning)

Animals in Spring by Rustad, Martha E. H. (Capstone Press)

Biggest, Smallest, Fastest, Slowest by Rigby Staff (Rigby/Steck-Vaughn)

Cacti by Rigby Staff (Rigby/Steck-Vaughn)

Changing and Growing by Rigby Staff (Rigby/Steck-Vaughn)

Claws by Rigby Staff (Rigby/Steck-Vaughn)

Do Animals Migrate? by Brynie, Faith Hickman (Rosen Publishing)

Do Animals Work Together? by Brynie, Faith Hickman (Rosen Publishing)

Frog Or Toad?: How Do You Know? by Stewart, Melissa (Enslow Publishers, Inc.)

Funny Fish by Rigby Staff (Rigby/Steck-Vaughn)

Hidden Insects by Rigby Staff (Rigby/Steck-Vaughn)

How are Plants Helpful? by MacAulay, Kelley (Crabtree Publishing Company)

How do Animal Babies Live? by Brynie, Faith Hickman (Rosen Publishing)

How do Plants Survive? by MacAulay, Kelley (Crabtree Publishing Company)

In Hiding: Animals Under Cover by Rigby Staff (Rigby/Steck-Vaughn)

Life In The Trees by Rigby Staff (Rigby/Steck-Vaughn)

Look at the Leaves by Rigby Staff (Rigby/Steck-Vaughn)

Smelly Skunks by Rigby Staff (Rigby/Steck-Vaughn)

Spots by Rigby Staff (Rigby/Steck-Vaughn)

Stinkers! by Rigby Staff (Rigby/Steck-Vaughn)

Using Leaves by Rigby Staff (Rigby/Steck-Vaughn)

Which Animals Are The Best Athletes? by Brynie, Faith Hickman (Rosen Publishing)

Level I

A Baby Lobster Grows Up by Marsico, Katie (Grolier/Scholastic Library Publishing)

A Look At Teeth by Fowler, Allan (Grolier/Scholastic Library Publishing)

All in the Family by Rice, Dona (Shell Educational Publishing/TCM)

Amazing Birds Of The Rain Forest by Daniel, Claire (Rigby/Steck-Vaughn)

Animal Families by Kalman, Bobbie (Crabtree Publishing Company)

Animal Helpers by Rigby Staff (Rigby/Steck-Vaughn)

Bug Senses by Guillian, Charlotte (Capstone Press)

Chameleons by Rigby Staff (Rigby/Steck-Vaughn)

Cool Crabs by Rigby Staff (Rigby/Steck-Vaughn)

Hidden Spiders by Rigby Staff (Rigby/Steck-Vaughn)

Horns by Rissman, Rebecca (Capstone Press)

Insect-Eaters by Rigby Staff (Rigby/Steck-Vaughn)

Insects that Use Color by Rigby Staff (Rigby/Steck-Vaughn)

It Could Still Be A Flower by Fowler, Allan (Grolier/Scholastic Library Publishing)

Living In A Desert by Fowler, Allan (Grolier/Scholastic Library Publishing)

Megamouths and Hammerheads by Rigby Staff (Rigby/Steck-Vaughn)

Raising Babies: What Animal Parents Do by Dona Herweck Rice (Shell Educational Publishing/TCM)

Senses by Lisa Greathouse (Shell Educational Publishing/TCM)

Spines by Rissman, Rebecca (Capstone Press)

Level J

Animals Grow And Change by Kalman, Bobbie (Crabtree Publishing Company)

Baby Birds by Kalman, Bobbie (Crabtree Publishing Company)

Baby Giraffes by Kalman, Bobbie (Crabtree Publishing Company)

Facts About Honeybees by Rigby Staff (Rigby/Steck-Vaughn)

From Tadpole to Frog by Zoehfeld, Kathleen Weidner (Scholastic, Inc.)

Leafcutter Ants by Rigby Staff (Rigby/Steck-Vaughn)

Snakes That Rattle by Rigby Staff (Rigby/Steck-Vaughn)

The Fastest Animals by Ipcizade, Catherine (Capstone Press)

What Is a Vertebrate? by Kalman, Bobbie (Crabtree Publishing Company)

Level K

Animal Headgear by Rigby Staff (Rigby/Steck-Vaughn)

Animal Tails by Rigby Staff (Rigby/Steck-Vaughn)

Camouflage by Rigby Staff (Rigby/Steck-Vaughn)

Living in the Rain Forest by Rigby Staff (Rigby/Steck-Vaughn)

Message Received! by Sharon Coan (Shell Educational Publishing/TCM)

Sea Habitats by Rigby Staff (Rigby/Steck-Vaughn)

The Stinkiest Animals by Miller, Connie (Capstone Press)

Underground Homes by Rigby Staff (Rigby/Steck-Vaughn)

What's On The Food Chain Menu? by Lundgren, Julie (Rourke Publishing)

Why Animals Live In Webs by Weber, Valerie J. (GarethStevens)

Level L

Animals Armed For Survival by Rigby Staff (Rigby/Steck-Vaughn)

Using a Beak by Rigby Staff (Rigby/Steck-Vaughn)

Using a Tail by Rigby Staff (Rigby/Steck-Vaughn)

Space Systems: Patterns and Cycles—Unit 6

Level F

How Do You Know It's Fall? by Fowler, Allan (Grolier/Scholastic Library Publishing)

How Do You Know It's Summer? by Fowler, Allan (Grolier/Scholastic Library Publishing)

Looking Up! by Torrey Maloof (Shell Educational Publishing/TCM)

Season To Season by Rigby Staff (Rigby/Steck-Vaughn)

Sun by Rice, William (Shell Educational Publishing/TCM)

Level G

I See Spring by Ghigna, Charles (Capstone Press)

I See Summer by Ghigna, Charles (Capstone Press)

I See Winter by Ghigna, Charles (Capstone Press)

Look at the Stars by Rigby Staff (Rigby/Steck-Vaughn)

My Book of the Seasons by Rigby Staff (Rigby/Steck-Vaughn)

Our Sun by Rice, William (Shell Educational Publishing/TCM)

Space, Stars and Planets by Rigby Staff (Rigby/Steck-Vaughn)

Stars in the Sky by Rigby Staff (Rigby/Steck-Vaughn)

The Man In the Moon by Rigby Staff (Rigby/Steck-Vaughn)

Level H

Looking at the Moon by Rigby Staff (Rigby/Steck-Vaughn)

Stars by Simon, Seymour (Harper Collins)

Sun up, Sun down by Gibbons, Gail (Houghton Mifflin Harcourt Publishing)

Level I

Asteroids and Comets by Rice, William (Shell Educational Publishing/TCM)

Energy From The Sun by Fowler, Allan (Grolier/Scholastic Library Publishing)

Measure the Weather by Michele, Tracey (River Stream)

Planet Earth by Rigby Staff (Rigby/Steck-Vaughn)

The Moon: Revised Edition by E. H., Rustad & Martha (Capstone Press)

The Stars: Revised Edition by E. H., Rustad & Martha (Capstone Press)

The Sun: Revised Edition by E. H., Rustad & Martha (Capstone Press)

Level J

Things With Wings by Rigby Staff (Rigby/Steck-Vaughn)

Level K

Earth and Moon by Maloof, Torrey (Shell Educational Publishing/TCM)

Seasons And Weather by Rigby Staff (Rigby/Steck-Vaughn)

Sky Changes by Rigby Staff (Rigby/Steck-Vaughn)

The International Space Station by Rigby Staff (Rigby/Steck-Vaughn)

Common Core State Standards
for English Language Arts

A correlation to the Next Generation Science Standards is located in the front of this Teacher Edition. Correlations for the Common Core State Standards for English Language Arts are provided on these pages.

Grade 1	Units/Lessons
Reading Standards for Informational Text	
Key Ideas and Details	
RI.1.1 Ask and answer questions about key details in a text.	Unit 5 Lesson 2
	Unit 5 Lesson 3
Writing Standards	
Text Types and Purposes	
W.1.2 Write informative/explanatory texts in which they name a topic, supply some facts about the topic, and provide some sense of closure.	Unit 1 Lesson 2
Research to Build and Present Knowledge	
W.1.7 Participate in shared research and writing projects (e.g., explore a number of "how-to" books on a given topic and use them to write a sequence of instructions).	Unit 2 Lesson 2
	Unit 3 Lesson 3
	Unit 4 Lesson 1
	Unit 4 Lesson 2
	Unit 4 Lesson 3
	Unit 4 Lesson 4
	Unit 5 Lesson 1
	Unit 5 Lesson 2
	Unit 6 Lesson 2
W.1.8 With guidance and support from adults, recall information from experiences or gather information from provided sources to answer a question.	Unit 1 Lesson 1
	Unit 5 Lesson 3
	Unit 6 Lesson 1
	Unit 6 Lesson 2

Grade 1	Units/Lessons
Speaking and Listening Standards	
Comprehension and Collaboration	

SL.1.1 Participate in collaborative conversations with diverse partners about grade 1 topics and texts with peers and adults in small and larger groups.
 	
   a. Follow agreed-upon rules for discussions (e.g., listening to others with care, speaking one at a time about the topics and texts under discussion).
 	
   b. Build on others' talk in conversations by responding to the comments of others through multiple exchanges.
 	
   c. Ask questions to clear up any confusion about the topics and texts under discussion.
	Unit 2 Lesson 1
	 Unit 3 Lesson 1
	 Unit 3 Lesson 2
	 Unit 3 Lesson 3

Common Core State Standards for Mathematics

A correlation to the Next Generation Science Standards is located in the front of this Teacher Edition. Correlations to the Common Core State Standards for Mathematics are provided on these pages.

Grade 1	Units/Lessons
Operations & Algebraic Thinking	
Represent and solve problems involving addition and subtraction.	
1.OA.A.1 Use addition and subtraction within 20 to solve word problems involving situations of adding to, taking from, putting together, taking apart, and comparing, with unknowns in all positions, e.g., by using objects, drawings, and equations with a symbol for the unknown number to represent the problem.	Unit 6 Lesson 2
1.OA.A.2 Solve word problems that call for addition of three whole numbers whose sum is less than or equal to 20, e.g., by using objects, drawings, and equations with a symbol for the unknown number to represent the problem.	Unit 3 Lesson 3
Number & Operations in Base Ten	
Extend the counting sequence.	
1.NBT.A.1 Count to 120, starting at any number less than 120. In this range, read and write numerals and represent a number of objects with a written numeral.	Unit 3 Lesson 2
Understand place value.	
1.NBT.B.3 Compare two two-digit numbers based on meanings of the tens and ones digits, recording the results of comparisons with the symbols >, =, and <.	Unit 2 Lesson 1 Unit 5 Lesson 3
Use place value understanding and properties of operations to add and subtract.	
1.NBT.C.5 Given a two-digit number, mentally find 10 more or 10 less than the number, without having to count; explain the reasoning used.	Unit 5 Lesson 3

Grade 1	Units/Lessons
Measurement & Data	
Measure lengths indirectly and by iterating length units.	
1.MD.A.1 Order three objects by length; compare the lengths of two objects indirectly by using a third object.	Unit 5 Lesson 1 Unit 5 Lesson 2
1.MD.A.2 Express the length of an object as a whole number of length units, by laying multiple copies of a shorter object (the length unit) end to end; understand that the length measurement of an object is the number of same-size length units that span it with no gaps or overlaps. *Limit to contexts where the object being measured is spanned by a whole number of length units with no gaps or overlaps.*	Unit 2 Lesson 2 Unit 4 Lesson 2 Unit 4 Lesson 4 Unit 5 Lesson 1
Tell and write time.	
1.MD.B.3 Tell and write time in hours and half-hours using analog and digital clocks.	Unit 3 Lesson 1
Represent and interpret data.	
1.MD.C.4 Organize, represent, and interpret data with up to three categories; ask and answer questions about the total number of data points, how many in each category, and how many more or less are in one category than in another.	Unit 1 Lesson 1 Unit 1 Lesson 2 Unit 4 Lesson 1 Unit 4 Lesson 3
Geometry	
Reason with shapes and their attributes.	
1.G.A.3 Partition circles and rectangles into two and four equal shares, describe the shares using the words *halves*, *fourths*, and *quarters*, and use the phrases *half of*, *fourth of*, and *quarter of*. Describe the whole as two of, or four of the shares. Understand for these examples that decomposing into more equal shares creates smaller shares.	Unit 6 Lesson 1

Math Correlations

Grade 1	Units/Lessons
Mathematical Practices	
MP.2 Reason abstractly and quantitatively.	Unit 6 Lesson 2
MP.4 Model with mathematics.	Unit 4 Lesson 4
MP.5 Use appropriate tools strategically.	Unit 5 Lesson 2

ScienceSaurus, A Student Handbook, is a "mini-encyclopedia" children can use to explore more about unit topics. It contains numerous resources including concise content summaries; an almanac; many tables, charts, and graphs; a history of science and a glossary. *ScienceSaurus* is available from Houghton Mifflin Harcourt.

Science Dimensions Grade 1	*ScienceSaurus* Topic
Unit 1 Engineering and Technology	
Lesson 1 Engineer It · How Do Engineers Use Technology?	Doing Science, Science is Observing
	Doing Science, Doing an Investigation
	Doing Science, Using the Design Process
Careers in Science & Engineering · Packaging Engineer	Doing Science, Science is Observing
	Doing Science, Doing an Investigation
	Doing Science, Using the Design Process
Lesson 2 Engineer It · How Can We Solve a Problem?	Doing Science, Science is Observing
	Doing Science, Doing an Investigation
	Doing Science, Using the Design Process
People in Science & Engineering · Mary Delaney	Doing Science, Science is Observing
	Doing Science, Doing an Investigation
	Doing Science, Using the Design Process
Unit 2 Sound	
Lesson 1 What Is Sound?	Physical Science, Energy
People in Science & Engineering · Ludwig van Beethoven	Physical Science, Energy
Lesson 2 Engineer It · How Can We Communicate with Sound?	Physical Science, Energy
Careers in Science & Engineering · Sound Engineer	Physical Science, Energy
Unit 3 Light	
Lesson 1 How Does Light Help Us See?	Physical Science, Energy
People in Science & Engineering · Thomas Edison	Physical Science, Energy
Lesson 2 How Do Materials Block Light?	Physical Science, Energy
Lesson 3 How Does Light Travel?	Physical Science, Energy
Careers in Science & Engineering · Camera Engineer	Physical Science, Energy

Science Dimensions Grade 1	ScienceSaurus Topic
Unit 4 Plant and Animal Structures	
Lesson 1 Engineer It • What Parts Help Plants Live?	Life Science, Living Things
	Life Science, Plants
People in Science & Engineering • Janine Benyus	Life Science, Living Things
	Life Science, Plants
Lesson 2 Engineer It • What Body Parts Help Animals Stay Safe?	Life Science, Living Things
	Life Science, Animals
Careers in Science & Engineering • Bioengineer	Life Science, Living Things
	Life Science, Animals
Lesson 3 Engineer It • What Body Parts Help Animals Meet Their Needs?	Life Science, Living Things
	Life Science, Animals
Lesson 4 How Do Plants and Animals Respond to Their Environment?	Life Science, Living Things
	Life Science, Environments and Ecosystems
Careers in Science & Engineering • Forest Ranger	Life Science, Living Things
	Life Science, Plants
	Life Science, Animals
	Life Science, Environments and Ecosystems
Unit 5 Living Things and Their Young	
Lesson 1 How Do Plants Look Like Their Parents?	Life Science, Living Things
	Life Science, Plants
People in Science & Engineering • Gregor Mendel	Life Science, Living Things
	Life Science, Plants
Lesson 2 How Do Animals Look Like Their Parents?	Life Science, Living Things
	Life Science, Animals
Lesson 3 How Do Animals Take Care of Their Young?	Life Science, Living Things
	Life Science, Animals
Careers in Science & Engineering • Zookeeper	Life Science, Living Things
	Life Science, Animals
	Life Science, Environments and Ecosystems

Science Dimensions Grade 1	*ScienceSaurus* Topic
Unit 6 Objects and Patterns in the Sky	
Lesson 1 How Do Objects in the Sky Seem to Change?	Earth Science, Space
People in Science & Engineering • Dr. Sarah Ballard	Earth Science, Space
Lesson 2 What Are Patterns of Daylight?	Earth Science, Space
Careers in Science & Engineering • Circadian Biologist	Earth Science, Space

Interactive Glossary

Teacher Notes

_____

_____

_____

_____

_____

_____

_____

_____

_____

_____

_____

_____

Interactive Glossary

This Interactive Glossary will help you learn how to spell and define a vocabulary term. The Glossary will give you the meaning of the term. It will also show you a picture to help you understand what the term means.

Where you see , write your own words or draw your own picture to help you remember what the term means.

adaptation

Something that helps a living thing survive in its environment. (p. 198)

behavior

A way an animal acts. (p. 256)

R1

Interactive Glossary

communicate

To share information. (p. 60)

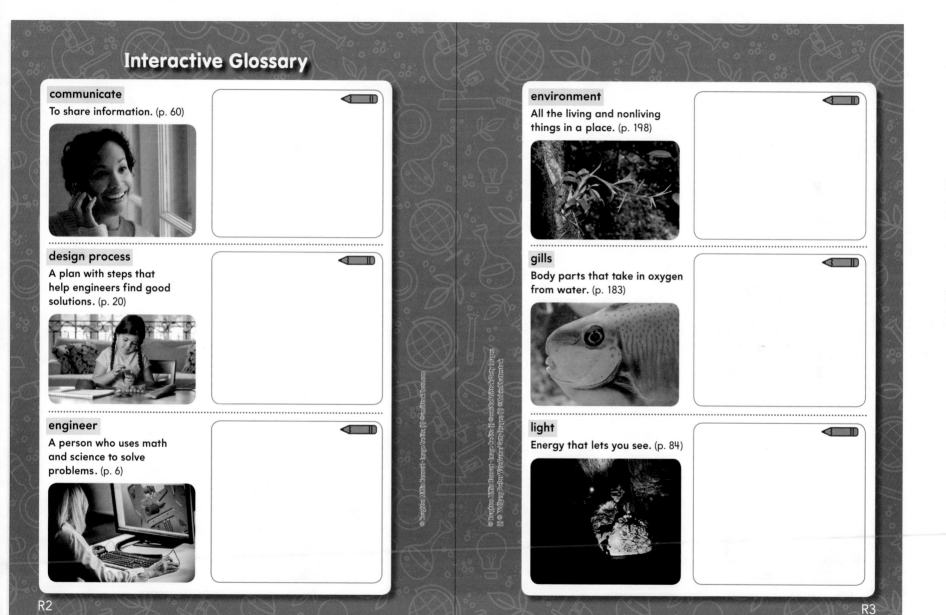

design process

A plan with steps that help engineers find good solutions. (p. 20)

engineer

A person who uses math and science to solve problems. (p. 6)

environment

All the living and nonliving things in a place. (p. 198)

gills

Body parts that take in oxygen from water. (p. 183)

light

Energy that lets you see. (p. 84)

R2

R3

Interactive Glossary

lungs

Body parts that take in air. (p. 183)

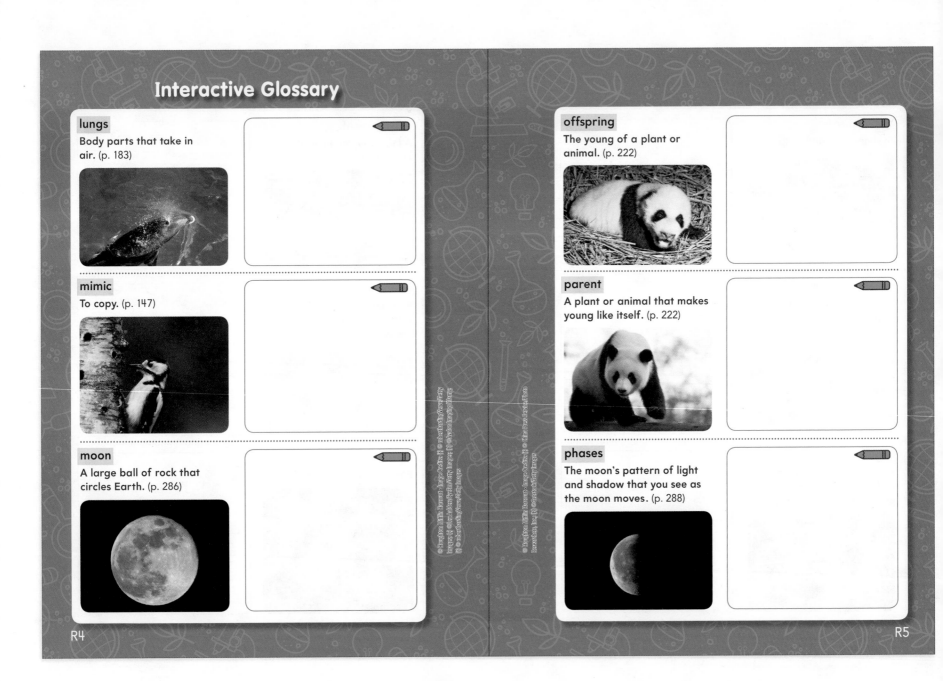

mimic

To copy. (p. 147)

moon

A large ball of rock that circles Earth. (p. 286)

offspring

The young of a plant or animal. (p. 222)

parent

A plant or animal that makes young like itself. (p. 222)

phases

The moon's pattern of light and shadow that you see as the moon moves. (p. 288)

Interactive Glossary

pitch

How high or low a sound is. (p. 47)

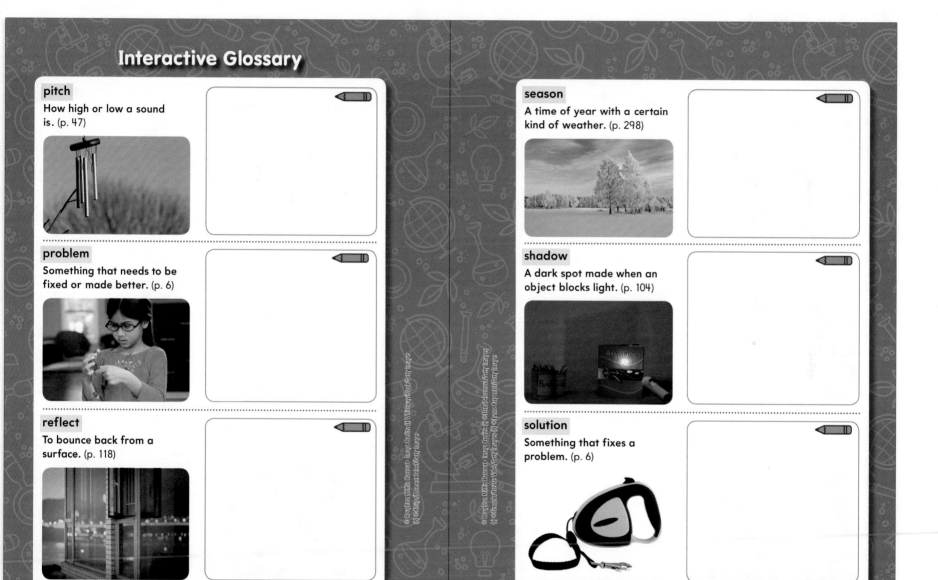

problem

Something that needs to be fixed or made better. (p. 6)

reflect

To bounce back from a surface. (p. 118)

season

A time of year with a certain kind of weather. (p. 298)

shadow

A dark spot made when an object blocks light. (p. 104)

solution

Something that fixes a problem. (p. 6)

Interactive Glossary

sound

A kind of energy you hear when something vibrates. (p. 44)

star

An object in the sky that gives off its own light. (p. 280)

sun

The star closest to Earth. (p. 280)

technology

What engineers make to meet needs and solve problems. (p. 9)

trait

Something living things get from their parents. (p. 231)

vibrate

To move quickly back and forth. (p. 44)

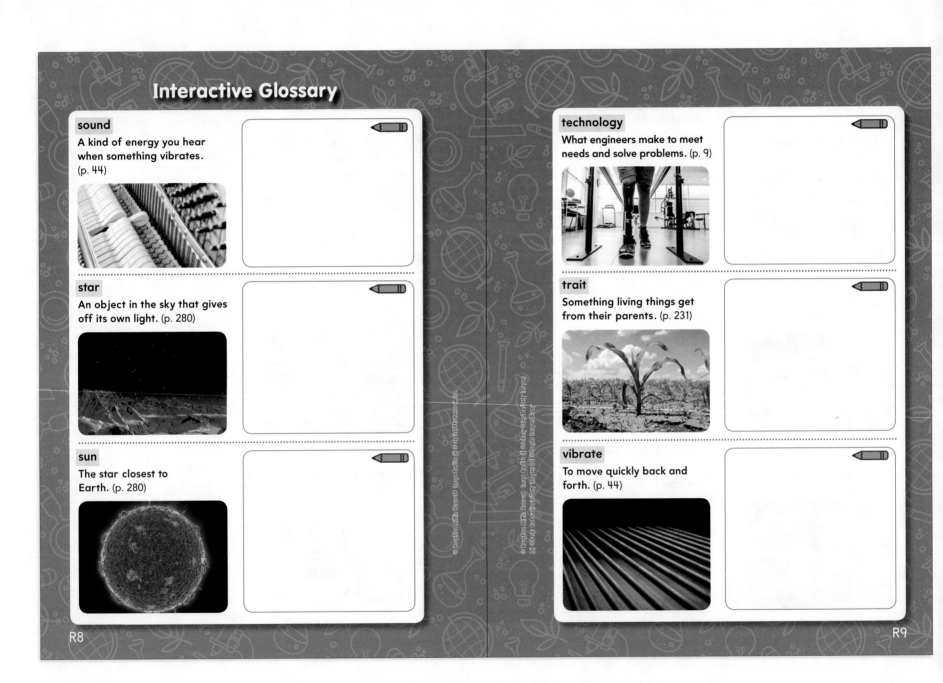

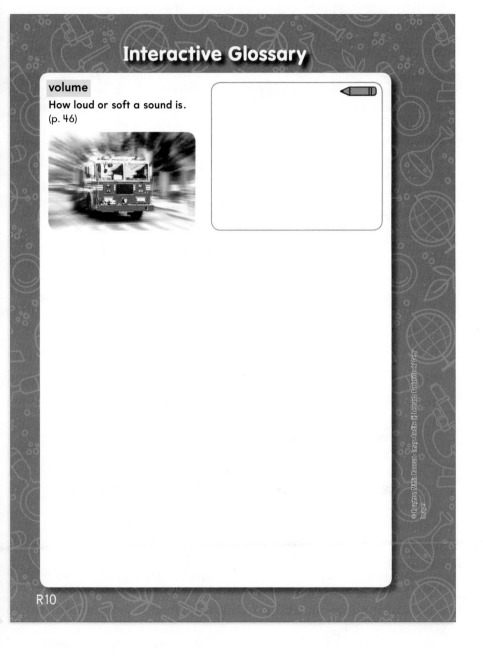

Interactive Glossary

volume

How loud or soft a sound is.
(p. 46)

R10

Index

Index

Index

Index

Index

M

Index

Index